An
ACCOUNT OF THE WAR IN INDIA

An ACCOUNT OF THE WAR IN INDIA

BETWEEN THE ENGLISH AND FRENCH, ON THE COAST OF COROMANDEL, FROM THE YEAR 1750 TO THE YEAR 1760

RICHARD OWEN CAMBRIDGE

GYAN

Published by

Gyan Publishing House
5, Ansari Road
Daryaganj, New Delhi-110002
Phone: 011-47034999, 9811692060
E-mail: books@gyanbooks.com

Distribution Network
gyanbooks.com
India, USA, Canada, UK, Australia, France

ISBN : 978-81-212-9648-9 (PB)
First Published, 1761

2nd Impression 2023

Printed at: Gyan Press, Delhi.

AN ACCOUNT OF THE WAR IN INDIA
Author: RICHARD OWEN CAMBRIDGE

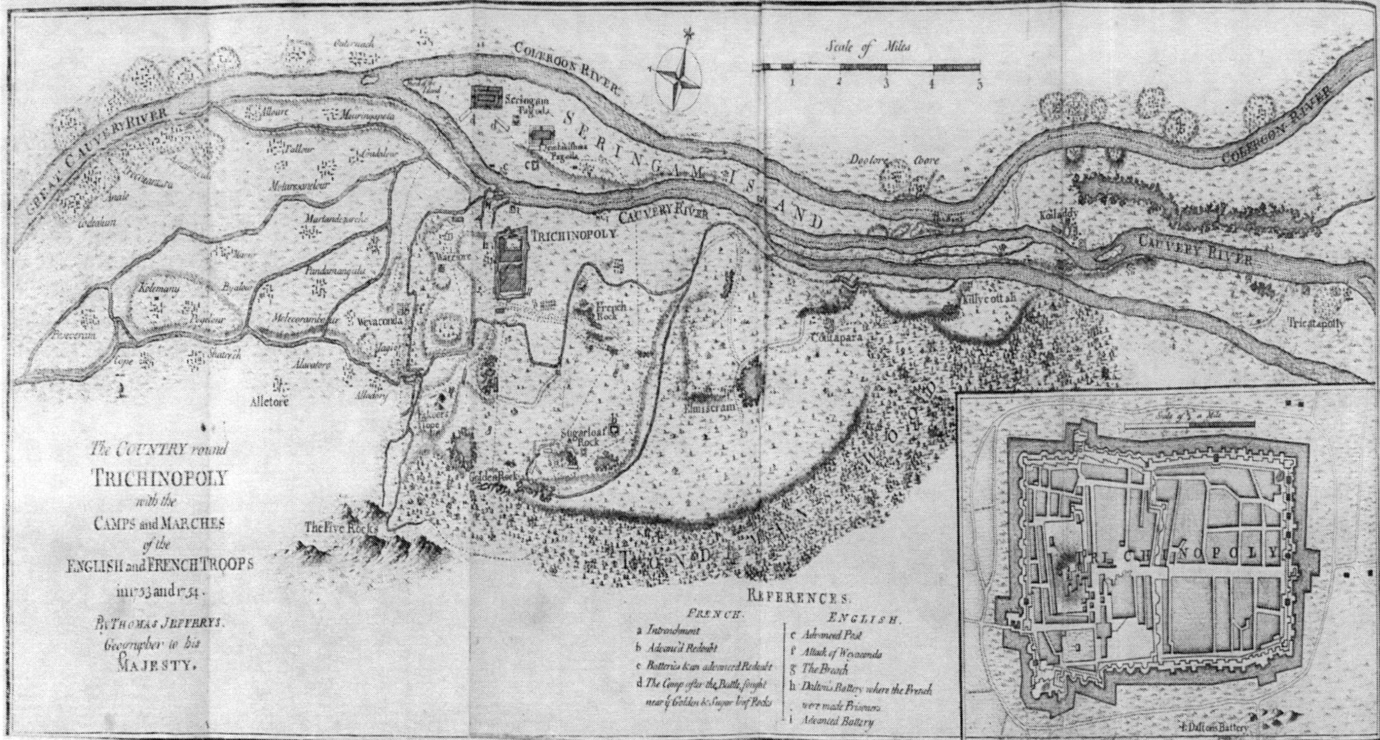
The COUNTRY round
TRICHINOPOLY
with the
CAMPS and MARCHES
of the
ENGLISH and FRENCH TROOPS
in 1753 and 1754.
By THOMAS JEFFERYS.
Geographer to his
MAJESTY.
Scale of Miles
1 2 3 4 5
COLEROON RIVER
GREAT CAUVERY RIVER
CAUVERY RIVER
SERINGAM ISLAND
TRICHINOPOLY
Seringam Pagoda
French Rock
Sugarloaf Rock
Golden Rock
The Five Rocks
Elmiseram
Weyaconda
Alletore
Killycottah
Coilladdy
Tricatapolly
Coiladdy
Dooloor
Coore
Conapara
REFERENCES.
FRENCH.
a Intrenchment
b Advanc'd Redoubt
c Batteries & an advanced Redoubt
d The Camp after the Battle fought near ye Golden & Sugar loaf Rocks
ENGLISH.
e Advanced Post
f Attack of Weyaconda
g The Breach
h Dalton's Battery where the French were made Prisoners
i Advanced Battery
TRICHINOPOLY
Scale of ½ a Mile
Dalton's Battery

AN

ACCOUNT

OF THE

WAR in INDIA,

BETWEEN THE

ENGLISH and FRENCH,

ON THE

COAST of COROMANDEL,

From the Year 1750 to the Year 1760.

TOGETHER WITH

A RELATION of the late Remarkable EVENTS

ON THE

MALABAR COAST,

And the EXPEDITIONS to

GOLCONDA and SURAT;

With the OPERATIONS of the FLEET.

ILLUSTRATED WITH MAPS, PLANS, &c.

The whole Compiled from ORIGINAL PAPERS.

By RICHARD OWEN CAMBRIDGE, Esq;

PREFACE.

THE importance and novelty of a ſubject, of which we have hitherto had imperfect and inaccurate accounts, induced me to ſeize every opportunity of making myſelf acquainted with the tranſactions in the Eaſt-Indies by the peruſal of authentic Papers. The ſatisfaction I received from thoſe I had already ſeen, excited an eager deſire for further enquiry, and urged me to agree to any conditions under which I might be enabled to gratify my curioſity.

Nothing but a determination to write ſome account of India, could have entitled me to the ſight of ſuch materials as I have been favoured with, or have properly introduced me to the free converſation of the perſons principally concerned; which, as it has afforded me the greateſt pleaſure, as well as inſtruction, I ought never to mention without due acknowledgments. As I eſteem it a ſingular honour to have been indulged ſo much beyond my expectation, by all whom I have taken the liberty to trouble on this occaſion, I am bound to declare, that every perſon to whom I have applied, without exception, has given me full ſatisfaction in every point on which I had occaſion to conſult him, and has done it with the utmoſt politeneſs.

After this, I need not dwell upon any further inducements to write; and yet the great reputation which the nation, and ſo many individuals have acquired in the Eaſt-Indies, has doubtleſs been another very inviting circumſtance.

There had been two very partial accounts published by the French; and as Mr. Dupleix also in his MEMOIRE has misrepresented many principal facts, it became necessary to state them in their true light.

Though nothing appears more impertinent than the prefixing an account of a work to the book itself; yet, as it is usual with most people to form a false conception of things, and then to be displeased if they do not find the realities exactly conformable to the opinions they have entertained, it may in some cases be pardonable to endeavour to remove such prejudices.

It will not appear strange, that the generality of the world, through the habit of reading novels, and works of imagination, should expect from an history of the East (which has generally been made the scene of most of their ideal stories) a tale of adventures full of wonder and novelty, and nearly bordering upon romance. Neither are we to be surprised if others of a serious cast, having also, at the same time, an elegant turn of mind and a taste for ornament, should have expressed an expectation, and, perhaps, hinted their advice, that, in order to engage the attention of the reader, the work ought to be embellished with the strange manners of a remote people, the works of art and the wonders of nature in so very distant and different a climate from our own.

It is sufficient to say, in answer to this, that the work before us is not a history of India, nor of war in the interior parts of India, but of war on the coast; of war between two European nations, who have not, till very lately, had any connection with the governing people of the country. It has been entirely owing to the war, that an European has been allowed to have any kind of familiar commerce with them, or that the servants of the company have been admitted to an acquaintance with their courts, the splendor of which has been greatly lessened by the war. The war alone has taught them the geography of the country, a hundred miles round their settlements; and, within these

these few years, those who had been at Madura, which is about that distance, were as eagerly listened to when they returned to Madrass, and their accounts were as new to all that heard them, as if they had come from Pekin: but it does not appear that those accounts were very amusing, or that they would afford any entertainment to make up for the interruption they would give to the thread of the history.

When the design of the work is once explained, it will then best be seen whether it has been properly executed. The two things chiefly proposed by it were, first, to make the generality of the readers acquainted with the geography of the country, of which they have as yet very imperfect and confused notions; and, in the second place, to lay before the more informed, an exact, clear, and impartial state of facts, drawn entirely from authentic papers, by which they may judge for themselves, without comment or reflections to bias them, whether the civil and military officers of the English, or French East India Company abroad, have acted with the most uprightness and bravery, in the course of the war, and the negociations relative to it.

This being the real design of the work, every kind of decoration that was not necessary to illustrate facts would have diverted the attention of the reader from a close view of the conduct of the two nations, by which he is to form his judgment.

Had these materials fallen into the hands of any person capable of rendering them more pleasing, by his superior taste in composition, and a happy elegance of stile, surely he would have employed those talents injudiciously, had he bestowed them on this work: for the greatest part of it (in order to support by authorities what is advanced as fact) is an assemblage of treaties, debates, grants, articles of war, and letters. These are here a necessary, but they are not a favourite part of any work: but there are two pieces that are the most valuable and essential to the whole. The ſiege of Fort St. George, which being a journal, muſt of courſe be dry; and Colonel Lawrence's own narrative of his campaigns, which, though full of inſtruction, was written in a camp, with the ſoldier-like plainneſs which is the diſtinguiſhing character of that excellent officer.

It is now ſubmitted to the public, whether it would have been proper to have given a different colour to the continuation of a narrative which had pleaſed all who had ſeen it, by its unaffected ſimplicity; and if, after what has been ſaid, I ſhall be convicted of an error in judgment, it will neither ſurprize nor give me any concern, provided I am not proved to have made any eſſential miſtake in matters of fact. And herein I flatter myſelf I cannot be greatly to blame, as I am certain that I have not put down any material circumſtance without the authority of authentic papers, or without conſulting with the ſeveral perſons concerned, and examining moſt thoroughly every thing that has appeared dubious.

As I have taken ſo much pains not to give credit too haſtily to any informations I may have received, I may be allowed to deſire the reader will not too raſhly give ear to ſuch teſtimony as he may think will confute them; and particularly, that he will not ſuppoſe a man the better acquainted with facts for having been in India, unleſs he has been in that very part which was the ſcene of the tranſaction in queſtion; for the ſeveral ſettlements being ſome as remote from others as England is from Turky or Africa, the people on one coaſt have ſomtimes no more knowledge of what is doing on the other, than we have at home.

It is alſo to be expected, that thoſe who have been witneſſes to any event which it has been thought proper to relate conciſely, will be ready to impute that brevity to a want of information; when, at the ſame time, the European reader will think that very narrative too long, and the detail too minute and unintereſting.

I have,

I have, therefore, in handling every new ſubject, endeavoured to confine myſelf to the moſt recent, as well as the moſt important events, alone; and have avoided going too far back in point of time, as that might occaſion a confuſion, by introducing a variety of perſons, and a multiplicity of ſtrange names; which would certainly give a heavineſs, if not a ridicule, to the whole.

This naturally leads to the mention of another difficulty.

The Aſiatic Monarchs are exceedingly fond of aſſuming new names, and frequently beſtow them on others as a very ſerious and important favour; and indeed they generally confer them engraved on a ſeal-ring, which exempts the wearer from all taxes, tolls, and impoſts, wherever he appears with it in the dominions of the Prince who beſtows it.

By this means it often happens, that different perſons have the ſame appellation, and that the ſame perſon is called by different names, which creates a confuſion not always in the power of the writer to prevent; ſince it is by no means proper to alter a name in the ſignature of original papers; and yet, when the reader ſees the ſame perſon ſigning a different name * from that which he is commonly diſtinguiſhed by, he will be apt to think there is ſome miſtake.

As it is impoſſible to find out any criterion to ſpell the Perſic and Indian names by, ſince they are ſo variouſly pronounced and ſo differently written by perſons of the ſame nation, I cannot pretend to be exact in this particular. The French having publiſhed an account of the war ſome years ago, many readers will have been habituated to ſee names of ſome of the principal perſons ſpelt after their manner; therefore, for the ſake of conformity, I have uſed the ſame conſonants as I find employed by M. Dupleix and his

 country-

* See page 323. The ſeveral names uſed by the Vizier, who is commonly called Shaw Abadin Cawn.

countrymen; but as their vowels are pronounced ſo very differently from the Engliſh, I have, for the moſt part, altered them accordingly. The word which ſignifies a warrior, is written by the Engliſh jung, jing, or jenk; but as the French, and particularly M. Dupleix, write it zing, I have done ſo likewiſe; for though many hold the other to be the true pronunciation, there are ſome who make it doubtful; eſpecially when they ſay the word Gentoo, or Jentoo, might be ſpelt with a z *; and it becomes the more a matter of indifference, when we call to mind the reciprocal letters of the Spaniards; who ſpell many words both with the x † and j, and give exactly the ſame ſound to the one as to the other.

I could hardly avoid ſaying thus much, on a ſubject very unintereſting in itſelf, and, poſſibly, tireſome to the generality of readers; I ſhall therefore purſue it no farther.

* In like manner, Jemidar is very often ſpelt Zemidar.

† The Spaniards in their voyage to Peru, having occaſion to mention our Ship the Chicheſter, write it Sixter; and as we have moſt of our ſpellings of eaſtern words from foreigners or inaccurate ſeamen and traders, it may be allowable to make ſome alterations; though, from the force of habit, ſome people will condemn thoſe which are made upon the beſt reaſons. The French having always been imitated by us in the ſpelling of Schah and Khan, though the words have for that reaſon often been pronounced wrong, the obvious ſpelling of theſe names with the w, which helps to give the true ſound to the vowel, will at firſt be thought a blameable ſingularity: to avoid a charge of that kind, I have not often deviated from the common ſpelling, but as it was neceſſary to do it ſometimes, I have particularly taken care to alter ſuch as might miſlead the reader into the ſuppoſition of falſe etymologies, and give him erroneous ideas of things: as in the uſual ſpelling of the word *Sea*-poy, which made it generally ſuppoſed, that the *Se*-poys, who are foot ſoldiers, were either ſailors or marines.

GLOSSARY

OF

PERSIC AND INDIAN NAMES.

Arzee, A REQUEST, or petition

Bang, An intoxicating juice of a vegetable

Batta, An extraordinary allowance to the army when abroad in the field, or in any country garrison where provisions are scarce

Betel, A leaf, not unlike that of a kidney-bean; it grows on a vine exactly in the same manner; and is in great use, from the prince to the beggar. They constantly chew it, mixed with Chinam and Betel-nut; for the Betel-leaf and the Betel-nut are from different plants. The farmers of Madrass pay the company from six to seven thousand pounds a year for the exclusive privilege of vending it

Bramin, A priest

Buckshee, Treasurer to the Mogul

Bunder, A custom-house

Chinam, Fine slacked lime

Chop, A small seal, on which is engraved the name of the Mogul and the year of the hegyra

Choultry,

GLOSSARY.

Choultry,	An open house for all travellers, the same as a Turkish caravanserai. A bramin resides always in or near it, to keep it clean, and to furnish travellers with water, &c. He is maintained by an endowment
Chout,	Properly a fourth, but commonly used to express the tribute which the Marattas claim and raise on all the governments in India
Circar, or Sircar,	A general name for the government, or persons concerned in the administration
Coffrees,	(By the French called Cafres) is now become the general name for all negroes who are brought to India from the Cape, the coast of Guinea, or any other parts of Africa, and chiefly from Madagascar; they are brave and steady in the field
Colleries,	Inhabitants of the woods under the government of the Polygars
Cooley,	A labourer of any kind
Coss,	A little more than two miles
Cowle,	A protection
Dooley,	A woman's chair, somewhat like a sedan
Durbar,	The court of a Mogul Prince, or place where they meet in council
Dustuck,	An order
Enam,	A gift
Firman, or Phirmaund,	A patent, or paper signed by the Mogul
Gentou, Zentoo,	Indians, Idolaters
Housbulhookum,	A patent or paper signed by the Vizier

Jaeger,

GLOSSARY.

JAGEER, or JAQUEER,	A territory or domain granted for a particular uſe, either to maintain a number of troops, or keep a fort in repair; and ſometimes as a penſion
JEMIDAR, or ZEMIDAR,	Officers of horſe or foot, and ſometimes people of rank employed about the perſons of the great in the adminiſtration
KILLEDAR,	A Governor of a fort
LACK,	Of roupees, above twelve thouſand five hundred pounds.
MAUND,	A variable weight; at Bengal, ſeventy-ſix pounds; at Surat, thirty ſeven pounds one-half; in Perſia, the Tabareſe Maund is only ſix pounds
MOORS,	The Mahometans improperly ſo called
NABOB,	A Governor of a province, appointed by the Souba, or Viceroy
NAIB,	A deputy
OMRAHS,	Privy Counſellors, men of the firſt rank in the empire; they are under the Vizier, but are moſtly concerned in all the revolutions of the ſtate
PADDY,	Rice in the huſk
PAGODA,	An Indian temple
PAGODA,	A coin paid by the Company at eight ſhillings, but intrinſically worth ſeven ſhillings and eight pence
PALLANKEEN,	A bed, ſupported by a wooden or ivory frame of ſix feet long, and near three feet broad, faſtened at each end with croſs ſticks to a bamboo fifteen feet long, which forms an arch over the pallankeen or bed, and is covered with a canopy of cloth lined with ſilk, and ſtiffened with ribs of the coconut tree
PARAGANA,	Any diſtrict of country

PARSEES,

GLOSSARY.

PARSEES,	Worſhippers of fire
PATAMAR,	A poſt or meſſenger ſent from place to place
PEONS,	A name for the infantry of the Deckan; they are armed with a broadſword, and ſomtimes with a matchlock
PERWANNA,	A paper ſigned by the Nabob
PETTAH,	The town ſurrounding an Indian fort
PHOUSDAR,	A renter
POLYGAR,	Lord of a ſmall territory
RAJA,	The higheſt title of the Gentoo princes
ROUPEE,	About two ſhillings and fivepence
SANEDS,	Commiſſions, or grants for particular countries
SARDAR,	An officer of horſe
SEPOYS,	Indian ſoldiers, which are entertained and diſciplined by Europeans
SHROFF,	A money changer or banker
SIRPAH,	A rich dreſs of the country
SOUBA,	Viceroy of one of the two great provinces
TANK,	A pond, or pool of water
TANKA,	The revenue appropriated by the Mogul for the maintenance of a fleet at Surat
TOM TOMS,	Drums
TOPASSES,	Black foot ſoldiers, deſcended from Portugueſe marrying natives, called Topaſſes becauſe they wear hats
VAKEEL,	An agent or miniſter for the Moors

Page 13.

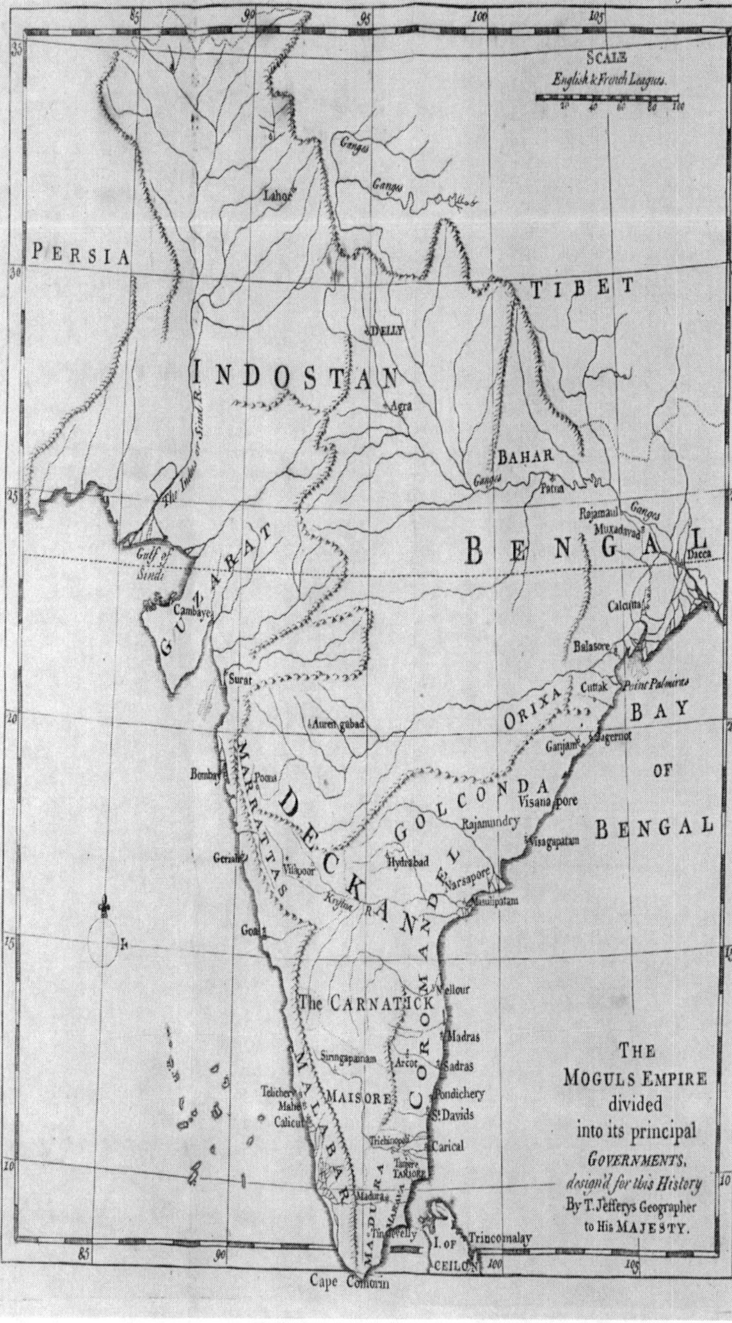
SCALE
English & French Leagues.
PERSIA
TIBET
INDOSTAN
Lahor
Ganges
DELLY
Agra
BAHAR
Patna
Rajamaul
Muxadavad
BENGAL
Dacca
Calcutta
Balasore
Gulf of Sindi
GUZARAT
Cambaye
The Indus or Sind R.
Surat
Cuttak
Point Palmiras
ORIXA
Aurengabad
Ganjam
Jagernot
BAY
OF
BENGAL
Bombay
Poona
MARRATTAS
DECKAN
GOLCONDA
Visanapore
Rajamundry
Visagapatam
Geriah
Visiapoor
Hydrabad
Narsapore
Masulipotam
Krishna R.
Goa
COROMANDEL
Vellour
The CARNATICK
Madras
Sadras
Seringapatnam
Arcot
Pondichery
St. Davids
Tellichery
Mahe
Calicut
MAISORE
MALABAR
Trichinopoli
Carical
Tanjore
TANJORE
MADURA
Madura
MARAVA
Tinevelly
I. OF CEILON
Trincomalay
Cape Comorin
THE
MOGULS EMPIRE
divided
into its principal
GOVERNMENTS,
design'd for this History
By T. Jefferys Geographer
to His MAJESTY.

INTRODUCTION.

FOR the better underſtanding any accounts of a country, with which the European reader is ſo little acquainted, it is neceſſary firſt to inform him of ſuch particulars as ſerve to explain the tranſactions and events in the work before him.

It is generally ſuppoſed, that the Peninſula within the Ganges is under the immediate government of the Mogul himſelf, and that the royal mandates from Delli are, according to the received notion of ſo arbitrary a dominion, obeyed in the moſt remote parts of the coaſt. This is ſo far from the truth, that a great part of that vaſt Peninſula never acknowledged any ſubjection to the throne of Delli, till the reign of Aurengzebe; and the revenues from thoſe Indian kings and Mooriſh governors, who were conquered or employed by him, have, ſince his death, been intercepted by the viceroys, which his weaker ſucceſſors have appointed for the government of the Peninſula: ſo that at this time neither can the tribute from the ſeveral potentates reach the Court of Delli, nor the vigour of the government extend from the capital to thoſe remote countries. And ever ſince the province of Indoſtan was ruined by Nadir Shaw, the weakneſs of the Mogul, and the policy and confirmed independency of the Viceroys have in a manner confined the influence of the government to its inland department.

Let it therefore be underſtood, that the Sovereign poſſeſſes a third only, and that the leaſt valuable part, of his own vaſt empire. Bengal, the ſmalleſt, but moſt fertile province, is governed by a Viceroy. The other diviſion, called the Deckan, extending from Balaſore

Balaſore Jagonaut (or thereabouts, for the geography is certainly not ſettled) to cape Comorin, is alſo delegated by the Mogul to another Viceroy, of exceeding great power, having within his juriſdiction ſeven large territories, to which he has the undiſputed right of nominating ſeven Nabobs, or governors of provinces. In all parts of India there are ſtill large diſtricts, which have preſerved, with the Gentoo religion, the old form of government under Indian Kings called Raja's. Such are Maiſſore, whoſe capital is Seringapatam, and Tanjore, whoſe capital is Tanjore. There are alſo among the woods and mountainous parts of the country ſeveral petty Princes, or heads of clans diſtinguiſhed by the name of Polygars. Theſe are all tributary to the Nabobs, and thoſe to the Viceroy, whoſe capital is Aurengabad. The Carnatick is that part of the Deckan which comprehends the principal ſettlements of the Europeans, Madraſs, and Pondichery, and alſo Arcot. To eſtabliſh the government of the laſt named province, and to oppoſe the hoſtile intentions of Mr. Dupleix, the Engliſh Eaſt-India company engaged in this war in ſupport of Mahomet Allee Cawn.

As it is neceſſary, that the reader ſhould be well acquainted with the geography of this country, without which he can never have any juſt notion of the government of it, the moſt accurate maps of particular ſpots have been procured, and diſtinctly engraved; and there is alſo prefixed an outline of the whole country unincumbered with the ſmaller diviſions, and containing only the names of ſuch places as are moſt frequently mentioned, in order to give at one view, a full idea of the whole empire of India within the Ganges, and to ſhew the conſequence of the two great viceroyalties, compared with that of the principal ſeat of government.

The chain of mountains which run through the peninſula from north to ſouth, are the cauſe of an extraordinary phenomenon in natural hiſtory. The

countries

countries which are ſeparated by theſe mountains, though under the ſame latitude, have their ſeaſons and climate entirely different from each other; and while it is winter on one ſide of the hills, it is ſummer on the other ſide. On the coaſt of Malabar a ſouth-weſt wind begins to blow from the ſea at the end of June, with continued rain, and rages againſt the coaſt for four months, during which time the weather is calm and ſerene on the coaſt of Coromandel: and towards the end of October, the rainy ſeaſon, which they term the Change of the Monſoon, begins on the coaſt of Coromandel: at which time, the tempeſtuous winds bearing continually againſt a coaſt in which there are no good ports, make it ſo dangerous for the ſhipping to remain there, for the three enſuing months, that it is ſcarce ever attempted. This is the cauſe of the periodical return of our ſhips to Bombay, where there is a ſecure harbour, and convenient docks.

When the reader has been made acquainted with ſo much of the geography of the country, as is abſolutely neceſſary for his underſtanding the nature of the government, it will be proper that he ſhould be ſatisfied in regard to certain doubts and difficulties that will naturally ariſe in the peruſal of the work.

Without a few previous explanations, he will never be able to conceive, by what means a handful of Europeans ſhould appear ſo reſpectable in the field, when oppoſed to a multitude of Aſiatics. As this is owing to a number of concurring circumſtances it will be requiſite to give ſome account of ſuch of their manners, habits, and prejudices, as may have a nearer or more remote influence on their military character.

Nothing appears a greater difficulty to the military men in this part of the world, than the poſſibility of ſubſiſting ſuch vaſt multitudes as the Aſiatic armies frequently conſiſt of, eſpecially with ſo large a proportion of horſe.

If

If it be matter of aſtoniſhment, that ſuch numbers of fighting men are frequently brought into the field, how will it appear when it is added to the account that every horſe-man has two ſervants, one to take care of his horſe, the other to procure him forage, and that all theſe are accompanied by their wives and children, that there always follows the camp a moveable town of ſhops, where every thing is to be ſold as in their cities, ſome hundreds of elephants for ſtate only, and a train of women (with their numberleſs retinue) belonging to the Prince and the great officers. For wherever the Sovereign moves, he is more taken up with a vain oſtentation of pomp and magnificence, than with the object of the war; and it is his pleaſure that his ſubjects ſhould abandon the capital in order to augment his * numbers.

To

* I took a view of the Leſker, or Mogul's camp, which is one of the greateſt wonders I ever beheld (and chiefly for that I ſaw it ſet up and finiſh'd in leſs than four hours) it being no leſs than twenty Engliſh miles in compaſs, the length ſomeways three coſſes (about ſeven miles) including the ſkirts: in the middle, where the ſtreets are orderly, and tents joined, there are all ſorts of ſhops, and ſo regularly diſpoſed, that every man knows whither to go directly for what he wants; each man of quality, and every trade being appointed how far from the King's tents they ſhall pitch, what ground they ſhall take up, and on what ſide, without ever altering. All which, as it lies together, is almoſt equal to any town in Europe for greatneſs: but no man muſt approach the royal quarter, by a muſket-ſhot every way, which is now ſo ſtrictly obſerved, that none are admitted but by name: and the time of the durbar in the evening is omitted, andſpent in hunting or hawking on pools by boat, in which the King takes wonderful delight and his barges are removed on carts with him.

Sir Thomas Roe's Journal.

In imitation of their Sovereign, and from the ſame motives of pride and vanity, the leſſer Princes and Viceroys, affect the ſame magnificence in the ſplendor of their camps and the number of their followers. Thoſe who were with Nazirzing in 1750, give the like deſcription of his camp, being well aſſured that it exceeded twenty miles in circumference; but as for the numbers, there is no way of aſcertaining them; therefore they only ſay, they were reported on the ſpot to have been 300,000 fighting men,

and

To provide for all these, the whole country is put in motion, and the strictest orders are given for all provisions to be brought into the camp. By these means, all the cities far and near are exhausted, but the camp for the most part, is plentifully supplied.

The forage is procured in the following manner. Every horse-man is allowed a man for the purpose, who is constantly employed in cutting turf, and washing the roots of it: and this is a more hearty food for a horse than grass. A shower of rain produces another crop in a few days time: and in case of continued dry weather, they move their camp to fresh ground *.

Many of the Indians abstain from all kinds of animal food, and the greatest part of them use rice, as their common and almost only sustenance: and as they have so great a veneration for Cows, they are all prohibited by their religion, from killing any of that species; therefore there generally is a sufficient sup-

 ply

and might possibly have been near 200,000; and the followers of the camp said to have exceeded a million, might possibly have amounted to half that number. Nazirzing's army being, at that time, in the heart of his own dominions, and undisturbed by marauders, was regularly supplied from all the neighbouring towns, which, by receiving ready money for their provisions, were enabled to pay the arrears of their revenues, so that the Viceroy maintained this amazing multitude by the collections and contributions which he raised in his march, without diminishing from the treasures which he always carried with him, and which served to fill twenty tents with gold and silver coin.

* They also feed their horses in the rice fields, and where meat is plenty, they boil the offal to rags, and mixing it with butter and some sorts of grain, make balls of it, which the thrust down the horses throat. In a scarcity of provisions, they give them opium, which has the same effect both on the horses and men, for at once it damps their appetites, and enables them to endure fatigue. The horses of the country, are naturally so exceedingly vicious, that they are not to be broke in the manage, and cannot be brought to act with the same regularity in the field, as a squadron of European cavalry. The Persian horses being more gentle and docile, and greatly esteemed, and often valued at a thousand guineas. Those of India, sell for fifty or a hundred.

ply of beef for the Mahometan ſoldiery, and the ſmall proportion of Europeans. But to leſſen the ſurprize of the more exact calculator, it muſt be ſuppoſed, that theſe numerous armies ſeldom keep the field any time, without great loſs by famine; for a very conſiderable diminution is ſcarcely felt, among ſuch numbers, and very little regarded from any notions of humanity: a famine is, therefore, neither conſidered as any thing extraordinary; nor will the memory of it ever prevent the aſſemblage of another multitude, who muſt alſo be liable to the ſame chances of ſubſiſting or ſtarving, as accident ſhall determine. In like manner, allowance muſt be made for the great loſs and damage they ſuſtain in men, beaſts, and all the implements of war, as often as they move in difficult roads and * defiles, and particularly in their method of paſſing over great rivers. For their rivers, when they are not fordable, in the rainy ſeaſon become torrents, being ſwelled to ſuch a degree, that they are not to be paſſed but ſlantwiſe, the landing place being frequently above a mile below the place of embarkation, and heavy veſſels, built of timber, could not be brought up againſt the ſtream to ſerve again.

They therefore make large boats of a kind of baſket-work, which they cover with ſkins. As there muſt always be great plenty of hides in ſo numerous an army, they are eaſily made. They are very light and

* We marched every other day about four coſſes only, with ſuch a train of baggage, as was almoſt impoſſible to be kept in order; we paſſed through woods, and over mountains thick of buſhes, where many camels periſhed; and many people tired with the difficulties of an impaſſible way, went away to Agra, and all complained. I loſt my tents and carts, but by midnight we met again. The king reſted two days; for the Leſkars could not in leſs time recover their order; many of the king's women, and thouſands of coaches, carts, and camels, lying in the woody mountains without meat or water. He himſelf got through on a ſmall Elephant that will climb up rocks, and paſs ſuch ſtraits, that no horſe or beaſt I have ſeen, can follow him.

Sir T. Roe's Journal.

and manageable, and yet will carry above fifty horſe, and are capable of tranſporting the heavieſt artillery.

It is owing entirely to an ignorance of the manners of the Aſiatics, that many people imagine they can never be made ſoldiers. It may perhaps be ſhewn that they never will, whilſt the ſame wretched government and abhorrence of innovation ſubſiſts: but thoſe are greatly miſtaken, who attribute their dread of fire arms, and particularly of artillery, to a daſtardly diſpoſition, and an invincible timidity.

The true cauſe lies in the inexperience of their leading men, who never underſtood the advantages of diſcipline, and who have kept their infantry upon too low a footing. Their cavalry (which are, among them, very reſpectable, and alſo well paid) though not backward to engage with ſabres, are extremely unwilling to bring their horſes within the reach of our guns; ſo that they do not decline an engagement ſo much through fear for their lives, as for their fortunes, which are all laid out in the horſe they ride on. As an inſtance of the affection they contract for ſo ſerviceable a creature, Morarow, the general of the Marattas, having had his favourite horſe ſhot, mourned for him three days, after their manner, that is to ſay, was ſo long without his turban.

Such of the natives as have been diſciplined and encouraged by Europeans, and formed into a regular infantry, under officers of their own, and generally known by the name of Sepoys, have familiarized themſelves to fire arms, and behaved well behind walls; and when we give them ſerjeants to lead them on, they make no contemptible figure in the field.

Nothing is ſo ruinous to their military affairs, as the falſe notion which is generally entertained among them, and chiefly by their commanders, in relation to artillery. They are terrified with that of the enemy, and fooliſhly put a confidence in their own; and what is the moſt fatal miſtake, they place their chief dependance on the largeſt pieces, which they neither know how to manage nor move. They give them pompous and ſounding names, as the Italians do to their guns, and have ſome pieces which carry a ball of ſeventy pounds. When we march round them with our light field pieces, and make it neceſſary to move thoſe enormous weights, their bullocks, which are at beſt very untractable, if a ſhot comes among them, are quite ungovernable; and at the ſame time are ſo ill harneſſed, that it cauſes no ſmall delay to free the reſt from any one that ſhall happen to be unruly or ſlain.

In war with the Aſiatics alone, we have a much greater advantage in their being ſo very tenacious of their old manners, than in their want of bravery. Not only the Prince himſelf, but every Raja, who has the command of all the forces he can bring into the field, be they more or leſs, always appears among them mounted on an Elephant, and is at once the General and enſign, or ſtandard of that corps, who keep their eyes conſtantly on him; and if they loſe ſight of him for a moment, conclude that all is loſt. Thus we find, Aurengzebe gained two battles by the treachery of thoſe who deſired his two victorious brothers to get down from their Elephants, mount their horſes, and purſue the vanquiſhed: their troops miſſing them, immediately diſperſed. The ſame practice, continued to this day, affords our engineers a fair opportunity of deciding the fate of a whole detachment, by one well directed diſcharge of a ſix pounder: and thoſe enormous beaſts, now ſeem to be brought into the field for no other end but to be a mark for our artillery. It is ſaid, they begin to ſee the danger of this practice, but ſurely that might have been found long ſince; for before the uſe of artillery, the General thus diſtinguiſhed, was in like manner expoſed to the arrows of a whole army, and yet we always find them in the ſame perilous ſtation. Porus is ſaid to have been pierced with nine arrows,

and

and to have ſunk from his Elephant with innumerable wounds. It ſhould ſeem probable, that not merely their regard for ancient manners, but the expediency of keeping their troops together by this ſignal, will induce them to continue the ſame method; the neceſſity of which will appear from the conduct and ſucceſs of Aurengzebe, who, when he found his army giving way on every ſide, ordered chains to be faſtened about the legs of his Elephant, to convince them that he would not give the example of flight; and that thoſe to whom his life was dear or intereſting, could preſerve it by no other means but firmly maintaining their ground It may perhaps be a farther illuſtration of this practice, to ſhew the conformity of cuſtoms among remote and different barbarous nations, unſkilled in the military ſcience.

In the hiſtories of America, we find Montezuma repreſented as performing no part of a general, but only ſitting in an exalted ſtage on men's ſhoulders, and ſerving as a conſpicuous ſtandard to his troops.

To ſhew that they themſelves are ſenſible of the danger of being thus expoſed, they will ſometimes avail themſelves of the only device that can afford them any ſecurity. For it has been obſerved, that ſeveral Elephants capariſon'd alike, with riders in the ſame rich and ſplendid habits, have appeared in different parts of the field on the ſame day.

Another great obſtacle to their ſucceſs in war, is their ſuperſtition, and particularly their ſtrict obſervance of lucky and unlucky days, which often prevents them from taking the moſt obvious advantages of an enemy.

Being fond of all kinds of beaſts of prey, they keep great numbers of them, and often viſit them before they give battle; and if they find them heavy and dull, they think it a bad omen, and a reaſon ſufficient to poſtpone their intended deſign of an action; and on the other hand, the accidental fury of the animal is regarded as a happy omen of ſucceſs. They have alſo a cuſtom of matching two wild beaſts, moſt commonly elephants; and having given their own name to the one and that of the enemy to the other, they bring them together to fight in preſence of their army: but in this cuſtom, they are not altogether to be condemned for ſuperſtitious folly, ſince they have the policy to make it a very unequal match, and to give their own name to the ſtrongeſt.

The art of influencing the vulgar to engage in any great undertaking, by the aid of theſe prejudices, is rare, where the chiefs are themſelves alſo ſuperſtitious: but it frequently happens that great obſtacles are by theſe means thrown in their way and many of their deſigns made to miſcarry by artful people. In order to give an authentick repreſentation of ſuch practices, the following extract of a letter from Colonel Laurence, to the Governor of Fort St. George, is here inſerted.

" We made one march nearer the enemy, and in-
" tended to have poſted ourſelves this day on the
" road between Wandewaſh and Pondichery, but
" were prevented by the following unforeſeen acci-
" dent. For ſome days paſt, the black people at-
" tending the camp, have been very ſickly, and ſome
" of them died every day, and that by almoſt inſtanta-
" neous deaths, owing partly to the ſeaſon of the year,
" and in ſome meaſure to bad water. A Bramin,
" moſt probably employed by the enemy, came into
" our camp, and by pretending inſpirations, he ga-
" thered about him a crowd of Malabar people;
" theſe he threatened with the vengeance of their
" gods if they followed the camp, and very artfully
" inſinuated, that the preſent reigning ſickneſs
" amongſt them, was a puniſhment inflicted on them
" by their god, who was offended at their remaining
" with the Engliſh. Upon this, all the * Cooleys
" deſerted.

But

* Blacks who are hired to carry the baggage, and ſometimes to draw the guns.

But what is the greateſt obſtacle of all, to their becoming a military people, is, that thoſe who have once had ſuch ſucceſs in the field, as to obtain the name of Fortunate, being thereby conſidered as invincible, and in conſequence unmoleſted for a time, are willing to ſave the needleſs expence of an army. For this reaſon there are few veterans, and moſt of their armies conſiſt of an aſſemblage of various people haſtily brought together from different parts; ſo that there can be no ſuch thing as diſcipline, without which, numbers are but an impediment, and bravery ineffectual.

Notwithſtanding they have ſo ſeverely ſuffered by being ſurprized in the night by the Europeans; they can never be brought to eſtabliſh either order or vigilance in their camp: and when they have acted with us as allies, the moſt earneſt remonſtrances could never prevail with them to be ſufficiently upon their guard, when in the neighbourhood of the French, or to quit their ground in the * morning, to co-operate with us in ſurprizing the enemy.

At the cloſe of the evening, every man eats an inconceivable quantity of rice, and many take after it ſome kind of ſoporific drugs; ſo that about mid-night, the whole army is in a dead ſleep: the conſequence of theſe habits is obvious; and yet it would appear a ſtrange propoſition to an Eaſtern Monarch, to endeavour to perſuade him that the ſecurity of his throne depended upon the regulation of the meals of a common ſoldier: much leſs would he be prevailed on to reſtrain him in the uſe of that opium, which is to warm his blood for action, and animate his ſoul with heroiſm. It muſt fill the mind of an European ſoldier at once with compaſſion and contempt, to ſee a heap of theſe poor creatures, ſolely animated by a momentary intoxication, crowded into a breach, and both

* See Page. 195

in their garb and impotent fury, resembling a mob of frantic women.

There is certainly an appearance of effeminacy in the Eastern dress, which has at all times greatly contributed to lessen their military character with the European nations, who, from their own habits and prejudices, will naturally receive a strange impression, upon seeing a body of horse in silk or cotton robes. These last mentioned particulars are not insisted on as any part of the argument; the foregoing accounts will sufficiently demonstrate, that a nation under such circumstances, can never become a military people.

And yet, there is no character they are so fond of as that of a warrior; and as they have no other notion of government, they have been, from time immemorial continually at war with one another. They will still talk in a very high strain of their passion for military glory; and as the word *zing*, in their language, signifies a soldier, it will appear, by the frequency of that termination to most of the names mentioned in the following sheets, how generally they affect the honour of that title.

Upon this occasion, it would be great injustice to our commanders on the coast of Coromandel, not to observe, that they have always had to contend with a superior body of Europeans, conducted by leaders of experience and rank in the French army.

Thus far it has been requisite to relate such of the Asiatic manners, as may give some light to the accounts of their military operations; and it might perhaps be not altogether unpleasing to the reader, nor useless on this occasion, to relate some farther particulars of the Moors, who are the governing people of India, and particularly of the Mogul. To enter into a minute description of the custom of the Indians, though they were the original inhabitants (besides that Bernier, Thevenot, Tavernier,

nier, and * others, have treated of them at large) is not the design of this work, and more particularly belongs to the commercial history of these countries. But for the illustration of the events of war, the manners of the † Moors who have usurped the government, are chiefly to be examined into.

It is extremely difficult to give any recent account of these princes, as they are by custom proud, have a contempt for other nations, and admit no one to their courts, unless it be such as by any peculiar talent may happen to administer to the gratification of some present fancy, or to the relief of any disorder they may labour under. They have an implicit faith in the abilities of the European physicians. It is owing to this opinion, that Bernier was enabled to give so ample and authentic an account of the life and manners of Aurengzebe. He travelled with him in his extraordinary journey to Cachemire, of which he has given a clear, comprehensive, and most entertaining journal. As Bernier's whole account of the Mogul Empire, is so full and instructive, it is much more proper to recommend the perusal of it to the reader, than to transcribe, as is too often the practice, from a book that is in every body's hands, and which is, throughout, full of use and entertainment.

But on the other hand, where there are books that, amidst a quantity of useless matter, have some few curious particulars; or when any scarce tract is either out of print, or only to be found among large collections; in such case, it may be allowable to give extracts of the most useful passages. The justness of

* There is a very good account by Terry, chaplain to Sir Thomas Roe's embassy, printed along with the English translation of Pietro de la Valle's travels to the Malabar coast.

† It is a great impropriety to call the Mahometan-usurpers of India by the name of Moors: and yet, as the writers of all nations have always given them that appellation, it would now be a greater impropriety to deviate from that usage.

of the foregoing obſervation, will be ſhewn, if the majority of readers ſhall happen to be unacquainted with the journal of ſo eminent a perſon as Sir Thomas Roe, who was ambaſſador from James I. to the Mogul Jehan Guire. As no Engliſhman has lately had the opportunity of ſo familiar an intercourſe with thoſe Monarchs, the accounts given by him of the ſplendor of the Mogul, ſo greatly diminiſhed of late years, with ſome particulars of his private life, may not improperly be here inſerted: and it is to be remark'd, that ſo ſtrict is their attachment to antient manners, that they never change their modes of life or faſhions; and therefore whoever reads a deſcription of them in any diſtant time, will have a moſt exact repreſentation of their preſent manners.

Extract of a Letter from Sir THOMAS ROE, to the Archbiſhop of *Canterbury*, dated *Adſmere*, *January* 29, 1615.

'THESE people have no Written Laws, the 'King's judgment binds; who ſits and gives 'ſentence once a week with much patience, both in 'civil and criminal cauſes, where ſometimes he ſees 'the execution done by his Elephants with too much 'delight in blood.

'His Governors of provinces rule by his Firmans, 'which are his letters or commiſſions authorizing 'them, and take life and goods at pleaſure.

'In revenue he doubtleſs exceeds either Turk or 'Perſian, or any Eaſtern Prince, the ſums I dare not 'name: but the reaſon, all the lands are his, no 'man has a foot. He maintains all that are not me-'chanics, by revenues beſtowed on them, reck-'oned by horſes; and the allowance of many is grea-'ter than the eſtates of German Princes. All men 'riſe to greater and greater Lordſhips as they ad-'vance in favour, which is got by frequent preſents, 'rich and rare. The Mogul is heir to all that die,

'as

'as well thoſe that gained it by their induſtry, as 'merchants, &c. as thoſe that live by him. He 'takes all their money, only leaving the widow and 'daughters what he pleaſes. To the ſons of thoſe 'that die worth two or three millions, he gives ſome 'ſmall Lordſhip to begin the world anew. The 'King ſits out in three ſeveral places three times of 'the day, except ſomething extraordinary hinders 'him: an hour at noon to ſee his elephants fight, 'from four till five to entertain all comers, to be ſeen 'and worſhipped; from nine till midnight amidſt his 'principal men in more familiarity, being below 'among them.

'All the policy of his ſtate is to keep the greateſt 'men about him, or to pay them afar off liberally *. 'There is no council, but every officer gives the King 'his opinion apart. He (meaning Jehan Guire, 'Grandfather of Aurengzebe) is of countenance 'cheerful, and not proud in nature, but only by ha-'bit and cuſtom, for at night he is very affable and 'full of gentle converſation.

'The buildings are all baſe, of mud, one ſtory 'high. I know not by what policy the King ſeeks 'the ruin of all the antient cities which were nobly 'built, and now lie deſolate and in rubbiſh. His own 'houſes are of ſtone, handſome and uniform. His 'great men build not, for want of inheritance, and 'as far as I have yet ſeen, live in tents or houſes worſe 'than our cottages.'

A Letter of the ſame date from Sir THOMAS ROE, to the Eaſt-India Company.

'AT my firſt audience, the Mogul prevented 'me in ſpeech, bidding me welcome as to the 'brother of the King my maſter: and after many 'com-

* And whether at home or abroad, to keep a great number of ſpies continually about them.

'compliments, I delivered his Majesty's letter, with 'a copy of it in Persian: then I shewed my commis-'sion, and delivered your presents, that is, the coach, 'the virginals, the knives, a scarf embroidered, and 'a sword of my own. He, sitting in his state, could 'not well see the coach, but sent many to view it, 'and caused the musician to play on the virginals, 'which gave him content. At night, having staid 'the coachman and musician, he came down into a 'court, got into the coach, and into every corner of 'it, causing it to be drawn about. Then he sent to 'me, though it was ten o'clock at night, for a ser-'vant to put on his scarf and sword after the English 'fashion, of which he was so proud, that he walk-'ed up and down flourishing it, and has never since 'been seen without it. But after the English were 'come away, he asked the Jesuit, whether the King 'of England was a great King, that sent presents of 'so small value, and that he looked for some jewels.

'There is nothing more welcome here, nor did I 'ever see men so fond of drink, as the King and 'Prince are of red wine, whereof the Governor of 'Surat sent up some bottles, and the King has ever 'since solicited for more: I think four or five casks 'of that wine will be more welcome than the richest 'jewels in Cheapside."

Extracts from Sir THOMAS ROE's Journal.

'THE King having been far gone over night in 'wine, some, however accidentally or malici-'ously, spoke of the last merry night, and that many 'of the nobility drank wine, which none must do 'without leave. The King forgetting his order, ask-'ed who gave it, and answer was made the Buckshee; 'for no man dares say it was the King when he 'makes a doubt of it. The custom is, that when 'the King drinks, which is alone, sometimes he will 'command the nobility to drink after him, which if they

'they do not, it is looked upon as a crime: and ſo 'every man that takes a cup of wine of the officer, 'has his name writ down, and he makes his obei- 'ſance, though perhaps the King's eyes are clouded 'The King not remembering his own command, 'called the Buckſhee, and aſked whether he gave 'the order, who falſely denied it, for he had it 'from the King, and by name called all that drank 'with the Embaſſador. The King then called for the 'liſt, and the perſons named in it, and fined ſome 'one, ſome two, and ſome three thouſand roupees; 'and ſome that were nearer his perſon, he cauſed to 'be whipped before him, they receiving a hundred 'and thirty ſtripes with a terrible inſtrument, having 'at the ends of four cords, irons like ſpur-rowels, ſo 'that every ſtroke made four wounds. When they 'lay for dead on the ground, he commanded the 'ſtanders-by to ſpurn them, and after that, the por- 'ters to break their ſtaves on them. Thus moſt cru- 'elly mangled and bruiſed they were carried out: 'one of them died on the ſpot, ſome would have 'excuſed it by laying it on the Embaſſador, but the 'King replied he only ordered a cup or two to be giv- 'en him. Drunkenneſs is a common vice, and an ex- 'erciſe of the King's, yet it is ſo ſtrictly forbidden, 'that no man can enter the Guzelcan when the King 'ſits, but the porters ſmell his breath, and if he have 'but taſted wine, he is not ſuffered to come in, and 'if the reaſon of his abſence be but known, it will 'be a difficult matter to eſcape the whip; for if the 'King once takes offence, the father will not ſpeak 'for the ſon.

'The ſecond of September was the King's birth- 'day, and kept with great ſolemnity. On this day 'the King is weighed againſt ſome jewels, gold, ſilver, 'ſtuffs of gold, ſilver, and ſilks, butter, rice, fruit, 'and many other things, of every ſort a little, which 'is all given to the Bramins.

'He

'He was so rich in jewels, that I own in my life I 'never saw such inestimable wealth together. The 'time was spent in bringing his greatest elephants be-'fore him; some of which being lord-elephants, had 'their chains, bells, and furniture of gold and silver, 'with many gilt banners and flags carried about 'them, and eight or ten elephants waiting on each of 'them cloathed in gold, silk, and silver.

'In this manner about twelve companies passed by 'most richly adorned, the first having all the plates 'on his head and breast set with rubies and emeralds, 'being a beast of wonderful bulk and beauty. They 'all bowed down before the King, making their re-'verence very handsomely: this was the finest show 'of beasts I ever saw.

'I found the Mogul sitting on his throne, and a 'beggar at his feet, a poor silly old man, all ragged 'and patched. The country abounds in this sort of 'professed poor holy men; they are called Fakeers *, 'and held in great veneration: and in works of mor-'tification and voluntary suffering, they outdo all 'that ever has been pretended either by Hereticks or 'Idolaters. This miserable wretch cloathed in rags, 'crowned with feathers, and covered with ashes, his 'Majesty talked with about an hour so familiarly, and with

* There are few books of Voyages among the Turks or Indians which do not make mention of the Fakeers or Joguies. The former is a Turkish word, and signifies poor, the latter is the Indian name for these extraordinary saints, for such they are esteemed, and are called Santos at Cairo, and in many other parts It is well known that the veneration paid to the numerous body of these worthless and insolent beggars, is owing to the opinion of extraordinary sanctity which a few of this sect acquire by the performance of certain singular and fantastical vows. Some have made a vow to hold their arms above their head till they contract a stiffness, and can never be moved: others to keep their hands clenched till their nails grow through them: others to sit in chairs full of sharp nails, to drag a heavy chain, to carry vast weights about their necks, or fire on their heads. Some years ago one of these made a vow to measure the length of the whole empire with his own body; and at this time there is a Fakeer who every day rolls himself round the rock at Trichinopoly, which is a mile in circumference.

'with such seeming kindness, that it must needs argue an humility not found easily among Kings. The beggar sat, which the King's son dares not do. He gave the King a present of a cake mixed with ashes, burnt on the coals, and made by himself of coarse grain, which the King willingly accepted, broke a bit and eat it, which a nice person could scarce have done; then he took the clout that wrapped it up, and put it into the poor man's bosom, and sent for an hundred roupees, and with his own hand poured them into the poor man's lap, and gathered up for him what fell besides. When his collation or banquet, and drink came, whatsoever he took to eat he broke and gave the beggar half; and rising, after many humiliations and charities, the old wretch not being nimble, he took him up in his arms, though no cleanly person durst have touched him, and embracing him three times, laying his hand upon his heart, and calling him father, left him and all of us in admiration.

'While the King appeared at the window, two eunuchs stood on two tressels with long poles, and feather-fans at the end of them, fanning him. He bestowed many favours, and received presents. At one side in a window were his two principal wives, whose curiosity made them break little holes in a grate of reed that hung before it, to gaze on me: I saw first their fingers, and then, they laying their face close, first the one and then the other, I could sometimes discern their full proportion. They were indifferently white, with black hair smoothed up: but if there had been no other light, their diamonds and pearls had sufficed to show them. When I looked up they retired, and were so merry, that I supposed they laughed at me. On a sudden the King rose, we retired to the Durbar, and sat on the carpets, attending his coming out. Not long after he came and sat about half an hour, till his Ladies at their door had mounted their elephants, which were

'about

'about fifty, all of them richly adorned, but chiefly 'with turrets on their backs, all inclosed with grates 'of gold wire to look through, and canopies over 'of cloth of silver. Then the King came down the 'stairs with such an acclamation of health to the 'King, as would have out-roared cannon. At the 'foot of the stairs, where I met him, and shuffled to 'be next, one brought a mighty carp, another a dish 'of white stuff like starch, into which he put his fin-'ger, and touched the fish, and so rubbed it on his 'forehead: a ceremony used presaging good fortune. 'Then another came and girt on his sword, and hung 'on his buckler, set all over with diamonds and ru-'bies, the belts of gold suitable: another hung on 'his quiver with thirty arrows, and his bow in a case, 'being the same that was presented by the Persian 'Embassador. On his head he wore a rich turbant, 'with a plume of Heron's feathers, not many, but 'long: on the one side a ruby unset as big as a walnut, 'on the other side a diamond as large; in the mid-'dle an emerald much bigger. His staff was wound 'about with a chain of great pearl, rubies and dia-'monds drilled. About his neck he wore a chain of 'three strings of most excellent pearl, the largest I ever 'saw. Above his elbows, armlets set with diamonds, 'and on his wrists, three rows of several sorts; his hands 'bare, but almost on every finger a ring; his gloves, 'which were English, stuck under his girdle. His 'coat of cloth of gold without sleeves, upon a fine 'semian as thin as lawn. On his feet a pair of bus-'kins embroidered with pearl, the toes sharp and tur-'ning up. Thus armed and accoutred, he went to 'the coach that attended him with his new English 'servant, who was cloathed as rich as any player, and 'more gaudy, and had broke four horses, which were 'trapped and harnessed in gold and velvets. This was 'the first coach he ever sat in, made by that sent out 'of England, and so like, that I knew it not but by 'the cover, which was a Persian gold velvet. He

'sat

'sat at the end, and on each side went two eunuchs, 'who carried small maces of gold set all over with rubies, with a long bunch of horse-tail to slap the flies 'away. Before him went drums, base trumpets, and 'loud musick; many canopies, umbrellas, and other 'strange ensigns of majesty, made of cloth of gold, 'set in many places with rubies. Nine led horses, the 'furniture all garnished, some with pearls and emeralds, some only with studs enamelled. The Persian Embassador presented him a horse. Next behind came three palankeens, the carriages and feet 'of one plated with gold, set at the ends with stones, 'and covered with crimson velvet, embroidered with 'pearl, and fringes of great pearl, hanging in ropes 'a foot deep, a border about it set with rubies and 'emeralds: and a footman carried a footstool of gold 'set with stones. The other two palankeens were 'covered and lined only with cloth of gold. Next 'followed the English coach newly covered and richly 'adorned, which he had given to Queen Nourmahal, who sat in it. After them a third, in which 'sat his youngest sons. Then followed above twenty 'elephants royal, led for him to mount, so rich in 'stones and furniture that they glittered like the sun. 'Every elephant had sundry flags of cloth of silver, 'gilt sattin and taffety. His noblemen he suffered to walk on foot, which I did to the gate, and 'left him. His Wives on their elephants were carried half a mile behind him.

'When he came before the door, where was his eldest son kept prisoner, he stayed the coach, and called for him. He came and made reverence, with a 'sword and buckler in his hand, his beard grown to 'his middle, a sign of disfavour. The King commanded him to mount one of the spare elephants, 'and so rode next to him, with extraordinary applause 'and joy of all men, who are now filled with new 'hopes. The King gave him one thousand roupees 'to cast to the people. His Jailor, Asaph Chan, and 'all those monsters, were yet on foot: I took horse 'to avoid the croud and other inconveniences, and 'crossed out of the Leskar before him, waiting till he 'came near his tents. He passed all the way between 'a guard of elephants, having every one a turret 'on his back, and on the four corners of each, four 'banners of yellow taffety, and right before a piece 'of cannon carrying a bullet as big as a tennis-ball, 'the gunner behind it. They were in all about three 'hundred. Other elephants of state went before, and 'behind, about six hundred, all of which were co- 'vered with velvet, or cloth of gold, and had two 'or three gilded banners: several footmen ran along 'the way with skins of water to lay the dust before 'the King. No horse or man was suffered to come 'within two furlongs of the coach, except those that 'walked by on foot; so that I hasted to his tents to 'attend his alighting. They were walled in about 'half an English mile in compass, in form of a fort, 'with several angles and bulwarks, and high cur- 'tains of a coarse stuff made like arras, red on the 'outside, and within figures in panes, with a hand- 'some gatehouse; every post that bore these up was 'headed with brass. The throng was great: I had 'a mind to go in, but no one was permitted, the 'greatest in the land sitting at the door; however I 'made an offer, and they admitted me, but refused 'the Persian Embassador. In the midst of this court 'was a throne of Mother of Pearl, borne on two 'pillars raised on earth, covered over with a high 'tent, the pole headed with a knob of gold: under 'that, canopies of cloth of gold, and under-foot 'carpets. When the King entered, every man cried '*joy and good fortune*, and so we took our places. 'He called for water, washed his hands, and depar- 'ted. His women went in some other way to their 'apartments, and his son I saw not.

'Within

'Within this inclosure where about thirty divisions with tents. All the noblemen retired to theirs which were in excellent forms, some all white, some green, some mixed, all inclosed as orderly as any house, in the most magnificent manner I ever saw. The vale showed like a beautiful city, for the baggage made no confusion; I was ill provided with carriages, and ashamed of my equipage; for five years allowance would not have provided me an indifferent tent answerable to others, and to add to the grandeur, every man has two, so that one of them goes before to the next ground and is set up a day before the King rises from the place where he is.

A Circumstance which may appear trifling will greatly contribute to compleat the idea which Sir Thomas Roe has given us of the Moors in India.

It happened there was among the presents, a picture of Venus leading a Satyr by the nose. The Mogul when he saw this, shewed it to his courtiers, and bid them remark the action of the woman, the blackness of the Satyr's skin, and other particulars, giving them to understand, he considered it as a reflection on the people of Asia, whom he supposed to be represented by the Satyr, as being of their complexion; and that the Venus leading him by the nose denoted the great power the women of that country have over the men.

It was indeed too apposite an emblem; and this, will give a just representation of the luxurious indolence in which they pass the greatest part of their lives, except when they are at war. As they sit for the most part (when they are not with their women) upon their sofas, smoaking, and amusing themselves with their jewels, taking coffee or sweetmeats, seeing their quails fight, or such like pastimes; nothing ſurprizes them ſo much as to ſee a European walk about a room; and none but their very young people ever ride for amuſement or exerciſe only.

Though Sir THOMAS ROE repreſents the pride of the Mogul as ſcarcely ſupportable to an Engliſhman, yet that Embaſſador appears to have been favoured in a very extraordinary manner. The extreme diſregard which the Aſiatic Sovereigns naturally have for Europeans, is fully ſet forth in the following extract from M. de Buſſy's letter publiſhed in Mr. Dupleix's Memoirs. It is a juſt and moſt authentic picture of the haughty demeanor and aſſuming arrogance of thoſe people, and will prove what has been advanced of the very little intercourſe we could have had with them.

Extract of a Letter from M. de Buſſy.

POUR bien apprécier l'etat préſent de la nation Francoiſe dans l' Inde, il faut ſe rapeller ces tems d' humiliations oú les Francois étoient forcés pour le bien de leur commerce, d'aller timidiment porter leurs preſens & leurs hommages á de petits chefs de Bourgades que nous n'admetons aujourd'hui a nos Dorbards, que lorſque nos intérêts l'exigent; Je ne parle pas d'un tems bien eloigné, il n'y a que ſix ans que ce changement a commencé; alors le Nabob d' Arcate tout petit Seigneur qu'il etoit, comparé au Souba du Dekam dont il n'étoit que le Fermier, traiter avec nous comme un Souverain avec ſes ſujéts. Il prenoit, en écrivant á nos Gouverneurs, un ton d'autorité bien humiliant pour la nation Francoiſe. Nous ne paroiſſions qu'en ſupplians, & toujours chargés de préſens qu'il exigeoit comme un tribut. Quelqu'un de ſes bas-officiers approchoit il de Pondichery, on envoyoit par députation le recevoir au loin, avec de grandes marques de conſidération. En un mot, quiconque ſe diſoit envoyé de ſa part, étoit aſſuré d'être craint,

craint, respecté, chargé de présens de la nôtre. Il falloit, disoit on, tout mettre en usage pour ne point irriter ces petits tyrans, dont le ressentiment pouvoit porter un préjudice considérable au commerce. Il etoit inoui alors qu'un Souba du Dekam abaissat sa fierté jusqu' â ecrire a un Commandant Général des Francois. Quand Nisam Elmoulouk; pere du Nabob régnant, vint dans la province d' Arcate pour reprendre sur les Marattes la ville de Trichenapoly toutes les nations Européennes s'empresserent á lui donner des marques de leur soumission & mirent tout en usage pour gagner sa bienveillance. Daigna-t'il écrire à aucun de ceux qui les représentoient? Non sans doute; il ne daigna pas même honorer d'un de ses regards les riches présens qu'on jettoit respectueusement á ses pieds, comme un hommage de dépendance. Quelles etoient les bornes des establissements de la compagnie avant l'expédition qui m'occupe depuis quatre ans? Pondichery, Carikal, Chandernagor en composoient á peu prés toute l'étendue. Pouroit-on franchir ces bornes sans faire des bassesies & des présens, pour en obtenir la permission des Faussedars où Fermiers du pays?

A Translation of the foregoing.

'TO form a true judgment of the advantageous 'change in the affairs of the French in India, 'we must go back to those times when they were 'obliged, for the interest of their commerce, in a 'servile manner to carry their presents, and pay their 'homage to those petty chiefs whom we do not at 'present deign to admit to our Durbar, except 'when some particular interest requires it. I speak 'not of distant times, this change is within these 'six years. It was no longer ago that the Nabob of 'Arcot, inconsiderable as he is in regard to the Souba of the Deckan, for he is but a farmer of his revenues, behaved to us as a sovereign to his subjects.

jects. His letter to our Governours ran in a ſtrain of authority opprobrious to the French nation. We never appeared beſore him but as ſuppliants carrying preſents, which he continually exacted from us. If any even of his inferior officers came towards Pondichery, formal deputations were ſent out to meet them with the greateſt marks of reſpect. The utmoſt care was taken to avoid giving offence to thoſe petty tyrants, whoſe reſentment might have prejudiced our commerce.

‘For a Souba of the Deckan to condeſcend to write to the Commandant General of the French, was a thing unheard of, and not to be expected. When Nizam al Mulk, father of the reigning Souba, came into the province of Arcot to retake Trichinopoly from the Marattas, the European nations ſtrove who ſhould give him the ſtrongeſt marks of their ſubmiſſion, and omitted no means of gaining his favour: yet he deigned not to write to any of the Governors who repreſented thoſe nations, and hardly honoured with a look the rich preſents, laid with all imaginable reſpect at his feet, as a token of their homage and dependence.

‘What were the bounds of the Company's eſtabliſhments before the expedition which has taken me up theſe four years? Pondichery, Carical, and Chandernagore, where the whole of their extent: thoſe bounds could not be paſſed without ſubmiſſion and preſents, to obtain leave from the farmers of the revenue.

IT is evident from this letter, how few Europeans have of late been acquainted with the interior parts of the country. But M. de Buſſy, by accompanying Salabatzing in all his motions, and ſome of our own countrymen, from their intimate and familiar intercourſe with the governing people in * Bengal, have had

* When they were at Patna, they had conſtant advices from Delli.

had all advantages of information; and it was from a certain knowledge, that the most ample and instructive materials for this purpose had been provided in the country, and were now actually in England, that I desisted from the design I had once entertained of entering on the affairs of Bengal. Besides, I had not engaged in any part of this work many weeks, before there appeared some Memoirs of the Revolutions in Bengal, published by a person principally concerned in them, which anticipated my purpose of giving a slight view of those affairs: And whenever the publick shall be favoured by those who are so capable and so well prepared thoroughly to explain not only the secret springs of the great events and revolutions, but also the civil, commercial, and natural history of Bengal, it will appear how much more properly the history of that province is left to those who had a personal share in the transactions, and had themselves seen and considered the state of the country. If, contrary to my apprehension, the same reasoning ought to have deterred me from attempting the relation of the war in the other parts of India, it will give me great pleasure to see the history of the Coast of Coromandel also laid before the publick in a manner more worthy their attention.

COLONEL LAWRENCE's

NARRATIVE OF THE WAR,

ON THE

COAST OF COROMANDEL,

From the Beginning of the Troubles to the Year 1754.

1730.

THE authority of the Nabob Mahomet Allee Cawn having been diſputed by the French, was the firſt cauſe of the war. I ſhall endeavour to ſhew how he founded his right, and with what juſtice the French ſupported his competitors. I ſhall trace it from the year 1730, as the different appointments, made ſince that time by the viceroys of the Deckan, have a neceſſary connection with many parts of this narrative, and lead to a knowledge of the perſons principally concerned in this ſcene of troubles.

The viceroy of the Deckan, in the year 1730, was called Nizam Almuluck. According to his right of of nominating a Governor of the Carnatick, now more generally known by the name of the Nabob of Arcot, he appointed Sadet Allee Cawn, who was succeeded by his nephew Deuſt Allee Cawn, who governed in the year 1740.

Chunda Saib, a man of no family or riches, but endowed by nature with talents, and a capacity that made ample amends for what fortune had denied him, had the command of a ſmall diſtrict of country, and could bring about an hundred horſe into the field. He ſerved under Deuſt Allee Cawn, to whom his genius ſoon made him known, and ſo uſeful, that he advanced him, and married him to one of his daughters.

The kingdom of Trichinopoly was then under the Gentou government. The king dying, left no children, and appointed his brother's ſon to ſucceed. The dowager queen, ſupported by her two brothers, put in a claim to the regency, till her eldeſt brother's ſon was of a fit age to reign. There was a third party formed, by a relation of the deceaſed king, who demanded the throne as his right, and brought a large army to ſupport his pretenſions *. The king's party was ſoon thrown out of the competition, and the diſpute continued between the queen and the king's relations. The queen applied to the Nabob of Arcot, and he came to her aſſiſtance, and with him Chunda Saib, as his general, who managed affairs ſo well, that, having weaken'd both, he formed a ſtronger party for himſelf, and waited with patience till his ſcheme was ripe for execution. Under pretence of a viſit to the queen, he introduced himſelf and ſome troops into the town, got poſſeſſion of it, put to death all the different competitors, plundered and impriſoned the queen, who, finding no reſource left, poiſoned herſelf; firſt burning the alcoran on which Chunda Saib had ſworn that his only views in this viſit were to

* The Gentou queen's name was Menachiama. Her competitor, the king's relation, Trimolanaik.

to ſhew marks of reſpect and regard. Thus the government of the kingdom of Trichinopoly was changed in 1738, and ſtill continues under the Nabob of Arcot; and is commonly given to one of his neareſt relations.

In the year 1740, the Marattas invaded Arcot; and overthrew Deuſt Allee Cawn in a battle which coſt him his life. His ſon, Subter Allee Cawn, on his father's death, fled to Madraſs, and there obtained the protection of Mr. Benyon, then governor. Soon after he received a grant from Nizam Almuluck, appointing him Nabob of Arcot; but, in the year 1744, he was treacherouſly murdered, at a feaſt made by his brother-in-law Mootis Allee Cawn, at Velloure, a ſtrong fort, twelve miles from Arcot.

Coza Abdallah Cawn ſucceeded him, and was himſelf, ſhortly after, ſucceeded by Anaverdy Cawn, our preſent Nabob's father, who was appointed, by the viceroy of the Deckan, nabob of Arcot, in the year 1745.

Chunda Saib remained at Trichinopoly till the year 1741, when the Marattas came a ſecond time into the country, beſieged the town, got poſſeſſion of it, and took him priſoner. He was carried to Sattarah, the Marattas' capital, and there confined till 1748, the year in which Nizam Almuluck died.

Nizam Almuluck left four ſons, Gauzedy Cawn, Nazerzing, Salabatzing, and Nizam Allee.

Though the ſucceſſion in this country is not hereditary, yet it commonly runs in the ſame family, eſpecially when the ſurvivors have power to make good their pretenſions, and money to ſecure the Mogul's appointment. Gauzedy Cawn, the eldeſt ſon, was then Bucſhee, or pay-maſter-general to the Mogul, the ſecond man in power, next to the Vizier, in this mighty empire. He having perhaps more ambitious views, refuſed the viceroyalty of the Deckan, but made over his intereſt to the ſecond ſon Nazerzing, who was appointed by the Mogul Shaw Hamet.

Nizam

Nizam Almuluck had alſo a nephew, Eradmoodin Cawn, commonly called Muzapherzing, who, on his uncle's death, laid claim to the Carnatick, founded, as he ſaid, on a promiſe from his uncle. But Nazirzing refuſed his conſent, and confirmed Anaverdy Cawn, agreeable to his father's appointment. On this refuſal Muzapherzing declared he would ſupport his pretenſions by open force. His firſt ſtep was to go to Sattarah, and apply to Ballazerow, chief of the Marattas, for aſſiſtance. There he ſaw Chunda Saib, who ſtill remained priſoner. Muzapherzing engaged to get him releaſed, and Chunda Saib, on his ſide, promiſed to go to Pondichery, and influence Mr. Dupleix to aſſiſt and ſupport him in his cauſe. The Maratta chief conſented to every thing, and promiſed his aſſiſtance. He kept his word in regard to the releaſing of Chunda Saib, but ſent no troops. Chunda Saib ſet out for Pondichery, in 1748, and Muzapherzing prepared to raiſe an army.

Chunda Saib ſucceeded, made ſome preſents, and promiſed much more; and, when Muzapherzing was ready, they were joined by ſix hundred French, and a train of artillery. In July 1749, they marched for Arcot, and there encountered Anaverdy Cawn, who loſt the victory and his life. His eldeſt ſon, Mauphus Cawn, was taken priſoner, and his ſecond ſon, Mahomed Allee Cawn, the preſent Nabob, made the beſt of his way to his government of Trichinopoly, waiting there for an opportunity to revenge his father's death. The victorious army purſued the blow, took Arcot, and over-ran the whole province. They afterwards returned to Pondichery, where Muzapherzing appointed Chunda Saib Nabob of Arcot.

They remained quiet at Pondichery, till Admiral Boſcawen ſailed for Europe, not daring to move till he was out of ſight. The day after October 21, 1749, they took the field, and raiſed contributions all over the country. The king of Tanjore, having refuſed to acknowledge Muzapherzing, or Chunda Saib, they marched and laid ſiege to his capital. The

French

French were commanded by Mr. Law, nephew of the famous Missisippi Law. They soon made a breach, but the troops within seeming determined to defend it, they were afraid to venture an assault. By protracting the siege, the people in the town were reduced to their last barrel of powder; but, however, they saved the place, by compounding for some lacks of * roupees in ready money, and a bill for seventy-five lacks more. The enemy raised the siege, but, after one day's march, the French army returned, and insisted on a sum of money for themselves, alledging that they had not received any part of what was paid. However, it was to no purpose, for the king of Tanjore, having received in that time a reinforcement of Sepoys and gunners, and a large quantity of powder from Trichinopoly, refused to give any more. Still the breach remained open, which the French would not attack. In the mean time, certain accounts came of Nazerzing's march from Aurengabad towards Arcot, in order to punish Muzapherzing, and Chunda Saib, for their rebellion. This obliged them to raise the siege a second time in good earnest, and return to Pondichery. This passed in January 1750.

Ever since Anaverdy Cawn's defeat, his son, Mahomed Allee Cawn, had desired our assistance It was necessary to put a stop to the progress of the French, whether in justice to assist the lawful prince against rebels, or as an act of self-defence, and to prevent an increase of power in an oppressive neighbour, that must at last, have proved our ruin. This determined us to protect the Nabob Mahomet Allee Cawn, till we could know Nazirzing's determination: captain Cope was therefore sent with a detachment to Trichinopoly.

Nazirzing had given orders to the Nabob to join him on his march, in obedience to which he set out from Trichinopoly, at the head of a large army of horse,

* A lack of roupees is about 12000 l. sterling.

horſe, and the Engliſh detachment commanded by Captain Cope, and joined Nazirzing at * Waldore, in February 1750. As it is cuſtomary amongſt all Eaſtern princes to make preſents on the firſt viſit, when the Nabob waited on Nazirzing, he aſked him what he had brought: the Nabob took Captain Cope by the hand, and, preſenting him, ſaid he had brought that gentleman and the aſſiſtance of the Engliſh nation. Nazirzing was pleaſed with the anſwer, conferred ſome honours on Captain Cope, and, a few days after, appointed Mahomed Allee Cawn to ſucceed his father, as Nabob of Arcot and Trichinopoly.

Muzapherzing and Chunda Saib marched out of Pondichery with their army, and two thouſand Europeans commanded by Mr. Dauteuil, with a large train of artillery, and a numerous body of Sepoys. They took poſt within a few miles of Nazirzing, at whoſe earneſt and repeated requeſt, I marched with ſix hundred men, accompanied with Mr. Weſtcott, one of the council, with a commiſſion to treat with Nazirzing, in which we were aſſiſted by Captain Dalton.

We joined him at Villanure, and were very graciouſly received, ſuitable to the dignity of an Eaſtern prince, at the head of three hundred thouſand men, of which he declared me Generaliſſimo. He propoſed to me to attack the enemy immediately; I told him, in the Eaſtern ſtile, that he muſt be ſure of victory wherever he fought, yet the attack might be attended with ſome difficulty, and coſt him the lives of many brave men, as the enemy were ſtrongly poſted†, and

* A fort ſome miles weſt of Pondichery.

† The French were entrenched, and had 20 pieces of cannon. Nazarzing had 800; but his principal officer of artillery was an Iriſhman, for the natives, in general, think every European an Engineer. I happened to find fault with this gentleman's diſpoſition of his artillery, which was in a hollow, where his cannon were hid. He gravely replied, "What, did I think him mad, or fooliſh "enough, to expoſe his excellency's cannon, by placing it on a "riſing ground?"

and had with them a large train of artillery. But that, if he pleaſed to march between them and Pondichery, he might, by cutting off their communication, oblige them to fight at a greater diſadvantage.

However juſt my propoſal might be, his anſwer was as follows: What! ſhall the great Nazirzing, the ſon of Nizam al Mulk, even for an advantage, ſeem to retreat before ſo deſpicable an enemy? no, he would march and attack them in front. I told him he might do as he pleaſed, I was ready to ſupport him.

The two armies were ſo near, that the next day we cannonaded, and were drawn out to engage.

In this ſituation, a meſſenger came to me from Mr. Dauteuil, to acquaint me, "That although we were "engaged in different cauſes, yet it was not his de-"ſign nor inclination, that any European blood ſhould "be ſpilt: but as he did not know our poſt, ſhould "any of his ſhot come that way, and hurt the Eng-"liſh, he could not be blamed." I ſent him for anſwer, "That I had the honour of carrying the "Engliſh colours on my flag gun, which if he plea-"ſed to look out for, he might know from thence "where the Engliſh were poſted;" and I aſſured him, I ſhould alſo be very loth to ſpill European blood; but, if any ſhot came that way, he might be aſſured I would return them.

To know, I ſuppoſe, whether I was in earneſt, a ſhot was fired from their battery over our heads: I ordered three guns to anſwer to it, and ſaw them well pointed. Mr. Dauteuil ſeeing us reſolved not to look tamely on, and probably fearing the ſucceſs of an action, thought it more prudent to retreat in the night. Leſt his heavy artillery ſhould retard him, he, for the greater expedition, left eleven pieces behind; and what was worſe, part of his artillery-men with them, the better to conceal his deſign; for he gave out, he was only going to alarm our camp in the night, and would be back in the morning.

Nazirzing

Nazirzing having immediate notice of his retreat, ſoon routed Muzapherzing's and Chunda's Saib's forces; fell in with the unfortunate French gunners left behind as a ſacrifice, and cut moſt of them to pieces. We ſaved as many as we could, taking them by force out of the hands of the Moors, got their wounds dreſſed by our ſurgeons, and took all the care of them that humanity required of us. In return, Mr. Dupleix wrote a long proteſt againſt me, for making French ſubjects priſoners in time of peace; but the poor fellows, more ſenſible of the obligations they were under to us, very gratefully acknowledged our tender uſage, and confeſſed it was entirely owing to us that they were ſaved.

The ſame night a large detachment of Marattas from Nazirzing's camp, commanded by Morarow *, were ſent in purſuit of Mr. Dauteuil. They came up with him the next day. Mr. Dauteuil formed his men into a ſquare. Morarow attacked and broke it with only fifteen men, imagining his whole party in his rear; but ſeeing his danger, he with that handful, when ſurrounded, boldly puſhed for it; and breaking through the oppoſite ſide, cleared his way with ſix men, having loſt nine in the attack.

On the retreat of the French and their army being diſperſed, Muzapherzing ſubmitted to, and implored the mercy of his uncle, who received him into his camp, and detained him as a ſtate priſoner; but Chunda Saib, whoſe ſole dependance was on Mr Dupleix, continued obſtinate, and retreated with the French to Pondichery. Muzapherzing's ſubmiſſion, as will ſhortly appear, was only

* Morarow, whoſe name often occurs in this narrative, is a Maratta, who by ſupporting the diviſions in the country, has made himſelf conſiderable from a ſmall beginning; he ſides with no party but as he finds his advantage in it, and as eaſily changes ſides; he commands about 3000 very good horſe. When he is not employed or paid by any prince, he ſcours the country for himſelf, and raiſes contributions where he can get moſt, and with leaſt riſque. His real maſter is the Nanah Shaw Raja; but he obeys his orders juſt as they are conducive to his own intereſt.

ly politic, and, that he might be nearer at hand, to concert a ſcheme, which in a few months was put in execution, at the expence of his uncle's life. The conſequence of the victory was the retaking of Arcot, which again acknowledged its lawful maſter.

Mr. Dupleix, after this diſgrace, wrote a long letter to Nazirzing, which he would not open or read but in our preſence. Though he pretended ſubmiſſion to the viceroy, he had ſtill the preſumption to dictate to him, and inſiſt, that none of the family of Anaverdy Cawn ſhould ever govern the province of Arcot. Ambaſſadors came alſo to treat publickly for an accommodation, but their real buſineſs was privately to concert meaſures with Shanavas Cawn, Nazirzing's prime miniſter and the * chiefs of the conſpiracy, which was firſt laid in Pondichery by Chunda Saib and Mr. Dupleix, who promiſed to aſſiſt them to the utmoſt of his power, as it plainly appeared afterwards. Though this was carried on with great ſecrecy, I had information that ſome deſign was on foot againſt Nazirzing, and that Shanavas Cawn was principally concerned in it. I therefore deſired my interpreter to acquaint Nazirzing with what I had heard, and in particular what concerned his prime miniſter. But ſo great were the apprehenſions of the perſon we employed as linguiſt, that he did not dare to ſay what I directed him, nor accuſe a perſon in ſuch high favour and power as Shanavas Cawn, who was preſent, ſo much did he dread his reſentment, which I plainly diſcovered from the anſwers I received from Nazirzing, and the confuſion of the interpreter..

D Part

* The two principals of which were the Nabobs of Cadapah and Condanore. Theſe Nabobs are under the viceroy of the Deckan ; their country is in the Subaſhip of Golconda ; they have in their pay numbers of Patans, who are reckoned the beſt ſoldiers amongſt theſe eaſtern moors : as the policy of this ill-ruled empire requires frequent aſſaſſinations, theſe Patans are eſteemed very uſeful in that kind of villainy.

Part of our instructions to Nazirzing were, to obtain an enlargement of our bounds round Madrass, which he frequently promised, and certainly intended to perform, had not his minister, who was in an opposite interest, contrived to disappoint us, by delaying and putting us off from time to time. Seeing ourselves only amused, we pressed our demands with more earnestness, and Nazirzing promised we should be immediately satisfied; but desired we would march with him to Arcot, a proposal we could by no means consent to, as it would have left our settlements and frontier bounds exposed to the insults of 2000 French, and Chunda Saib, who at this time was raising another army. We also endeavoured to make him sensible, that his march to Arcot removed him too far from his enemies, who were only waiting for a favourable opportunity to renew the troubles. That it was easy for him, by staying where he was, to finish the business effectually, and to distress his enemies, by cutting off their communication with the country, and thereby oblige them to accept of whatever terms he would please to offer them. But the more we urged against his march to Arcot the more his favourite pressed him to it. Our removal from him was the great object of the party, that had resolved his ruin.

Finding all our endeavours were of no weight against a determined scheme, we marched to our settlements, and Nazirzing to Arcot, where, lulled into a security, by what he was willing to look upon as a victory, he gave himself up entirely to the pleasures he was fondest of, women and hunting. Nothing was omitted by the faction to amuse him, and take off his attention from business, or whatever might lead to a discovery of the designs which were carrying on against him.

The detachment commanded by Morarow, sent in pursuit of the French, when they retreated from Nazirzing encamped near Pondichery, with their usual carelessness.

careleſſneſs. The French attacked them in the night, when they little expected, and were as little prepared for an enemy, and eaſily put them to the rout, killed a great many, and got poſſeſſion of their camp and baggage. This ſucceſs animated the French, and they once more took the field with Chunda Saib, and marched for Trividy, a fortified pagoda, ſituated about ſixteen miles weſt of fort St. David, which being garriſon'd only by country troops, they ſoon got poſſeſſion of it.

The Nabob, Mahomet-Allee Cawn, who had attended Nazirzing to Arcot, and was conſtantly preſſing him to return to the charge, deſired a party from the army, to oppoſe and puniſh the French, and Chunda Saib: and at the ſame time applied to the Engliſh for a body of Europeans, and a train of artillery. Captain Cope therefore, with 400 of the military, and a body of ſepoys, marched to his aſſiſtance; and in conjunction they moved towards the enemy. I ſhould at that time have taken the field myſelf, but the chair becoming vacant by the removal of Mr. Floyer, I was obliged to take the government till Mr. Saunders, who was appointed to ſucceed, could come from Vizagapatam, and ſoon after his arrival, I embarked for England.

The Nabob had agreed to pay the whole expence of our troops in the field; but a large preſent to Nazarzing for his commiſſion having exhauſted his treaſury, inſtead of money, we got only trifling excuſes, with which he put us off from day to day, till at laſt the expences falling entire upon us, and the Nabob, for want of magazines and money, being unable to march his army between the French and Pondichery, Captain Cope had orders to return.

The very next night after, the French and Chunda Saib attacked the Nabob in his camp. It could not be called a battle, but a rout; the troops, inſtead of fighting, running away in ſmall parties, every thing fell into the victor's hands; even the Nabob, with difficulty made his eſcape, almoſt ſingly, and unattended, to Nazirzing.

The enemy did not remain idle, but followed the blow; and partly by threats, partly fair promiſes, got poſſeſſion of Gingee, a place exceeding ſtrong by nature, and not ill fortified, according to the eaſtern manner. They took care to ſecure their new conqueſt by a ſtrong garriſon, ſupporting it well with artillery and ammunition.

Nazirzing, rouzed from his lethargy by the loſs of Gingee, and reflecting on its conſequences, immediately marched from Arcot to retake that important place, declaring he would ſucceed or never return. Muzapherzing and his faction now thought it a proper time to put their ſchemes in execution; Nazirzing with his army ſurrounded Gingee; the French, and Chunda Saib were encamped under the walls.

Nothing now was wanting but to ſtrike the blow, which was concerted in the following manner. The French were to attack that part of the camp which the Nabobs of Cadapah and Condanore occupied, and their troops had inſtructions to make no reſiſtance. The Nabobs had engaged on their part to aſſaſſinate Nazirzing at his firſt appearance, on the alarm. The attack was no ſooner begun, but the two Nabobs made directly for Nazirzing's tent, and meeting him as he came out, they intreated him to mount his elephant and puniſh the rebels. The unfortunate prince was diſpoſing himſelf to follow their advice, when the ſtroke was given, the one ſtabbing him with a poniard, while the other ſhot him with a piſtol. His head was ſevered from his body, fixed on a ſpear, and brought to his nephew Muzapherzing, who being immediately releaſed, and mounted on his late uncle's elephant, was proclaim'd through the camp Viceroy of the Deckan. Little or no reſiſtance was made any where; ſo general was the conſternation, that every body thought of ſaving themſelves, not knowing who were friends or enemies, nor how to oppoſe a ſucceſſion

ceſſion they ſo little expected. The French puſhed their way to Nazirzing's tents, where was found an immenſe treaſure, in money and jewels, by which many made their fortunes, but none ſo largely as Mr. Dupleix, a fortune, by all accounts, not to be equalled at that time, by any ſubject in Europe.

To perpetuate the memory of this famous victory, which the French had boaſted of as ſuperior to any thing of the kind recorded in hiſtory, Mr. Dupleix, near the place where the maſſacre was committed, cauſed a town to be built, called Dupleix * Fateabat, and to record the ſhare the French had in it, a pillar now lies at Pondichery, deſigned to be erected in the market place, with a pompous Latin inſcription, giving an account of the engagement, and the French valour. Unluckily future ages will not be the wiſer for it; for captain Clive, a year after, in retaking the Arcot country, burnt the town, and deſtroyed the monument on which the Pillar was to have been erected.

The victorious army returned to Pondichery in January 1751, with a moſt ſumptuous train of the princes of the Deckan, and divided the ſpoil. Muzapherzing declared Chunda Saib Nabob of Arcot, and all its dependencies, and aſſociated Mr. Dupleix in the government with himſelf. On this Mr. Dupleix aſſumed the ſtate and formalities of an eaſtern prince. He held his Durbar in the palace at Pondichery, and ſuffered neither the natives, nor his own countrymen to approach him without a preſent after the eaſtern manner, he mounted his elephant, and was proclaimed Nabob. Mahomed Allee Cawn eſcaping with the utmoſt difficulty, and without attendants, made the beſt of his way to Trichinopoly, notwithſtanding the great ſearch made to ſeize his perſon.

It was agreed at Pondichery, that Chunda Saib ſhould raiſe an army, and aſſiſted by the French, endeavour to make good his appointment to the government

* The place of victory.

vernment of Arcot under Mr. Dupleix: that Muzapherzing ſhould march with the late Nazirzing's army to Aurengabad, the uſual reſidence of the princes of the Deckan; accompanied by Mr. Buſſy, at the head of 600 French, 3000 ſepoys, and a large train of artillery. They began their march the beginning of 1751, and on the road the two Nabobs of Cadapah and Condanore, jealous of Muzapherzing and the power of the French, and not thinking themſelves ſufficiently rewarded, upon various pretexts fomented a quarrel, till at length they proceeded to farther outrages, which produced an engagement. The Patans advanced to attack the French, but were unable to ſtand the cannonade. After they were obliged to retire, they fell upon Muzapherzing's flank, routed his troops, and in ſome meaſure revenged Nazirzing, in the death of his nephew, the chief of the conſpirators. A great many of the Patans were killed, and among the reſt the Nabob of Condanore.

The next day, the chiefs of the army proclaimed Sallabatzing, brother to Nazirzing viceroy of the Deckan, though there was a ſtrong party for the ſon of Muzapherzing. At this time the troubles at the court of Delly, prevented the Mogul from ſettling the affairs of the Deckan; he only made an appointment of Gawzedy Cawn to the government, and reſolved to ſupport him with an army, when the ſtate of his affairs would permit. The new prince * ſent Saneds to Mahomed Allee Cawn in the month of March, confirming him Nabob of Arcot.

Upon the death of Nazirzing, captain Cope was again ſent in January 1751, with a ſtrong detachment, to ſupport the Nabob in Trichinopoly, after an offer made to Chunda Saib and his allies, of the quiet poſſeſſion of the whole province, except that fort and its dependencies.

Chunda

* Saneds are commiſſions or grants for particular countries.

Chunda Saib and the French treated this propoſal with the higheſt contempt, and immediately raiſed troops and took the field. We collected about five hundred men from all our garriſons, and ſent them under the command of captain De Gingins to obſerve their motions, who finding their intentions were for Trichinopoly, moved that way alſo; and at the ſame time, a party from that garriſon, of about 110 men, marched to meet captain De Gingins, followed by what troops the Nabob could raiſe, commanded by his brother Abdiel Vahob Cawn. The firſt party met captain De Gingins at Verdachilum, and from thence the army moved in conjunction to Volconda, where they were alſo joined by the Nabob's forces, amounting in the whole to about 2000 horſe, 3000 ſepoys and 600 Europeans.

Volconda is a conſiderable town about 45 miles from Trichinopoly, in the road to Arcot. The governor at firſt ſeeming in our intereſt, amuſed us for two days, with promiſes to deliver up the fort; but ſoon after Chunda Saib and the French appearing, he threw off the maſk, and declared againſt us. The next night we attacked the fort without ſucceſs, and the army, after ſome loſs, was obliged to retreat to Outatour, 17 miles from Trichinopoly.

The enemy's army, conſiſting of about 6000 horſe, 4000 ſepoys, and 600 Europeans, followed our army to Outatour, and encouraged by the ſucceſs of an ambuſcade, in which ſome of our men fell, by following too cloſely a party of Chunda Saib's horſe, they attacked our camp, but were repulſed: however, not thinking our poſt tenable, ſhould the enemy repeat their attack, we retreated to the banks of the Coleroon, facing Trichinopoly. Chunda Saib's army increaſing daily, our people thought themſelves obliged alſo to quit that poſt, and to croſs the river to the iſland oppoſite Trichinopoly. The enemy ſtill following, we abandoned that poſt, and paſſing the river Cauvery the 17th of July, we encamped under the walls of Trichinopoly.

Chunda Saib and the French immediately took poſſeſſion of our poſt, and raiſed ſome batteries againſt the town, from acroſs the river; but finding the diſtance too great, even for a ſhot at almoſt its greateſt range, they left a party to ſecure Seringam Pagodas and croſſing the river, encamped on the plain on the eaſt ſide of the town, at the French Rock, and there contented themſelves with cannonading and throwing in ſome ſhells.

The Nabob beginning then to be in want of men and money, applied to the King of Maiſſore, who ſupplied him indeed with both, but in ſmall parties, and ſmaller ſums at a time, the common way of doing buſineſs in this country. Thus remained affairs at Trichinopoly, the enemy contenting themſelves with a uſeleſs cannonade, which however they adorned with all the terms of the moſt regular ſiege; and we waiting for our promiſed reinforcement, encamped under the walls of the fort, to keep our communication as open as poſſible.

The French bringing almoſt their whole force into the field with Chunda Saib, and leaving Arcot but poorly defended, a ſcheme was laid to reduce part of that country to the Nabob's obedience. Captain Clive commanded the party. This expedition was attended with uncommon ſucceſs, which ſome people were pleaſed to term fortunate, and lucky; but, in my opinion, from the knowledge I have of the gentleman, he deſerved, and might expect from his conduct every thing as it fell out. A man of an undaunted reſolution, of a cool temper, and a preſence of mind, which never left him in the greateſt danger. Born a ſoldier, for without a military education of any ſort, or much converſing with any of the profeſſion, from his judgment and good ſenſe, he led an army like an experienced officer, and a brave ſoldier, with a prudence that certainly warranted ſucceſs. This young

young man's early genius ſurpriſed and engaged my attention, as well before as at the ſiege of Davecottah, where he behaved with courage and judgment, much beyond what could be expected from his years, and his ſucceſs afterwards confirmed what I had ſaid to many people concerning him.

Captain Clive, in the month of Auguſt, having joined a detachment of our army at Trichinopoly, was ſoon recalled for the intended expedition; and being arrived at Madraſs, he marched with 300 Europeans, and about 500 ſepoys. His officers were chiefly Writers, or other ſervants of the company, never before employed in a military capacity; and yet, with this force, he ſurpriſed and took Arcot, the capital of the province, on the firſt of September. The French truly ſenſible of this diſgrace, and knowing the importance of the place, concerted meaſures to retake it, and collected all the men they could ſpare under Raja Saib, ſon to Chunda Saib, who, with a large detachment from his father's army, marched and inveſted Arcot the twenty third of September. During the ſiege, which laſted two months, they diſmounted two eighteen-pounders, upon which Mr. Clive, wrote the governor of Madraſs word that he was mounting the laſt eighteen-pounder he had left, but that he had ſtill three months proviſions, and thought himſelf able to defend a breach whenever the enemy ſhould make an aſſault. A party was detached from the army at Trichinopoly to ſupport him, on notice of whoſe approach, the enemy reſolved to make their laſt effort; they attacked the breach, and the fort in three different places; at every attack they were beat off with conſiderable loſs, and captain Clive taking advantage of their confuſion ſallied out, and following the blow, took all their cannon, levelled their trenches, and returned to the fort.

The party by this time came up, as alſo a detachment of Maratta's commanded by Budgerow a brother of Morarow, which enabled captain Clive to take

take the field He marched out of Arcot in ſearch of the French and Chunda's Saib's ſon, never giving them time to reſt, but purſuing his good fortune, he took the forts of Timery, Cauvery-pauk, Aranie and Conjeveram, and compleated it by a total defeat of the enemy at Cauvery-pauk in the month of March 1752. Their army was entirely deſtroyed and Raja Saib obliged to take ſhelter in Pondichery, where M. Dupleix refuſed to ſee him. By this victory, a large part of the Arcot country was recovered for the Nabob.

Before we enter on the affairs of Trichinopoly the chief ſcene of our military operations, it will be requiſite that the reader ſhould be well informed of the ſingular circumſtances of the Plain in which it is ſituated. By comparing the following deſcription with the accurate map annext; the importance of the poſts and other objects contended for, will be readily conceived and underſtood.

Trichinopoly is ſituated on a plain which once was crowded with rich villages and plantations of trees, but ſince the war, hardly a trace of either is left. The town is in form of an oblong ſquare, the longeſt ſides of which are Eaſt and Weſt. On the North runs the river Cauvery, leſs than half a-mile from the fort. The town was formerly no more than a wall round the foot of a rock, in circumference about twelve hundred yards. As the inhabitants increaſed, the town was augmented to half of the preſent oblong, with a croſs wall, the traces of which ſtill remain ; the third augmentation was made to the ſouthward, and incloſes the town as it now ſtands. It is at preſent near four miles in circumference, with a double enceinte of walls with round towers at equal diſtances according to the Eaſtern method of fortifying. The ditch is near thirty feet wide but not half ſo deep ; and at different ſeaſons it is more or leſs ſupplied with water, but never quite dry. The outward wall is built of a grayiſh ſtone, each

ſtone

ſtone from four to five feet long and all laid endways. It is about eighteen feet high, and four or five thick, without parapet or rampe, nothing but a ſingle ſtructure of ſtone, and is very properly called a wall: the other is more properly a rampart. The diſtance betwen them is about twenty-five feet, the height of the rampart thirty. The rampe is equal in

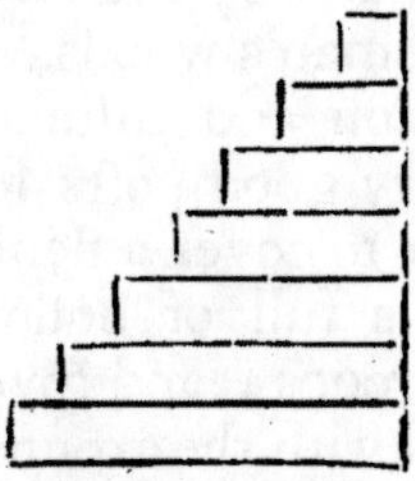

thickneſs at bottom with the height of the rampart, 30 feet, decreaſing in thickneſs like the profile in the margin. The terre-plein of the parapet is about ten feet, and the parapet is for the moſt part, ſeven or eight feet high, covering the men entirely, with loop-holes to fire thorough. Some baſtions have been conſtructed by us, as regular and good, as the ground would admit of, built on the foundations of the round towers. They are moſtly on the angles of the ſquare and on the Weſt face, about the middle of the curtain called Dalton's battery, even with the outward wall. The town is very well ſupply'd from the river, by water courſes which direct the water into large ſquare ponds or tanks that have communication by aqueducts.

A moſt extraordinary rock ſtands in the middle of the old town, and is about 300 feet high; on the top of it is a pagoda which was of ſingular uſe to us the whole war; its height commanding even as far as Tanjore which is forty miles. Here was conſtantly ſtationed a man with a teleſcope who gave us by ſignals and writing an account of all the enemy's motions. The buildings on this rock and thoſe which are cut out on the ſides of it are very ſurpriſing works in a country where they have ſo few tools to facilitate their labour.

The ſoil on the Eaſt and Weſt ſides for two miles round, and on the North ſide as far as the river is rich and good, but does not run deep. After digging a foot or two you find it rockey, and to the ſouth

ſouth face, there is ſo little mould that it will not admit of cultivation; but every other part, in time of peace, produces rice in great plenty. The plain runs in length from eaſt to weſt about 19 miles; from the boundaries of the Tanjore kingdom, to the head of the iſland weſterly. Its breadth is unequal, from 7 to 12 miles. On the north it is bounded by the river Cauvery, and on the ſouth by Tondeman's woods.

The different rocks, whoſe ſituation and diſtance are deſcribed on the map, afford very good poſts for an army, either as advanced ones, or to cover a flank. The plain, though ſeemingly level, is full of hollow ways, ſufficient to conceal or cover troops; and gives a perſon who is thoroughly acquainted with the ground, great advantages. Water is always to be had on the plain, by ſinking wells, and in ſome places it is collected in baſons, either formed by nature or art. This element is ſo great and uſeful a bleſſing in this country, that no pains are ſpared in ſaving and keeping all that falls. However, the water on the plain is very unwholeſome, as ſtanding waters generally are; beſides, it is ſo impregnated with ſaltpetre, with which the earth abounds, that in ſome places it is too brackiſh to be drank, and moſt commonly occaſions bilious diſorders.

The iſland of Seringam is formed about 6 miles north-weſt of Trichinopoly, by the river Cauvery, which divides itſelf into two branches. That to the northward takes the name of the Coleroon, that to the ſouthward preſerves its old name the Cauvery. Each of theſe rivers, after a courſe of about 90 miles, empty themſelves into the ſea. The Coleroon at Davecotah, the Cauvery near Tranquebar, at about 20 miles diſtance from each other.

This iſland 15 miles eaſt of Trichinopoly, is ſo narrow, that both the rivers would rejoin in the ſame channel, were they not prevented by a high bank, which keeps them aſunder. This bank was made at a great expence, and is conſtantly kept in repair by the

the kings of Tanjore. The uſe of it is to direct the courſe of the river Cauvery through that kingdom, by the means of water courſes and canals, which diſtribute it into proper channels all over the country, and are the ſource of riches and fertility. The river, by its natural courſe, waters the north ſide of the kingdom, and by a large channel which they have made near the bank, the ſouthern ſide receives alſo a ſufficient quantity of that uſeful element, without which, in this part of the world there can be no fertility.

The bank is about ſeven feet wide at top; it riſes from the foundation with a ſlope on each ſide. This bank is as ſtrong as wood, ſtone, earth, and ſtraw can make it, and ſufficient to ſupport, and confine the currents on each ſide. Its height from the common level of the water is near 20 feet, to which the river can never riſe; ſo that there is no danger of an innundation. It is about a mile in length; afterwards the land naturally widening, there need no more precautions to prevent the rivers from joining. A number of people are conſtantly employed, to ſee that the water makes no encroachments, and if it does, to apply a remedy immediately. The repairs each year are paid by a general tax on the country, which amounts to about 20000 pounds annually. The bank forms on the iſland, what I have called, in my narrative, the Paſs; and by its poſition and ſituation it will appear how capable it is of defence, with a ſmall number of men, even againſt an army. Above a mile diſtant from it, to the eaſt, was a fort called Koiladdy, which being built for the preſervation of the bank, was deſtroyed by the enemy, about the time we laſt marched to Tanjore. The enemy had often threatened to cut the bank if the king would not comply with their meaſures; at laſt they carried their threats into execution in the year 1754; but luckily at a ſeaſon when it was leaſt detrimental, for in three months, with our aſſiſtance, it was repaired.

However

However the damage in that little ſpace of time, and the coſt of repairing it, amounted to fifty thouſand pounds; from whence may be ſeen how eaſily the maſters of that bank may give law to the king of Tanjore; and how much it is his intereſt to be a friend to the Nabob of Trichinopoly, to whom he is obliged to pay tribute for the bank, three lack of rupees yearly. In this iſland, facing Trichinopoly, ſtand the famous Pagodas of Seringam; ſome others, but not ſo remarkable, called Jembikiſhna, are at half a mile diſtance to the eaſt. Seringam is little more than a mile diſtant from Trichinopoly. The Pagodas are ſurrounded by ſeven ſquare walls of ſtone; each wall has a gateway in the middle of each ſide of the ſquare, pointing to one of the four cardinal points. The gateways are ornamented in the manner of that country, with crouded emblematical figures of their divinities. The principal gateway in the outward wall, which faces Trichinopoly, is a curious piece of architecture, though yet unfiniſhed. It is formed by pillars 32 feet high in the ſhaft, with capitals. Four of theſe pillars are of one ſtone each, but the largeſt ſtones are thoſe which are laid acroſs the top of the gateway; they meaſure 33 feet long, and five and an half one way, and four feet ten inches the other. The ſpace between the outward and ſecond walls meaſures 310 feet, and ſo proportionably between the reſt. No Europeans are admitted into the laſt ſquare, it being the Sanctum Sanctorum, and few have gone farther than the third.

Seringam was the poſt occupied by the enemy all the war; once indeed they ſuffered by taking ſhelter there, but that was owing to our having the Marattas on our ſide, and a ſufficient number of troops to cut off their communication, and for want of proviſions, obliging them to ſurrender. We never ſince had the fortune to be equal to them, much leſs ſuperior, and by that means it has proved a ſure refuge to them on many occaſions, and we have never had it in our

power

power to dispossess them, since the Maissoreans took possession, in consequence of their agreement with the Nabob. It is an excellent post for an army that can keep their communication open. The ground about it is so full of difficulties, by hollow ways, and water courses, that a besieging army must run the hazard of losing a great many men before they can carry their point. Jembikishna has but a single enciente of wall, and nothing remarkable but its magnitude and vicinity to Seringam.

Adjoining to Trichinopoly is the kingdom of Tanjore, bounded on the north by the Coleroon, on the east by the sea, on the south by two countries which belong to two powerful Poligars, the one called Marravar, the other Tondeman, and on the west by Trichinopoly. The boundaries commence at 14 miles distance from the fort last mentioned. Near the mouth of the Coleroon, we have a fort called Davecotah, which once belonged to the kingdom of Tanjore, but was taken by us while I commanded in the year 1749. The possession of this has enabled us to support the Nabob and king of Tanjore, who is well pleased with its being in our hands, and has therefore granted it to the company, with some territory annexed. The next settlement on the coast, given also by the king of Tanjore, belongs to the Danes, and is called Tranquebar. Next to that, the French have one called Carrical; and to the southward of it the Dutch have another, called Negapatam. Thirty miles from thence is a place called Adriapatam, which finishes the territories of the king of Tanjore along the sea coast. The distance of the first, Davecotah, from the last is about 90 miles, which is the broadest part of his kingdom. It decreaseth by degrees in breadth, and near Trichinopoly is 30 or at most 40 miles wide. Its length from the west to the sea is about 100 miles. The revenues of this small kingdom, well managed, may produce near a million yearly. The king was a friend to us and

and the Nabob the whole war; that is, he found it his interest to be so, because he knew well the French and Maissoreans wanted nothing less than his country, and we found it much our interest to keep him our friend. His country was the only communication we had left with the coast; for since the Maissoreans and Marattas had joined the French, they were masters on the north side of the Coleroon. What confirmed him the more in our interest, was the just fear he had, that if the Maissoreans were once masters of Trichinopoly, they would willingly extend their dominions to the sea, and his kingdom was too easy and beneficial a conquest to remain long unattempted: besides, he hated the French since their setting up Chunda Saib, and laying siege to his capital.

At Trichinopoly we were in daily expectation of the king of Maissore's troops, who marched out of Seringapatam, the capital of the Maissore kingdom, to a place called Carroor, about 50 miles from Trichinopoly. The king of Maissore, besides his own proper forces, had also engaged Morarow and his Marattas to come to our assistance. Twelve hundred of these joined us in November, and another party, as I have already said, were with captain Clive in the Arcot province. The Nabob's brother and a party of Europeans marched to hasten the junction of the Maissoreans. Thus ended the year 1751.

In January we were joined by another party of Marattas, and 4000 Maissore horse, besides 3000 irregular troops called * Colleries, who live on plunder, and are notorious thieves, particularly for stealing of horses, in the practice of which they are both daring and expert. They creep along the woods with a spear, 18 or 20 feet long, trailing on the ground, which they manage on occasion with great dexterity. They

* The Colleries are inhabitants of the woods, under the government of the Polygars, another name for the Gentou governors. The greatest in power are the Rajahs, the least the Polygars.

They are troublesome in the field by giving frequent alarms, and in their woody country it is dangerous to attack them.

The Maissore general (commonly called the Dolaway) * Nanderauze, had not yet joined us with the remainder of the army. The enemy had sent a party on his road, who took post in a village, by which he was obliged to pass. We sent another party to dislodge them, commanded by captain Cope. Our first Attack was unsuccessful, partly owing to captain Cope being mortally wounded in the beginning of the engagement, and our having been misinformed as to the enemy's strength and number. However, the party being reinforced, we carried our point. Nanderauze and Morarow, with about 2000 horse, joined us the 26th of the month, and our party returned the 28th with the rest of the army.

The king of Tanjore after many solicitations, sent also his troops, under the command of his general Monagee; and Tondeman came likewise in to our assistance.

In this situation were affairs when I landed from England the 15th of March; captain Clive was then just ready with a party to march to Trichinopoly. On the 17th I joined him, and took the command. The party consisted of 400 Europeans, and 1100 sepoys.

The situation of our affairs made it highly requisite to hasten the march with all expedition; fatal spirit of division having unhappily crept in amongst our officers, so that many opportunities and advantages were lost, which gave the country alliance but an indifferent opinion of our conduct.

On the 27th of the same month, being arrived within 18 miles of Trichinopoly, I was met by the command-

* The king of Maissore was a minor; the kingdom was then governed for him by his two uncles, the one, called Nanderauze, commanded the army, the other ruled in the cabinet.

commanding officer of artillery, who brought me intelligence, that the enemy had poſted a ſtrong party at Koyladdy, within cannot-ſhot of the road I was to paſs the next day.

In order to join the army as ſoon as poſſible, I diſpatched my guides to find out another road, judging it of conſequence to avoid the enemy's poſt, eſpecially as I had a very large quantity of ammunition and ſtores, part of which I laid up in Tricatapolly, a fort belonging to the king of Tanjore, that it might not retard my march the next day.

By ſome miſtake of my guide, we were led within reach of the very poſt I wanted to avoid. To draw off the fire of their battery from my party, I ordered ſome guns from my rear diviſion to anſwer theirs, and leaving a guard to ſupport them, the main body were directed to move on ſlowly, inclining to the left, which, with a ſmall loſs, brought us out of reach of their guns: upon which we halted till the party and guns came up. We then continued our march without interruption, and incamped that night within ten miles of Trichinopoly.

The next morning we were joined on our march by the troops, and about 200 ſoldiers, commanded by the captains Clarke and Dalton, within four miles of Trichinopoly. Captain De Gingins ſent his adjutant to inform me, that the whole of the enemy was in motion towards me. Their right was at their incampment of Chucklepollam, a village on the banks of the river Cauvery, and facing the paſs: Their left extended almoſt to the French Rock, a ſtrong poſt in their poſſeſſion. Their cavalry was on the left of their infantry, extending all the way to Elmiſeram, another very ſtrong poſt on an inacceſſible rock, on which they had mounted ſome large cannon. As I had no intention to engage, till my entire junction was made, and till I had lodged my ſtores in the fort, I marched round Elmiſeram, purpoſing to come in by the Sugar-loaf Rock. Our baggage on the left flank

was

was ſecured by the march of the army, which kept moving, ready to form, with their front to the enemy.

The enemy advanced and began to cannonade. We immediately halted behind a large bank, which covered our party from their guns, but which was eaſily got over, if they ſhould advance and appear determined to attack.

The artillery was poſted on the top of the bank, which was high and commanded all round. Their cavalry came on near enough for grape-ſhot to do execution. They ſtood for ſome time, till Allum Cawn, the officer who commanded them, was killed, and above 200 more; on which they retreated. The reſt of the army choſe to follow their example; the French bringing up their rear, moved back to their camp, and left us to finiſh our march to Trichinopoly.

I waited the next day on the Nabob, the Maiſſore general, and the reſt of the alliance, in order to ſettle the plan of operations for the enſuing campaign *. There it was agreed to attack the enemy in their camp; and in caſe they choſe rather to retreat to the iſland than ſtand an engagement, to take ſuch meaſures as entirely to cut off their communication with the country; which we effected ſoon after, and obliged them to ſurrender for want of proviſions.

Ready and reſolute as theſe country people appear in councils, they are ever dilatory and ſlow in execution, ſuperſtitiouſly tied down to faſts and feaſts, lucky and unlucky days: nothing ſpurs them on to act, till thoſe ridiculous cuſtoms are complied with, which ſeldom happens before the opportunity is loſt. Thus three or four days were thrown away in theſe

 trifling

* The army conſiſted of 1200 Europeans, and Topaſſes in battalion; ſepoys in our pay 2000. The Nabob's Maiſſore Marrattas and Tanjore forces above 1500 horſe. Their infantry of all ſorts 10,000.

trifling delays; and the enemy apprifed of our defign, prudently as we then thought, determined to retreat to the ifland for their greater fecurity, burning and deftroying a large magazine of provifions, intended for the fiege of Trichinopoly. By this fudden and unexpected retreat, we had a more compleat victory, which made fome amends for what I before was concerned at, the not having it in my power, to attack them as we propofed.

This retreat to the ifland was on the 3d of April. The army under Mr. Law confifted of 600 Europeans, Topaffes, and Coffrees, 1800 French fepoys, and about 15,000 black cavalry and infantry; Mr. Dupleix's account fays 20,000 in all.

We now endeavoured to cut off their fupplies, which they moftly received from the other fide of the Coleroon, their communication being open that way quite to Pondichery. Promifing myfelf great fuccefs from the activity and vigilance of captain Clive, I detached him with 400 of my beft Europeans, 1200 fepoys, and 4000 horfe, to take poft on the other fide. He croffed the two rivers, about feven miles below Seringam, at a pafs near Dolaways Choultry.

I alfo fent captain Dalton to take the poft of Elmiferam where the enemy had cannon. The place furrendred after a faint refiftance. Captain Clive having acquainted me that he had taken poft at a village and a Pagoda, called Samiaveram, about ten miles from Seringam, and on the high road to Arcot and Pondichery, through which their convoys muft pafs, I paid him a vifit the 8th of April, after Elmiferam was reduced, to concert what further meafures were proper to be purfued. We agreed that he fhould make an attack on Pitchunda, a place which they had fortified, fituated on the bank of the Coleroon, oppofite to Seringam, and commanding the pafs of that river. But it was firft neceffary to ftorm Lalgoody, a mud fort, where the enemy had a large magazine of grain, and this captain Clive executed three

three days after, while the neceſſary diſpoſitions were making for the ſiege of Pitchunda. Having received intelligence that a party of the enemy were at Outatoor, 15 miles from Samiaveram, with a large convoy of ſtores, captain Clive marched the 15th of April to intercept them, leaving only a ſmall party to ſecure his poſt till his return. The French being adviſed of his march, thought ſo good an opportunity of retaking a poſt of that conſequence ought not to be neglected. They therefore formed a detachment from their army, who had orders to march after dark, that their attack might be made at day-light, on the party which were left in the Pagoda.

On captain Clive's arrival at Outatoor, he found no enemy nor convoy, and ſuſpecting the report to have been a fineſſe of the enemy, in order to draw him from Samiaveram, he reſolved, after refreſhing his people, to return immediately to his former poſt. He arrived near the Pagoda about eleven at night, his men, fatigued with ſo long a march, went to reſt, and captain Clive retired to his pallankeen *.

The French, ignorant of captain Clive's return, began their march in the night from their army, and arrived about four in the morning at Semiaveram, where they found every thing as quiet as they could wiſh: their guides led them directly to the Pagoda. On their approach, the 16th of April, the party left there in the morning challenged, and were anſwered Friends, by ſome deſerters from us. This contented our people, who imagining them ſome of captain Clive's returning party, were not convinced of their miſtake till the ſepoys began to fire.

 Captain

* A pallankeen is a bed ſupported by a wooden or ivory frame, of ſix feet long, and near three feet broad, faſtened at each end with croſs ſticks to a bamboo arched in the middle, 15 feet long which forms an arch over the palankeen or bed, and is covered with a canopy of cloth lined with ſilk, and ſtiffened with ribs of the coconut tree.

Captain Clive awaked, and alarmed at the firing, ran immediately towards it, by which means he joined the French ſepoys, who were puſhing into the Pagoda, and imagining them his own troops, who endeavoured to ſcreen themſelves from an attack, began to reprimand them in the country language, angrily demanding, what they were firing at. The ſepoys in this confuſion paid little regard to him, till one of their officers ſuſpecting him to be an Engliſhman, drew his ſword and cut at him, which he parried, by advancing forwards and receiving the blow from near the hilt; another officer of our ſepoys accidentally coming to his aſſiſtance, cut the fellow down, and diſengaged captain Clive, who by this time perceiving his miſtake, and by great good fortune getting out of their hands, went in ſearch of his detachment, which he found under arms; but in the mean while his own party in the Pagoda was diſlodged, and the French were in poſſeſſion of the poſt.

He therefore inſtantly formed his detachment, and marched to the Pagoda, and finding the enemy in poſſeſſion, he immediately ordered the gate to be ſtormed. The officer who attempted it was received by a platoon of the enemy, who killed him on the ſpot, and many of his people.

On this it was thought neceſſary that our cannon ſhould be ſent for, and a ſummons was made to the French commanding officer, ſignifying, that as it was impoſſible to eſcape, it was moſt prudent for him to ſurrender. The French officer bravely endeavoured to diſengage himſelf, by ſallying out of the Pagoda; but being killed in the attempt, with ſome of his foremoſt people, the reſt ſurrendered at diſcretion. The French ſepoys without the Pagoda ſeeing it ſurrendered, endeavoured to ſteal off; but the day beginning to dawn, they were perceived and purſued by the Maratta cavalry, who riding in amongſt them, inhumanly cut them all to pieces.

Monagee

Monagee with the Tanjore troops undertook to retake Koiladdy. He ſucceeded April 21ſt, and the Nabob gave the king of Tanjore a grant of it, as it guarded the bank, which conveyed the river Cauvery into his country.

As nothing now remained to obſtruct our deſigns on Pitchunda, I took poſt on the iſland to cover the cannon and ammunition neceſſary for the attack of it. The garriſon conſiſted of 72 Europeans, 49 * Topaſſes, and ſome ſepoys; and on the defences were mounted three pieces of cannon and two mortars.

Receiving intelligence that the enemy had a party at Outatoor, I ſent captain Dalton with 150 Europeans, 400 ſepoys, and 1000 horſe to diſlodge them; he came up and had ſome ſkirmiſhes with them, but expecting to renew the fight the next day, the 2d of May, he found the place abandoned.

Monſ. D'Auteuil and his party marched off in the night, left the greateſt part of their convoy of ſtores, with which captain Dalton returned to captain Clive, who by this time had laid ſiege to Pitchunda. I therefore ordered him to continue with Mr. Clive; and a battery being opened on the 8th, on the 10th the garriſon ſurrendered priſoners of war, and were ſent to the Nabob at Trichinopoly. Thus their communication was entirely cut off from the other ſide the Coleroon, Monagee having taken Koiladdy. I detatched our Coffrees † with two guns, to ſecure the paſs on the iſland, who threw up an intrenchment, which might alone have defended them againſt the whole body of the enemy's army; ſo inacceſſible is

* Topaſſes are the deſcendants of the Portugueze who firſt ſettled in India, and married with the natives. They differ very little in colour from the Indians themſelves. They have the name of Topaſſes given them from their wearing hats.

† Coffrees (by the French called Cafres) is now become the general name for all negroes who are brought to India from the Cape, the coaſt of Guinea, or any other parts of Africa, and chiefly from Madagaſcar. They are brave and ſteady in the field.

this paſs, any where but in front, and there it does not admit of more than two men abreaſt. I then encamped at Chuckleypollam, facing the paſs of the Cauvery.

The Maiſſoreans and Marattas on our right extended to Warriore Pagodas, and from thence a chain of cavalry to the extremity of the iſland, to prevent any ſupplies ſlipping through, Monagee and the Tanjore troops on our left, the main body at Dolaways Choultry, to defend that paſs between them and us, all Tondeman's and the other Polygar's Colleries. Such was our ſituation. The enemy who encamped till then on the iſland, ſtruck their tents the 18th of May, and took ſhelter under cover of the walls of Seringham, giving out that they would receive us there. To diſtreſs them the more, we paſſed the Cauvery to the iſland, and encamped on the eaſt ſide of Jembikiſhna, where ſome days after we threw up an entrenchment quite acroſs from river to river, intending to wait there till we could get up ſome heavy cannon from Davecotah; having but one 18 and one 12 pounder, artillery not ſufficient to make a breach. Monagee took poſſeſſion of my poſt at Chuckleypollam. We were in this ſituation when intelligence came that Mr. D'Auteuil, who was lately driven out of Outatoor by captain Dalton, was then at Volconda, with a large quantity of ſtores. Captain Clive, on the firſt notice, formed a party, and marched the 27th. He returned the twenty ninth with Mr. D'Auteuil and his whole party priſoners. They conſiſted of three officers and fifty men, 300 ſepoys and as many horſe.

At this time the enemy were ſo reduced for want of proviſions, that the Indian army, on pardon and protection promiſed by the Nabob, came over to us in great numbers; one of their generals in particular, named Coop Saib, joined us, with a thouſand horſe, a large body of ſepoys, and 14 elephants.

Chunda

Chunda Saib dispirited and reduced to the greatest extremity, and without money to pay his troops, willing to try if he had a friend in Monagee the Tanjore general, demanding leave to pass through his camp to Tanjore, which was very readily granted; and, as is too much the custom in like cases, the moment he was in the power of his enemy he was made a prisoner. He might, no doubt, have escaped to Pondichery, but in these circumstances he dreaded Mr. Dupleix.

Next day, June 1st, the Nabob, the Maissore and Maratta generals, Monagee and myself, being assembled, it was debated how to dispose of him. I was silent on this occasion, and they were of different opinions. The Nabob and Monagee judged it very dangerous to let out of their hands a man who had already given them so much trouble. The Maissore general and Morarow were for having him in their possession. Finding they could not agree, I proposed that we should have the care of him, and keep him confined in one of our own settlements; this was by no means approved, and we parted without coming to any resolution; but some of Monagee's people put an end to the dispute by cutting off his head, which was done the 3d of June *

Thus did Chunda Saib pay the just price of his ambition and presumption. In private life he is said to be a man of great benevolence, humanity, and generosity: with regard to his public character; in this country, ambition being a venial fault, every man who succeeds is a great man; if he fails he is only reckoned unfortunate.

Mr. D'Auteuil was brought prisoner to Trichinopoly, and on giving his parole not to serve against the Nabob, was released. The enemy became so much straitened

* Mr. Dupleix, in his Memoire, falsely asserts, that Col. Laurence himself ordered the death of Chunda Saib, notwithstanding that caluctny had been clearly refuted in the country.

ſtraitened for want of proviſions, that they could hold out no longer. Mr. Law therefore thought in earneſt of ſurrendering, and to that end deſired our mediation with the Nabob. We met in conſequence, and explained to him the Nabob's terms, which were in general;

That the Pagodas of Jembikiſhna and Seringam ſhould be delivered to the Nabob, with all the guns, ſtores, and ammunition. That the Europeans, Topaſſes, and Coffrees, ſhould be priſoners of war. That the officers ſhould give their parole not to ſerve againſt Mahomed Allee Cawn and his allies, and the deſerters be pardoned.

Theſe articles being ſigned by Mr. Law on the 3d of June, captain Dalton took poſſeſſion of Seringam, and the French marched out, being about 600 Europeans and 300 ſepoys. The reſt of their allies accepting of the Nabob's cowle or protection, ſeparated and diſperſed. In Seringam we found thirty pieces of cannon, ten of which were 18 and 12 pounders, the reſt field-pieces, two large mortars, a number of cohorns, and a great quantity of ammunition, and all kind of millitary ſtores.

Captain Campbell with a party eſcorted the priſoners to fort St. David. The Pagodas being thus ſecured, and every thing ſo happily finiſhed to the ſouthward, I imagined we had only to put the Nabob in quiet poſſeſſion of his territories to the northward, where many places ſtill remained with the French, but Gingee was the only fort of conſequence which could give us any trouble.

On my repreſenting the ill conſequence of our delays, and preſſing the Nabob to march with his allies, and reduce the reſt of the province, I perceived in him much unwillingneſs and unaccountable backwardneſs; but this myſtery was at length explained. The Maiſſoreans refuſed to march till the Nabob had delivered up Trichinopoly, which they demanded, as they ſaid, according to agreement; inſiſting, that as they

they had performed their part of the treaty, it was but just the Nabob ſhould fulfil his alſo.

The Nabob juſtly objected, that it was neither their agreement, nor reaſonable, that the fortreſs of Trichinopoly ſhould be the price of its relief, but that when the king of Maiſſore had ſettled him in quiet poſſeſſion of all his other dominions, he ſhould then be ready and willing, according to his real intention and meaning, to give up that place.

The Maiſſoreans ſeeming ſatisfied, promiſed to march and remove this objection. In confidence that they would follow, we marched with our Europeans to Outatoor the 16th of June, but not finding our allies or the Nabob follow us, we returned the 18th of June, hearing that Morarow with his Marattas intended to put a ſtop to the Nabob's march.

I endeavoured to reconcile the chiefs; but I found Morarow wanted no leſs than Trichinopoly for himſelf; an agreement therefore between the two contending parties never could procure it him, wherefore he ſeparately adviſed both not to give up their pretenſions; hoping a breach would give him an opportunity to effect what he ſaw was not to be obtained by any other method.

The Nabob, by giving up Trichinopoly and its dependancies, without being in poſſeſſion of the reſt of the Arcot countries, quitted for ever that part which alone, of all his pretenſions he was actually in poſſeſſion of. The king of Maiſſore's friendſhip and alliance was of great conſequence, but it alſo might be purchaſed too dear; for however he might promiſe to aſſiſt the Nabob in the recovery of his other countries, when he was once in poſſeſſion of the place, if he ſhould refuſe to fulfil this part of the engagement, who could force him? Other compenſations were propoſed, and the Nabob even offered to give him a promiſe under his hand, to deliver Trichinopoly in two months, if he would but march with and aſſiſt him.

Nanderauze

Nanderauze promiſed he would follow, and join the Nabob with his troops, in order to march towards our ſettlements. The Maiſſoreans and Morarow remained encamped under the walls of Trichinopoly, ſeemingly friends, and every day talked of following the Nabob. Monagee with the king of Tanjore's troops returned home, and Tondeman followed them. The Tanjoreans could never be brought to conſent to the giving Trichinopoly to the Maiſſoreans.

On the 28th we marched from Outatoor through Volcondah and Verdachilum, and arrived before Trivedy on the 7th of July. The enemy had left there a ſmall party, which, on the Nabob's ſummons, ſurrendered There I left the army, under the command of captain De Gingins, being in ſo bad a ſtate of health that I could not keep the field.

It will not be improper to ſhew what the French were doing at Pondichery. To give Dupleix his due, he was not eaſily caſt down; his pride ſupported him, and at the ſame time his mind was full of reſources; the injuſtice of his cauſe never diſturbed him; and, provided he could gain his ends, the means never gave him any concern. His council was chiefly compoſed of his own creatures, who never diſputed what he propoſed. He was married to a woman endowed with as much ſpirit, art and pride, as himſelf; born in the country, miſtreſs of all the low cunning peculiar to the natives, and well ſkilled in their language.

The ſurrender of Mr. Law happened at that ſeaſon of the year, when the ſhips arrived from Europe, and brought a large reinforcement, to which Mr. Dupleix added all the ſailors from the company's ſhips, ſending Laſcars on board to navigate them to China. Thus he collected new troops; and not to want a pretender to the government of Arcot, on Chunda Saib's death, he proclaimed Raja Saib his ſon, Nabob of the province; but afterwards, that he might ſeem to have an undoubted right of appointing whom he

pleaſed,

pleaſed, he gave out that the Mogul had ſent him Saneds or commiſſions, declaring him governor of all this part of the Carnateck, from the river Kriſtnah to the ſea. Theſe Saneds were proved to be a forgery, and the whole contrivance detected in the moſt public manner, as will appear.

The ſuppoſed meſſenger from Delly was received with all the honour and ceremony uſually paid to an ambaſſador from the Mogul; and that nothing might be wanting to compleat the farce, Mr. Dupleix himſelf, in the country manner, with muſick and dancing-girls before him, mounted on an elephant, received with due reverence from the hands of the pretended ambaſſador, his commiſſion from the Mogul, and in conſequence of his appointment, gave out all orders from that time as ſuch; he even kept his Durbar or court, ſat on a ſofa, and received preſents from his council as well as the natives, like a Prince of the country; and thus endeavoured to ſupport the character of Subah of the Deckan.

Mr. Dupleix, to return to my ſubject, finding that Chunda Saib's ſon would be of little uſe to him, by his intereſt in the country, or his money, offered the Nabobſhip of Arcot to the governor of Velloure, Mootis Allee Cawn, a man every way fit for his purpoſe, and beſides, very rich. Mootis Allee Cawn was to find money, and Dupleix Europeans. Under different pretences, and at different times, he got from him about three lack of roupees; but the titular Prince finding he was only amuſed, demurred till Dupleix would give him better proofs of making good his promiſes. As there was no more money to be got, Dupleix had no further occaſion for him, and left him where he found him, only ſomething the poorer.

As I have ſaid before, there was ſtill a good deal of the Arcot province in the hands of the French, and Chunda Saib's friends, which we ſhould have endea-

voured

voured to recover. Our forces were not very confiderable; we had loft a great many men; there was a ftrong garrifon left in Trichinopoly, and we had but few recruits that year. The French had many more, befides preffing the feamen into their fervice. However, enough might have been fpared to go with the Nabob and gather his rents, and to recover the greateft part of the country. Inftead of beginning by degrees, which at that time was all our ftrength would admit of, the governor of Madrafs refolved to attack Gingee.

Gingee is fituated to the weft of Pondichery. It is furrounded with mountains, and the roads, or more properly paffes, leading to it, begin between thofe mountains, at about ten miles diftance. An army within thofe paffes may be eafily blocked up, unlefs they can afford to fecure themfelves, and keep their communication open with the country. It confifts of two towns, called the Great and little Gingee. The firft to the fouthward, the other to the northward. They are both furrounded by one wall, three miles in circumference, which inclofes the two towns, and five mountains of ragged rock, on the fummits of which are built five ftrong forts. The two towns are divided from eaft to weft by a wall lined with cannon, which one of thofe five rocks defends as a citadel. The place is inacceffible, except from the eaft and fouth-eaft. Four roads lead to it, by the one our army marched, the other faces towards Arcot, the third to Wandewafh, and the fourth to Pondichery. The place was well fupplied with all manner of ftores, and garrifoned by 150 Europeans, and fepoys and black people in great numbers. Such was the ftate of Gingee when we refolved to befiege it. Ill as I was, at that time, with the fever, I fet out from Fort St. David for Madrafs, to fee the governor, and try if I could diffuade him from the attempt.

I repre-

I repreſented the ſituation and ſtrength of the place, compared to the force we could ſend, and even allowing that we could have marched our whole force, the number would not be ſufficient for the attack, and at the ſame time to provide for our ſecurity, by keeping the paſſes open, and protecting our convoys of proviſions, which muſt come from Fort St. David, as no ſupply could be expected from a country diſaffected by its neighbourhood to Pondichery. Beſides, we had alſo an enemy at our back, with a force ſufficient, at leaſt, to ſtop our convoys. I repreſented to him that the Nabob's affairs alſo required our ſettling other places firſt, where we were ſure of ſucceſs; and we ought to conſider what an impreſſion the leaſt check would make on the minds of theſe fluctuating, and yet unſettled people.

Theſe, with ſeveral other reaſons determined me to diſſuade the governor from the attempt; but he declared to me, that he had ordered a party, and it muſt go.

Major Kinneer was ſent with a detachment, from the army at Trivedy, of 200 Europeans; the Nabob alſo ſent his troops, about 600 horſe, and 1500 Sepoys.

They marched the 23d of July, and arrived before the place the 26th. A ſummons was ſent, which the French anſwered very civilly, by ſaying, they kept it for the King of France, and were reſolved to defend it. Soon after, intelligence was brought that a party marched from Pondichery of 200 Europeans, and 1500 Sepoys. Two pieces of battering cannon, ammunition, &c. were ordered out, under an eſcort of 150 Europeans. The French poſted themſelves on the road our convoys were obliged to paſs, upon which Major Kinneer judged it better to leave Gingee, againſt which he had no proſpect of ſucceſs, and meet the French; finding it of moſt conſequence to keep his communication open.

The

The French had made choice of a good poſt, with a river and the village of Vickarivandy in their front, and ſeven pieces of cannon well diſpoſed. Our men attacked, but were very warmly received, and galled by a briſk fire from behind walls. A blundering commander of our artillery, (a Frenchman who had deſerted and was taken into our ſervice) contrived to poſt our cannon ſo, that they could not favour the attack; which Major Kinneer endeavouring himſelf to rectify, was wounded in the leg, and many of the men and officers killed; which obliged him in the end to retreat, but in very good order. Thus ended the expedition againſt Gingee. Poor Major Kinneer was almoſt recovered of his wound, but fretting at his diſappointment, was ſeized with a fever and flux, which carried him off ſome time after.

The French, animated as uſual upon the leaſt ſucceſs, joined this party with all the force they could bring into the field. The marched cloſe to the bounds of Fort St. David. I was ſtill at Madraſs, but having received an account of their motion, orders were ſent to our troops in St. David's, to march out and encamp. Captain Schaub's company of Swiſs was alſo ſent by ſea from Madraſs. The party went in boats, though I deſired they might be ſent in a ſhip which was in the road, as well for the ſafety and eaſe of the troops, as a ſecurity againſt any attempts of Mr. Dupleix, who, I very well knew, was capable of doing any thing to anſwer his preſent purpoſes.

Mr. Dupleix, on notice of the embarkation, ſent a ſhip out of Pondichery road, and took captain Schaub and his whole company, and carried them into Pondichery, and there detained them priſoners of war. An action againſt the law of nations, and an open violation of the peace then ſubſiſting between us and the French; ſacred here, as well as in Europe, though we were allies in different cauſes. Immediately

ately on news of this, ill as I still continued, I embarked with captain Gaupp's Swiss company, on board the Bombay Castle, the ship I had asked for the other party.

I arrived at St. David's the 16th of August, and the 17th took the field with 400 Europeans, 1700 Sepoys, and 4000 of the Nabob's troops, and nine pieces of cannon. I found the enemy encamped within sight of us, and after reconnoitring their situation, I resolved to attack them the next morning; which they either got information of, or suspected, for they marched off that night to Bahoor. I followed them the next day, for they still retreated, till they came very near their own bounds, with the village of Villanour in their front, three miles from Pondichery.

Mr. de Kerjean, a nephew of Mr. Dupleix, commanded this army. By his uncle's order, he protested in a long letter, against our entering their bounds, forbidding us to follow the Prince of the country even in his own territories. The absurdity of these protests, to which we had too long paid some regard, was greatly increased since Mr. Dupleix had thrown off the mask, by taking captain Schaub and his party prisoners.

I was encamped at a Pagoda called Trichanky, from whence I had a view of their camp, consisting of 400 Europeans, 1500 Sepoys, and 500 cavalry. In hopes of bringing them to an engagement, I attacked their advanced post at Villenour; but as they would not support it, I could do no more than drive out that party, my orders not permitting me to follow them into their bounds.

Finding it impossible to bring on an engagement, I marched back and incamped at Bahoor, two miles from Fort St. David, to see if my retreat would encourage De Kerjean to follow us. As no people are naturally more elated with trifles, (I mean when they have not at their head a man of ſolidity, experience and judgment) I had hopes this ſcheme might take. The event more than anſwered my expectation. Mr. Dupleix ordered De Kerjean to follow us, conjuring him to improve the minute, and make the proper uſe of our fears. De Kerjean, ſuſpecting it might be otherwiſe, repreſented his thoughts of our retreat, which only procured him a more peremptory order, to march after us immediately; for Mr. Dupleix told him, he was convinced we would not fight; that he expected the * Prince every hour with Mr. De la Touche, who ſhould inſtantly ſuperſede him. He was therefore obliged to obey, and accordingly encamped next day, within two miles of us, and I made a diſpoſition for attacking him the morning after.

On the 26th of Auguſt, at two in the morning, our little army was under arms; our Sepoys in front in one line, our battalion formed a ſecond, with the artillery divided on our flanks. A high bank on our left flank, extended to the French camp, and behind it were poſted the cavalry, with orders to march as we did; and if they ſaw the enemy in any confuſion on our attack, they were immediately to make the proper advantage of their diſorder. The ground permitting us, we marched in that order, and came up in time to begin our attack, a little before dawn of day. Our Sepoys were challenged by the enemies advanced poſt, and not anſwering, received their fire and returned it, ſtill marching on. The Europeans followed in good order, and kept ſhouldered while our Sepoys were engaged with theirs. The day juſt then beginning to break, we ſaw the French battalion drawn out a little upon our left. On their right was the bank I mentioned before, and on their left a tank or pond of water,

* The Prince was a very large French company's ſhip, with 700 men, and preſents from the French king for the Mogul, Salabatzing and Chunda Saib: ſhe was burnt in her paſſage to India, and ſcarce a man ſaved.

water, which obliged us to incline, to make our front equal to theirs. We then advanced, while they continued all the time a very brisk fire from their cannon. The small arms soon began: our men advanced firing; and the French stood their ground, till our bayonets met. The violence of the attack was made by our grenadiers and two platoons, who threw the enemy into disorder, and soon after their whole line was broke. They then threw down their arms, and ran for it. Every moment our cavalry was expected to charge; but they, instead of pursuing, employed themselves in plundering the camp, which gave time to many of the French to retreat to Areacopong. The action, however, ended greatly in our favour. Mr. Kerjean, fifteen officers, and 100 private men were made prisoners, and many more were wounded, or fell in the engagement. Their artillery, consisting of eight pieces of cannon, with all their ammunition, tumbrils, and stores, fell into our hands. We had one officer killed, three or four wounded, and seventy eight men killed and wounded. The Nabob, highly delighted at our success, though displeased at the behaviour of his own people, returned with me to Fort St. David, where we received accounts that three thousand Marattas were on their march from Trichinopoly to join the Nabob; but we had reason to suspect their intentions; they were to have joined the French, if our success had not prevented them. Nanderauze, the Maissore general, still remained before Trichinopoly, with Morarow, outwardly our friend, but ready to seize the first opportunity to get possession of the town: they therefore kept captain Dalton continually on the watch, the more so as it was necessary to seem as if we did not suspect them, or know any thing of their treating with the French. Mr. Dupleix did not lose so fair an opportunity of endeavouring to bring the Maissoreans to his interest. He therefore promised Nanderauze not only Trichinopoly, but gave him hopes that the kingdom of Tanjore might also be added to it.

On the news of our victory, 3000 Marattas joined us, commanded by Innis Cawn, the next in rank to Morarow, who, according to cuſtom, ſwore fidelity to the Nabob, and we marched to Trivedy the 17th of September.

To improve the remaining part of the ſeaſon, the monſoon * coming on, captain Clive was ſent with a ſmall detachment to take Covelong, a fort ſixteen miles to the ſouthward of Madraſs, and Chengalaput, about forty. The laſt mentioned fort was exceeding ſtrong, being almoſt encompaſſed by a moraſs, and ſurrounded with two walls, the ramparts of which are ſixteen feet thick, a wet ditch faced with ſtone ſixty feet wide, quite round the outward fort, and another half round the inner. Chengalaput capitulated the 1ſt of October. It ſhould be remarked, that the officer who commanded was then priſoner on parole.

Having performed this ſervice, and the monſoon now approaching, I propoſed returning to winter quarters, at Fort St. David, to give our men, who who were ſufficiently harraſſed, the ſmall refreſhment of two months reſt, and good quarters, during the rains, which fall heavily in this country; but I had orders to canton the troops at Trivedy: the Nabob did the ſame.

Notwithſtanding theſe ſeeming advantages to the northward, our ſituation in general was very diſcouraging. The Nabob's money at this time began to fail, and what is a natural conſequence, his troops left him. Beſides, they had never been uſed to keep the field at this ſeaſon of the year; Morarow, on a pretended diſpute with the Maiſſoreans for want of pay, marched off to Pondichery, and declared for the French; Innis Cawn decamped alſo at the ſame time.

All

* A ſeaſon of heavy rains and ſtorms which begin about this month, and generally continue to December.

All this was a ſcheme concerted by Nanderauze, to ſee if he could not gain Trichinopoly. He would not break openly with the Nabob, for then all his hopes were gone; but if he could create us ſuch a number of enemies, he concluded neither the Nabob nor the Engliſh could poſſibly ſupport the war. He thought therefore, in ſuch diſtreſs, he might make his own terms for the aſſiſtance we ſhould want, and which he alone could give us. This, in reality, was the intention of his pretended quarrel with Morarow.

The Maiſſorean, to ſave appearances, and act with ſome ſhow of juſtice, ſaid he would return to his own country, if the Nabob would pay him his expences in ready money. The ſum he aſked was as impoſſible for the Nabob to raiſe, as for us to advance, which he very well knew. Countries were offered as ſecurities; but nothing leſs than ready money would ſatisfy, or what he choſe rather, the being put in poſſeſſion of Trichinopoly, which he had attempted to ſurpriſe in the following manner.

A Neapolitan named Clement Poverio, who had been a long time in India, and knew the country language very well, had taken ſervice with the Nabob, and commanded a company of Topaſſes. This man ſerved as interpreter between captain Dalton and Nanderauze, who thinking it not difficult to bribe ſuch a perſon, offered him a conſiderable ſum of money, if he would be inſtrumental in lending him aſſiſtance to get poſſeſſion of the town. The man deſired ſome time to conſider of it, and on his return honeſtly diſcovered the whole to captain Dalton, who, after returning him thanks for his fidelity, and promiſing a reward, ordered him to carry on the ſcheme with Nanderauze, and on his next viſit to aſſure him he was ready to obey his orders. The fellow returned with his leſſon, and acted his part naturally, ſo as to avoid the appearance of double dealing. The ſcheme concerted between Nanderauze and Morarow was, that Poverio, with part of his Topaſs company, ſhould ſecure a gate for the entrance of the troops. The French priſoners that we had taken at Samiaveram and Volconda, were to be armed, and ſet at liberty, by the remainder of his company, who were to attack the guard over them. Six reſolute fellows undertook to diſpatch captain Dalton on his firſt appearance, after the alarm given. Every thing, in ſhort, was ſettled, and the night appointed for the execution. Captain Dalton appriſed of this, to ſcreen Poverio from ſuſpicion, made the neceſſary diſpoſitions for his defence, with the greateſt ſecrecy, till the evening came, on which the plot was to take place. He then informed the Nabob's brother-in-law, the governor of Trichinopoly, of their deſigns, and the plan he had laid to defeat them. Terrified at the thoughts of an attempt, and conſulting nothing but his fears, to prevent all riſque, the governor ſent a meſſenger to Nanderauze, informing him of the diſcovery of the whole plot, and our having taken proper meaſures to prevent its execution; adding to it all the circumſtances that Dalton had told him, that the Maiſſorean might not doubt in the leaſt, the truth of the diſcovery. When he had done this, he acquainted captain Dalton with it, not a little pleaſed with himſelf, and thinking he had acted with uncommon diſcretion in the affair to prevent the Maiſſorean's deſigns by ſuch a prudent ſtep. Nanderauze wiſely deſiſted from the attempt, but offered large ſums for Poverio, dead or alive. It was on the diſcovery of this, that I propoſed Dalton ſhould ſeize on the Maiſſorean and Morarow, which he might eaſily have done, by a ſurpriſe, as he often had conferences with them; and I muſt own, I thought in juſtice it would have been right to have done it: but the Preſidency were of another opinion. Before we cloſe the year 1752, it will be neceſſary to ſay what was doing by Salabatzing and Mr. Buſſy to the northward.

At

At the end of the year 1751, we left the French with the Viceroy of their own appointing, Salabatzing marching to Aurengabad: they were ſoon after diſturbed by Ballazerow the chief of the Marattas, who came down with a large army againſt them.

The war continued till October 1752, when Gawzedy Cawn, the elder brother of Salabatzing, whom the Mogul had appointed Prince of the Deckan, marched to take poſſeſſion of his government; but he died in fourteen days after his arrival at Aurengabad, poiſoned by his own ſiſter. After his death, Salabatzing concluded a treaty at Hydrabad with Ballazerow; but the Mogul, on the death of Gawzedy Cawn, appointed his ſon Shaw Abadin Cawn to ſucceed. He accordingly informed the Nabob, Mr. Saunders, and Mr. Dupleix of the Mogul's appointment, and raiſed a large army to come and take poſſeſſion: but he was ſoon obliged to drop that deſign, the Mogul's affairs requiring his preſence with the army at Delly. Salabatzing now left at large, at the earneſt ſolicitation of Mr. Dupleix, gave all our ſettlements to the northward to the French, who, however, for the preſent, did not attempt to take poſſeſſion, except of Divi Iſland. Mr. Buſſy frequently quarrelled with Salabatzing, and as often again aſſiſted him with his Europeans in collecting his revenues; by which conduct he ſometimes promoted the intereſt of the company, always his own, and is thereby become one of the richeſt ſubjects in Europe.

Before the beginning of the new year the Maiſſoreans had declared againſt us, and being in poſſeſſion of Seringam Pagodas, captain Dalton beat up their camp in the night, and killed ſome people.

Two days after this, the Maiſſoreans recovering themſelves, attacked his advanced poſt, on the other ſide the Cauvery, within cannon-ſhot of the fort. It was defended by a redoubt, in which he had poſted ſixty Europeans, and ſome Sepoys. The enemy came on with extraordinary reſolution, through the fire of our muſquetry to the very parapet. A panick ſeized our people, and inſtead of truſting to the redoubt, and waiting for a reinforcement from the town they abandoned the poſt, and attempted to croſs the river. The cavalry ſeeing their confuſion, followed them into the Cauvery, and there cut every man to pieces. This obliged captain Dalton to keep within his garriſon, which was ſtill very ſufficient; and as we apprehended no ſcarcity of proviſions, we were not concerned on his account, being determined our efforts ſhould ſtill be exerted in this part of the province.

In conſequence of our reſolution, and hearing the French were marched with Morarow from * Waldore, towards Trivedy; we ſet out from Fort St. David the 6th of January, with 350 Europeans, 700 Sepoys, and joined the Nabob and our other forces at Trivedy. Our army conſiſted of about 700 Europeans, 2000 Sepoys, 1000 of the Nabob's cavalry, and our own little troop of twenty. The Nabob had neither money nor allies, except the King of Tanjore, who promiſed very fairly, but never ſent any aſſiſtance. The French, conſiſting of 500 Europeans, 2000 ſepoys, a troop of horſe commanded by Mr. Maiſſin, and 4000 Marattas, intrenched themſelves on the banks of the river Paniar in ſight of Trivedy. Morarow, with his Maratta horſe, ravaged and deſtroyed the country, attacking our convoys, and obliging us to march our whole force, to bring our proviſions and ſtores from Fort St. David.

On the ninth of January in the morning, the Marattas, who had a train of artillery, and two companies of Topaſſes, brought down three pieces of cannon, and begun to cannonade the village of Trivedy. I ordered the grenadiers and ſome ſepoys to attack their

* A fort 12 miles weſt of Pondichery.

their battery, and followed with our whole body to ſupport them. The party buſhed on briſkly, and got poſſeſſion of their artillery before they had time to fire a ſecond round. As the cavalry ſtill kept their diſtance but within cannon ſhot, we followed them with ſome field-pieces about two miles, and were preparing to return when they ſurrounded and attacked us on every ſide. Our cannon did great execution with grape-ſhot, and our men kept their fire admirably well. Finding they could not ſucceed, they left us to purſue our march to camp, with the three pieces of cannon our grenadiers had taken in the morning.

The King of Tanjore having promiſed us a body of cavalry, I ſent a party of infantry, with two pieces of cannon to favour their junction. They came on ſome part of the way, but thinking us in a bad condition, and fearing the Marattas, they amuſed us only with promiſes, and obliged our party to return to the army without them.

The enemy were ſo ſuperior to us in cavalry, that we were obliged often to march our whole body to eſcort ſtores and proviſions from St. David's to our camp; always haraſſed more or leſs by the Marattas. On the 1ſt of April in particular, returning from St. David's, they attacked us in ſmall parties the whole day, till within three miles of Trivedy, and there a large body attacked our front with great briſkneſs, but they were repulſed with the ſame ſpirit. We then perceived the whole body of the enemy on the right of the road, within a mile of Trivedy. Our convoy very luckily marched on the left flank, near the bed of a river. The enemy advancing, we came preſently near enough for cannon, and kept advancing, and firing, with a ſeeming reſolution on both ſides to come to an action. They had a hollow way in their front, which they imagined we could not paſs; but as ſoon as we came to a proper diſtance to make a puſh, I ordered my ſepoys and artillery to halt, and keep

keep the cavalry clear of my convoy. Then marching on briskly with the main body of Europeans, we crossed the hollow way, so much to the surprize of the French, that they gave us only one fire, and ran away. We were too well satisfied with our victory to pursue, as we had the convoy to take care of: our men, besides, were almost exhausted with fatigue, having been under arms from 3 o'clock in the morning, and the day so excessively hot, that some of our Europeans dropt down dead on the march, with the heat and want of water. The Marattas hovered about us till the close of day. We killed a great many of them, and in particular Budgerow, Morarow's brother.

The same day, on our march, we were joined by captain Polier, and his company of Swiss. With this reinforcement I determined to try if it was possible or warrantable to attack the enemy, who could not be brought out of their entrenchments to an engagement. In consequence of this resolution, I made a march nearer them.

In the front of their camp was a village where lay an advanced party. Our grenadiers and 100 of the battalion were ordered to attack it; they succeeded, and drove the enemy out, who returned to their main body. A little beyond this village, within 700 yards of their camp, was a convenient and safe post to make a battery. We had brought with us two 24 pounders, which we mounted, and began to cannonade their camp, which was surrounded with a parapet cannon proof, and with redoubts at proper distances, mounted with 30 pieces of cannon, and a very broad and deep ditch, with a good glacis. We continued cannonading for some time; but to so little purpose, that we thought proper to desist; besides, our march from Trivedy increased our difficulties with regard to provisions. The Marattas were indefatigable, who being joined by a small party from

Pondichery

Pondichery, ſurprized a fort called Bonnagery, from whence we drew our ſupplies of grain. Finding I could not bring them to an engagement, and that an aſſault was impracticable, from their numbers, which in Europeans were almoſt equal to our little army; we returned to Trivedy, and captain Killpatrick marched with a detachment to retake Bonnagery, which the enemy abandoned in the night.

Captain Dalton, ever ſince the loſs of his party, had been ſhut up in the fort. The main body of the enemy was at Seringam, and their cavalry continually ſcouring the plain, prevented any proviſions from coming in. The inhabitants and garriſon were ſupplied from the magazines which were under the care of the Nabob's brother, who had always declared there was ſufficient for a long time. Though there was no appearance of ſcarcity, captain Dalton thought it neceſſary to know the real quantity in ſtore; and making an examination, to his great ſurprize, it appeared there was only ſufficient for three weeks, and no hope of a ſupply from the country, a party lately ſent into Tondeman's diſtricts not being able to get any, or even to return. He immediately diſpatched a meſſenger with an account of his ſituation, who reached me late at night, the 20th of April at Trivedy. Aſtoniſhed at this intelligence, we ſaw the neceſſity of an immediate march to Trichinopoly, which we begun the 22d. inſtant in the morning, leaving captain Chaſe with 150 Europeans and 500 ſepoys for the defence of Trivedy; and as I intended paſſing through the Tanjore country, letters were diſpatched by the Nabob and me to the King, acquainting him with our march, and inviting him to join us on our approach, to his capital. Though we proceeded as expeditiouſly as poſſible, we were obliged to halt every third or fourth day, on account of the hot winds, which were ſo powerful at this ſeaſon, that notwithſtanding all our care, our little army was greatly

greatly diminiſhed. We marched by Chillambrum, a ſtrong Pagoda, in which we had a ſerjeant, and a few gunners. A place of ſo much conſequence for preſerving our communication by land between St. David's and the Tanjore country, ſhould have been reinforced; inſtead of that, our men were withdrawn, and it fell into the enemy's hands ſoon after our departure. On our entering the Tanjore country, the King ſent his prime miniſter Succogee, to compliment the Nabob and his allies. He received our force, and promiſed very fairly on the part of his maſter, to whom he ſoon returned. We purſued our march to Condore the 3d of May. On our arrival, the King deſired to meet the Nabob and me half-way. I ſet out the 4th, in company with the Nabob and Mr. Palk, who had been with me from my leaving Madraſs. The King met us at the place appointed, attended by his whole court, who on the occaſion made a very magnificent and ſplendid appearance. He was eſcorted by 3000 horſe, well mounted, and a great many elephants in ſilver trappings. After ceremoniouſly paſſing each other in our Palankeens, we were conducted to a pleaſant garden, and there received by the King, under a pavilion, ſupported by pillars of ſilver, elegantly covered, and furniſhed. There we renewed our aſſurances of friendſhip and protection, and all our former engagements; and it was determined that the King ſhould ſupport the Nabob, and join him the next day with 3000 horſe, and a like number of ſepoys. After a refreſhment of fruits, a ſhower of roſe-water, and being anointed with otter of roſes, we were diſmiſſed with preſents of elephants, horſes and * ſirphas, and eſcorted to our camp by a brilliant party of the Rajah's cavalry.

On the 5th, the horſe and ſepoys joined us, according to agreement; but, as we ſoon after experienced, only

* A rich dreſs of that country.

only to make a parade, for they left us the ſame day. We remonſtrated, and very warmly preſſed their junction, but they excuſed themſelves with promiſes of returning. Unwilling therefore to loſe time, and ſuſpecting that they wanted only to amuſe the Nabob and us, we marched, and arrived the 6th of May at Trichinopoly, much decreaſed in numbers through fatigue; and notwithſtanding we frequently ſent the ſick back to our ſettlements, the hoſpitals were filled at our arrival. We had even left our tents behind, and took only with us what baggage was abſolutely neceſſary, that nothing might retard our relieving Trichinopoly, which indeed was of ſo great conſequence, that every thing was to be riſqued for it. The enemy made a ſhow of oppoſition when we approached the fort. The whole plain was covered with their cavalry and ſepoys, but a few ſhot from our field-pieces ſoon determined them to retreat to Seringam. As we ſent 100 men to the hoſpital upon our arrival at Trichinopoly, the remainder of my force, with what the garriſon could ſpare, when muſtered, amounted to no more than 500 men in battalion, and 2000 ſepoys. Nanderauze was on the iſland, and had with him 10,000 cavalry, 6000 Black infantry, and about 100 Europeans, with a good train of artillery. After giving the men two days refreſhment, I croſſed the Cauvery to the iſland together with the Nabob, intending to attack the enemy if we found a favourable opportunity; but their ſuperiority, and the advantage of their ſituation, made it impracticable. It was as much as we could do, by a very briſk fire of our artillery, to keep our flanks clear from the cavalry that ſurrounded us, and at every motion we made were ready to charge. Nor were the enemy's cannon ſilent; ſo that after a very fatiguing day, I was obliged at night to retreat, and repaſs the river. In this attempt we had two officers killed

killed, and three wounded, and but very few men in proportion; the enemy's cavalry ſuffered greatly.

We then encamped on the plain, about four miles ſouth-weſt of the fort, at a place called the Fakeers's Tope, to keep our communication open with Tondeman's country. This Polygar ſtill remained a friend to the Nabob. He ſometimes ſent his troops, and all our proviſions came from his country. Beſides what was neceſſary for our daily conſumption, our deſign was, if poſſible, to lay up a year's ſtock of grain in Trichinopoly; as without this ſupply our military operations muſt entirely be confined to this ſpot; but all our endeavours to this purpoſe were ineffectual. The King of Tanjore, or Tondeman, could eaſily have ſupplied us with the quantity wanted, if they had been willing; but they were apprehenſive, that if once Trichinopoly was well ſupplied, we might think an army needleſs there, and march towards the coaſt, and by that means leave their country expoſed to the inſults of the enemy. In vain were all our promiſes, that the ſafety of their countries ſhould be our firſt care: In vain did the Nabob and I repreſent to them the advantage it would be for the common cauſe to have an army at liberty to move where we pleaſed, which was not poſſible, while the magazines remained unfurniſhed with grain. All theſe reaſons were to very little purpoſe; they judged of the Engliſh by themſelves, apprehending that if once we could carry a point, promiſes made to gain it would be no longer in force. By theſe means we were kept in Trichinopoly above a year, never able to get three months proviſions into the fort; I mean for the garriſon only without conſidering the inhabitants, who were now obliged to leave their dwellings and ſettle in Tanjore, and other places: by this means the town, lately ſo populous, became almoſt uninhabited. About this time I was commiſſioned with Mr. Palk to treat with the King of Maiſſore. We accordingly wrote

wrote to him, and desired an interview, which his French allies would not permit him to give us. He only recapitulated in a letter, six feet long, the agreement between the Nabob and him, the many injuries he had received from us by being kept out of the fort, and insisted on Trichinopoly or his expences.

The day we left Trivedy the enemy came out of their entrenchments, and encamped near the fort. A part of the garrison made a sally, and, flushed with their first success, they imprudently pursued too far: the enemy getting between them and the town, cut off their retreat; and after some resistance, the whole party, which consisted of two officers, 60 Europeans, and two companies of sepoys, was either put to the sword, or made prisoners of war.

The French now erected a battery, and began to cannonade the place. The garrison was still sufficient to make a good defence, had not a mutiny arose, in which the men got possession of the Arrack in the garrison, and, mad with liquor, obliged the commanding officer to capitulate, by which means he and all the rest of the garrison were made prisoners of war. This gallant young man, whose lenity, in not putting a stop to the first appearance of the mutiny, had been attended with such bad consequences, was so sensibly affected with his misfortune, that it threw him into a fever, of which he died soon after at Pondichery.

Chillambrum and Trivedy being reduced, the Marattas, French, and Maissoreans all joined at Seringam, and being also reinforced from other parts, their battalion outnumbered ours. With this superiority they crossed the Cauvery, and encamped to the westward of us, on the plain.

I was obliged, a little before that, to go into the fort on account of my health; and by a mistake of the gentleman who commanded, and to whom I had given directions for securing a post in his front at the Five Rocks, which he neglected, the enemy posted themselves

themſelves between us and Tondeman's country. That our communication might not be quite cut off, I ſent orders to ſecure the Golden Rock, which was accordingly done by two companies of ſepoys. The enemy reſolving to gain that poſt alſo, ſent a party early in the morning, June 26th, to attack it, and had almoſt begun their attack before we perceived their motion, it being ſcarce day-light. As ſoon as ever we diſcovered the fire, I came out of the town, having diſpatched a meſſenger firſt with orders to the commanding officer to detach the picquet, and endeavour to ſupport the ſepoys. The enemy moved at the ſame time, but before either had got half-way, the party which had attacked our ſepoys in the morning had carried their point, and drove them from their poſt. It was expedient immediately to attempt regaining it; we therefore moved our whole body: the enemy did the ſame. Being come near enough, as I imagined, to make my puſh, I ordered the firſt diviſion of the grenadiers, and the picquet ſent in the morning, (who had halted for my coming up) to march on briſkly, and attack the party on the Rock, while I followed ſlowly with the remainder to ſupport them. The enemy had ſent a reinforcement to thoſe on the Rock, and with their remainder were drawn up on the right of it. As ſoon as our firſt diviſion was engaged, I advanced, and attacked their battalion; the firſt diviſion had gained their point almoſt inſtantly, ſo that the enemy found themſelves between two fires; in which ſituation they did not long remain, but retreated, or rather ran away as faſt as they could, leaving us maſters of the poſt, and three pieces of cannon.

While we were purſuing our ſucceſs, the whole body of Marattas and Maiſſoreans rode in between us and them, ſo that our attention was afterwards ſufficiently taken up in ſecuring our return to camp, which we effected without difficulty, though they made

two

two or three briſk attacks; but our men had been long accuſtomed to preſerve their fire: and as our cannon were well ſerved, the cavalry thought proper to retire. Their loſs on this occaſion was not inconſiderable: amongſt the reſt a nephew of Morarow, called Ballapa, was killed. He commanded the Marattas, as their chief was yet in the Arcot province. I had known this young man when he was on our ſide, a youth of great ſpirit and courage, and an excellent horſeman. His body being found in the field, was ſent back in my pallankeen to his friends: a reſpect I thought juſtly due to ſo gallant an officer; and they were very thankful for the favour. He was ſhot by one of our grenadiers, being advanced ſo near us that he cut one of our men in the ranks, tho' accompanied by only four horſemen. Had all the reſt behaved with the like reſolution, we ſhould have found much more difficulty in our return to camp. Thus was this great object of the war again ſaved by our ſucceſs, but the numbers of the enemy were ſo great, that a victory or two more would have left all my men on the plains of Trichinopoly. I therefore thought in earneſt of a reinforcement, eſpecially as the neighbourhood of the enemy, with their large body of cavalry, began to make my ſtay on the plain very inconvenient, without horſe to oppoſe them. The Nabob and I determined to move towards Tanjore, to try what our preſence would do with the King, and if poſſible perſuade him to ſend the troops he ſo often promiſed, to our aſſiſtance. We marched the 2d of July and encamped at a place called Conandercoile, half-way between Trichinopoly and Tanjore. I choſe this road rather for ſecurity, than ſhortneſs; it being moſt of the way through thick woods, and ſafe from the cavalry. There we halted till we received intelligence from Mr. Park, that he had prevailed on the King to ſend out Monagee his general at the

G head

head of 3000 horſe, and 2000 ſepoys, to join us, which was compleated in ten days.

Some of our ſhips at this time being arrived on the coaſt from England with recruits, a detachment of 170 men, and ſome ſepoys were ordered to march and reinforce us, under the command of lieutenant Repington, who joined us on the 3d of Auguſt, and on the fifth we ſet out for Trichinopoly in company with the King's horſe, commanded by Monagee. The enemy at this time alſo received a reinforcement, and were in battalion ſuperior; however, as Trichinopoly was ill ſupplied and diſtreſſed, we were obliged to march. On the 7th we arrived at Dolaways * Choultry, about ten miles eaſt of the town. A heavy rain falling kept us there the next day; but the ninth, in the morning. we began our march, with a convoy of ſome thouſands of bullocks, laden with proviſions. By the ſignals made from the Obſervatory, on the top of the rock of Trichinopoly, we were given to underſtand that the enemy ſeemed determined to oppoſe us; and by the ſame ſignals we were enabled to judge of their diſpoſition, which we ſoon diſcovered more plainly as we advanced. They had extended themſelves from the French Rock to the Golden Rock; at each of which ſome of their infantry was poſted. At the Sugar Loaf, as between both, and readieſt to oppoſe us, if we attempted to paſs, was their battalion, with the artillery planted to advantage. All the cavalry was between theſe rocks, and in different parties, forming a chain, and waiting our motions. In conſequence of this diſpoſition of the enemy, I ordered our march. Our proviſions and baggage on the left flank with the Nabob, Monagee, and

* An open houſe for all travellers, the ſame as a Turkiſh Caravanſerai. A Bramin reſides always in, or near it, who keeps it clean, and provides water. He is maintained by an endowment from the founder of the charity. On moſt publick roads there is a Choultry every five or ſix miles.

and the Tanjore troops. Half our ſepoys in front, and after them, a party of Europeans, and an advanced guard to the firſt diviſion of artillery. After them followed the battalion, and in their rear my ſecond diviſion of guns, ſupported by a piquet; the other half of our ſepoys brought up the rear of the whole.

As my intention was to avoid an engagement, if poſſible, having ſo large a convoy under my care, I directed the march ſo as to be out of the reach of their guns, intending to go round by the Golden Rock. This put their whole body in motion; they detached a party of their battalion to reinforce that poſt, where they had a great many ſepoys, their main body alſo made a motion to ſupport them, and attack us as we came round. Finding it impoſſible to avoid an action, I reſolved to prevent that party's reinforcing the other on the rock; and ſince we were obliged to engage, I reſolved to diſpoſſeſs the enemy, as the gaining of that poſt would give me an advantage. I therefore ordered the grenadiers, the picquet, and our advanced ſepoys to puſh for it; their party did the ſame to ſupport it, but not with the ſame vigour or ſpirit, for we out-marched them, and drove off the party which were in poſſeſſion. On this, their advanced party halted, and preſently after the whole body, which had moved but a little way from the Sugar-Loaf Rock to ſupport them. When our whole force had reached the Golden Rock, I ordered our baggage in the rear of it, unwilling to expoſe them to the cannonade, and our cavalry to ſtay by, and ſecure it; being determined to attack the enemy, and if poſſible, to drive them out of the field, for without it we could not finiſh our march. As I have ſaid before, the firſt party of the enemy had halted between the two rocks, but imprudently, nearer to us a good deal than to their own body. So favourable an opportunity was not to be loſt. The picquet, grenadiers, and four platoons were immediately ordered to attack them, and according to their ſucceſs, I was ready to move with the remainder, either to ſupport, if repulſed, or to join, and puſh the advantage to their main body, by driving on them their beaten party. Our artillery was poſted clear of the flanks of the party, as they marched, to keep the cavalry at a diſtance. The officer who was ordered for the attack, inſtead of following my orders, ſent me word, he could not execute them without cannon, and that he was halted, waiting for it. The leaſt delay was ſufficient for the enemy to ſee their blunder, and in conſequence to repair it, by moving up to their party, which would oblige me to do the ſame; and by this means, the affair might become more equal, and indeed with more advantage on their ſide, as they were ſuperior. On this meſſage I left the main body, and galloped to the head of the party, and there ordered him back to the poſt I had left, deſiring him to leave this with me. Captain Kirk, at the head of the grenadiers, captain Killpatrick with the picquet, and myſelf at the head of four platoons, marched on, the line keeping in admirable order, in ſpite of a very ſmart fire from the enemy's artillery, which coſt us ſome men, and in particular captain Kirk, who was killed at the head of his favourite grenadiers. The brave fellows, by whom he was much beloved, could not ſee his death without ſome emotion. Captain Killpatrick, who ſaw him fall, and his men at a ſtand, immediately put himſelf at their head, and deſired them, if they loved their captain, to follow him, and revenge his death. Theſe things on the ſpot have generally a very great effect, when delivered from a perſon, whoſe ſpirit and courage is known: the fellows, rouſed in an inſtant, ſwore after their manner, they would follow him to——; and in that diſpoſition attacked the enemy, who were unable to ſtand the ſhock. The main body ſeeing our ſucceſs, (according to the directions I had

had left) marched to ſupport us, and purſued the blow. The enemy at laſt moved to the aſſiſtance of their party; but too late. The briſkneſs of the attack gave no time for rallying, but on the contrary, the pannick ſpreading through the whole, the batallion did not even ſtay to give or receive a fire, but ran off in great confuſion, round the Golden Rock, and away to the Five Rocks. To increaſe their diſtreſs, our rear diviſion of guns which we had left at that poſt, with moſt of our ſepoys, and cavalry, to ſecure our baggage and proviſions, cannonaded them ſeverely in their retreat; and had the Tanjore horſe done their duty, few could have eſcaped. The Tanjore chief alledged that he was afraid to leave the convoy, expoſed to their large body of cavalry, which remained in good order, and conſtantly near us; but this was but a bad excuſe, for orders had been ſent him, on the enemy's retreat, to purſue, and we were marching back to ſecure the convoy. The enemy, who were encamped almoſt in the order in which they drew up to oppoſe my march, ſtruck their tents at the beginning of the attack, and left us little elſe on the field of battle beſides their killed and wounded, with three pieces of cannon. We had not more than 40 men killed and wounded; the enemy above an hundred.

I cannot help mentioning one particular circumſtance in this affair, to ſhew the extraordinary behaviour of the French; the boys with my palankeen had ſtraggled a little out of the line of march, and were picked up by the Marattas. It was the ſame in which I had ſent back the body of Morarow's nephew: I therefore deſired the Maratta chief to return it, and I would pay the price to the horſemen who had taken it; but the French had got it out of their hands, and would not ſuffer them to ſend it back, but carried it to Pondichery, where, by Mr. Dupleix's order, it was carried about the town in triumph. At the ſame time it was reported that I was killed, and that we had loſt the victory, of which the palankeen was a trophy.

The enemy retreated to Alletore, very near the head of the iſland. The two next days were employed in putting proviſions into the fort; when that was done, we marched and encamped at the Five Rocks, which was in their rear; upon which they retreated to * Moutehillenour, and in ſo great a hurry, that they left behind them a nine pounder, and ſome ammunition. Elmiſeram ſurrendered the 11th to Monagee. The ſtrength of the ground they occupied, made it impoſſible for us to attack them; beſides, they received in the mean time a reinforcement of Europeans from Pondichery; and Morarow returned to them with all the reſt of his cavalry. We then marched to cover our convoys from Tanjore, which their ſuperior numbers of cavalry made it difficult to bring in. Several of our parties were attacked; in particular one on the 28th, by a large body of Marattas, and Maiſſore horſe. They came ſo near the picquet, which was ſent to the ſupport of the convoy, that the ſoldiers in the front rank wounded ſome of the horſe with their bayonets, and yet, by not parting with their fire, brought in the convoy ſafe.

A number of our men falling ſick, by the badneſs of the water, we moved our camp to the French Rock the 1ſt of September. The enemy made a motion alſo upon this, and encamped with the Sugar-Loaf on their right, and the Golden Rock on their left. We were joined in this camp by another reinforcement from the ſettlement, commanded by captain Ridge, with ſome men and officers from Europe, about 150 Europeans, and 300 ſepoys. This gave us great ſpirits, and determined us to attack the enemy. Our neceſſities indeed obliged us to it. We had a ſcarcity of every thing in camp, not above three days proviſions,

* Situated upon the river, about ſeven or eight miles from Trichinopoly.

ons, and no convoys could come without the risque of an engagement. I thought it more adviseable, therefore, by attacking them, to engage while I could be master of my own disposition. Having refreshed the troops with two or three days rest, we moved nearer the enemy; and in order that they might imagine the motion was made only to try if they would decamp on my approach, I sent to Trichinopoly for an eighteen pounder, and with it cannonaded their camp, as if we meant no more than to make them uneasy.

The following was the enemy's disposition, and my order of attack for the next morning. As I have said before, they were encamped with the Sugar-Loaf Rock on their right, having thrown up intrenchments in their front and rear, but none on the left, where were posted the Maissoreans and Marattas, extending almost to the Golden Rock, on which they had a party of 1500 sepoys, 100 Europeans, and two guns. Our battalion of 600 rank and file was ordered into three divisions; to march in the rear of each other, just at a proper distance to form the line when necessary. Our sepoys followed in the rear, to the right and left of the divisions, and the Nabob and Monagee with the cavalry brought up the whole, our cannon being divided on our flanks.

September 21st at four in the morning, we marched directly forward to the Golden Rock. Our front division, which was according to custom, composed of the grenadiers, picquet, and two platoons were ordered to attack it briskly. The enemy were so much surprized, that even they forgot to fire their two pieces of cannon, which were loaded with grape; and their infantry, so great was their pannick, fired without any order, little to our prejudice. We got possession of the rock in an instant. No time was lost to increase the confusion these runaways must create. After dismounting the two pieces of cannon, and our front division again being formed, we marched on in the same order for the French battalion. As I wished and expected, the beaten party carried their confusion to the black troops in camp, who in crowds ran for safety towards the French, and increased their disorder. The enemy soon perceived by the runaways where they might expect our attack, and in consequence also found out that their intrenchments were of no use, which obliged them to form opposite to where we were marching. In this situation we passed the Black camp easily, and were with the French in less than half an hour. The day then began to dawn: Their cannon fired very briskly, as we approached; but, I suppose, in the hurry, they forgot to point them, so little damage did we receive. We found them drawn up rather on our right, and still inclining that way, with an intention, I supposed, to fall on the flanks of our divisions. As a large body of their sepoys were posted on their left, I sent orders to ours on the right in my rear, to move up equal with the right of my first division to oppose theirs, and secure that flank. We formed our line as we marched, and attacked as we formed. Our right soon drove their left, and our center and rear divisions, the right and center of their line. Another body of their sepoys, in possession of the Sugar-Loaf Rock were routed by our division of sepoys, on the left of my last division. In short the affair was soon decided every where: they attempted to rally, and make a stand again, near a little breast-work, but were quickly obliged to abandon it, leaving behind them their camp standing, all their artillery, (eleven pieces of cannon, with their commandant Mr. Astruc) and nine officers prisoners, and about 100 men killed and wounded on the field of battle, and almost as many prisoners. In this action we had 70 men and six officers killed and wounded. I received a slight wound in my arm, and captain Killpatrick a shot through his body; concluding it must be mortal, he would not permit any of his people to stay by him, but sent them on to join their company in the pursuit of the enemy. Some straggling Maratta horse came

came up in the mean time, according to cuſtom, cut him with their ſabres as they paſſed, which would have been repeated by others, but the ſurgeon by accident ſeeing him in that danger, ſtaid and protected him, till the ſucceſs of the day cleared the field of the enemy. The garriſon made a ſally, and picked up ſeveral priſoners, who were making their eſcape over the river to the iſland, where they at laſt collected their ſcattered army, leaving us maſters of the plain, and an open communication. The Nabob's cavalry were few; but had our Tanjore horſe behaved as they ought, we muſt have deſtroyed many more of the French battalion. Nor had they now any excuſe as formerly, the enemy's horſe having kept their diſtance on our firſt attack in the morning; but the Tanjoreans were too buſy in plundering the camp to think of a purſuit. We had not ſufficient force to follow the blow on the iſland, but were obliged to reſt contented with our ſucceſs, and endeavour to perſuade the King of Tanjore and Tondeman, to make uſe of this favourable opportunity to throw in proviſions.

The enemy had left a party at Weyaconda, which we were obliged to attack, and batter in breach. The breach was ſcarce practicable, when our ſepoys perceiving the enemy ſtealing off by another gate, clambered up as well as they could, and cut the garriſon to pieces; it conſiſted of two hundred Black infantry. Upon this we marched and encamped at the French Rock, and diſpatched an officer to the King of Tanjore, to haſten the important article of proviſions, who ſucceeded in part, and we got ſtores for three months into the place.

The monſoon ſeaſon coming on, it was high time to think of cantoning our troops. The Nabob and I therefore fixed upon Koiladdy, about fifteen miles eaſt of Trichinopoly, as it commands the paſs on the iſland. We ſhould have remained nearer Trichinopoly, or perhaps in the town itſelf, but that would have

have occaſioned a very great conſumption of proviſions. Therefore after leaving a ſufficient garriſon in Trichinopoly and the fort of Elmiſeram, we marched for Koiladdy, and provided againſt the ſevere rains which generally fall about this ſeaſon of the year. In our cantonments we were very ſickly; we loſt ſix officers in as many weeks, and a great many ſoldiers. The Nabob continued with us, but Monagee and the Tanjore troops returned home. Being pretty well acquainted with the nature of the people, notwithſtanding their promiſes of coming back; I wrote to the preſidency, to ſend Mr. Palk, who had before ſo well managed for us, to keep that court firm in our intereſt, I was the more ſollicitous becauſe I knew the king's prime miniſter was our enemy, and conſtantly endeavouring to keep his maſter neuter or rather a ſeeming friend to both, and if at any time we were unſucceſsful, Succojee was ſure to be in the intereſt of the enemy. Nanderauze ſent an ambaſſador to the king of Tanjore making large promiſes if he would leave us, and threatening on the contrary, if he did not, that the Marattas ſhould ravage and lay waſte his country, and puniſh him with fire and ſword, and that the Nabob governor, meaning Dupleix, ſhould alſo bring down Salabatzing againſt us. Succojee the miniſter had been brought over to the French cauſe by a large bribe, and by his intrigues removed Monagee from his maſter's favour.

The enemy remained ſeemingly very quiet on the iſland, and had received ſome reinforcements from Pondichery, but none came to us from Madraſs, to put on an equality. Mr. Dupleix generally obliged the inhabitants of Pondichery to mount guard and do the duty of the garriſon, but we could not in like manner truſt Fort St. George without regular troops. On the 28th in the morning, our out-guards reported that in the night they had heard a great firing towards Trichinopoly. We remained in ſuſpence till the evening, when the following account came from captain Killpatrick,

Killpatrick, who ſucceeded captain Dalton in that command.

The enemy's whole army under Mr. Maiſſin croſſed the river the 27th at night. Their forces were diſtributed agreeable to the different falſe attacks they were to make. The real one was to be made by the French battallion, on that battery, which is in the center of the Weſt face; and as I obſerved before was called Dalton's battery. They had 800 men, 600 were to eſcalade, and Mr. Maiſſin with 200 more and a body of ſepoys to wait the event, prepared to ſecond, and join the firſt party, when they had got over the wall. At three in the morning they paſſed the ditch which was almoſt dry. They placed their ladders, and mounted to the Number of 600 on the battery, without interruption, or the leaſt alarm in the garriſon. The guard appointed for the battery was of 50 ſepoys, with their officers and two European gunners. The rounds had gone at twelve o'clock, and found them preſent, and alert. However when the French came they were moſtly abſent or with the two European gunners aſleep. By this time, two or three ſhot were fired, which alarmed our piquet. The French, perſuaded that firing alone would frighten the garriſon, turned two of our twelve pounders on the battery, againſt the town, and diſcharged them with a volly of ſmall arms, their drums beating, and the ſoldiers crying out, *Vive le Roy*.

Captain Killpatrick was then ill of his wounds. The next officer in command came to him for his orders. He bid him march inſtantly with the picquet, reſerve, and what ſepoys were not poſted, to the place where the attack was made, and to order every man alſo to their reſpective Alarm Poſts, and not to ſtir from them on pain of death. The French after their diſcharge, came down from the battery; and were between the two walls. There was a ſlight gate in the inner wall, which led into the town. The man who

who was their guide knew where it was, they had two petards ready to clap to it, and at the ſame time to amuſe us, another party was to eſcalade the inner wall. The ſcheme was well laid, and had not the French petulance, made them too ſoon diſcover themſelves, they perhaps might have had time to execute their deſigns, and have entered the town. When our officer came to the place attacked, it was not eaſy for him to diſcover the ſituation of the enemy: but however in the hurry and confuſion, he did not forget the gate, on the flanks of which he poſted a number of men, with plenty of ammunition, to fire from thence inceſſantly, whether they heard or ſaw any thing of the enemy or not. And luckily he did, for the guide and petardier were found killed within ten yards of the gate. The eſcaladers had ſo far ſucceeded in their deſign as to have fixed ladders againſt the inner wall, and began to mount. The commanding officer of this party, preceeded by his drummer were the firſt perſons who attempted to enter, in which the latter loſt his life, and the officer receiving a ſhot and cut at the ſame time, was pulled within the town. The frequent flaſhes of fire, occaſioned by the briſkneſs of the attack and defence, were the only guide our artillery officer had to direct the pointing of his guns; with which he ſo well ſucceeded, having loaded them with grape, as to ſhatter the ladders, kill a number of men and entirely diſappoint their well concerted ſcheme. They now only thought of making their eſcape, or ſcreening themſelves from our fire. This firſt was impracticable, their ladders being moſtly deſtroyed, and they within the firſt wall: yet ſome attempted leaping off the battery, into the ditch, but the greater number lay hid under the parapet. The long wiſhed for day at laſt came and diſcovered where the enemy were, who made uſe alſo of the light to beg for quarter, which was granted them. They loſt

loſt in that affair * 364 Europeans taken priſoners, 65 of which were wounded. Eight officers alſo priſoners, and moſt of them wounded, beſides forty private, and one officer killed, and they acknowledged themſelves that many more were wounded, or lamed, who were carried off to the iſland. We found two petards, one as I ſaid before, with the petardier within ten yards of the gate, the other at a little diſtance from it.

I gave orders for marching the next day, but firſt ſent a reinforcement to captain Killpatrick, as the number of his priſoners was much greater than his European garriſon, and the enemy threatened the place with another general aſſault. We arrived at the French Rock without oppoſition, the enemy keeping cloſe to the iſland.

The king of Tanjore after a great many difficulties, ſent out ſome of his troops to Tricatapoly ; eighteen miles from Trichinopoly, and made no ſmall merit of what he had done, for the Nabob. But the truth was, he had certain intelligence, that the enemy were forming a party of Marattas, to enter his country, and he therefore prepared to oppoſe them. Succogee had ſo effectually irritated the king againſt Monagee, that the command of the troops was given to Gauderow, an officer of no ſkill or judgment, but a creature of Succogee's, and uncle to the king. We deſired that Monagee might be ſent, well knowing his merit as a ſoldier, and his ſtrong attachments to the common cauſe, which he always thought his maſter's intereſt. On our writing preſſingly for him, Succogee repreſented to the king that Monagee was too much in our intereſt not to be ſuſpected, and that it was poſſible, with our aſſiſtance, he might endeavour to make himſelf too powerful.

* It may ſerve as a ſpecimen of Mr. Dupleix's manner of relating theſe affairs, both in his Memoire and the little Hiſtory which he cauſed to be publiſhed in the year 1757, to cite the following words from the Memoire, where ſpeaking of this loſs of ſo large a party of Europeans, he ſays, Il fallut donc ſe retirer *et meme avec perte*.

powerful. Being acquainted with this, I was obliged to desist even from mentioning Monagee's name, or the consequence might have been fatal to him. Not to drive things therefore to extremities, I wrote to the king that he might send whom he pleased to command his troops, I was satisfied.

Thus ended the year 1753, in which had we been able to pursue our fortune, our advantages would have been real: but instead of it our successes were only a respite, and we soon had the same to go over again, having, however, the consolation to think we had done all we could against so great a superiority. A superiority indeed which I am often ashamed to mention, for fear my veracity should be called in question.

Mr Bussy with his army was still attending and supporting Salabatzing to the northward. Shaw Abadin Cawn the son of Gauzedy Cawn, who had been appointed by the Mogul prince of the Deckan, had too much employment on his hands, as chief Bucshee of the empire, to think at that time of making good his pretensions.

The latter end of this year the Mogul Shaw Hamet was deposed, and succeeded by Allum Geer. This change was occasioned by the following event. The Mogul sent Shaw Abadin Cawn, the Bucshee, at the head of 90000 horse, to suppress an irruption of the Rashpoots, who are reckoned the best soldiers in Indostan. In this expedition he succeeded, but on his return to Delly, an uncle of his taking the advantage of his absence, persuaded the Mogul that he had always been his enemy, and intended making use of his army to dethrone him. The Mogul was the easier persuaded, as the Bucshee had obtained the post he enjoyed, more through power than favour, and had ever spoke freely of the Mogul's dissolute way of life, which was generally spent in debauchery. It was therefore agreed, that Shaw Abadin Cawn should be put to death, but as they rightly judged it could not be done openly, the fol-

following ſcheme was laid for the execution of their deſign.

The Mogul went out of Delly, at the head of 25000 horſe, in order as he ſaid to do honour to Shaw Abadin Cawn, and reward him for his ſervices. At their meeting, the blow was to have been ſtruck. The Bucſhee having intelligence of all that paſſed, came readily to meet the Mogul, but brought with him 30000 Marattas; who in caſe of any attempt were to protect him. The Mogul's party hearing that ſuch precautions were taken, not knowing what might be the conſequence, and afraid to offend a man ſo powerfully ſupported, diſbanded and returned to Delly, leaving their ſovereign almoſt without attendants: who therefore immediately followed his troops. Whether Shaw Abadin Cawn thought this a favourable opportunity to dethrone a man who was a ſcandal to the dignity of the throne; or whether it was the reſult of a premeditated deſign, he followed the Mogul, entered Delly, and went immediately to the palace, where after making his obeiſance, and ſitting down a little while at the Durbar with the Mogul, he ordered his people to ſeize on and impriſon him; he then aſſembled the Omrahs *, placed on the throne, Allum Geer a near relation to the late Mogul. The depoſed Prince, according to the cruel policy of their government was immediately deprived of his ſight.

The Marattas as they had threatened, ſlipped by Gauderow, who was encamped on the frontiers, entered the Tanjore country, and began according to cuſtom to plunder and burn the villages, cut the grain, and drive off the cattle. The king preſſed by neceſſity, found at laſt, that no body but Monagee, could put a ſtop to the miſchief. He applied alſo to me, but the

* Privy counſellors, men of the firſt dignity and family in the empire. They are under the Vizir, but are moſtly concerned in all the revolutions of the ſtate: and commonly their intereſt elects and depoſes the Moguls.

the violent rains had ſo ſwelled the rivers between us, and the roads were ſo bad that it was impoſſible for us to move. Monagee came out of Tanjore, with what troops he could raiſe, and Gauderow had orders to join him, and give up the command. Monagee came up with the Marattas on the 4th of January, drew them into an ambuſcade, took from them 800 horſe, and made a great many priſoners, and cut to pieces the remainder of the party. I flattered myſelf ſuch a piece of ſervice, might reinſtate our friend Monagee, and reſtore him to favour, and that after ſo much ſucceſs, perhaps he would join me, but I was greatly miſtaken. On his return to Tanjore, he was very graciouſly received, but told at the ſame time, that the enemy being now ſubdued, there was no further occaſion for his ſervice; and conſequently the troops were diſbanded. All this was the effect of Succogee's envy, which increaſed in proportion with the other's merit. He perſuaded the king, that keeping up troops was too heavy an expence; that the Engliſh would do the reſt, that it was our buſineſs to fight and not his, who had juſt gained a glorious victory, with which he might ſit down in ſafety and content.

During this time the two governors, Mr. Saunders and Dupleix were endeavouring to negociate. After many altercations, and a tedious correſpondence, it was agreed on between them to ſend commiſſaries from each nation, and hold a congreſs at Sadraſs *, at which place matters might more eaſily be adjuſted. Accordingly commiſſaries were appointed. Thoſe on our ſide were Mr. Palk and Mr. Vanſittart; on theirs the father L'Avaur, ſuperior general of the Jeſuits in India, and Meſſieurs De Kerjean and De Bauſſet, who aſſembled at Sadraſs in January.

We

* A Dutch ſettlement ſituated between Madraſs and Pondichery.

We proposed for the basis of the treaty, the Nabob being acknowledged, and the king of Tanjore to remain in peaceable possession of his country. But their proposals in answer to ours were as follows:

1st, The restitution of the French prisoners.

2dly, That Madrass, which used to pay to the Duan of Arcot, 4000 pagodas yearly, should be independent, and all our arrears forgiven.

3dly, That the company should be lawfully entitled to Ponamalley and all its dependencies.

4thly, That the Nabob should have some establishment elsewhere, if the preliminaries were received, and that his differences with the Maissoreans, with regard to Trichinopoly, should be reconciled.

5thly, That the English should evacuate all the places taken from the French, to whom they belonged, whether by grant or conquest, as well as all the places in the Carnatick, without opposing the disposition and arrangement of Salabatzing, who had an undoubted right, and who had associated the Marquis Dupleix in the government of the Deckan. Such were Mr. Dupleix's proposals.

It has been before said, that Mr. Dupleix would willingly make the world believe he had received grants from the Mogul and Salabatzing appointing him governor from the river Kristna to Cape Comorin, and as such he was proclaimed in the usual form. In consequence of this pretended authority, these articles were made. But an unlucky mistake proved it all to be a forgery. The French commissaries came equipped with what they called Des pieces authentiques

 from

from the Mogul, and other officers under him, constituting and appointing Mr. Dupleix governor general from the river Kriſtna to the ſea, and the French commiſſaries agreed (leſt our gentlemen ſhould doubt it) they ſhould examine, and take copies of theſe grants.

A Perſian interpreter was ſent for, from whom they learned that the ſeven firſt ſaneds or grants were only copies, though produced as originals: to which the French commiſſaries anſwered, that Mr. Dupleix kept the originals at Pondichery, and if required, they ſhould be ſent for; but that theſe papers, atteſted by a Caudy *, were of equal validity. This cauſed ſome diſpute, but our gentlemen dropt it; and on further examination it appeared to Mr. Vanſittart (who underſtood enough of the Perſian language) to be a falſe ſeal fixed to the ſaned, called the Mogul's, the firſt having no date †. On that the French immediately objected to our proceeding any further; for unleſs we could produce Nazirzing's ſaneds to the Nabob, they could not admit of theirs being copied. We told them, that Nazirzing ſupporting him, was a ſufficient ſaned in his favour. That it was their firſt propoſal, as well as Mr. Dupleix's, all along to Mr. Saunders, to begin with an examination of their own ſaneds, and we could not help being ſurprized at their declining it, after ſome copies had been taken. That pieces of ſo publick a nature, we apprehended, might be expoſed to all the world. But we could not help remarking, that the firſt of thoſe ſaneds was without date; and the only original they produced, et le plus authentique, as it is termed, was a manifeſt forgery; for it had no ‡ chop of the Mogul or his Vizier; it had no ſign manual,

* Caudy a perſon who adminiſters juſtice, and by whom copies of all public papers are atteſted.

† Mr. Dupleix is ſilent on this ſubject in his Memoire.

‡ A ſmaller ſeal on which is engraved the name of the Mogul. Every grant is generally authenticated, not only with this ſeal of the Mogul, but alſo that of his Viziers.

manual, and from other manifeſt tokens, it was evident that it had been borrowed from ſome old ſaned, eſpecially as the number 3 is annexed to it, which was the third year of the reign of the laſt Mogul.

I have dwelt ſo long on this affair, only to give an idea of what ſhuffling conduct Mr. Dupleix was capable, in order to carry a point, and ſhew a real cauſe why the congreſs came to nothing. The commiſſaries were recalled on each ſide, and the war as likely to continue as ever.

We remained near Trichinopoly, and the enemy on the iſland, but they were well ſituated, having a large body of cavalry, and the river fordable every where to incommode us very much. All the country round, after being the ſeat of war for ſo many years, was ruined; our proviſions coming moſtly from Tanjore, we were obliged to ſend large parties to eſcort them, for the merchants with grain would not come within eighteen miles of us without a party to protect them. We were obliged alſo to ſend five or ſix miles for firewood, while the enemy's cavalry were continually in motion on every ſide. At that time we had troops enough on the coaſt, which might have joined us, with whoſe aſſiſtance we ſhould have been able, at leaſt, to have protected our convoys with leſs fatigue and riſque, as the event too fatally ſhewed.

In the month of February we ſent a party for proviſions and ſtores, and for fear the enemy might at laſt be tempted to attack them, I made it ſtronger than any I before had ſent. It conſiſted of two captains, ſix officers, and 180 men rank and file, four pieces of cannon, and 800 ſepoys. The commanding officer had orders, if he ſaw or heard any of the enemy coming to attack him, to take poſt immediately and defend himſelf, till we could come to his aſſiſtance. * It will be needleſs to enter on the particu-

 lars

* They were attacked on their march from Killycottah, and within

lars of this affair, as one can hardly do it without blaming, at leaſt pitying the commanding officer, who is ſince dead, and who certainly, from his miſconduct, loſt his party ; and what ſtill added to the misfortune, our brave company of grenadiers, who had ever behaved well, and ſucceſsfully, were amongſt them. They were either taken, or cut to pieces, and both their officers killed. In this unhappy affair, 134 men were priſoners, 100 of which were wounded. Of the eight officers four were killed, and three wounded, one only eſcaping ; our four pieces of cannon, and about 7000l. in money, with a large convoy of proviſions fell into the hands of the enemy. The party was attacked by 120 French infantry, two companies of deſerters about the ſame number, the French troop of about 80, 6000 ſepoys, all the Maiſſore cavalry, and the Marattas, who came in at the latter end of the fray, in all about 10000, and ſeven pieces of cannon.

We began our march to their relief, but too late, as they had not followed the propoſed diſpoſition, and particularly had not taken poſt agreeable to their orders, but endeavoured to march on, covering their convoys with their force ſo divided and ſeparated, that they were not able to ſupport each other, ſo that the cavalry, who ſaw their confuſion, had an eaſy conqueſt, and not much more than the buſineſs of a minute to cut them to pieces, which was the fate of every man, except thoſe whom the French troops ſaved, and even of theſe there were few who did not bear marks of their defeat. This was a moſt heavy ſtroke upon our little handful of men, above a third, and I cannot help repeating it, our beſt troops, for ſo with reaſon I reckoned our grenadiers, who had always behaved ſo well on every occaſion where bravery and reſolution were to be ſhewn. Soon

within a mile of that place. There was a village before them called Coutapara, a little below Elmiſeram. The men who were at that poſt on the attack, ſecured the village for our people with ſome ſepoys ; and had they been in a body, and puſhed for it, agreeable to their orders, the enemy could not have hurt them.

Soon after this misfortune we received intelligence, that one of the Nabob's brothers, Mauphus Cawn, was in the Arcot province, and marching to our aſſiſtance with 2000 horſe, which determined me to try every method to maintain my ground ſome time longer, and to leave a party of 180 men, which was at Davecotah, to ſtrengthen Mauphus Cawn, who wanted ſome Europeans to eſcort him to camp. We therefore opened our communication with Tondeman's country for proviſions, as no merchant could be perſuaded to venture the other way with grain from Tanjore. The enemy continued on the iſland, not yet chuſing to encamp on the plain; beſides, they had ſuffered as well as we in the laſt affair. Their whole attention was taken up in ſchemes to ſurprize our parties, but we ſo often changed our roads, and the time for bringing in our proviſions, that they never ſucceeded. We were greatly aſſiſted in this by a Moorman, who for his deſerved merit was made commander of our ſepoys.

Mahomed Iſouf Cawn, commonly called the Nelloure Subadar, from the place whence he came, had firſt a company of ſepoys in our ſervice, which were raiſed by himſelf. He is an excellent partizan, knows the country well, is brave and reſolute, but cool and wary in action. He was never ſparing of himſelf, but out upon all parties, and by his good intelligence brought in proviſions to keep us tolerably well ſupplied. He is born a ſoldier, and better of his colour I never ſaw in the country.

Mr. Palk, who was now at Tanjore, found affairs, juſt as I had repreſented them: Monagee a priſoner, the King difficult of acceſs, and his miniſter ſtrong in the Maiſſore intereſt, oppoſing all our meaſures, and ever throwing in obſtacles to prevent Mr. Palk's ſeeing his maſter; and when, after ſome days, he was admitted to an audience, he found the King wavering and irreſolute, one hour ſeemingly convinced by his arguments, the next liſtening to, and approving of Succogee, and upon the whole determining nothing. Add to all theſe difficulties another, which as we did not ſuſpect it, was the moſt dangerous. It was no leſs than the treachery of our linguiſt, who of courſe was acquainted, and knew all our deſigns and motions. This man being in treaty with Nanderauze, diſcovered to him all he knew of our affairs. It was a moſt intricate piece of villainy, and with no ſmall difficulty traced to the bottom, ſo carefully had the fellow laid his ſchemes. When the fact was proved againſt him, he was blown away from the mouth of a cannon, the common puniſhment of traitors.

In this ſituation did we remain till ſome time in May, ſtill waiting for Mauphus Cawn, and in hopes that his coming would determine the King of Tanjore to return to our alliance; but another accident helped to bring it about more effectually. On the 12th of May, I ſent a party out in the morning to take poſt on the plain, and wait for a convoy of proviſions from Tondeman's country. The party was commanded by a diſcreet and gallant officer, captain Caillaud, who with 120 men, two guns, and 500 ſepoys marched from camp about four o'clock in the morning. The Nelloure Subadar, who was in the front of his advanced party, on getting over a little riſing ground, was ſurpriſed by his horſe neighing, who was immediately anſwered by many others. When he got to the top of the bank, he diſcovered a part of the enemy poſted; the French troop in particular, who mounted on his appearing, firſt diſcharging their carbines, on hearing which captain Caillaud halted, formed his party, and rode up to his advanced guard. He met the Nelloure Subadar, who told him, the enemy were on the road, and had poſted themſelves, as well as he could diſtinguiſh, in the ſame place where it was intended to wait for the proviſions. The enemy had a bank in their front, which formed a parapet, and it was agreed to attack them, immediately on their flank

flank, with the Europeans on one ſide, and the ſepoys on the other. They quickly drove the enemy, and obliged them to leave a tumbril of ammunition behind, and ſome of their men. The poſt was immediately taken, and there the party waited agreeable to their orders. By this time it was broad day-light, when we diſcovered the number of the enemy, which was much ſuperior to our party, even in infantry, beſides all the Maiſſore cavalry. Captain Caillaud therefore employed a black fellow to ſlip through the enemy that had ſurrounded him, and ordered the proviſions to return. The enemy continued at a little diſtance from the poſt, and contented themſelves with a cannonade. The moment the firing was heard in the camp, the little army being under arms, marched to ſupport the party. The whole body of the enemy were ſeen likewiſe on the plain. Captain Polier commanded (I being much indiſpoſed at the time, and ſcarce able to move out of bed.) As our diſtance was leſs than that of the enemy, we were firſt joined. Captain Caillaud having reported what he had done with regard to the proviſions, it was agreed to return to camp, and, if poſſible, to avoid the enemy, then haſtening to cut off our retreat.

In the morning, one of the gun-carriages was rendered uſeleſs, by the enemy's cannonade. The ſame accident alſo happened to captain Polier, who not caring to leave the cannon behind, ſpent ſome little time in fixing them on ſpare carriages, to bring them off, this being done, they began to move, the ſepoys divided in front and rear. The enemy had now alſo joined, and were marching down in very good order, and ſo near, that it was impoſſible to avoid an engagement. The French battalion, as our people marched by files, was on the right flank, the ſepoys in our rear, and the cavalry ready to charge on the right, and in front.

Our army marched on very quick to gain a more advantageous piece of ground a little way before them, which the moment they were in poſſeſſion of, the men

 were

were halted, and faced the French; the ſepoys in the rear were drawn up fronting thoſe of the enemy, to keep them off our right flank, ſo that our little body was formed in half a ſquare. The ſepoys on the left, with one piece of cannon, had orders to keep off the cavalry. Our two remaining pieces (for we carried out but five in all), were in the front of the battalion oppoſite the French. Never, I believe, were two pieces better ſerved: they were of the ſhort ſix pounders, that take in a large quantity of grape, ſo that when they were near enough, every ſhot took place in the French battalion. The enemy were ſo much galled by the briſkneſs of this cannonade, that they began to give way, which we ſaw, in ſpite of all the efforts of their officers to keep them up. The lucky minute was improved, by our men advancing and giving them a fire, which compleated what the cannon had begun, and left us at liberty to finiſh our retreat. We ſuffered moſtly from their ſepoys, who, though they fired at a great diſtance, annoyed us very much in wounding our men, and moſt of our officers; captain Polier received two wounds, and was obliged to give up the command to the next officer, captain Caillaud, who began the march on the retreat of the French, and brought the party home with the two diſmounted pieces of cannon.

Our forces, that day, when joined, conſiſted of 12 platoons in battalion 360 men, 1500 ſepoys; and as to our cavalry, we had our troop of about 11 men, and a few of the Nabob's horſe: our artillery five pieces of cannon, two of which were rendered unſerviceable by the accidents before related. The French had 500 Europeans, their two companies of deſerters, their troop of about 50, near 5000 ſepoys, and all the Maiſſore cavalry. About 6000 of the Marattas the day before luckily croſſed the Coleroon, on ſome diſpute between them and the Maiſſoreans.

Our loſs in battalion was ſix officers wounded out of nine, 59 private men killed and wounded, and about

about 200 ſepoys. The enemy's loſs was much more conſiderable.

I expected the French would have encamped where we had fought, which, had they done, we muſt have run the chance of another battle, either to have marched away towards Tanjore, or to have convoyed in proviſions; but they luckily for us choſe to return to the iſland, and our communication being open, the proviſions came in that night. I now determined to march towards Tanjore, and there wait for Mauphus Cawn; beſides, I was in hopes my preſence with an army might do ſomething in favour of Mr. Palk's negociations. I wrote to him, however, to apprize the King of my intentions, and to ſee how he took it. While I was waiting for his anſwer, an event happened which made our army as welcome as we could wiſh. The enemy, the ſecond night after our engagement, took all their Europeans, 3000 ſepoys, and 2000 horſe, and marched away for Tondeman's country, with an intention to burn and deſtroy every thing they could, to deter that Polygar from ſending any more proviſions.

The country people alarmed, drove all their cattle, and valuable effects into the woods, where it was impoſſible to follow them; and this expedition of the enemy's ended in nothing, but burning a few empty villages, and taking a gun of ours in the woods, which the ſepoys had to protect our convoys. After three days they returned, but vexed at their diſappointment, and finding the King of Tanjore would not declare, they loſt patience, and fell furiouſly upon the frontiers of his country, took Killycottah, a fort on the borders, and marched to Koiladdy, which they alſo took, and by that means made themſelves maſters of the bank on the iſland, which carries the water into the Tanjore country, and began to cut it in three or four places.

In theſe circumſtances, without waiting for Mr. Palk's anſwer, for I knew the King would be glad to to ſee us in his country to defend it, we marched immediately to Tanjore, through Tondeman's woods, dividing our force, and leaving half with captain Killpatrick in Trichinopoly. I wrote alſo for the party from Davecotah to march, and meet us at Tanjore, for I found that Mauphus Cawn, for whom we waited, was not moved from Arcot. On my firſt day's march, as I expected, I had a letter from the King, begging me to come, and wiſhing me joy on the late victory. Mr. Palk alſo wrote to me, that things were much altered in our favour ſince this expedition of the enemy's, and that the King had ordered his horſe out under Gauderow. Mr. Palk adviſed him to ſend his cavalry to meet us, that when joined, we might ſoon drive the enemy out of his kingdom. Inſtead of that, he ordered 1200 horſe to go to Tricatapolly to puniſh the enemy, as he ſaid.

Morarow, who ſtill remembered the ſhame of his defeat, ſome months before, thought it now a good time to be revenged of the Tanjore troops, eſpecially when Monagee was not at their head. He therefore croſſed the Cauvery, and at day-break fell upon Gauderow's party, who made as little reſiſtance as ſurpriſed troops commonly do: Gauderow and 200 of his men only eſcaped, the reſt were either killed, wounded, or taken priſoners. We arrived two days after this fray near Tanjore, and there met the party from Davecottah, and 500 ſepoys. The King came out of his fort to meet me, but I was ſo ill, that I was obliged to ſend captain Caillaud to make my apology.

The next grand point we had for Mr. Palk to endeavour at, was the removal of Succogee from the King, and Monagee to be reſtored to favour and power. The circumſtances were favourable for us, and Mr. Palk and captain Caillaud managed ſo ſucceſsfully, that they convinced the Tanjorean, that to his miniſter, and his bad counſels muſt be attributed all his misfortunes; and that, had he continued ſteady dy to the Nabob and the Engliſh, the war might have been happily finiſhed, and the enemy could not have dared to enter and lay waſte his country, nor the bank have been deſtroyed. But ſtill it was not too late; every thing might be recovered if Succogee was removed from his perſon and councils, and Monagee reſtored to his former rank, who had given ſo many convincing proofs of his ſtrong attachments to his maſter's intereſt. The king was deeply concerned: he would fain employ both; he was unwilling to part with his favourite; but when he was convinced that our friendſhip depended on it, Succogee was removed, and Monagee inveſted with the ſole and full management of his kingdom, and appointed once more commander in chief of his forces. New troops were raiſed to make up for their late loſs, and every thing promiſed well from ſo lucky a change in our favour.

At this time we were acquainted from Madraſs, of the arrival of a detachment ſent us from Bombay, by that preſidency, at the requeſt of our governor and council; and indeed I muſt do governor Bourchier the juſtice to ſay, that he was always inclined to give us any aſſiſtance in his power. Some ſhips from Europe arrived alſo with recruits.

Mauphus Cawn was then at Conjeveram, 60 miles weſt of Madraſs, but he wanted money and ſome Europeans to enable him to join us. My opinion was aſked, what ſhould be done in this affair. I gave it for advancing him the ſum required, a lack of roupees, and that a party of 500 Europeans, conſiſting of the Bombay detachment and the recruits lately arrived, ſhould immediately march and take Mauphus Cawn under their eſcort. All this was agreed to, and the party marched accordingly.

Morarow, on ſome diſpute between him and the Maiſſoreans, had croſſed the Coleroon before the 12th of May, as I have before obſerved. He repaſſed it to perform that exploit againſt the Tan-

jore

jore troops; and having ſtruck the ſevere blow aforementioned, he returned to the other ſide of the Coleroon again, and continued at a diſtance from the Maiſſore camp. He then propoſed to the Nabob, that if the payment of three lack of roupees could be ſecured to him, he would return to his own country, and never more be an enemy to him, the Engliſh, or the Tanjoreans. The Nabob having no money, applied to the King of Tanjore, and after a great many meetings, it was agreed to, and the articles drawn up and ſigned. In the mean time Morarow gave Nanderauze to underſtand, that he was in treaty with the Nabob, but that if he would pay him the money then due, he would return to his aſſiſtance. Nanderauze ſent him all the money he could ſpare; and Morarow finding there was no chance for more from that quarter, agreeable to his treaty with the Nabob, marched off. Part of the money was paid by the king of Tanjore on his going, the reſt to be paid on his arrival in his own country.

Another detachment came from Davecottah, commanded by captain Zeigler, conſiſting of about 80 Europeans and Topaſſes, and 400 ſepoys. As my health was much impaired, and therefore my continuing with the army very precarious, the governor and council, at my requeſt, ſent captain Killpatrick a major's commiſſion, and conſented to his ſucceeding to the command, if I ſhould be obliged to leave it. I was not a little chagrined to find the Tanjore troops ſo long aſſembling, being anxious to march. The enemy were now again encamped on the plain, and had ſo cloſely beſet Trichinopoly, that our communication was quite cut off. At laſt Monagee ſet up his ſtandard, and joining us on the 25th, we marched. My intentions were to have proceeded directly to Trichinopoly; but in a council of war next day, I found Monagee unwilling to proceed, till we were joined by our other party, who were eſcorting Mauphus

Mauphus Cawn. With all the reaſons I made uſe of, I could not convince him of the neceſſity of an immediate march. We were therefore obliged to wait, but on theſe conditions only, that he ſhould in the interim collect a magazine of grain equal to the conſumption in Trichinopoly, to enable us, on our arrival, to replace what had been ſpent in our abſence.

Mauphus Cawn was then advanced as far as Fort St. David, where, contrary to his agreement, he wanted all his money before he paſſed the Coleroon, and even ſaid that this would not be ſufficient to pay his troops, inſiſting on a further ſum. Finding he trifled with us, I ordered captain Forbes not to wait for him, but to join me with his Bombay detachment, and our recruits, as expeditiouſly as poſſible, which he completed on the 14th. The 15th I reviewed the army, which conſiſted of about 1200 men in batalion, 3000 ſepoys, and 14 pieces of cannon. Monagee had with him 2500 horſe, 3000 infantry, and ſome field pieces. On the 16th we marched, and the 17th reached Trichinopoly.

The enemy had been joined the night before by 200 Europeans, and their whole body appeared on the plain in order of battle; their battalion and ſepoys with the Sugar-Loaf Rock on their right, and the cavalry on their left. I ordered our advanced guard to take poſſeſſion of a bank which commanded the entrance to the plain. As we advanced, the enemy began to cannonade. When I had paſſed the bank, we formed, and faced the enemy. Monagee's troops made up the ſecond line, and covered our baggage and proviſions. The enemy kept moving on; and we likewiſe, our cannon anſwering theirs. We expected nothing but an engagement, and were not a little ſurprized, at once, to ſee their battalion go to the right about, their cannon drawing off, and the whole retreating very regularly. They killed us a captain and 15 men, and ſuffered themſelves ſomething

thing more. The enemy had another party of Topasses and sepoys marching to join them from the island, which when perceived by Major Killpatrick, he sallied out with part of his garrison, and obliged them, after a severe cannonade, to retire to the island.

We halted next day to refresh our men, and to put our heavy baggage into the fort, resolving not to give the enemy rest, till they had quitted the plain. They had the first day gone to the Five Rocks, but on our marching to the Fakeer's Tope, they moved off, and encamped at Mootachillenour. We followed them, and in the night they thought proper to cross the river, and encamped behind their Pagodas on the island. We then retook our post off Elmiseram, and sent a detachment to cover the king of Tanjore's workmen, repairing the bank near Koiladdy, the enemy having also abandoned that place.

About this time our fleet, under the command of admiral Watson, arrived with colonel Adlercron's regiment, and the French ships had brought Mr. Godeheu, commissary-general and governor-general of all their settlements, with 1500 Europeans. Upon his arrival he wrote to Mr. Saunders to acquaint him with his inclination to pursue pacific measures, introducing his proposals for a suspension of arms, by sending back the troops which Mr. Dupleix had caused to be stopped in their passage from Madrass to Fort St. David. The governor and council, pleased to find they had now to deal with a person who appeared to concur with them in pursuing the true interest of the two commercial companies, were not long in sending their answer, and both sincerely labouring to hasten the conclusion of an event so much to be wished. A Suspension of arms was agreed on, and actually took place on the 11th of October 1754.

The

The ARTICLES were as follow.

ARTICLE I.

To begin from the 11th of October, the day on which THE SUSPENSION OF ARMS ſhall be publiſhed to all the troops, in all the forts, and actual poſſeſſions of the two contracting nations in the Carnatick; all acts of hoſtility ſhall ceaſe between the French and the Engliſh.

II. During the courſe of this ſuſpenſion, which ſhall be for three months, their troops ſhall not act againſt each other, not only as principals, but even as auxiliaries.

III. The two nations ſhall oblige their allies to enter into the ſame agreement.

IV. If either of the two nations, French or Engliſh, ſhall commit any act of hoſtility, poſſeſs themſelves of any place; or either occaſion any damage to the other after the day of the publication of the ſaid ſuſpenſion, both oblige themſelves to make reparation proportionable to the damage, and to the entire reſtitution of whatever was taken.

V. If the allies or other troops in the pay of either nation, ſhall commit any act of hoſtility, or plunder the territories of which either nation is now in poſſeſſion, it ſhall be lawful for both nations to repulſe their inſults by force; by which the injured nation ſhall not be deemed to have infringed the preſent agreement.

VI. If the allies or auxiliary troops of either nation, ſhall take arms or inſult the countries of which the nation they were allied to is now in poſſeſſion, the two nations ſhall ſuccour each other in this caſe to oppoſe this enemy, who ſhould become thereby a common enemy to both.

VII. The troops of the two nations ſhall be employed during this ſuſpenſion of arms, to ſecure their ſettlements and preſent poſſeſſions; they may be tranſported freely, and without any difficulty, from one place to another at the pleaſure of the governors, generals, commanders, &c. of each nation; and

and all persons actually under the protection of either flag, may in like manner go and come where they think proper, without being disturbed either in their effects or persons.

VIII. There shall be a free commerce throughout the Carnatick, and in all the countries to the northward on the Coromandel coast, for the two contracting nations; they may bring goods from all the places in the dependencies of either nation or their allies, and transport them freely and without any duty whatever through the respective territories and * Jageers.

IX. As soon as the suspension is proclaimed, the mutual exchange of prisoners shall be set about, and the necessary measures taken in an amicable manner to soften the fate of those that shall remain, by putting them together into places where they may feel less of the rigour of a long captivity.

Mr. PALK and Mr. VANSITTART were sent to Pondichery, and returned with the following Treaty and the Truce.

ARTICLES of a provisional Treaty, concluded and agreed on between us Thomas Saunders, Esq; President for the Honourable English Company on the coast of Coromandel and Orixa, Governor of Fort St. George, &c. and the Sieur Charles Robert Godeheu, Commissary for his most Christian Majesty; Commander General of all the settlements of the French Company on both sides the Cape of Good Hope, and at China; President of all the councils there established, and Director General of the India Company of France.

ARTICLE I.

The two companies, English and French, shall renounce for ever all Moorish government and dignity, and shall never interfere in any difference that may arise between the princes of the country.

All

* Jageers are lands granted by the Mogul or his representatives.

All places, except thoſe which ſhall be ſtipulated in the definitive treaty, to remain in the poſſeſſion of the two aforeſaid nations, French and Engliſh, ſhall be delivered up to the Moors.

II. In the Tanjore country, the Engliſh ſhall poſſeſs Davecottah, and the French Karical; each with their preſent diſtricts.

III. On the Coromandel coaſt, the French ſhall poſſeſs Pondichery, the diſtricts of which are to be ſpecified in the definitive treaty. The Engliſh ſhall poſſeſs Fort St. George, and Fort St. David, with the diſtricts likewiſe to be ſpecified.

The French ſhall form a limited ſettlement, the ſituation of which ſhall be choſen between Nizampatam, and the river of Gondecama excluſively; as an equivalent for the difference there is between Davecottah, and Fort St. David together, compared with Karical:

Or elſe,

The diſtricts of Pondichery ſhall be made equal to thoſe of Fort St. George and Fort St. David together, and in this caſe the French ſhall abandon the Point D'Appuy, propoſed above. The alternative ſhall be left to the determination of the two companies.

IV. Mazulipatam and Divy ſhall be neuter, leaving to the two companies the choice of making a partition; each nation ſhall have a houſe for commerce at Mazulipatam, with an equal number of ſoldiers to guard it, in caſe the town ſhould remain neuter. Divy ſhall be delivered to the Engliſh, if the French reſerve Mazulipatam. And if the French keep Divy, the Engliſh ſhall have Mazulipatam. In theſe two laſt caſes, equal diſtricts ſhall be annexed to the poſſeſſions.

V. The navigation of Narzapore river ſhall be free; the Engliſh may carry their ſettlement upon the banks of the ſaid river, or keep Bandermalanka; but they ſhall poſſeſs only one of thoſe two places; the French ſhall have a ſettlement

 on

on the ſame river. The diſtricts ſhall be equal between the two nations.

VI. The entrance of Ingeram river ſhall be free, neither the French nor the Engliſh ſhall poſſeſs the iſlands of Coringe and Yellacatippa. The Engliſh ſhall have their factory at Suncrapollam, with its diſtricts, and a warehouſe at Nellepely, the fortifications of which ſhall be razed. The French ſhall have their factory at Yanam, with diſtricts equal to thoſe of Suncrapollam, and they ſhall be at liberty to have a ware-houſe on the Terra Firmâ in caſe they judge it neceſſary, for the convenience and eaſe of their trading buſineſs.

VII. In the Chickakul country, as the Engliſh have Vizagapatam, the French may ſettle a factory where they pleaſe, to the ſouthward of Pondemarka, or the northward of Bimlepatam, whether at Gangam or Maſouſbunder, on an equality with Vizagapatam.

VIII. Theſe conditions accepted on both ſides, although they are not to be a law for a definitive treaty in Europe, they ſhall nevertheleſs produce a truce between the two nations and their allies, until news is received in India of the anſwers made in Europe concerning this agreement; which anſwers we promiſe bonâ fide to communicate to each other as ſoon as they ſhall be arrived by the ſhips of either nation.

IX. Neither nation ſhall be allowed to procure, during the truce, any new grant or ceſſion, or to build forts for the defence of new eſtabliſhments. It ſhall only be lawful to rebuild and repair the fortifications now ſubſiſting in the eſtabliſhments they poſſeſs at this time, in order to prevent their entire ruin.

X. Until the arrival of anſwers from Europe to theſe articles, which ſhall be diſpatched thither by the firſt ſhips, to be ſubmited to the deciſion of the two companies, under the pleaſure and approbation of the two crowns, the two nations ſhall not proceed to any ceſſion, retroceſſion, or evacuation of what they now poſſeſs, every thing being to remain on the footing of uti poſſidetis.

XI. With

XI. With regard to the indemnification, the two nations may expect for the expences of the war; this article shall be amicably adjusted in the definitive treaty.

Done at Fort St. George, 31 Decemb. 1754.

(L. S.) (Signed) THOMAS SAUNDERS.

(In English and French) (Under the English)

(L. S.) (Signé) GODEHEU.

(Under the French)

Examined with the original, and attested to be a true copy.

Dated at Pondichery, 26 Dec. 1754. HEN. VANSITTART, JOS. DU PRE', } Secretaries.

ARTICLES and Stipulations, of a Truce, concluded between us Thomas Saunders, Esq; President, &c. &c. &c. and the Sieur Charles Robert Godeheu, Commissary, &c. &c. &c. in virtue of a provisional treaty which we have signed the same day, to promote the re-establishment of tranquillity in this part of India.

ARTICLE I.

To take place on the 11th of January, 1755; the day of the expiration of the suspension of arms, proclaimed the 11th of October, 1754; all hostilities shall cease between the English and French.

II. During this truce, which shall be in force until we are informed in India of the answers made in Europe concerning the said provisional treaty; the troops of the two nations, French and English, shall not act against each other, either as principals or auxiliaries.

III. The two nations, English and French, engage to oblige their allies to observe all that is stipulated for the accomplishment of the truce by virtue of the treaty; and whoever shall dare to infringe it shall be reputed a common enemy, and shall be reduced to good order by the force of arms.

IV. If either of the two nations, French or English, or either auxiliary troops or allies, shall commit any act of hostility, possess themselves of any place, or any one shall cause any damage to another during the said truce; both oblige themselves to make reparation proportionable to the damage, and to the entire restitution of whatever shall be taken.

V. If the allies or other troops in pay of either nation, shall be guilty of any act of hostility, or commit any pillages in the territories whereof either nation is now in possession, it shall be lawful for both nations to repulse their insults by force, by which the injured nation shall not be deemed to have infringed the present agreement.

VI. If the allies or auxiliary troops of either nation, shall take up arms and insult the countries of which the nation they are allied to is now in possession; in this case, the two nations shall assist each other against this enemy, who shall thereby become the common enemy of both.

VII. The troops of the two nations shall be employed, during this truce, in the care of their present establishments and possessions; they may be transported freely, and without any difficulty, from one place to another, at the pleasure of the governor, generals, commanders, &c. of each nation; and all persons actually under the protection of either flag, may likewise go and come at pleasure, without being molested either in their effects or persons.

VIII. Trade shall be free throughout the Carnatick, and in all the countries to the northward of the Coromandel coast, for the two contracting nations; they may fetch merchandizes from all the places in the dependance of each other, and transport them freely, without any restraint, through the respective jageers and territories.

IX.

IX. All common enemies, or the particular enemies of either nation, who ſhall come to attack the Engliſh and French in their preſent poſſeſſions, and trouble the tranquillity which is to reign in India, ſhall be repulſed by the united force of the two nations, French and Engliſh.

X. As ſoon as the truce is proclaimed, the mutual exchange of priſoners ſhall be ſet about, man for man; and means ſhall be reſolved on for the eaſe of thoſe which ſhall not be exchanged.

XI. Commiſſaries ſhall be appointed on both ſides, to examine into the infringements committed by each party, or their auxiliary troops or allies, and ſettle the reſtitution to be made of all the places taken, during the truce, againſt the tenour of the ſuſpenſion of arms; as likewiſe of all that may have been taken from them by the ſaid auxiliary troops, in merchandizes, effects, money, &c. and farther, to ſettle in a fixed method, for a guide, during the whole time of the truce, all the names, and the extent of every country, * paragana an village, under the power, and in the poſſeſſion of the two nations, Engliſh and French.

XII. It is agreed, that whenever, in the courſe of the truce, any complaint ſhall be made by either of the ſaid nations of an infringement of the 4th article, the ſaid commiſſaries on each ſide appointed, ſhall certify and examine the fact, that juſtice may be done accordingly to the injured nation, either by reſtitution or reparation, according to the nature of the injury received.

Done at Fort St. George, 31 Dec. 1754. Signed as before.

Dated at Pondichery,
26 Dec. 1754.

* A Paragana is any diſtrict of country.

Additional Articles and Stipulations to the foregoing Truce.

ARTICLE I.

If any nation ſhould attempt to erect a ſettlement within the bounds of the preſent poſſeſſions of either of the two companies; both Engliſh and French ſhall jointly oppoſe and hinder any ſuch undertaking.

II. The cuſtom-houſes and † juncans ſhall remain on the ſame footing as before the war; and no alteration ſhall be made in the duties paid on the importation and exportation of goods of the produce or manufacture of the coaſt.

Done at Fort St. George, 31 Dec. 1754. Signed as before.

Dated at Pondichery,
4 Jan. 1755.

† A Juncan is a toll or duty on every thing that paſſes.

TRAN-

TRANSACTIONS

ON THE

COAST of COROMANDEL,

In the Year 1755.

THE suspension of arms was accompanied with another event of great importance to the tranquillity of India, the departure of Mr. Dupleix, who being removed from the government, returned with the next ships for Europe.

Here it may be proper to take a view of the several provinces and governments of the Deckan, their present interests and designs. This will not be a mere recapitulation of what has been said in the Narrative; for as the princes of that country are continually agitated by the passions of avarice, ambition and jealousy; they are every moment prompted by suspicion or the love of intrigue, to enter into new quarrels, form different connexions, and by their restless and uncertain spirit, create the utmost perplexities to their allies. Fond of compliments, ceremonial and repeated professions of friendship, they have little regard for truth or gratitude; nor have they any consideration for the future more than the paſt, ſolely occupied with what they imagine will advance their preſent views. This character of the Aſiaticks in general will be exemplified by a review of the preſent ſituation and deſigns of the ſeveral powers of the Deckan, as they appeared in the year 1755.

Salabatzing was induced by his incapacity and ſloth, to ſubmit himſelf entirely to the councils of the French for the ſake of their protection and aſſiſtance. Bound by no ties of affection, he was now meditating the removal of thoſe very perſons with whom he had ſo lately been ſharing the greateſt power and wealth, without the leaſt regard to their having aſſiſted him in that uſurpation.

The king of Tanjore, a ſubtle prince, lived in a continual jealouſy of the Engliſh and French, who had both ſettlements in his dominions, well knowing that either of theſe ſingly was able to give law to him, and always apprehending moſt from the ſide to which the balance of power ſeemed to incline. From a diffidence of the French, and a better opinion of the Engliſh faith, he had, for the moſt part, ſhewn a regard for our alliance, but it required great addreſs to manage his irreſolution, to divert his partiality for a treacherous favourite, and keep him firm to his engagements. His moſt dangerous neighbours were the Maiſſoreans, a rich people, and formidable from their being undiſturbed at home. He knew they had long formed deſigns againſt Trichinopoly, and at this very time, were in treaty with the French for that end. The knowledge of this determined him to enter into the ſtricteſt bands of friendſhip with us, and yet, at the ſame time, his ſuſpicion of our entering into any alliance with the governor of Marava, (a country bordering on his dominions to the ſouth), threw him into the moſt precipitate reſolution of carrying fire and ſword into that country. It was in vain to remonſtrate to him, that ſo raſh a proceeding would only facilitate the deſigns of the Maiſſorean, by leaving Trichinopoly ly defenceleſs. The Maravar was the preſent object of his jealouſy.

Tondeman a Polygar, whoſe woods, adjoining to Tanjore, had been an uſeful protection to our convoys during the war, was alſo uneaſy at our ſuppoſed intentions of alliance with the Maravar.

The king of Maiſſore, young, and in a manner confined to his ſeraglio, gave up the direction of affairs to his uncle, who was prime miniſter and brother to Nanderauze. They were both, at this time, purſuing their ſcheme on Trichinopoly, in which they ſuffered ſo many repulſes, and ſaw their extravagant projects ſo often defeated, that they were ready to ſeize any pretext for abandoning their enterprize. They ſoon relinquiſhed it on good reaſons, and from thenceforth became leſs formidable neighbours to the king of Tanjore.

Mootis Allee Cawn, governor of *Velloure, a powerful and deſigning man, had the addreſs to murder two Nabobs with impunity; and during this long war, to keep himſelf clear of its calamities. Mr. Dupleix uſed to call him his deputy in his province. Though no confidence could be placed in the friendſhip of this artful man, it was imprudent to have him for an enemy; therefore his offers to acknowledge the Nabob were gladly accepted, but there was little ſincerity in his profeſſions of ſubmiſſion.

The Marattas have always had ſo conſiderable a ſhare in the diſturbances, and were at this time taking ſo large a part in the politicks of theſe countries, that it is requiſite, for the explanation of the affairs of the peninſula, to give as many particulars of this extenſive people as can be aſcertained; for as they have no written hiſtory, and ſcarce any tradition, that we know, of their former ſtate, it is impoſſible to procure a full and ſatisfactory account of ſo numerous a nation,

* Within twelve miles of Arcot, the ſtrongeſt fort in all that diſtrict.

nation, once ſettled, then diſperſed, and now re-eſtabliſhing themſelves throughout all parts of the Mogul's empire: a people who have had, from time immemorial, ſettlements to the north of Delly, great part of which they ſtill poſſeſs, though ſo great were the numbers that were driven out from thence, by Aurenzeb, that he employed above twenty years in fruitleſs endeavours to reduce them in their new ſettlements in the mountainous parts of the Deckan.

They have had continued wars ever ſince, with all the Moguls, Subahs and governors, and made innumerable treaties of peace with them, which they never obſerve any longer than they think it their intereſt. They have themſelves had ſtrange internal revolutions; and what is moſt ſtrange, the preſent governing men among them are Bramins or prieſts, hated by the true Marattas, but followed by them for pay.

Their Raja or Prince is ſacred: and they hold that he ought to be a kind of idol, ſhut up and fed at the publick expence, and the executive power lodged in ſome other branch of his family, at leaſt, ſuch has been the eſtabliſhment on the Malabar coaſt: but this was ſubverted by the uſurpation of the two Bramins, the one called Peelagee, and the other Budgerow. Peelagee governed Guzarat, and Budgerow the country to the ſouthward. His ſon, who ſucceeded him, is known by his name Balazerow, on the Coromandel coaſt: On the Malabar he is called the Nanna, for that is the title by which the acting head of the government and general of the forces is diſtinguiſhed. The nominal prince, or the idol, as he has been deſcribed, is ſtiled Ram Raja and Saha Raja. All theſe names, indiſcriminately uſed and ſtrangely ſpelt, occaſion no ſmall difficulty to the reader, who is here alſo deſired to take notice, that though all writers ſpeak of Sattaarah, as the capital of the Maratta's country, the reſidence of of the Bramin their ſovereign is * Poona, where all the buſineſs of the government is carried on.

What proves that they have formerly been powerful over all the Mogul's empire, though now diſunited, is the univerſal acknowledgment of the *Chout*, or tribute paid to them of a fourth of the revenues of every Raja or governor. This they ſtill collect in all parts, taking what they can get of it in ready money, and leaving the ballance in arrear, which will ſerve them at leaſt as a pretence for another incurſion, whenever they want employment for their troops.

It may ſeem ſtrange that theſe Marattas, who are Bramins, and ſo ſtrict obſervers of the Gentou religion, and the tenets of the Tranſmigration of ſouls, that they will never kill the moſt offenſive animals that crawl about them; ſhould, without any ſcruple, eagerly employ their ſabres to the deſtruction of their fellow-creatures. The ſalvo for this extraordinary contradiction, is a device of their prieſts, who, by the ſacrifice of a Buffalo, with many miſterious and enthuſiaſtick ceremonies, abſolve their warriors from the reſtrictions which bind the vulgar.

It ſhould be here obſerved that the Marattas mentioned ſo often in the narrative, were only a body of horſe, freebooters, who alternately took the pay of the higheſt bidder. They were ſuch as Morarow had picked up to follow his fortunes, and till he attempted to make himſelf independent, they had no ſettled habitation, and no profeſſion but war, if it may be called a profeſſion where they have neither art nor diſcipline, and yet they are formidable to the Moors, who carrying ſuch numerous and incumbered armies to the field, are the eaſier harraſſed, and even ſtarved by them. For theſe pillagers, continually galloping round the country, cut off the convoys, and as

* Poona is about a hundred miles eaſt-ſouth-eaſt of Bombay. D'Anville ſays, the ſituation of Sattarah is not aſcertained, and therefore he has not put it in his map.

as moſt of their parties carry with them neither baggage, nor proviſions, they eaſily elude all purſuit, and in an inſtant retire to their faſtneſſes, or even, if occaſion requires, to their own country. They ride a hardy horſe inured to fatigue, and for the moſt part fed with ſtanding corn. The common men have no cloathing but a turban on their head, and a ſaſh round their waiſt: inſtead of a ſaddle they uſe ſuch a kind of pad as is recommended by Marſhal Saxe. Truly formidable with their ſabres, they are fatal to troops that are once broke.

The Marattas, though not without trade and manufactures, have principally enriched themſelves, by obliging the wealthy and more reſpectable powers their neighbours to be tributary to them. It will naturally be aſked, why do the opulent ſtates ſubmit to be tributary? and what ſecurity have they that theſe licentious plunderers will abide by their agreements, and not continually encroach upon them, and raiſe their demands? The reaſon is plain: it is leſs expenſive, and a lighter tax upon trade, to agree to ſome certain payment, than to engage in the unknown expence of armies, to free themſelves from ſo irregular a foe: and as to greater exactions, if the chief has once ſettled the *Chout*, he will hardly venture to ſtruggle for more, as the money agreed on goes into his own pocket; and were he to proceed to the more violent method of compulſion, by invading the country, the ſpoil would all become the property of his troops, under the article of plunder, and his own ſhare would come very ſhort of the ſum ſtipulated; beſides, they have the prudence to conſider, that a country ravaged by their troops, will produce neither tribute nor plunder again for ſome time.

They are a deſtructive foe and an unſerviceable friend. They ruin their enemies by burning their country, and their allies by their avaricious demands for money. Inſtead of meriting their pay, which they might eaſily do after a defeat, by cutting off all the

the broken troops, they fly to the camp, where every man procures a good burthen for his horſe, and walking on foot, drives him away loaded with the ſpoil.

Such has been, in a great meaſure, the ſtate of the Maratta people; but about this time it will appear, that they entertained various deſigns of extending their territories in ſeveral parts of the country, and alſo on the ſea coaſt. They took large diſtricts from the Viceroy of the Deckan, marched to Delly and made a Mogul, and after driving out Angria by our ſtrength, beat the Portugueze by their own. They had generals who ſet up for themſelves in the remote countries that they had conquered, and were giving ſome other indications of their return from a vagabond life of rapine and diſorder, to a more ſettled ſyſtem of policy.

Of all the Princes of the Deckan, there are none ſo free from the faults of the country as the Nabob Mahomed Allee Cawn; having always experienced the invariable friendſhip of the Engliſh, he has been taught the true value of honour and conſtancy, and throughout his conduct, manifeſted uncommon gratitude and fidelity to his engagements. The ſums we had expended in the ſupport of his cauſe, inſtead of raiſing in him the expectation of being farther burthenſome to us, lay like a heavy weight upon his mind; and the diſtreſs he was in for money, with the impoſſibility of paying any conſiderable part of his debt to the company, viſibly affected his health: his brothers who accompanied him, having a ſeparate command, would each of them keep up as many attendants, and as large an expence as the Nabob himſelf. Exhauſted by this unneceſſary profuſion, he was not able to furniſh the workmen and materials with which he had engaged to ſupply our engineers for compleating their fortifications, nor even to find money for his own troops to prevent them from diſbanding. Upon conſideration of this ſtate of the Nabob's affairs, it was prudently determined to take an exact account of his revenues, which were mortgaged to the

the company, in order to judge what ſums might be actually forth-coming for their uſe, after a due proportion ſhould be allotted for the maintenance of himſelf, and the ſupport of his dignity.

It was at the ſame time recommended to him, to ſettle as ſoon as poſſible at Arcot, his capital, with all his family, as well to ſave expence, by reducing their ſeveral retinues to one houſhold, as for the credit of his government. But it was of great conſequence to his revenues, before he left the countries of Madura and Tinevelly, which uſed to produce an immenſe income, to collect the tribute which had not been paid during the troubles, and alſo to induce the ſeveral Polygars, and all ſubordinate governors to acknowledge the Nabob's right, by receiving grants from him for the countries they held under his government.

It was neceſſary on this, as on all other occaſions, to have at hand a ſufficient force; for in this country, we are to look upon an army as a proper formality uſually attending a meſſage to a friend, a ſubject, or an enemy. From theſe conſiderations, an expedition was ordered into the Madura and Tinevelly countries to collect the revenues, under the command of Alexander Heron, lieutenant colonel in his Majeſty's ſervice, and major of the company's forces, attended by Mr. Maunſell, to act together with the Nabob's Vakeel, (or agent) as commiſſaries for the adminiſtration of the monies received. Colonel Heron, the latter end of January 1755, marched to Manapar, a village about thirty miles from Trichinopoly. Soon after his arrival, he was joined by the Vakeels of four neighbouring Polygars, who came to ſettle their accounts, promiſing ſoon to pay the ballances that were due; they alſo ſigned a paper, acknowledging themſelves under the Nabob's government, independant of any other power whatſoever; and that they enjoyed their lands in right of his grants only. At the ſame time the Nabob received letters of the like purport from the

the three principal men in the Madura and Tinevelly countries. But upon the return of the officers, one of the four Polygars, by name Lachynaig, who had paid part of his tribute, and given a bill for the reſt, refuſed to pay the remainder; wherefore, at the inſtance of the Nabob, colonel Heron, on the 10th of February, moved with the army cloſe to a fort, which was one of the barriers of his country. All that day and the next, he endeavoured, both by fair means and threats, to make him comply, but could get no ſatisfactory anſwer. He then determined to attack the fort the next morning, in which he ſucceeded with little loſs: and alſo the ſame day took another fort, which gave him poſſeſſion of all the country of that Polygar, except the tops of the hills, where the inhabitants had taken ſhelter. In theſe two affairs he loſt fourteen ſepoys and ſome few * colleries.

Here the Nabob left colonel Heron, and his brother Mauphus Cawn accompanied him in the expedition. The roads were exceſſive bad through the woods for the carriage of the heavy cannon. Some breaſt-works thrown up in the narrow paſſes, were abandoned on the army's nearer approach, though not till part of the ſepoys had given their fire, which was returned, but without any effect. Beyond the woods was a ſtone-fort, which, had it been quite finiſhed, would have been of conſiderable ſtrength for that part of the country. The Madura people who were fortifying it, abandoned it immediately. There was found in this fort ſome grain, ammunition, and four Pieces of cannon. The colonel left ſome troops in poſſeſſion, and advanced towards the town of Madura; upon which the garriſon retired a little farther into the country, to a ſmall fort, whither they carried their moſt valuable effects, and military ſtores. The greater part of the inhabitants remained, and ſeemed very well ſatiſfied with the change of government. Being then the ſeaſon for gathering in the grain,

* See page 64 and 65.

grain, and collecting the revenues, it was refolved to quarter the army there. Madura is a ftrong Indian town, encompaffed with a wall like Trichinopoly, but being of much greater extent, would require a very large garrifon to defend it.

Colonel Heron, having wrote circular letters to all the neighbouring Polygars, as well as to the People of Tinevelly, marched for the fort to which Myana the late governor of Madura had retired. It was a ftrong Pagoda, which he had fortified in the beft manner he could, but on the expectation of an attack, he and all his horfe fecured themfelves by a timely retreat, and carried with him his elephants, camels, treafure, and the greateft part of his valuable effects; he left a few fepoys to defend the fort, who fired very brifkly for fome time, but on our returning it with cannon and fmall arms, they furrendered. Here were found three brafs and iron cannon, a number of Malabar guns, and a great quantity of ammunition. After taking two other fmall forts, the army marched for Tinevelly, and arrived the 25th; fome of the Polygars came in, others fent their Vakeels to fettle every thing amicably.

The greateft difficulty arofe from the good inclinations of the Polygar of * Marava. He offered a free paffage through his country for the Englifh troops, employed his intereft with the other Polygars, and fent his brother, who advanced within five miles of the army, with three thoufand men and fome pieces of cannon, tendering his fervice, and preffing us to make fettlements in his country. The news of this caufed fo great jealoufy, and worked upon the King of Tanjore and Tondeman, in fuch a manner, that they fent a proteft againft our treating with the Maravar, and even raifed forces, and were actually marching into his country; Monagee, it feems, while out of

* Marava is a large county on the fea-coaft to the fouth of our fettlements, and to the eaft of Madura.

of favour, had received ſome perſonal affronts from the Maravar: this might be in fact the inſuperable difficulty; but the reaſon given out was the friendſhip that had ſubſiſted between the Maravar and the Maiſſoreans; but at this critical time, the very fear of the Maiſſorean was a reaſon for letting all preſent jealouſies ſubſide: therefore all endeavours to mollify the king of Tanjore and Tondeman being vain, orders were diſpatched to colonel Heron, to break off all further treaty with the Maravar.

At the ſame time, advice being received of the approach of Salabatzing, with Mr. Buſſy, the army was ordered to return as ſoon as poſſible to Trichinopoly. The news of Salbatzing's march was true, but it had not the conſequence that was apprehended; for he entered Maiſſore, where he levied the revenues of that rich province, and returned, carrying with him fifty-two Lack of roupees. Meſſrs. Buſſy and Law were both with him; the latter made a demand in the name of the French Company for ſeven lack for the loſs he had ſuſtained when he was taken in Seringam. The money was refuſed, and at Mr. Buſſy's requeſt, Law deſiſted from his demand.

Colonel Heron had very little advanced the company's affairs by his conduct at Madura and Tinevelly. The monies he collected did not amount to the charges of the expedition, and the terror of his arms was ſo little reſpected in the country, that Myana, the late governor of Madura, having cut off a party that was ſent to ſurprize him, had the boldneſs to come to the very gates of Tinevelly while the army was there, and plunder the villages round. The colonel having received his orders, ſet out the 22d of May, and in his way, at the deſire of Mauphus Cawn, inveſted a fort, which for want of heavy cannon, he was obliged to leave and continue his march to Madura, where he arrived the 26th of May. He left it the 28th, and calling at Colguddy Pagoda, ſeized a large number of religious images, and demanded five thouſand roupees for their ranſom, which being refuſed, he put them into his tumbrils, and was carrying them off. The Colleries were eaſily inſtigated by the Bramins to reſcue their gods; and taking the opportunity when the baggage was paſſing ſome ſtrong defiles in the Natam woods, they ruſhed from the thickets in great numbers, recovered their idols, deſtroyed ſeveral carriages, ſtabbed a hundred bullocks, killed ſome men, and carried off a quantity of baggage. The army purſued their march, without any thing farther to be remarked, till they reached Trichinopoly the 6th of June. Colonel Heron was tried by a court martial for miſconduct in this expedition. It was proved that he had given in falſe accounts, had ſecreted part of the money received, and for this purpoſe, inſtead of collecting the revenues in concert with Mr. Maunſel, had entered into a private agreement with the Nabob's brother, Mauphus Cawn, and farmed out the countries to him at half their value, not paying a regard to the inſtructions ſent him by the Nabob himſelf.

Trichinopoly being looked upon as the main ſecurity for the Nabob's debt, colonel Heron was ordered to leave there a garriſon of five hundred men, under the command of major Killpatrick. Nanderauze, the Maiſſorean general, who lay encamped near the town, was continually practiſing every kind of ſtratagem, and contriving the moſt chimerical deſigns to make himſelf maſter of it. He employed a Bramin in the town, who conſtantly ſent him intelligence, and gained him ſome friends in the place, and having prepared four hundred ladders, and concerted every thing for an eſcalade in the night, he made a propoſal to Mr. De Sauſſay, commander of the French at Seringam, to join him in the attempt. Mr. De Sauſſay, expreſſing his ſenſe of ſo treacherous a proceeding in the time of a ſuſpenſion of arms, Nanderauze urged him with repeated ſolicitations, and even offered

offered him three lack of roupees, provided he would feign a quarrel, march off, and thereby leave him at liberty to pursue his designs. Mr. De Saussay having rejected these offers with disdain, was soon after informed by a friend he had in that general's councils, that in case of his refusal, the next project was to surprize the French, and endeavour to cut them off. He wrote to major Killpatrick to send him a trusty person, to whom he communicated the whole, and moreover assured him, that in case the Maissorean made any motion towards the town, he would immediately attack his rear, and make a signal on the sight of which the major might sally, and put the enemy between two fires.

While the French and English chiefs were interchanging their assurances of mutual assistance against this Indian politician, he suddenly decamped and hastened his march home, not altogether, as some imagined, from disappointment, but rather from having received accounts of the march of Salabatzing towards his country. Soon after his return, he stirred up a rebellion, which threw the kingdom of Maissore into confusion.

The enemy being removed, and no farther obstacle remaining to delay the necessary measure of conducting the Nabob to his capital, a proper escorte was ordered: and captain Polier having prepared every thing for that purpose, they began their march the 9th of July, and proceeding in the slow manner which the burthensome pomp of eastern state must always occasion, arrived at Condor, and forded the Cauvery on the 16th. They halted the next day, and Monagee, with a numerous train, paid the Nabob a visit. At this interview, the strongest protestations of an inviolable friendship were made on both sides. Monagee assured the Nabob, most particularly, from the King of Tanjore, that he would never forsake him, and had five thousand horse ready at his order, if he needed them in the Arcot country. The Nabob having thanked Monagee for the promised aids and for his love and friendship, which he always relied on, at the same time whispered captain Polier in English, *'Tis all a lie.* The captain took up the discourse, assuring Monagee that the English, as they had hitherto constantly supported the Nabob, would continue their protection to him, as also their friendship inviolably with the King of Tanjore, so long as he remained firm to the Nabob. Monagee declared the King of Maissore had offered his King sixty lack of roupees, provided he would forsake the Nabob, but he rejected the proposal. With a few more civilities, and some useful orders about provisions, Monagee concluded his visit.

The Nabob continuing his march, arrived within a mile of Arcot the 19th of August, where he resolved to wait for a lucky day to make his entry into the city. Here he was met by colonel Lawrence, Mr. Palk and Mr. Walsh, deputed to invite him to Madrass. He readily consented, and at the same time desired those gentlemen to mention aloud at his Durbar, that now the army was arrived there, the Polygars and his other tributaries should be first invited to settle accounts, and pay off their arrears, but if that they did not comply without delay, they should be forced to it. As they were sensible this must have a good effect, they took an opportunity of doing it at a full assembly, on which among the rest, Abdiel Vahob Cawn, and the governor of Velloure's Vakeel were present.

On the 21st the Nabob made his entry into Arcot in a very splendid manner, and the 30th he visited Madrass, and was received at the Company's garden-house by the governor, the admirals Watson and Pocock, and most of the gentlemen of the place. During his stay there, the proper measures were concerted for collecting his revenues, and towards the latter end of October he set out for that purpose, accompanied by major Killpatrick with a detachment of three hundred Europeans, and fifteen hundred sepoys, together

together with Mr. Percival, who was appointed commissary general for the Company. He was alſo to be preſent at every tranſaction, it being agreed with the Nabob, that half the money to be collected from the ſeveral Polygars ſhould be paid to himſelf, and the other half to the Company.

To enter into an exact detail of their proceedings with the ſeveral petty Polygars would be very tireſome and unintereſting to moſt readers. Therefore, not to take up their time with a catalogue of uncooth names, which will never occur again in the ſubſequent relation of theſe affairs, it ſhall ſuffice to ſay, that from the 20th of October to the end of the year 1755, the army was either encamped or in motion about the diſtrict of Arcot; and that the Polygars and governors, in proportion, to the remoteneſs or ſtrength of their little forts, were more or leſs backward in ſettling their accounts, and all dealt evaſively. No hoſtilities were however committed againſt any of them, although it was a conſiderable time before ſome of them came to ſuch terms as the Nabob would accept, and ſeveral held out beyond the end of the year; but thoſe being the leaſt able to continue their oppoſition, were left to be reduced by the forces of the Nabob.

Mootis Allee Cawn having been mentioned in the narrative, and his character diſplay'd within a few pages, a particular detail of his conduct ſhall here be given; as it will fully ſerve to convey a general idea of the chicanery of all Aſiatic governors, as well Moors as Indians, when called upon for the arrears of their tribute.

This crafty politician having the mortification to find himſelf outwitted by Mr. Dupleix, addreſſed himſelf to the Nabob, who was then, it is to be obſerved, at a diſtance, acknowledging his right, and offering to ſettle the tribute due from him for the diſtrict of Velloure. He atteſted the ſincerity of his intentions with his hand on the Alcoran, calling God

 and

and the Prophet to witneſs to his truth. But when the Nabob, upon his arrival at Arcot, ſent to claim the performance of theſe ſolemn engagements, it too plainly appeared, that they were meant only to amuſe and deceive him: it was therefore thought neceſſary to ſtrike a terror into him for an example, as, both in riches and power, he was the moſt conſiderable of all the chiefs in the province. Accordingly, on the 19th of January 1756, the army was reinforced with the grenadiers; and another company, with two eighteen-pounders, was detached after them. Major Killpatrick advanced within five miles of Velloure the 30th; and found it to be, as it had been reported, the ſtrongeſt fort in the province.

The next day the Governor of Madraſs received a letter from Mr. De Leyrit, diſputing the Nabob's right to Velloure, and threatening to oppoſe all our proceedings; and intelligence came, at the ſame time, that a party of three hundred French and three hundred Sepoys, were actually marching from Pondichery. Theſe advices were diſpatched the ſame night to Major Killpatrick, with directions to continue negotiations with Mootis Allee Cawn; and in caſe the French ſhould actually approach, to ſend a meſſage to the commanding officer to retire, and if he ſhould pay no regard to the meſſage, but proceed to ſuccour Velloure, or commit any diſturbance in the Nabob's diſtricts, then to oppoſe him by force. Major Killpatrick had advanced within cannon ſhot of the fort when theſe diſpatches reached him; and, during ſeveral days that he remained in his encampment treating with the Governor, different advices came of parties moving from Pondichery and Villanour to Gingee, and from thence, by Chetteput road, towards Velloure. It was, therefore, to be apprehended, that the Governor might be prevailed on by the French, to admit their troops, for the defence of his fort, and theſe if once admitted, it was foreſeen, would not be withdrawn again from ſo valuable a poſſeſſion.

poſſeſſion. The Governor had ſent his Vakeel to Madraſs, where he was at this very time, to deſire that ſome Engliſh gentleman might be ſent to Velloure, with power to ſettle affairs amicably.

The reduction of the fort was now, by the interpoſition of the French, rendered impracticable, and the ſtay of the army, with any other object but that of an accommodation, a uſeleſs expence: it was therefore reſolved to accede to the propoſal of the Vakeel, and a proper perſon was accordingly deputed. While this meaſure was prudently concerting at Madraſs, Mootis Allee Cawn, finding that our army remained cloſe to his walls, notwithſtanding all the motions of the French, agreed with Major Killpatrick to pay one hundred thouſand pagodas, and twenty-five thouſand roupees, for the removal of our troops, deſired to enter into friendſhip with us; and, by way of earneſt, ſent out twenty thouſand roupees.

No ſooner was this money paid, than Mootis Allee Cawn (informed by his Vakeel that a deputation was ordered on that very day) withdrew from his engagements; and, perſuaded that he might compound for leſs than he agreed the day before to pay to Major Killpatrick, refuſed the next day to comply with the terms. Whatever Major Killpatrick could urge, he would only anſwer, that, as a deputation was ſent from Madraſs, he ſhould not do buſineſs in any other way; and not only perſiſted obſtinately in his refuſal, but flatly denied his agreement made on the 9th of February. The collected army of the French lay, during all this time, encamped between Gingee and Chetteput, at the diſtance of about thirty-five miles from Velloure; it conſiſted, according to the beſt intelligence, of about ſeven hundred French and fifteen hundred Sepoys. It was therefore thought adviſeable to wait for an opportunity when the Governor might be in a more complying humour: and the event juſtified this prudent determination. Major Killpatrick having remained near Velloure with the army till the 24th, and receiving no offers that he could accept, without establishing a precedent of the most pernicious consequence, moved that day for Arcot, where he quartered the troops.

Mootis Allee Cawn, after repeated evasions and delays, at last put an end to this tiresome negociation by a compromise with the Nabob, and payment in part, without military compulsion; but not before the beginning of August 1756. The same shuffling conduct was practised, in a degree, by all the lesser governors, who entrenched themselves for a while in the several fortresses with which this country abounds; but, in their turn, they followed the example of Mootis Allee Cawn, in his compliance; as they had attempted to imitate him, according to their abilities, in his chicanery and resistance.

The Fleet having no other object during the truce it was agreed to employ it in the reduction of a piratical state on the Malabar coast, which had for a long time infested the trade of Bombay. Admiral Watson undertook this expedition with the same zeal which he shewed on every occasion for the service of his country, and the benefit of the Company in the Indian seas.

The Admiral had sailed to Trincomalay, the 6th of April, chiefly to avoid the risque of bad weather during that month. On the 13th of May he returned to Fort St. David, where he remained three months, it being the windward port both to Madrass and Pondichery. He came to Madrass on the 19th of August, and sailing with the whole squadron for Bombay the 10th of October, arrived there the 10th of November.

His force consisted of the Kent, of sixty-four guns, Capt. Speke; the Cumberland, of sixty-six guns, Capt. Harrison; the Tyger, of sixty guns, Capt. Latham; the Salisbury, of fifty guns, Capt. Knowler, the Bridgewater, of twenty Guns, Capt. Martin; and the King's-fisher sloop, of fourteen guns, Capt. Smith.

Smith. Rear Admiral Watſon's flag was hoiſted on board the Kent, and Rear Admiral Pocock's in the Cumberland.

For the better underſtanding the purpoſe of this expedition, it will be neceſſary to explain the nature of the enemy they were going againſt, and by what means a ſmall neſt of pirates, as they originally were, grew to a conſiderable ſtrength, and at laſt became a little empire, like the piratical ſtates of Barbary.

About a hundred years ſince, Conajee Angria, from a private Maratta, had been employed as a General and Admiral, under the Saha Raja, in his wars with the Seedee, or Mogul's Admiral. Being afterwards made Governor of Severndroog, upon the firſt favourable opportunity, he ſeized many of the veſſels he had formerly commanded; with theſe he began to commit acts of piracy, confining himſelf, however, to this iſland, till he had, by repeated ſucceſſes at ſea, rendered himſelf more formidable. The Marattas were alarmed, but had no means of getting at him in his iſland, he having now taken the greateſt part of their fleet. They therefore built three forts upon the main, within leſs than point-blank ſhot of his little territory, which was a ſmall, rocky, well-fortified iſland, of about one mile in circumference. By means of theſe forts they hoped to reduce him to obedience; but he having the ſea open, and being much ſuperior to his countrymen in ſkill and bravery, attacked and took ſeveral of their ſea ports, and at length carried his conqueſts from Tamana to Rajapore on the ſea coaſts; an extent of country of near ſixty leagues in length, in which are ſeveral commodious harbours. He alſo poſſeſſed himſelf of a great part of the inland country, in ſome places for twenty miles back, and in others thirty; ſecuring it to himſelf by building little forts, upon ſuch eminences as commanded the narrow paſſes and defilès. His ſucceſſors, ſtrengthening themſelves continually, by engaging every deſperate fellow they could ſeduce from the

the European ſettlements, grew to be ſo powerful, that the Marattas thought proper to agree to a peace with them, on condition that they ſhould acknowledge the ſovereignty of the Raja, and pay him an annual tribute. Being maſters of the coaſt, they made many conſiderable captures on the ſeas. From the Engliſh Eaſt India company (beſides veſſels of leſs note) they took the Darby, richly laden, from Europe, with one hundred and fifty men; and alſo the Reſtoration armed ſhip, of twenty guns, and two hundred men, fitted out purpoſely to cruize againſt them. They took alſo, from the French, the Jupiter, of forty guns, with four hundred ſlaves on board; and had the preſumption to attack Commodore Liſle, in the Vigilant of ſixty-four guns, the Ruby of fifty guns, and ſeveral other ſhips in company, when the Commodore was leaving the Malabar coaſt.

The Dutch too ſuffered in their turn; and, about twenty years ago, in reſentment, ſent ſeven armed ſhips from Batavia, and two bomb-veſſels, with a number of land forces, and attacked Geriah, but without ſucceſs. Angria growing more and more powerful, could brook no kind of ſubjection, and at length threw off his allegiance to the Marattas. Upon this he received ſome remonſtrances and threats from the Nanna; but was ſo far from regarding them, that he ordered the ears and noſes of the ambaſſadors who brought them to be cut off, in contempt of their Prince and his authority. Exaſperated at this inſult, the Marattas meditated his ruin, and repeatedly applied to the Governor and Council of Bombay, for the aſſiſtance of their marine force to extirpate him.

The piracies of all the ſucceſſors of Angria, who being of his family ſtill bore the ſame name, greatly annoyed not only the natives both by ſea and land, but alſo all European and Moors ſhips, going down that coaſt. As they put the Eaſt India company to a continual expence in keeping a marine force at Bombay,

Bombay, to protect their own and all English country ships, the destruction of so troublesome a neighbour had been the object of the government of Bombay for near fifty years, and immense sums had been expended on expeditions which hitherto had all proved fruitless. Commodore Matthews, in 1722, with his squadron and a small Portuguese army, joined the Bombay land and sea forces in an expedition against a fort called Colabiey, but this was defeated by the treachery, or rather cowardice of the Portuguese, who patched up a peace with Angria; and the ships and troops returned to Bombay, except the Shoreham man of war, who had her bottom beat out on the rocks. In the year 1751, Commodore Lisle being at Bombay, the Governor proposed to him the reduction of Geriah; which he promised to attempt, as the Nanna had engaged to attack the place by land, but a rupture between the Moors at Aurengabad and the Nanna, happened at that time, which put a stop to the enterprize. The Governor being thoroughly persuaded that the most effectual way of destroying Angria, would be by the assistance of the Marattas, kept up a strict friendship with the Nanna, who assured him that he should be joined by a powerful army as soon as ever a scheme could be agreed on for the reduction of Angria's forts on the coast. Upon these assurances, a treaty with the Marattas was concluded, and articles were signed by the Nanna on his part, and by the Governor of Bombay on that of the company.

While this treaty was in agitation, an event happened which shewed the necessity of carrying it into immediate execution. In February 1754, Angria's fleet attacked three Dutch ships, one of fifty, one of thirty-six, and one of eighteen guns; burnt the two former with three of his own vessels, and took the latter. Upon this success he grew insolent, and having built several vessels, and set upon the stocks two ships, one of which was to carry forty guns, he boasted

that

that he ſhould ſoon be ſuperior to whatever could be brought againſt him in the Indian ſeas. In the year 1755, at a time when the greateſt part of the company's forces were abſent on ſervice, the Marattas notified that they were then diſpoſed to join in the neceſſary buſineſs of humbling this common enemy, ſo formidable to the whole Malabar coaſt. Commodore James, who was commander in chief of their marine force in India, being then at Bombay, ſailed on the 22d of March, in the Protector of forty-four guns, with the Swallow of ſixteen guns, and the Viper and Triumph bomb veſſels, being all the force that could be collected together at that time.

The next day he ſaw off Rajapore ſeven ſail of Angria's grabs and eleven gallivats, and chaſed them to the ſouthward; and the day after, the Maratta's fleet came out of Choule, and joining the Commodore with ſeven grabs and ſixty gallivats, proceeded to Commoro bay, where they landed, and trifled away thirty hours; for it is uſual with them to land frequently, as they are prohibited by their religion to eat on board, and alſo enjoined waſhing, and other ceremonies, which can only be performed on ſhore. Landing again the next day, they received intelligence that Angria's fleet was in the harbour of Severndroog. The Commodore at length brought up his dilatory aſſociates; and immediately upon his approach, which was on the 29th, Angria's fleet ſlipt their cables, and run out to ſea, the gallivats towing their larger veſſels. This gave them a great advantage over our ſhips, as there was little wind. The chaſe continued from break of day till the afternoon; and it was obſervable, that our friends the Marattas, who being light, and built floaty for ſailing large, and in light gales, and who had, during all the preceding days, ſailed better than any of our veſſels, were now all aſtern, while their countrymen ſhewed a dexterity in their flight which we could not but admire. They threw out every thing to lighten their veſſels with amazing in-

duſtry

duſtry and readineſs, and ſpreading all the ſails they could crowd on the yards, they faſtened to the flag-ſtaves their garments, quilts, and even their turbans extended to catch every breath of air. By this manœuvre they gained their point, and drew the Commodore ſo far from his ſtation, that he was obliged to give over the chaſe and return to Severndroog.

The fortreſs, which bore that name, was ſituated on an iſland within muſket-ſhot of the main land, with no more than two fathom and an half in the frith. It is ſtrongly, but not regularly fortified; the greateſt part of the works being cut out of the ſolid rock, and the reſt built with ſtones ten or twelve feet ſquare; on the baſtions were fifty-four guns. The largeſt of the forts on the main land is called fort Goa, built in the ſame manner, with large ſquare ſtones, and mounting forty guns. The other two mounting above twenty guns each, were conſtructed in a leſs artificial manner, with ſtones of an irregular ſhape.

On the ſecond of April, the Commodore began to cannonade and bombard the iſland fort; but finding the walls on the ſide where he firſt made his attack, of extraordinary ſtrength, for they were fifty feet high and eighteen thick, he moved his ſtation ſo as to reach fort Goa with his lower deck guns, while he plyed Severndroog with his upper tier. About noon, the north-eaſt baſtion of the latter, and part of the parapet were laid in ruins, when a ſhell ſet fire to the houſes, which the garriſon were prevented from extinguiſhing by the inceſſant fire from the round-tops. The wind being northerly, communicated the fire all over the fort; one of their magazines blew up, and a general conflagration enſued. A multitude of men, women, and children, running out on the farther ſide of the iſland, embarked in boats, but were moſt of them taken by the Swallow, who was ſtationed to the ſouthward to prevent any ſuccours from being thrown into the iſland on that ſide. The Commodore

dore then turned all his fire on fort Goa; and after a ſevere cannonade, the enemy hung out a flag of truce; but the Governor, with ſome choſen Sepoys, croſſed over to Severndroog, which was entirely evacuated upon the blowing up of their ſecond and grand magazine. The Governor was now in poſſeſſion of the iſland fort, and the commodore of the other three; from whence he kept a ſmart fire on Severndroog. The Governor truſting to the natural ſtrength of the place, was reſolved to maintain it till he ſhould receive ſuccours from Dabul. As this appeared from all his anſwers to the ſummons and meſſages that were ſent him, a number of ſeamen were landed, under cover of the fire from the ſhips and the ſhore, who reſolutely ran up to the gates, and being determined to carry their point, with their axes cut open the gate of the ſally port, and procured an entrance with very little loſs.

On the 8th of April, the Commodore anchored off Bancote (now called fort Victoria) the moſt northern port of any conſequence of all Angria's dominions, which ſurrendered the next day upon a ſummons. This place the Eaſt-India Company, having the free conſent of the Marattas, have ſince taken into their hands, as it is a good harbour, and there is a great trade for ſalt and other goods, which are ſent to that port from Bombay; and what is ſtill more eſſential, the country about it abounds with cattle, which are much wanted for the uſe of the garriſon and ſquadron at Bombay. Of all proviſions, beef is the moſt difficult to be procured from any part of the continent; for, excepting Rajapore, which joins to Bancote, and is poſſeſſed by Mahometans (being the port of the Seedee) the coaſt is all inhabited by Gentoos, who never kill any living creature; and as they worſhip the cow, are particularly forbid by their religion to ſuffer the death of any kind of cattle. As all other places were by treaty to be given up to the Marattas, the Commodore cauſed the Engliſh flag, which

which had been hoisted on all the forts for a few days, to be struck on the 11th, and delivered them to be garrisoned by the Marattas. On the 14th he anchored at Dabul, with an intention to attack that place; but next morning received orders to return to Bombay, as the season was thought to be too far advanced for him to attempt any thing farther.

The squadron under the command of rear Admiral Watson, arrived at Bombay in November following: While they were cleaning and repairing, Commodore James in the Protector, and the Revenge and Bombay frigates under his command, was sent to reconnoitre Geriah, the capital of Angria's dominions, and to sound the depths of water at the entrance of the harbour; which service he performed, and returned to Bombay the last of December. The Admiral then sent the Bridgewater and King-fisher sloop, and some of the company's armed ships, to cruize off that port, who were joined on the 27th of January, 1756, by Commodore James in the Protector, and Guardian frigate, and remained on this station till the 11th of February, when the Admiral and the whole squadron arrived.

Upon the appearance of the English fleet, Angria, who had flattered himself that he should never see so large a force upon the coast, was terrified to so great a degree, that he abandoned his fort in hopes of purchasing his peace with the Marattas. They knew how to make their advantage of his present situation and perturbation of mind, and immediately turned their thoughts to the riches of their prisoner; for as such they then considered him; and that they might solely possess the plunder of the place, insisted on his sending an order to his brother, who was left in command, to put them in possession of the fort. The Admiral having information of these clandestine proceedings, sent a summons the next morning to the fort; and receiving no answer, he weighed in the afternoon, and stood in to the harbour in two divisions,

the

the Bridgewater leading that of his Majesty's ships in the following order: Bridgewater, Tyger, Kent, Cumberland and Salisbury, with the Protector of forty guns, belonging to the East India Company. The King's-fisher led those of the Company, consisting of the Revenge, Bombay, Grab, and Guardian frigates; the Drake, Warren, Triumph, and Viper bomb-ketches. As soon as the ships were properly placed, they began such a fire as soon silenced both the batteries and the grabs. About four o'clock a shell was thrown into the Restoration, an armed ship taken by Angria some time ago from the East India Company, which set her on fire; and very soon after his whole fleet shared the same fate. In the night the Admiral landed all the troops, under the command of Colonel Clive, suspecting the enemy would endeavour to let in the Marattas; which supposition was verified by a deserter, who informed Mr. Watson, that Angria had sent orders to his brother, who commanded the garrison, on no account to suffer the English to come in. The next morning the Admiral sent a message to the Commandant, declaring, that if he did not, in an hour's time, deliver up the place, and let the English march in, the attack should be renewed, and he must then expect no quarter. In answer to this, he desired a cessation 'till the next morning; giving for a reason, that it was not in his power to deliver up the place without Angria's permission, which he was only waiting for.

These were apparently trifling pretences to gain time, and to wait for an opportunity of giving the Marattas possession of the place; therefore the Admiral renewed the attack about four in the afternoon, and in less than half an hour the garrison flung out a flag of truce. It was then expected that their colours should be hauled down, and our troops admitted: but as they did not comply with this demand, the Admiral repeated the attack with so terrible a fire, that the garrison cried out for mercy, which our troops were then near

enough

enough to hear diſtinctly; and ſoon after they took poſſeſſion of the fort.

The loſs on both ſides was very inconſiderable: our people found their ſafety in their own bravery and ſpirit, and by driving the enemy from their works with the briſkneſs of their fire. The garriſon, having once abandoned the batteries, were ſafe in the extraordinary height and thickneſs of their walls; for all their ramparts which were not hewn out of the ſólid rock, were built of maſſy ſtone, at leaſt ten feet in length, laid endways; ſo that the greateſt weight of metal made no impreſſion, and would never have effected a breach. It is evident, therefore, that the garriſon was ſubdued by the very terror of ſo unuſual a fire.

There were found in the place upwards of two hundred guns, ſix braſs mortars, and a very large quantity of ammunition of all kinds, and, in money and effects, above one hundred and twenty thouſand pounds. The grabs, which were burnt, conſiſted of eight ketches, and one ſhip, beſides two others which were building (one of which was to carry forty guns) and a conſiderable number of ſmall veſſels called gallivats.

Colonel Clive, with his troops on ſhore, blockaded the fort; and, at the ſame time, by his poſition, prevented the Marattas from getting poſſeſſion of the place in a clandeſtine manner; this was proved to be their deſign, by an offer they made to the Captains Buchanan and Forbes, of fifty thouſand roupees, if they would ſuffer them to paſs their guard; but they, rejecting the offer with indignation, diſcloſed it to Colonel Clive: after which, the Marattas found it as impoſſible to elude the vigilance of the commander, as to corrupt the integrity of his officers.

Soon after the ſuſpenſion of arms was agreed on and publiſhed, Mr. Saunders made a complaint to Mr. Godeheu, deſiring redreſs, on advice that Nanderauze, the Maiſſore General, had taken Tinnevelly, was

was attacking Madura, and had ſtopped a quantity of our cloth. Mr. Godeheu immediately wrote to Nanderauze, requiring him forthwith to ceaſe from all hoſtilities, and warning him, withal, that, unleſs he readily conſented to reſtore every thing that he had taken, he muſt expect to be compelled to it by every power that had any ſenſe of juſtice; and that none of his allies could think it conſiſtent with their honour to ſupport him in diſturbing the preſent tranquillity.

At the ſame time the King of Tanjore, inſiſting on the reſtitution of ſome countries which the Polygar of Marava had taken from him at the beginning of the war, was on the point of proceeding to hoſtilities; but, by our intervention, the Polygar delivered up the countries, and ſatisfied the King.

He then demanded of Tondeman two ſmall diſtricts, which he thought were unjuſtly diſſevered from his kingdom; for his miniſter Monagee, in conſideration of his having been aſſiſted in a favourite enterprize by this Polygar, had formally made them over to him in the name of the King his maſter, without his conſent or knowledge. Captain Caillaud was ſent to learn the truth of this matter; and alſo, if poſſible, to reconcile the difference. He had firſt an interview with Monagee, who confeſſed to him, that he had privately made uſe of the ſeal and authority of the King, and had, for a long time, contrived to conceal this affair from him; but, upon being diſgraced ſome years ſince, he had taken refuge with Tondeman, and then it was diſcovered: that, ſince he had been reſtored to favour, his maſter had been perpetually urging him to endeavour to regain theſe countries; and therefore, while the King's jealouſy of Tondeman ſubſiſted, though he knew the diſtreſs of the country in maintaining the troops he now kept on foot, it was unſafe for him to diſmiſs them. He then entreated, with tears in his eyes, that the Engliſh would not forſake him, declaring, that his ruin was inevitable,

ble, unless they would find some way, for the present at least, to quiet the King's impatience.

This mediation, dextrously managed by Captain Caillaud, who soon after had an interview with the King, served to prevent hostilities for a time; but all endeavours for an accommodation would have proved ineffectual, had not the want of money to equip the army for the field had the desired effect of maintaining peace.

The Danes, some time ago, asked from the King of Tanjore an enlargement of their bounds, as part of their fort was washed down with the sea. Being refused their request, they marched with two hundred Europeans, five pieces of cannon, and some Peons, and attacked two pagodas belonging to the King of Tanjore, about three miles from Tranquebar. They took one, and attempted the other without success; for a detachment of horse and Sepoys having arrived there from Tanjore, had attacked the Danes, killed them about forty men, and wounded an hundred more; the rest escaped to the other pagoda, which they were fortifying. These differences were also referred to, and accommodated by the Governor and Council of Madrass.

The tranquillity on one side of the country, was no security to our extensive concerns and interests in other parts. A letter from Mr. De Leyrit, successor to Mr. Godeheu, gave great concern to all who had at heart the true commercial interests of the settlements, and the duration of the late treaty: but if the letters of Mr. De Leyrit were alarming, how much more was to be apprehended from the conduct of M. De Bussy, who was every day enlarging the valuable and extensive possessions which the French held in the north. It was now apparent, that the use they had been endeavouring to make of their influence over the Viceroy, ever since the truce, was to acquire to themselves the dominion of all the provinces of the Deckan. They began to manifest these intentions, by making ſuch exorbitant demands of poſſeſſions from Salabatzing as might well alarm him. One, among others, was, that they ſhould be put in poſſeſſion of the fort of Golconda.

In order to ſhew by what means this important fortreſs was ſaved from falling into the hands of the French, who ſeldom give up a point of this nature which they have once attempted, it will be neceſſary to give a ſhort account of one of thoſe rebellions which are ſo frequent in this country, that they are ſeldom taken notice of but for their conſequences.

It was about this time that Morarow, the Maratta freebooter, attempted to make himſelf independent, and to ſtrengthen himſelf in the fort of Savanore, by the concurrence of the Nabob of that diſtrict. Ballazerow, the chief of the Marattas, prepared to reduce him, as a rebel to that ſtate, and applied to the Governor of Madraſs for ſome Engliſh gunners. Before he could receive an anſwer to his letter, Salabatzing, conſidering alſo the Nabob of Savanore as a rebel, made it a common cauſe; and, joining Ballazerow, they ſoon obliged Morarow to come out of the fort and make his ſubmiſſions; not forgetting, at the ſame time, to call the Nabob of Savanore to account, for the protection he had given him in his fort.

The French accompanied the Viceroy in this expedition, and their aſſuming behaviour did not eſcape the diſcerning eyes of Ballazerow; who looking upon the French as a diſgrace to the Viceroy, and a great obſtruction to all his own views, remonſtrated to Salabatzing the danger and ſhame which the influence of a handful of Europeans, thus arrogantly giving law to a great Prince, muſt bring on his character and government.

The good council of Ballazerow, as it came very opportunely for the preſervation of the fort of Golconda, was not thrown away. Salabatzing repreſented the unreaſonableneſs of ſuch a demand: he told M. De

De Buſſy, that the countries which had been already given him were more than ſufficient for the pay and expences of his troops, and deſired to entertain them no longer upon ſuch extravagant terms. M. De Buſſy replied in a haughty ſtile to this expoſtulation, and only grew more preſſing in his demands, till Salabatzing was obliged to order him immediately to return to Pondichery. M. De Buſſy was now under a neceſſity of withdrawing his forces; and he began his march, as he pretended, for Maſſulipatam, by the way of Hydrabad, the capital of Golconda.

Upon the departure of M. De Buſſy, Salabatzing wrote to the Governor of Madraſs, requeſting ſome troops, to prevent the French from inſulting him in his government. In the mean time, the French having committed ſome diſorders in the countries they were paſſing through, the Viceroy detached a party of Maratta horſe to keep near them on the road, and prevent further diſturbances. M. De Buſſy, however, arrived ſafe at Hydrabad, and took poſt with his troops in a large houſe in the town, where he had mounted ſome guns, and prepared to defend himſelf againſt an attack.

M. De Buſſy had ſecured a good ſtock of proviſions of all ſorts, by plundering the Bazars: his force conſiſted of four hundred Europeans, and three or four hundred Sepoys, and the French had embarked from Pondichery four or five hundred men, to be landed at Maſſulipatam, and to march from thence to ſuccour M. De Buſſy. The march from Maſſulapatam to Hydrabad may be reckoned about fifteen days.

As the French had made ſo large a draft from Pondichery, there was the leſs danger to our ſettlements of any enterprize from thence; therefore it was agreed, that about four hundred Europeans, including the train of artillery, and four hundred Sepoys, might be ſent with ſafety to the aſſiſtance of Salabatzing: for although M. De Buſly, if he ſhould be joined by all the detachments ſent from Pondichery, would have

 near

near one thouſand men, yet, as he had no black troops, he would be liable to be continually harraſſed and ſtarved, while our party, joined by fifty thouſand horſe, had no ſuch difficulties to apprehend. Salabatzing had himſelf pointed out the road by which our detachment ſhould march, and ſent orders to all the Polygars and other officers reſiding in the adjacent countries, to furniſh ſufficient proviſions.

Every thing being thus ſettled, the neceſſary preparations were making for the march of the troops, when the news came of the ſurrender of Coſſembuzar and the danger of Calcutta. Immediately upon this advice, Major Killpatrick was ſent with two hundred and fifty men for Bengal. Freſh applications came from Salabatzing, and it was reſolved; notwithſtanding the detachment to Bengal, to continue the expedition to Golconda, when the account came of the loſs of Calcutta and all the ſubordinate factories. The neceſſity of re-eſtabliſhing the ſettlements in Bengal ſuperceded every other conſideration: therefore it was reſolved, in this moſt critical juncture, to ſend ſix hundred Europeans, and a thouſand Sepoys, under the command of Colonel Clive, for that important ſervice, which was ſo happily effected

As the Engliſh were thus prevented from ſupporting the Viceroy in his meaſures, he was obliged to alter his reſolutions, and finding that M. De Buſſy was joined by five hundred Europeans under Mr. Law, he ſoon hearkened to terms of accommodation; and the French were again admitted into the ſervice of Salabatzing.

In conſequence of this, about the beginning of the next year, the factories of Ingeram, Bandermalanka, and Vizagapatam, were taken by the enemy. As theſe events were not unforeſeen, immediately upon the re-commencement of hoſtilities, the greateſt part of the Company's effects were ſhipped off, particularly from the two former places. The latter was by no means provided to reſiſt ſo large a force as M. De Buſſy

Buſſy brought againſt it: For he paſſed the Chicacole the 20th of June with ſix hundred Europeans and ſix thouſand Sepoys, and thirty pieces of cannon. He had alſo obliged the Raja to furniſh him with four thouſand pikemen. The garriſon conſiſted of one hundred and forty Europeans, and four hundred and twenty Sepoys and Topaſſes.

On the 24th, about three in the afternoon, a large party of horſe being the van of the army, approached the town, in order to take a view of ſome of the out-works; but being fired at from the Black-Rock battery, retired to a great diſtance. Next morning the whole army was come up within two miles, and a conſiderable party encamped very near the town. In the afternoon M. De Buſſy ſent the following ſummons to the Chief of the factory.

SIR, French Camp, June 25, 1757.

" It is, I believe, needleſs to tell you what brings " me before your place; but I think it neceſſary to " acquaint you of it, by ſummoning you to ſurren- " der it up, and not expoſe your ſelf and your gar- " riſon by a miſtaken bravery, to all the fury which " follows an aſſault or eſcalade; an evil which I ſhould " not be able to put a ſtop to, having in my army " barbarous and undiſciplined nations.

" You will avoid this in ſurrendering, and may de- " pend upon all the good treatment and generoſity, " on which my nation piques itſelf in ſuch a caſe, and " particularly, Sir,

" Your moſt humble and

" Moſt obedient ſervant,

" DE BUSSY."

 A capitula-

A capitulation was accepted, in which it was agreed to deliver up the place, the fortifications, the artillery, marine, and military ſtores, arms, ſhip ſtores, &c. to the Company of France; as alſo all that ſhould be found in the different magazines belonging to the Engliſh Company.

The Chief, the Council, and all thoſe employed in the Engliſh Company's ſervice, the officers and all others, both civil and military, to be priſoners of war on their parole.

All the ſoldiers, ſailors, and other Europeans, to be priſoners, as long as the war ſhould continue between the King of France and the King of England, or till they ſhould be exchanged.

The Capture of this place gave the French the entire poſſeſſion of the coaſt from Ganjam to Maſſulipatam.

While the affairs in the north took this unfavourable turn, the Company received very little benefit from the ſouthern provinces, which were thought to have been peaceably eſtabliſhed.

In March, 1756, advice was received from the Nabob, that the Polygars, who were united againſt his brother Mauphus Cawn, had obtained ſeveral advantages over his troops, and had blocked up a large party in a ſtrong fort, between Madura and Tinnevelly. He requeſted that an European force might be ſent to ſupport his brother. It being thought imprudent at that time to part with any number of Europeans from Fort St. George, or to give the French a pretence for marching to the aſſiſtance of thoſe factious Polygars, Mahomed Iſout Cawn, the Nelloure Subadar who had a commiſſion as commander over all the Company Sepoys) was ſent with a thouſand Sepoys and the Coffree Company from Trichinopoly.

The day before he began his march, advice was received that Mauphus Cawn had obtained a compleat victory over the rebels, killed the General, and two thouſand

thouſand Colleries, and taken three hundred horſe, with all the baggage, guns, and ſome elephants: the battle was fought within ſeven miles of Tinnevelly. This victory was ſo far from producing the quiet which might naturally be expected from it, that it ſerved only to enable Mauphus Cawn to put in execution the deſign he had all along entertained, of making himſelf independent of his brother and his allies. He accordingly began to ſtir in the Tinnevelly province; having already, under falſe and frivolous pretences, obliged our Sepoys to leave the fortreſs of Madura. He could then no longer conceal his intentions, and therefore, without pretending to diſguiſe them, he put himſelf at the head of his troops, reſolving to oblige Iſouf Cawn entirely to quit the country, as he had already driven him out of Madura.

In the beginning of the year 1757, Captain Caillaud, who then commanded in Trichinopoly, was ordered to march from thence to the aſſiſtance of Iſouf Cawn, with one hundred and twenty Europeans, five hundred Sepoys, and two pieces of cannon. As Madura was now in the poſſeſſion of the enemy, he was obliged to take a large circuit to get into the Tinnevelly province by another road. Mauphus Cawn, did all in his power to oppoſe his march, but to no purpoſe; for, on the 17th of March, Captain Caillaud reached Tinnevelly, and joined Iſouf Cawn. His army then conſiſted of a few more Europeans and Sepoys, three additional pieces of artillery, and about five or ſix hundred cavalry. With this force he marched in queſt of Mauphus Cawn, whoſe troops conſiſting of cavalry, eaſily made their eſcape among the woods. Captain Caillaud, knowing it was in vain to purſue them in that country, employed himſelf more uſefully, in ſettling accounts with the renter, and remitting ſome money to the Company after he had provided for the payment of the army.

Having

Having finiſhed this neceſſary preliminary, he marched the beginning of May for Madura, the conqueſt of which was of the greateſt conſequence to the affairs of the two provinces, and arrived before it the twelfth of May. It is a large town, fortified in the old way, with two walls, and round towers at proper diſtances for flanking, and a ditch.

Mauphus Cawn had a garriſon there, and on hearing of the march of our troops, he threw in another reinforcement; ſo that in all, they had eight or nine hundred cavalry, and about three thouſand black infantry, moſt of them with fire-arms, fourteen pieces of cannon, with powder and ammunition in plenty. Captain Caillaud had no artillery with him; he therefore ſent to Trichinopoly for ſome battering cannon; and, in the mean time, was making all the neceſſary preparations for the attack, when he received a letter from the Preſidency of Madraſs, acquainting him that the French were in motion, their intentions not known, but ſuſpected to be againſt Trichinopoly; that, if this was confirmed to him, he was, before all things, to conſult the ſafety of that place.

He did not, however, think it neceſſary, upon a meer report, to abandon his enterprize, but reſolved to wait; and, in the mean time, made his diſpoſitions for the worſt that could happen; but as the call for his forces might be ſudden, he took a reſolution to make himſelf maſter of Madura by ſurprize: he was the rather encouraged to it, by obſerving a place which ſeemed to him, on reconnoitring, very fit for an eſcalade. The ditch was dry, the firſt wall very low, and, by intelligence from within, he knew it was thinly guarded; he therefore made all neceſſary preparations for the attempt.

Every thing went on at firſt with extraordinary ſucceſs; the advanced party, with their ladders, had got over the firſt wall unperceived and unheard, and were pulling over the longer ladders, to mount the inner wall.

wall. The unavoidable noiſe of their arms and implements, the grating of the ladders againſt the walls, together with the breaking of one of them, alarmed the centry, who immediately challenged and fired. The guard which was neareſt hoiſted ſome blue lights (a compoſition they make in that country, of ſulphur and antimony, which throws an exceeding clear light all around) by which they ſaw the aſſailants cloſe under the wall, preparing for the eſcalade, and many more on the glacis, ready to ſupport them; the main body was in a hollow way, out of their ſight, but within two hundred yards of the wall. The alarm was given in an inſtant, and they began to fire very ſmartly from the walls; none of the troops lay far from their poſts, ſo that the fire encreaſed every minute, therefore the retreat was ordered, and performed with a very inconſiderable loſs; which was the more extraordinary, as the men were ſo much expoſed.

Captain Caillaud received a letter that very day from the Preſidency, to inform him, that they did not imagine the French had deſigns on Trichinopoly, from the late intelligence received of their motions; and that they had ſent from Fort St. George a ſmall reinforcement to that garriſon: he therefore thought he might have time to finiſh the ſiege, when the heavy cannon ſhould arrive, and had given directions to the officer who commanded in his abſence at Trichinopoly, to ſpare no money nor pains for good intelligence, that he might be in time apprized of the enemy's deſigns and motions: but, notwithſtanding theſe precautions, the firſt intelligence he received was, that the French were in ſight of Trichinopoly: however, as his orders obliged him to hold his troops in readineſs againſt all events, his diſpoſitions were made accordingly, and he began his march immediately on receiving the news. He left behind him a good part of his army to blockade the place, taking with him all the Europeans, and one thouſand of the beſt Sepoys, with four days proviſions in their knapſacks.

Madura

Madura is an hundred miles from Trichinopoly, and the French, under the command of M. D'Auteuil, had then invested the place. They had nine hundred men in battalion, three or four thousand Sepoys, about one hundred European cavalry and hussars, and a much greater number of the country horse. It was no small difficulty to get into the town, as the enemy knew of his march, and made, as they thought, a disposition that could not fail of preventing him. Captain Caillaud was aware, that, if any misfortune should befal his party, Trichinopoly must inevitably be lost; but he had an advantage in his knowledge of the country, and also of the proper methods of procuring intelligence. He had by this means a true account of the dispositions of the French.

They had formed themselves in four divisions which made a chain quite a-cross the plain, in the front of which their cavalry was advanced, and divided into small parties, to possess the roads and posts all round. One part they had neglected, as thinking it impracticable for troops to march that way: it was a tract of land extending about nine miles to the west of the town, wholly consisting of plantations of rice. As the grain will not grow in this country, unless the soil be overflowed with water, the fields must of consequence be one continued slough, through which it is impossible to march without being above the knee in mud at each step. Captain Caillaud finding, as has been said, every other avenue stopped, resolved to take his rout by this difficult, and therefore unsuspected, way. About two in the afternoon he set out on the direct plain road, and continued to pursue the same course for some miles: this he did to deceive the enemy, and prevent the danger of a discovery, if it should have happened that they had any spies among our people. At the close of the evening he struck out of the road, and about ten o'clock got into the rice fields, and, for the next seven hours, the troops pursued their fatiguing march, till the long wish'd-for day

day appeared; they were then within cannon ſhot of the fort, which they ſoon reached, with no ſmall joy and ſatisfaction. Captain Caillaud had previouſly detached two companies of Sepoys to the right, in order to give the enemy an alarm that way, and ſtill keep up their attention on that ſide. Thoſe two companies executed their orders perfectly well, ſet the enemy in motion, and then retired to the woods, from whence they eaſily found their way into the town the following night.

The French could not at firſt believe the party was got in, but were ſoon convinced of it, and that very night repaſſed the river, and went on the iſland of Seringham. M. D'Auteuil was greatly blamed for his bad manœuvre, and ordered to return to Pondichery: upon his arrival there the command of the army was taken from him.

The manner in which the French came ſo unexpectedly upon Trichinopoly is too artful to be paſſed over unnoticed.

The declaration of war in Europe had to this time produced very little alteration in the affairs of the Coaſt; for, after parting with ſo conſiderable a portion of our ſtrength for the Bengal expedition, which reduced us to an equality with Pondichery, we could not hope to obtain, by a commencement of hoſtilities, any advantage equivalent to the expence of taking the field; and therefore our endeavours had been to preſerve the tranquillity of the province, to the end that the collection of the revenues, in which the Company had now ſo great a concern, might not be interrupted, and the French receiving no ſupplies from Europe to render them greatly ſuperior to us, had remained alſo quiet; reaſoning, no doubt, upon the ſame principles. At laſt, upon the arrival of two ſhips, which landed at moſt two hundred men, they grew impatient of repoſe, and though not daring to avow their deſigns, they found it no difficult matter to form a pretext for taking the field: for while the two companies,

companies, for fear of giving each other alarm, forbore to quell the irregularities of the petty Governors by force of arms, thoſe turbulent chiefs, who knew no other law than the ſword, had made continual invaſions on the countries adjacent to their little forts, and grievouſly oppreſſed the inhabitants with their depredations and exactions.

They had practiſed theſe outrages, with impunity, for the reaſons abovementioned, and might ſtill have continued the ſame, but that the French, to conceal their intended ſurprize of Trichinopoly, choſe to give out that M. D'Auteuil, who marched firſt with only two hundred men, had no other purpoſe than to demand ſatisfaction of Meer Saib, the Governor of Ellavanaſore, for ravages he had committed on ſome of their neighbouring villages. The more effectually to diſguiſe their real deſigns, they actually advanced near the fort of Ellavanaſore, and being repulſed by Meer Saib might have paid dear for their attempt, had not that reſolute Chief received a wound, of which he died a few Days after. The conſternation his death occaſioned, being increaſed by a reinforcement which M. Auteuil received from Pondichery, determined Meer Saib's brother to abandon the fort, and the French took poſſeſſion of it the 13th of April. For the ſame purpoſe, alſo, they pretended diſputes with Worriarpollam, and other places lying on that road.

M. Dauteuil, leaving a ſmall garriſon at Ellavanaſore, moved with the body of the army, firſt, to Verdachilum, where being joined by a reinforcement from Pondichery, Karical, and all their other garriſons, he marched the 4th of May and encamped near Worriarpollam, and on the 7th made an attack upon one of the paſſes of the woods, but was repulſed. He then accommodated matters with the Polygars, who were maſters of thoſe paſſes, on the promiſe of a ſum of money; and moved on with ſuch expedition, that an advanced party encamped near Seringham the 12th; and on the 13th M. D'Auteuil croſſed the river with the

the whole army, and took poſt at Worriour, a pagoda two miles and a half weſt of Trichinopoly.

The deſigns of the French, which had been ſuggeſted by private intelligence, were now too apparent; therefore, on the 11th of April, a reinforcement of fifty men were ordered from Fort St. David, to march with all ſpeed to Trichinopoly.

The great conſequence of that place, from the ſtrength of the fortification, the large tract of country it commands, as it may be called the key to Madura and Tinnevelly, and, above all, the number of four hundred French priſoners which were there confined, determined the Preſidency of Madraſs, upon the firſt news of the march of the enemy from Worriarpollam, to make all the efforts in their power for its ſafety. They could take their meaſures with the leſs riſque, ſince the French had drained all their garriſons ſo far, that Pondichery itſelf was left with very few Europeans fit for duty: therefore, having already ſent a detachment from Fort St. David to Trichonopoly, in order to cauſe a diverſion they prepared three hundred Europeans to march from Madraſs, with five hundred Seapoys, to be joined by a party under Colonel Forde. The Colonel had been ſent, at the requeſt of the Nabob, againſt his * brother, Nazeabulla Cawn, Governor of Nelloure; who having refuſed to be accountable for his arrears, had entered into a correſpondence with the French Chief at Maſſulipatam, and procured from him an aſſiſtance of ſeventy or eighty military, and ſome Sepoys. Abdul Vahab Cawn, who was left there with the Nabob's troops, not being able to collect money to pay them, was obliged to come away, ſo that Nazeabulla Cawn had the entire poſſeſſion of the country. He had not admitted the French party into the fort, but kept them with his army, which he then employed in ſubduing the neighbouring Polygars. It was to be feared they would find an opportunity of taking poſſeſſion of the fort, unleſs we took ſome ſteps to prevent them; for Nazeabulla Cawn, in return

* He was a natural ſon of the Nabob's father.

return for the aſſiſtance received from the French, had already made over to them ſome ſhare of his country, and particularly the ports of Ramahatam and Kiſtnapatam; places with which the Madraſs-merchants have a conſiderable commerce.

Colonel Forde was ordered to Nelloure with a detachment of one hundred Europeans, fifty Coffrees, and three hundred Sepoys; with two field pieces, one eighteen-pounder, and three royals. The Sepoys were ſent over-land to Kiſtnapatam, and Colonel Forde proceeded by ſea, with the reſt of the detachment, for the ſame place, where he diſembarked the the troops, and was joined by the Sepoys, and Abdul Vahob Cawn; who, after the uſual delays of thoſe people, ſupplied him, at laſt, with bullocks and other neceſſaries for his march.

The fort of Nelloure, which is twelve miles from Kiſtnapatam, is about twice as large as Madraſs. It has five gates, two large and three ſmall ones, and is ſurrounded by a mud wall, which is very broad at the bottom, and about three feet thick on the top of the rampart. It is almoſt ſurrounded by a dry ditch, except on the north ſide, where is a river, which in the rainy ſeaſon only, has water in it.

Colonel Forde having battered the fort three days, at length made a practicable breach on the 5th of May, and began the aſſault at break of day, in the following order: The Coffrees, Enſign Elliot at their head, marched with great reſolution to the foot of the breach, three companies of Sepoys followed them very cloſe till they came within ſixty paces of the breach, and then lay down in a ditch, and could not be got to advance a ſtep farther, ſo that the Europeans were obliged to march over them to the breach; where joining the Coffrees, they advanced to the top of it; but were ſo warmly received by the people in the fort, with pikes, firelocks, and ſtones, that it was impoſſible for them to get over. In this ſituation the fight was continued three quarters of an hour, and then

then the Sepoys ran away as faſt as they could towards our battery. The Colonel, now convinced that nothing could be done with his force, deſerted by the Sepoys, againſt ſo gallant a defence, ordered a retreat, which was conducted with ſuch good order, that not a man was hurt after they had left the attack; but, while they continued in the breach, the action was uncommonly briſk. Our people behaved with great reſolution, and had forty killed and wounded, with about fifty Coffrees and Sepoys: all theſe men were wounded in ſuch a manner as to be rendered unfit for preſent action; but there were ſcarce any of the aſſailants who came off without bruiſes and contuſions, from ſtones, pikes, or clubs; for, with ſuch weapons, numbers of the people in the place oppoſed and greatly incommoded them.

Colonel Forde, having no dependance on any but his own people, and thoſe being greatly reduced, and alſo great part of the ammunition expended, he ſtopped all further proceedings till he heard from the Preſidency of Madraſs, whom he immediately acquainted with the foregoing particulars. At the time theſe advices arrived at Madraſs, the French were encamped nearer to that place than our troops would be when before Nellour: therefore it was judged more prudent to give up that undertaking, than to hazard a detachment to the northward; whereas, by marching to the ſouthward, they could at once prevent the deſigns of the enemy on Trichinopoly, and ſerve as a barrier between them and Fort St. George; therefore they ſent out three hundred Europeans to the ſouthward, and diſpatched orders to Colonel Forde to join them with all his force.

While the neceſſary preparations were making for the march of the forces from Madraſs, Captain Polier was ordered from Chengalaput and Carangoly, to endeavour to reduce Outremalour, a fort poſſeſſed by the French, ſituate about fifteen miles from Chengalaput, and eight from Carangoly. On the approach of the party from Carangoly, the French garrison, which consisted only of Sepoys, abandoned the fort before Captain Polier's arrival: he left about forty Sepoys in charge of it, and then returned towards Chengalaput, near to which he encamped, in readiness to join the army from Fort St. George. By this time the French garrison of Allumparva, being reinforced by sea from Pondichery, so as to make up about one hundred Europeans and Topasses, and three hundred Sepoys, marched from thence, and retook Outremalour.

Colonel Adlercron resolving to command in person the intended expedition for the relief of Trichinopoly, marched from Fort St. George the 26th; and, lest the French redoubts of Waldour and Villenour should cause any delay in his passing by the direct road to Fort St. David, he took the rout of Chengalaput and Wandewash; and as he judged it necessary to halt at some place for Colonel Forde to come up with his party, it was recommended to him to employ that spare time in a second reduction of Outremalour, and in demolishing that fort. It was hoped that they might then be able to garrison Chengalaput and Carangoly, in such manner as to cover all those districts; which, thus protected, would bring a considerable revenue to the Company. On the approach of Colonel Adlercron, the garrison evacuated the place and threw themselves into Wandewash.

While the Colonel was detained at Outremalour, in destroying the fortifications of that place, he received letters from the Presidency, to acquaint him, that, since Capt. Caillaud had succeeded in throwing succours into Trichinopoly, they were no longer in pain for that fort; and therefore requested him immediately to invest the fortress of Wandewash, and to push the attack with the utmost vigour, that he might get possession of it before the French army could come to its relief. They were urgent for this undertaking, on account of the Governor's behaviour, who had

had paid the Nabob no tribute ſince the year 1752; and alſo, during that time had been a conſtant favourer of the French, who, under cover of that fort, had been enabled to make the moſt ſudden incurſions into all the diſtricts of the Arcot province. The reduction of this fortreſs would not only have prevented this inconvenience for the future, but the place itſelf would have been of the utmoſt conſequence to the Nabob and his allies, as being productive of large revenues, and alſo capable of ſerving as a barrier for the neighbouring countries.

Colonel Adlercron marched with the army on the 5th of June to Wandewaſh, and the next day entered the town; but, before the heavy cannon could come up, the greateſt part of the French army from Trichinopoly reached Pondichery, and marched out again to the relief of Wandewaſh: whereupon Colonel Adlercron, judging it impracticable to execute the plan which had been concerted at Madraſs, reſolved to wait for directions from thence; and, in the mean time, withdrew from the town, and encamped a few miles off. The Preſidency, being ſenſible that the collected force of the French would exceed our numbers, could not reaſonably hope to obtain any conſiderable advantage by keeping the field, and were therefore deſirous of putting an end to the expence; accordingly, they wrote to Colonel Aclercron to return with the army to Madraſs. They imagined that the French would alſo conſider, that our force was ſufficient to obſtruct any attempt on their ſide, and would therefore recall their troops to Pondichery.

Before Colonel Adlercron began his march for Madraſs the enemy's army had reached Wandewaſh; and, a very few hours after he left Outremalour, a party of French took poſſeſſion of it. Notwithſtanding the enemy moved ſo cloſe after him, Colonel Adlercron neither adviſed the Preſidency of their proceedings, nor waited to ſtop their progreſs, but continued his march towards Madraſs: the conſequence of which was,

 that,

that, on the very day he left Chengalaput, they made a forced march from Outremalour to Conjeveram, plundered the town, and attacked the fort, or walled pagoda; which was, however, so well defended by a Serjeant and two companies of Sepoys, that they were repulsed, with the loss of an officer and six Europeans killed, and about ten wounded. When this news reached Madrass the army was arrived within six miles of that place. The Governor and Council thought it highly necessary they should immediately march again, to protect their possessions from further devastations.

Colonel Lawrence, who on every occasion shewed the most earnest disposition to contribute in any shape to the advancement of all military operations, offered to join the army as a volunteer; and, when it was imagined Trichinopoly would have been the scene of action, his intention was to proceed with the troops from Fort St. David for the defence of that place. Afterwards, when the French army returned from Trichinopoly and were collected at Wandewash, he offered to embark with all the men that could be spared from Fort St. David, and to land at Sadrass, in order to join the army in the most expeditious manner. Being sensible how much his abilities and experience would contribute to the regulation and good conduct of the army, and judging Fort St. David to be free from all danger, as the whole French force was on the other side, the Presidency approved of this proposal, and Colonel Lawrence accordingly landed near Sadrass, with about one hundred men, the 22d of June, three days after the march of the army; which he joined on the other side of Chengalaput.

The army then advanced towards the enemy. and took post the 10th of July within four miles of them. The French were strongly intrenched about a mile from Wandewash. As their troops were manifestly discontented, which appeared by their frequent desertion, and our men were all in good spirits and eager for

for an engagement, all possible endeavours were used to induce the enemy to come out of their entrenchments. On the 17th some of the Nabob's horse, supported by a small party of Europeans, were sent within cannon shot of their camp, in hopes that a detachment would be sent out against them, and a general action brought on by that means, but all was in vain; and, as their entrenchments were defended by several batteries, and they had a great superiority also in the number of their troops, it was judged that they could not be attacked in such a post without too great hazard. The continuance of the army in their encampment in this state of inaction, was only a useless expence; therefore, to reduce it as far as prudence would admit, Colonel Adlercron was desired to send part of the army to Chengalaput and Carangoly, and the remainder to Conjeveram. This place, being situated in the center of our possessions, was a convenient station for the troops to move from, which ever way the enterprizes of the enemy might make it necessary.

The enemy remained about Wandewash till the 20th of September, when they moved against Chetteput with a body of eighteen hundred Europeans. Nizar Mahomed Cawn, assisted with a Serjeant and sixteen men from Fort St. George, defended the place to the last extremity, and even after the enemy had got possession of the fort he fought them in the streets till he was killed with a musket ball; his family then destroyed themselves, and a vast slaughter was made among his troops. This obstinate defence cost the besiegers also a great number of men.

The French withdrawing from the neighbourhood of Trichinopoly, left Captain Caillaud at liberty to proceed for the reduction of Madura; but, as the enemy found employment for all the troops that could be spared from Madrass, it was impossible to reinforce him with such a strength as should secure him success.

Without waiting for farther ſupplies, he took with him ſuch a force as he thought might be ſpared from Trichinopoly without weakening the garriſon too much, and marched the 27th of June with ninety military, four hundred Sepoys, and two twenty four pounders; with theſe he joined Lieutenant Rumbold, who had maintained his poſt before Madura with the Coffrees and Sepoys left und r his command. It took up ſome days to make the neceſſary preparations for erecting a battery, which was opened on the 9th, and a breach made before noon. Captain Caillaud thought it adviſeable to aſſault the breach without delay, leſt the beſieged ſhould throw up ſome works within during the night.

The diſpoſition being made, he began the attack at two in the afternoon; but the breach was ſo vigorouſly defended, that the beſt of his troops were either killed or diſabled in the attempt; the reſt fell back, and it was impoſſible to prevent a general retreat, or to perſuade the remains of the army to a ſecond attack: neither was it adviſeable, at a time when the beſieged were elated with having killed and wounded, upon this occaſion, between thirty and forty Europeans and Coffrees, and a hundred Sepoys.

Captain Caillaud reſolving to wait for an opportunity to renew his attempt, in the mean time, made the proper diſpoſitions for reducing the place by famine; but as this method might take up ſo much time as to prolong his ſtay till the arrival of the French fleet, he eagerly caught at the firſt opening for a treaty, and though the propoſals of Mauphus Cawn's people were moſt exorbitant, he did not raſhly reject them, but by degrees abating the terms, reduced them at length to a hundred and ſeventy thouſand roupees. He then concluded the bargain, and Madura was delivered up to him juſt at the time that the French fleet arrived. This event making it neceſſary to provide for the defence of all the garriſons; orders were ſent to withdraw

draw the troops from the Tinevelly country, and Captain Caillaud returned to Trichinopoly; leaving a large garriſon of Sepoys at Madura, under the command of Iſouf Cawn.

Mauphus Cawn being now maſter of all the revenue of Tinevelly, the diſtricts of Madura alone were not ſufficient to defray the expence of maintaining the fort.

The coaſt was at this time in danger of being diſturbed by other powers as well as the French.

The Marattas, who are continually traverſing theſe immenſe countries with their vaſt bodies of horſe, in a moſt incredible manner, having, within the laſt two years, conquered large diſtricts in many diſtant parts of the Deckan, had alſo entered the kingdom of Maiſſore, and at each time carried away upwards of thirty lack of roupees. The Nanna Balazerow, in his return, poſſeſſed himſelf of the fort and country of Serah, the next province to Cadapah. He left Balaventerow, his General, with about eight thouſand horſe, at Cadanattam, a place about eighty miles from Arcot. His orders were to demand the Chout of the Arcot and Trichinopoly countries, which had been unpaid for ſome years paſt. For this purpoſe he ſent a Vakeel to the Nabob, and another to Pondichery. Balazerow made a demand of forty lack of roupees; but, upon the repreſentation of the Nabob, who deſcribed to the Vakeel the ſtate of his country for ſome years paſt, and aſſured him that not only the whole revenues of the diſtricts in his poſſeſſion, but every roupee he could borrow beſides, had been ſpent in oppoſing the deſigns of the French, who would otherwiſe have ſubdued the whole Carnatick, the Vakeel reduced the demand to three lack; and, upon the Nabob's further inſtances, to two lack and a half, one half to be paid immediately, the other in one month. The Nabob thought this a more reaſonable accommoda-

 tion

dation than could have been expected; but not being able to raiſe that ſum himſelf, recommended to the Preſidency to conſent to theſe terms, and advance the money. The low ſtate of their treaſury put it out of their power to comply with this requeſt; nor could they, at any time, with prudence, pay ſuch a ſum upon a mere demand, without making ſome agreement, or terms of alliance, for the good of their affairs. In hopes to gain time, as ſhips from Europe were every day expected, they wrote to the Maratta Vakeel at Arcot, deſiring him to come and ſettle the affair in diſpute at Madraſs; and, at the ſame time, recommended to the Nabob to accompany him.

Although the Vakeel had told the Nabob that the French had offered four lack of roupees to the Maratta General, to engage him in their alliance, and hinted, that the conſequence of our not complying immediately with the terms offered, would be the ruin of the countries in our poſſeſſion, yet it was not apprehended that the Nanna had impowered this officer to proceed to ſuch extremities: neither could it be ſuppoſed that the French were able to make good ſo large an offer as four lack, having reduced their own finances to as low an ebb as thoſe of their neighbours; but it is natural to the Moors, in all their tranſactions, to mix a proportion of falſhood, and, if they fancy they can carry their point by it, they pride themſelves in the conceit of their art and cunning.

The Nabob arrived at Madraſs the 8th of Auguſt 1757, with Amoortarow, the Maratta Vakeel, and ſome days were employed in repreſenting to Amoortarow the vaſt expence which the Nabob and the Company had been at to preſerve the country from the entire dominion of the French; but the endeavours of the Preſidency, by that argument, to avoid the payment he demanded, were fruitleſs, and all their remonſtrances

remonstrances of very little weight, the Nabob having absolutely engaged with Amoortarow, before he left Arcot, to pay the sum of two hundred and fifty thousand roupees. Whenever it was proposed to Amoortarow to abate in his demand, his answer was, constantly, that he had the Nabob's promise, and should get the money from him. The Maratta seemed determined, in case it was not paid, to lay waste the countries in the possession of the Nabob and the Company, which was certainly in the power of an army of eight thousand horse. Such a force was then within eighty miles of Arcot, and might have seized a sum far exceeding their demand, as it was the time of the * Tripety feast, during which solemnity the greatest part of the revenues are usually collected at the pagoda. The Presidency therefore agreed, upon these considerations, to enable the Nabob to pay the sum in question, by allowing it to be deducted out of the second half of his assignment of eight lack to the Company.

Notwithstanding the power of the Marattas was so well known, and had been of late so universally felt, such is the restless spirit of all the Indian as well as Moorish Chiefs, that Morarow, who had, not long since, brought himself and the Nabob of Savanore to the necessity of imploring pardon from the Nanna, was now proposing a league, between himself, the Nabobs of Cadapah and Canoul, and the King of Maissore, with intent to retake Serah from the Nanna, and

* Tripety is a pagoda situated upon a hill about one hundred and fifty miles N. N. W. of Madrass. It is held in the same veneration by the Gentoos, as Mecca is by the Mahometans. An annual feast is held at Tripety, in the month of September, at which time a great number of devotees resort to the pagoda; and from the presents made by such a multitude of votaries, a large revenue accrues to the Nabob. None but Gentoos, of different tribes, are permitted to ascend the sacred hill on which the pagoda stands.

and prevent his getting any footing in the Carnatick. Could this treaty have been accomplished with any prospect of success, it must be granted, that it might have been a glorious barrier against the inroads of that destructive power. The proposal was specious, and would have had the approbation, and, possibly, the concurrence of the English, could it have been considered as a system of cool and lasting policy; but it was rather to be suspected of having its foundation in ambition or revenge, and as it proved, was only a means of provoking the Marattas to make those countries the seat of war, and of throwing them the sooner into their hands. Upon the first advice of this intended confederacy, Balaventarow marched against the Nabob of Cadapah, and killing him in a battle, took the greatest part of the country into his own hands; but Abdul Mahomed Cawn, with some of the relations and troops of the late Nabob, throwing themselves into Sydoat fort, maintained themselves for a time; but were at last obliged to accommodate with the besiegers for a sum of money, and the delivery of half the country to the Marattas.

During the time these transactions were on foot, Amoortarow the Vakeel, with a part of the Maratta troops, went against Trepalour, which is also in the dependency of Cadapah; but he was less successful than his master, for having attempted an assault, he met with so vigorous a repulse that great part of his forces were cut off, and himself mortally wounded and carried prisoner to the fort, where he died a few days after. The Marattas, during their stay in those parts, collected several sums of money from the different Polygars to the northward; and then went off towards Poona, to join Balazerow.

From these, and many more instances, it has been shewn how great a check the Marattas have been upon the Moorish Government, and that it is owing to their arms alone that the Mahometans have been prevented

vented from the usurpation of the whole peninsula.

As the Moors are a luxurious people, in a few years of peace they grow enervated by their debaucheries, and soon degenerate into sloth and effeminacy. It may also be added, that a general corruption of manners, and treachery to one another, would greatly conduce to render them an easy prey to the Marattas, whenever they should take the resolution to expel them the country. And though there is not a Governor, in the highest rank of power and independency, but what stiles himself, a thousand times in the ordinary transaction of the day, THE SLAVE OF THE MOGUL, there is not one of them in the whole empire that pays the least regard to the most solemn orders of that monarch, or that will march his troops to quell any dangerous commotion, or stir for the preservation of the life or throne of his master.

The only balance to the power of the Marattas is a race of northern people, inhabiting the mountains of Candahar, commonly known in India by the name of Pattans, though they are more generally called Agwans on the other side of the country; and under that name conquered Ispahan in the year 1722. They are Mahometans, yet no less enemies to the Moorish government than the Marattas, or other Indians. They are said to have been descended from an ancient colony of Arabians, who entered the country four hundred years before Tamerlane, and built the city of Massulipatam; from thence extending their conquest northward, they founded Patna in Bengal, and at last overran the whole country to the west, and were masters of Delli when Tamerlane first appeared in India. As they were always reckoned good soldiers, they are now considered as the very best infantry in the whole empire; and it is natural to suppose they should be such, since they have been inhabitants of the northern mountains.

This

This warlike nation made themſelves formidable to Nadir Shaw, in his march; and after that conqueror had left the Mogul empire in the weak and indefenſible ſtate to which he had reduced it, the Pattans invaded it, on a ſuppoſition that it was then in too low a condition to be able to reſiſt the force which he at that time thought was ſufficient to bring againſt it.

As ſoon as the Emperor was apprized of their march, he aſſembled his council, and ſitting on his throne, ſurrounded by his Generals and twenty-two principal Omrahs, held in his hand a betel, which, according to the cuſtom of the country, he offered to that chief who ſhould immediately engage to take the command of the army and repulſe the enemies of his country. So univerſal was the effeminacy or treachery of the courtiers, that not one of them advanced to take the betel as a pledge of their fidelity; which the young Prince, being then about eighteen, obſerving with extreme concern, preſented himſelf to his father, with earneſt entreaties that he might be permitted to receive it.

His father refuſed him, repreſenting to him, that it was not proper for the heir of the empire to expoſe himſelf in ſo perilous an enterprize, while there were ſo many experienced Generals more fit for that ſervice. On the other hand, the Omrahs all maintained, that, as his ſon had offered to take the betel, he alone ſhould put himſelf at the head of the troops; and joining with the Prince in ſolicitations, prevailed at length upon the Emperor, who immediately gave his orders for the raiſing of three hundred thouſand men.

The Omrahs, withdrawing from court, entered into a conſpiracy, and gaining the Chiefs of the ſeveral corps which compoſed this army, ſo haſtily aſſembled, concerted with them to betray the Prince.

The young hero, being informed of the plot that was laid againſt his life, a little before he gave battle to to the Pattans, had the addreſs privately to ſecure the perſons of thoſe treacherous commanders; he then attacked the enemy, and, gaining a compleat victory, obliged them to quit the country by a precipitate flight. While the Prince was thus gloriouſly delivering his country from the Pattans, the conſpirators in the capital cauſed it to be reported, that he was fallen in battle, and, entering the palace, ſeized on the Emperor, and ſtrangled him, giving out that he had poiſoned himſelf in a fit of deſpair, occaſioned by the loſs of the battle and the death of his ſon. This horrible aſſaſſination could not be concealed from the Prince, who was now returning in triumph to Delli. He was ſenſible of the danger that threatened his own life from ſo formidable a conſpiracy, and to avoid it, adopted the ſtratagem which his great grandfather Aurenzeb practiſed on another occaſion. He appeared inconſolable for the loſs of his father, pretending to believe that he died a natural death: he tore off his garments, and took the habit of a Fakeer, declaring publickly, that he renounced the world, and that he would never more have concern in the government.

A Court of juſtice for a ſtate criminal is a thing unheard of in theſe lawleſs governments; and there is no way of puniſhing a traitor but by turning againſt him his own arts of treachery and deceit.

The Prince acted his part ſo well, that he deceived the conſpirators, who went out to meet him, with aſſurances of their readineſs to acknowledge him for their maſter and King. He received them with a declaration of his intentions to give up the crown, and even to retire from the world. He told them, that, as it was neceſſary ſo vaſt an empire ſhould not be deſtitute of a head, he muſt entreat their aſſiſtance to direct him in the choice of an emperor, deſiring that they would aſſemble in his palace that evening, to deliberate on this important affair. The Omrahs retired flattering themſelves that they ſhould now have an opportunity of ſetting up a creature of their own

own; while Amet Shaw, for that was the name of the young Emperor, entered the royal palace, and prepared a number of trusty persons, whom he placed on each side of the doors of the several avenues which led to his inner court.

The entrance to the apartments of Eastern Princes is so disposed, with a view to prevent the sudden irruption of assassins, that there is no approaching the presence chamber but through long oblique passages, wherein, at intervals, there are recesses for the posting of guards. This contrivance at once secures the monarch from the attempts of the most determined villains; and, at the same time, affords him an opportunity for executing his purposes on those who have incurred his displeasure.

Every thing being disposed for the reception of the Omrahs, they were each introduced, as they arrived to these fatal avenues; and, as they stooped to pass the curtains, which are generally kept lowered, they were seized by the guards, and immediately received the just reward of their crimes.

Thus the Emperor Amet Shaw established himself, for a while, in the quiet possession of the throne, by triumphing at once over his foreign and domestick enemies. But it was not long before the peace of Delli was more fatally disturbed; for the Pattan Chief retiring to Lahore, in a little time assembled a much more formidable army, and entering Delli, gave up the town to be plundered three days by his soldiers. In the mean time, he took to himself all that was to be found in the royal treasury, and required of the collectors of the publick revenues, that they should be accountable to him for all they had received. He then marched home, being supposed to have taken away more riches, except jewels, than Nadir Shaw carried out of the country. He made no revolution, and, it is said, no alteration in the government of Indostan, and yet he assumed a kind of sovereignty over it; but when he returned to Lahore,

hore, he drew a line from north to ſouth, aſſuming to himſelf a vaſt extent of country to the weſt of that line, which was before, at leaſt nominally, dependent on the emprie of Indoſtan; there he left his ſon Timur as Governor of his new dominions, and gave no further diſturbance to Indoſtan till the year 1757.

Before we enter on the moſt important of all the military operations on the Coromandel coaſt, it may be uſeful to take a view of the ſtrength of the reſpective Companies.

The French had nineteen hundred Europeans on the coaſt, excluſive of thoſe with M. De Buſſy, before the arrival of their ſquadron in September. This fleet brought a reinforcement of one thouſand military, which, added to a number of ſailors that were landed, nearly compleated three thouſand five hundred men. The Engliſh having no more than one thouſand three hundred of the Company's troops, had encreaſed them by enliſting three hundred and thirty-four of Colonel Adlercron's regiment, when that officer, with his corps, was ordered home; and as the China ſhips brought them only eighty-four ſoldiers, their whole force amounted to no more than one thouſand ſix hundred and eighteen men.

In conſideration of this vaſt ſuperiority on the part of the enemy, the Preſedency judged it neceſſary to ſuſpend all operations of the field, and keep the troops collected in the ſeveral garriſons. Conformably to this plan, they drew the army from Conjeveram into Madraſs, ordered back Major Polier, who was marched to the northward, to protect Tripety againſt the threatened attack of Nazeabulla Cawn from Nelloure; and directed Captain Caillaud (who having taken poſſeſſion of the fort of Madura, was preparing to march for Tinnevelly) to return to Trichinopoly with all his Europeans, and as many Sepoys as he ſhould think neceſſary; leaving Iſouf Cawn,

Cawn, with the rest of the Sepoys, to protect Madura and Tinnevelly.

While we continued thus waiting the motions of the French, and surprized that they should remain inactive for so many months after the taking of Chetteput, a fleet of eleven sail, commanded by M. D'Aché, appeared off Fort St. David early in the morning of the 28th of April: two of them proceeding to Pondichery, landed M. Lally, while seven anchored in Fort St. David's road, and two farther off to the eastward. The Bridgwater and Triton being surrounded in St. David's road, were obliged to run ashore, in order to save their crews and stores. Next morning a large detachment from Pondichery entered the bounds of Fort St. David, and were to have been joined by the troops from the ships; but the unexpected appearance of the English squadron to the southward at the same instant, putting them into confusion, prevented the disembarkation.

Admiral Pocock being joined by Commodore Stevens, who arrived in Madrass road on the 24th of March, with the Elizabeth, Yarmouth, Weymouth, and Newcastle, on the 28th hoisted his flag on board the Yarmouth, and, after having put the squadron in the best condition possible for the sea, sailed on the 17th of April, in order to get to windward of Fort St. David, to intercept the French squadron, which, by intelligence, he had reason to expect.

His whole force now consisted of the Yarmouth, sixty-four guns, five hundred and forty men, Capt. John Harrison; the Elizabeth, sixty-four guns, four hundred and ninety-five men, Commodore Stephens, Capt. Kempenfelt his captain; the Cumberland, sixty-six guns, five hundred and twenty men, Capt. Brereton; the Weymouth, sixty guns, four hundred and twenty men, Captain Nicholas Vincent; the Tyger, sixty guns, four hundred men, Captain Thomas Latham; the Newcastle, fifty guns, three hundred and fifty

fifty men, Captain George Legge; and the Salisbury, fifty guns and three hundred men, Captain John Somerset; with the Queenborough and Protector store-ships.

The 28th at noon the Admiral made Negapatam, and the next morning, at half an hour past nine o'clock, in running down to St. David's, saw seven ships in that road getting under sail, and two cruizing in the offing, which, by their not answering his signal, he concluded were enemies, and made the signal for a general chace. They then stood off shore to the eastward, under top-sails, with the wind at south; and at noon, being joined by the two ships in the offing, and forming the line of battle a-head, with the starboard tacks on board, the Admiral found it necessary to make the signal to form his line also; and when all his ships came up and got into their station, which was a little before three o'clock in the afternoon, and nearly within random shot of the enemy, who continued under their topsails, he bore down upon the Zodiaque, on board of which ship M. D'Achè wore a cornette at the mizen-top-mast head, keeping a little a-head of him. The French began to fire upon him as he approached them; notwithstanding which, he forebore to throw out the signal for engaging till he came within half musket shot of the Zodiaque. A little after three, perceiving the ships were not all got near enough to the enemy, the Admiral made the signal for a closer engagement; which, was immediately complied with by the ships in the van. At half an hour past four, observing the rear of the French line had drawn up pretty close to the Zodiaque, he made the Cumberland, Newcastle, and Weymouth's signals to make sail up, and engage close. A few minutes after M. D'Achè broke the line, and shot up under the lee quarter of his second a-head, and then put before the wind: his second astern, who kept on the Yarmouth's quarter most part of the action, then came up along-side, gave his fire, and bore away; the two other ships in the rear came up in like manner, and then bore away. The Admiral observing the enemy's van to bear away also, hauled down the signal for the line, and made the signal for a general chase. At six, the enemy joined two ships about four miles to leeward, and at the same time hauledtheir wind, and stood to the westward, with the larboard tacks on board.

The Yarmouth's masts, yards, sails, and rigging, as well as the Elizabeth, Tyger, and Salisbury, were damaged so as to prevent their keeping up with the other ships that were in the rear during the action, and had suffered but little. From the condition of these ships, and, more especially, as the night approached, the Admiral thought it necessary to haul close upon a wind, and stand to the south-west, in order, if possible, to keep to windward of the enemy, in hopes of being able to engage them next morning if he could be so fortunate as to prevent their weathering him in the night. He ordered the Queenborough a-head to observe their motions, and continued endeavouring to work up after them till six in the morning of the first of May; when finding he lost ground considerably, for the enemy had received little damage in their rigging, he came to an anchor about three leagues to the northward of Sadrass, and sent an officer to the Chief of that settlement for intelligence. From thence he was informed, that the Bien aimè, of seventy four guns, had received so much damage in the action, that the enemy was obliged to run her ashore a little to the southward of Alamparvey, where the French squadron was then at anchor. The action was about seven leagues west by north of that place.

Admiral Pocock, in his letter to the Secretary of the Admiralty observed, that Commodore Stevens and Capt. Kempenfelt, Capt. Latham, and Capt. Somerset, who were in the van, and also his own Captain

Captain, Capt. Harriſon, and all the officers, and men belonging to the Yarmouth, by their endeavours to come to an engagement with the enemy and their conduct in action, gave him a ſenſible ſatisfaction.

It was confeſſed by ſeveral French officers, that they had ſix hundred men killed in the action and many wounded. Our loſs was only twenty-nine men killed and thirty wounded; which diſparity can only be accounted for by the enemy's endeavouring to diſmaſt our ſhips, while we fired at their hulls: and this will alſo account for the deſtruction of the Bien-aimè, and the eſcape of all the reſt, who got ſafe to Pondichery the 5th of May. The French had in the engagement eight ſhips of the line and a frigate. The Zodiaque of ſeventy-four guns, on board of which M. D'Achè, as it has been ſaid, wore a cornette on the mizen-top-maſt head: Le Bien-aimè, alſo of ſeventy-four guns, Le Vengeur, and Le St. Louis of ſixty-four, Le Duc d'Orleans and Le Duc de Bourgogne of ſixty, Le Condè and Le Moras of fifty, and Le Sylphide a frigate of thirty-ſix guns. After the engagement they were joined by the two ſhips which had been at Pondichery to Land M. Lally: they were Le Compte de Provence of ſeventy four guns, and Le Diligent of twenty-four.

Admiral Pocock having received one hundred and twenty recovered men from the hoſpital, and above fourſcore Laſcars from the governor of Madraſs, and having fiſhed his maſts, and repaired his moſt material damages, tried for ſome days to work up ſhore, but without ſucceſs. He then put off the land; and on the 10th of May ſtretched as far to the ſouthward as the latitude of nine degrees and thirty minutes north, by which he hoped to fetch to windward of Fort St. David; but upon ſtanding in again he met with ſuch ſtrong weſterly winds, and the Cumberland's leak increaſed ſo as to prevent her keeping the wind, therefore being able to reach no higher than Alamparvey, he anchored off that place the 26th of May. The 30th he got up in ſight of Pondichery; and the 1ſt of June in the morning the French ſquadron weighed, and ſtood out of the road, conſiſting of ten ſail. Admiral Pocock being conſiderably to leeward, expected that they would bear down and engage him; but they kept cloſe to the wind, and plyed away from him, notwithſtanding his endeavours to get up with them, which was prevented in a great meaſure by the Cumberland's bad ſailing. The ſecond and third day, the current ſetting ſtrongly to leeward, our ſquadron, not having any land or ſea winds, loſt ground conſiderably. The 6th, the Admiral received a letter from the ſelect committee of Fort St. George, acquainting him, that St. David's ſurrendered the 2d, and that it was probable Fort St. George would ſoon be inveſted, which would put it out of his power to ſupply the fleet with water. The Admiral finding this reaſoning to be juſt, returned and anchored in Madraſs road, where he ſupplied his ſquadron with water and other neceſſaries.

Having related the whole progreſs of the fleet to their return to Madraſs, it is now time to ſhew by what ſteps the French became maſters of Fort St. David.

The 29th of April the French horſe came into the bounds of Fort St. David; and preſently after them five hundred men of the regiment of Lorrain, and about two hundred of the Company's troops, with a number of Sepoys, artillery-men and eight pieces of cannon. They cut off and diſperſed ſeveral of our Sepoys. and plundered the villages. Their motions were ſo ſudden, they very much alarmed the inhabitants of Fort St. David, ſo that many of the Laſcars, Sepoys, and moſt of the artificers left the place. The enemy having ſummoned Cuddalore, it was ſurrendered on the 3d of May, on condition that the garri-
ſon

ſon ſhould have liberty to retreat, with their arms, to Fort St. David the next morning.

The enemy having withdrawn almoſt every man from their garriſons, to make themſelves as ſtrong as poſſible for the ſiege of Fort St. David, formed a very conſiderable army, amounting to three thouſand five hundred Europeans, and began to fire upon the place with two guns from Cuddalore the 16th, and with five mortars from the new town the 17th. On the 26th they opened a battery of ſeven guns and five mortars to the weſtward, at the diſtance of about eight or nine hundred yards; and on the 30th one to the north, of nine guns, and three mortars, at the diſtance of ſeven or eight hundred yards, and another to the north-eaſt of four guns, at about the ſame diſtance.

The beſieged had loſt the greateſt part of their black forces by deſertion, when they imprudently defended the out-poſts; which, conſidering the weakneſs of the garriſon, ſhould have been abandoned and deſtroyed. Thoſe who remained in the place, as well Europeans as others, were little diſpoſed to the obſervance of diſcipline and regularity; for having too free acceſs to the ſeveral ſtorehouſes of arrack and other ſtrong liquors, they were never in a condition properly to do their duty.

The enemy had not yet made any breach, but had diſmounted and diſabled thirty guns and carriages, and ruined ſeveral of the works, ſo that many of the parapets and platforms were deſtroyed by the ſhot and ſhells. The tanks, or reſervoirs, had ſuffered by the bombardment, ſo that there was no water to be had fit for uſe, but what came out of the covered way; from which they could only be ſupplied by night; and the beſt well there was likewiſe deſtroyed by a bomb. They were alſo ſhort of ammunition, having expended a great deal in firing away inconſiderately, before the enemy had begun to make their approaches.

This being the ſtate of the place on the 1ſt of June, at the requeſt of Major Polier, the Deputy Governor

 called

called a council of war; and it was unanimously agreed to surrender upon the following articles of capitulation.

ARTICLES OF CAPITULATION.

By which Alexander Wynch, Esq; acting Deputy Governor, and the Gentlemen of the Council at Fort St. David, in behalf of the United Company of Merchants of England trading to the East-Indies, are willing to surrender the Fort of St. David to M. Lally, Lieutenant-General in his most Christian Majesty's Service, and Commander in Chief of the French forces in India.

I. That all acts of hostility shall cease, until the articles of capitulation are agreed upon and signed.	I. Accordè.
II. That the Deputy Governor shall march, at the head of the garrison, drums beating, colours flying, out of the barrier into the advanced covered way, where the garrison shall ground their arms, and surrender themselves prisoners of war, on condition of being immediately exchanged for an equal number of his Most Christian Majesty's subjects, now prisoners in our garrisons on the coast of Coromandel; and, as soon as the exchange takes place, the garrison to be transported to such of our settlements as our President	II. Accordè pour la partie des honneurs, mais la garnison sera conduite prisonnier a Pondichery, ou elle restera jusques a ce qùelle soit changèe contre pareil nombre d'officiers et soldats de S. M. T. C. actuellement au Trichinopoly, et quand les dits soldats de S. M. T. C. seront arrivez a Pondichery, la ditte garnison de Fort St. David, sera conduitte a Madrass ou a Devicota a mon choix.

and

and Council of Fort St George may think proper.

III. That Fort St. David, and its out-works, ſhall not be demoliſhed; but remain in their preſent ſtate, until the concluſion of a peace.

III. Je ne m éngage a rien ſur cet article c'eſt le ſort de la guerre qui en decidera, et non celuy de la paix.

IV. That all the garriſon, including all the ſubjects of his Britannick Majeſty, as well civil as military, ſhall have all their baggage and effects ſecured, with liberty of removing and diſpoſing of them as they ſhall think proper; and that they be ſupplied with boats or proper conveyances for that purpoſe.

IV. La garniſon, et les ſujets de ſa Majeſté Britannique n'émporteront avec eux que leur vaiſſelle, chevaux, hardes ou meubles domeſtiques, et il leur ſera fourni des batteaux pour les tranſporter a Pondichery, bien entendu que les dits batteaux ſeront viſité par un commiſſaire de nos troupes, en preſence d'un commiſſaire Anglois nommez a cet effet.

V. That the Deputy Governor and Council, and the Company's ſervants be exchanged againſt an equal number of the French Eaſt India Company's ſervants made priſoners by Admiral Watſon at Chandernagore; and, until the exchange takes place, that they be permitted to go on their parole to Fort St. George.

V. Accordè, quoy que je n'aye pas lieu d'etre content de Mr. Wynch, qui a manqué a ce qu'il me devoit ainſi qu'aux regles de la guerre.

VI. That the ſick in the hoſpital which cannot be removed, have liberty to remain, under the care of

VI. Accordè.

 their

their own ſurgeons; and that they be ſupplied with proper proviſions and neceſſaries on paying for the ſame.	
VII. That a Capt. and fifty of the Engliſh troops ſhall remain in the Fort, to deliver it up, and that ſtrict diſcipline be obſerved, that no irregularities be committed; and, after the ſurrender, to take the fate of the reſt of the garriſon.	VII. Un officier, et dix hommes, ſuffiront a cette operation parceque je ne feray entrer qu'une compaignie de grenadiers dans le fort juſques a ce qu'il ſoit evacué.
VIII. That two commiſſaries ſhall remain, to deliver up all the magazines, ammunition, cannon, mortars, and goods, and point out to the engineers all the mines and ſubterraneous works.	VIII. Accordè.
IX. That no Company's ſervant, civil or military, be removed from the coaſt of Coromandel, until the the exchange ſhall take place.	IX. Accordè mais ceux qui s'en abſenteront ſans un paſſeport de moy, ſeront traittez comme eſpions.
AR. WYNCH. P. POLIER DE BOTTENS. RICH. FAIRFIELD. Fort St. David, 2d June 1758.	LALLY.

Separate

Separate article.

That the deserters which were in the English service at the time of the cartel settled between the Governors of Fort St. George and Pondichery, shall be deemed as prisoners; and those which have deserted since the present war, be pardoned, and return to their colours.

AR. WYNCH.
P. POLIER DE BOTTENS.
RICH. FAIRFIELD.

Fort St. David,
2d June 1758.

Accordè.

La garnison sortira a cinque heures apres midy par la porte de L'Ouvrage á corne ou elle deposera ses armes et il sera permis aux officiers militaires et civils, de rester jusques a demain dans le fort, la compagnie des grenadiers de seconde battaillon de Lorraine prendra possession de la porte de L'Ouvrage a corne, et de celle du fort qui y communique et s'y tiendra jusques a nouvel ordre.

LALLY.

The loss of St. David's gave a great and just alarm to the government of Madrass; as a much more resolute and obstinate defence had been expected, from the known bravery of Major Polier, who commanded the troops there: but it appeared, that very little care or œconomy was used in the management of their artillery and ammunition, as one officer only of that department was in the place; the men who composed the garrison were drunk and disorderly, and fully sensible of the little discipline they were under.

A court of enquiry was ordered at Madrass, to examine and report facts: Lieutenant-colonel Draper, the Majors Brereton and Caillaud composed this court.———They reported, That Major Polier's personal behaviour was much to be commended, but that he was injudicious in defending two outposts at some distance from the town, as his numbers

bers were but weak, having only two hundred Europeans and eighty invalids, and about thirty of the artillery, whom he could properly call his garrison; the seamen from two frigates which had been run on shore and burnt, made the majority of his troops: the black forces deserted in great numbers. However, it was judged that the place might have held out much longer, and that the terms on which it surrendered were shameful, as the French were not masters even of the outward covered way, had made no breach, had a wet ditch to fill up and pass, before the town could possibly be assaulted. The want of ammunition and water were urged as the principal excuses for its surrender; and that the powder with which all the mines were loaded were supposed to be spoiled by the dampness.

Major Polier, to wipe off the disgrace, was from that moment for fighting upon every occasion, whether proper or not; and, like other men in such situations, ran from one extreme to the other.

He desired to go a volunteer with Colonel Draper in the first sally made during the siege of Madrass, and was mortally wounded. He was a brave man, but very hasty, passionate, and suspicious, which oftentimes occasioned much uneasiness both to himself and every one else. He had served the company on several occasions with much reputation and conduct; and, it is thonght, the ill opinion he entertained of his garrison was his motive for consenting to the giving up of St. David's.

M. Lally's answer to the third article of the capitulation too plainly implied the inevitable destruction of the fortifications of St. David's. The works have since been blown up, and the whole reduced to an heap of ruins. The prejudice and partiality of the conquered, however they may complain, cannot justly condemn a General for an act of this nature; for, surely, the destruction of an enemy's fortress is one of the great ends of war. But the ruin of villas,

and

and the injury done to many beautiful ſtructures in the neighbouring country, will be a laſting reproach of wanton barbarity to the French. As for the devaſtations they committed in their march from St. David's, by plundering and burning the villages they paſſed through, they were immediately reſented by the people of the country. The ſufferers on this occaſion had it in their power to take their revenge, and, by cutting off the ſupplies of the army, ſoon reduced them to ſuch a ſtate that they were almoſt exhauſted by famine as they lay before Tanjore.

On the 25th of July Admiral Pocock ſailed with the ſquadron under his command, and ſtood to the ſouthward, along ſhore, with the ſea and land breezes, and anchored on the evening of the 26th off Alamparvey; and ſeeing a ſnow and ſeven chelingas near the fort, cloſe in ſhore, ſent the boats manned and armed, who burnt and ſunk the chelingas, and brought off the ſnow; the chelingas were all empty, and had been ſent from Pondichery with cannon and ordnance ſtores, which were all landed the day before; the ſnow was loaded with firewood for Pondichery.

The 27th in the evening the ſquadron got up within three leagues of Pondichery road, where the French fleet was at anchor, conſiſting of eight ſhips of the line and a frigate. Our fleet conſiſted of only ſeven ſhips, being the ſame that were engaged in the laſt action, but ſome of them now differently commanded: Captain Martin, who had before been left ill at Madraſs, now took the command of the Cumberland. Captain John Stukley Somerſet was advanced from the Saliſbury to the Weymouth, Captain Colville had the Newcaſtle, and Captain Brereton the Saliſbury. Next morning, about ten o'clock, the enemy got under ſail, and ſtood to the ſouthward with the land breeze. Admiral Pocock made the ſignal to chaſe, in hopes of being able to get up with, or weather them if poſſible, that being the moſt probable means of bringing them to action; but they kept to windward, and the next

morning

morning anchored to the ſouthward of Porto Novo. They then weighed and ſtood to windward with the land breeze, and about eight o'clock were out of ſight. At four o'clock in the afternoon, the Admiral diſcovering a ſhip in the ſouth-eaſt quarter, gave chaſe; at five ſhe hoiſted French colours, and ſtood for the land; he ſoon after run her on ſhore about two leagues to the northward of Porto Novo, and ſent the boats on board to endeavour to get her off, but finding it impracticable without loſing too much time, ſet her on fire. She proved to be the Reſtitution, bound to Pondichery from Carical, where ſhe had been ſent with ordnance ſtores and other materials for M. Lally's army. This ſhip had been ſent from Bengal laſt October with French priſoners, who mutinied, and taking the command of the ſhip from the maſter, carried her to Maſſulipatam, from whence ſhe was ſent to Pondichery; where the Governor and Council, contrary to the law of nations, made a prize of her.

On the 1ſt of Auguſt, at ten o'clock in the forenoon, the Admiral came in ſight of the French ſquadron, as they were getting under ſail off Tranquebar, and ſoon after they formed the line of battle a-head, with the ſtarboard tacks on board, and ſeemed to edge down towards him; but when he made ſail and ſtood for them, they hauled upon a wind till one o'clock, when they formed the line of battle a-breaſt, and bore down upon him with an eaſy ſail. At half an hour paſt one he made the ſignal, and formed the line of battle a-head with the ſtarboard tacks on board, and ſtood to the eaſtward under his topſails, ſometimes the main-topſails ſquare, as the ſhips ſtations required in the line, waiting for the enemy. At five the enemy's van was abreaſt of our center, at about two miles diſtance; they ſtood on till their van was abreaſt of ours, and kept about the ſame diſtance till half an hour paſt ſix, when they hoiſted their topſails, ſet their courſes, hauled cloſe upon a wind, and ſtood

to

to the ſouth eaſt. The Admiral then made the ſignal for our van to fill and ſtand on, and make ſail to the ſouthward, keeping in a line till twelve o'clock; and judging by the enemy's ſignal guns that they had tacked, made the ſignal to wear, and ſtood to the weſtward after them, but at daylight ſaw nothing of them.

In the evening he deſcried four ſhips in ſhore to the north-weſt, on the 3d at five in the morning, ſaw the enemy off Negapatam, about a league to windward, formed in the line of battle a-head with their ſtarboard tacks on board. He made the ſignal and formed his line a-head, with the ſtarboard tacks on board, and ſtood to the ſouthward with an eaſy ſail. At ſeven o'clock, obſerving the enemy kept their wind, he made the ſignal for making more ſail, in order to get to windward, for that was the only probable means of bringing them ſoon to action, as they ſailed better in general than our ſquadron. At half an hour paſt eight they began to edge down upon him, and at nine were at about three miles diſtance. He then made the ſignal for the Elizabeth and Tyger to change places in the line, apprehending the enemy's leading ſhip in the van might be an over match for the Tyger. At ten the enemy bore away, and ſteer'd for our rear, by which means on the ſea breeze ſetting in about noon, our ſquadron got the weather gage of them; and at twenty minutes after the Admiral made the ſignal for the leading ſhip to ſteer ſix points from the wind, and at one o'clock got near, within random ſhot of them; their line being then in the form of a half moon, their van and rear being to windward of their center. About twenty minutes after, obſerving the enemies ſhips in the van begin to fire on the Elizabeth, who was within muſket ſhot of her, the Admiral made the ſignal for battle, and began the engagement with the whole ſquadron. Mr. D'Aché, who was then under his topſails, in about ten minutes after ſet his foreſail, and

and kept more away ; his ſquadron did the ſame, and continued a running fight in a very irregular line till two o'clock, when the Comte de Provence, the Enemies leading ſhip put before the wind, having cut away her mizen-maſt on account of taking fire in the mizen top eight minutes after ; the Zodiaque and the ſhips a-head of her kept more away, and were immediately followed by the ſhips in the rear, which continued in an irregular line a-breaſt, and increaſed their diſtance a little from us ; on which Admiral Pocock made the ſignal for a cloſer engagement, in order for his all line to bear down as ſoon as poſſible and rake them, which was immediately obeyed ; and we were able to keep within gun ſhot of them till three o'clock, when obſerving they began to make more ſail, the Admiral hauled down the ſignal for the line, and cloſer engagement, and made the general ſignal to chaſe ; on which the enemy cut away their boats, and made all the ſail they could, and ſtood about north north weſt ; our ſquadron purſued them with all the ſail they could croud till near dark, when the enemy got off by outſailing us, and we were obliged to leave off chaſe; and at eight o'clock anchored off Carical.

The damage we received was, chiefly in our maſts and rigging, for the enemy's endeavours were (as in the former action) to diſmaſt us. They did not appear to have ſuffered much in their rigging, but they had about five hundred and forty men killed and wounded ; among the latter were Mr. D'Aché and his Captain. There were no more than one and thirty Engliſh killed, and one hundred and ſixteen wounded. Commodore Stevens received a muſquet ball in his ſhoulder, Captain Martin a wound in his leg by a ſplinter.

The Admiral had the pleaſure, on this occaſion, of writing to the board of Admiralty, that the behaviour of all his officers and men was, in this action, entirely to his ſatisfaction.

On

On the 5th the Queenborough intercepted a French ſnow, named the Ruby, of about one hundred and twenty tons. She ſailed from the iſlands the 1ſt of July, and was bound to Pondichery, loaded chiefly with ſhot and medicines.

The French ſquadron continued in Pondichery road from the laſt action till the 3d of September, when they ſailed and proceeded directly to the iſlands. Upon advice of their being ſailed, the Admiral ſent the Queenborough off Ceylon; for as it was very early in the ſeaſon, it was probable they might have been gone to cruize thereabouts. She returned the 17th without ſeeing them.

The French were at this time driven to ſuch ſhifts for want of money, that on the 7th of Auguſt they ſeized and carried into Pondichery a large Dutch ſhip from Batavia, bound to Negapatam, and having taken for their own uſe all the money, to the amount of ſeven or eight lack of roupees; they unloaded the cargo and detained the ſhip. It is ſaid M. Dupleix did the ſame laſt war.

The ſquadron having embarked Major Caillaud, with two hundred and fifty men (from Trichinopoly) at Negapatam, landed them at Madraſs the 25th of September. They remained there, taking in their water and ſtores, till the ſeaſon called upon them to proceed to Bombay. The Admiral, before his departure, in conſequence of an application from the ſelect committee, landed a Captain and Lieutenant, with a hundred and three marines, as a farther ſtrength to the garriſon.

The French had withdrawn their whole garriſon from Seringham, except a few Sepoys, who were left to deliver the place to the Maiſſoreans: but Captain Caillaud, before his departure from Trichinopoly, had made a diſpoſition for attacking it before the troops arrived from Maiſſore; and the French Sepoys, upon his approach, abandoning the place, he took poſſeſſion of it without any loſs.

Upon

Upon the news of the ſurrender of Fort St. David, the troops which garriſoned Arcot, Chengalaput and Carangoly, were ordered into Madraſs; for it was expected the enemy would attack that place next; but in caſe they ſhould go to the ſouthward, and inveſt Davecotah, which proved to be their deſign, the Chief there had orders to abandon the place, and if the the ſquadron ſhould be near him, to go on board with his garriſon, in order to come to Madraſs, if not, to retire to Trichinopoly; which laſt he effected without any difficulty, by paſſing through the Tanjore country. The French took poſſeſſion of Davecotah; and ſoon after M. Lally croſſed the Coleroon with his whole army, except ſeven or eight hundred men, which he left with M. Soupire; a part of theſe afterwards were ſent to the ſouthward. M. Lally marched by Tranquebar, and the Danes ſupplied him with ſome ammunition and field pieces. He then encamped in the bounds of Negapatam, and demanded of the Dutch a loan of money, and alſo of cannon, ammunition and proviſions; but the Dutch denied that they aſſiſted him with any thing, except proviſions, of which they ſent him continual ſupplies during the expedition to Tanjore. The firſt act of hoſtility committed by the French againſt the Tanjoreans, was the taking poſſeſſion of Nagore, their ſea port, and ſelling to Mr. Fiſher, Colonel of Huſſars in their ſervice, for two lack and a half of roupees, all the effects that were found there belonging to the country merchants from all parts of India, to the value, as was cómputed, of twice that ſum.

From Negapatam they marched to Trivalour, a pagoda, about fifteen miles on the road to Tanjore; there they eſtabliſhed a magazine, and from thence ſent deputies to demand of the King of Tanjore the payment of a note forced from him by the French army, and Chunda Saib, in the year * 1749, for ſeventy lack

* See page 44.

lack of roupees; and alſo a free paſſage through his country, for the army to march againſt Trichinopoly. Captain Caillaud, who commanded in that place, being directed by the Preſidency of Madraſs to uſe all his endeavours to prevent the King of Tanjore from being frightened into a compliance with theſe demands, had the ſatisfaction to find that the behaviour of the French at Nagore had provoked the King's reſentment, and he had already ordered Monagee with his troops to oppoſe the march of the French. One thouſand Sepoys, and five hundred Colleries, were ordered to reinforce the Tanjoreans from Trichinopoly; but as it was not ſafe to part with any Europeans from that garriſon, Monagee, with his country forces alone, was obliged to retreat before ſo large a body of regulars. It was then to be feared that they would be reduced to the neceſſity of an accommodation; but ſuch was the opinion they had formed of the French, that they choſe rather to ſtand a ſiege, than enter into a treaty with them. M. Lally, preſuming that the conſtancy of their reſolutions might be ſtaggered by their late repulſe, ſent an embaſſy to Tanjore of two officers and a prieſt, to demand a paſſage for his army, by the neareſt road to Trichinopoly; deſiring at the ſame time the aſſiſtance of his troops. The King conſented to a paſſage through his country, but not by the road which was deſired. He alſo offered ſome money, but indeed a very ſmall part of the ſum demanded. As for the aſſiſtance of his troops, he abſolutely refuſed it. With this anſwer the officers returned to camp, leaving behind them the prieſt, who ſome time after aſked a ſecond audience; at which, he not only inſiſted on the two former articles, but added to them the immediate payment of five lack of roupees. The King expreſſed great ſurprize at the preſumption of the prieſt, but conſented to give four lack; out of which he required ſome deduction ſhould be made for the damage done at Nagore; and as to the other articles, he gave the ſame anſwer as before. While they were treating, the army ſtill kept advancing; which juſtly increaſing the ſuſpicions of the King, he ordered the prieſt to be diſmiſſed. At night the advanced guard of the French army fired ſome ſhot againſt the town, from two pieces of cannon, which of conſequence put an end to all negotiation.

The French loſt every day ſome Europeans, by the frequent ſallies from the town; at length they brought up their whole force againſt it, which amounted to two thouſand three hundred and ſeventy regulars, and a great number of diſciplined Sepoys. The artillery which was already brought up, conſiſted of fourteen field pieces, and three of heavy cannon, and they had fourteen more at Trivalour. All this was not leſs yet ſufficient to deject the Tanjoreans. At this very time they had ſent out a body of horſe, joined with the Polygars of the country, to cut off the communication of the French with Carical; and had already deſtroyed ſome convoys of proviſions. Captain Caillaud having had the good fortune to keep the King of Tanjore ſteady to his true intereſts, had alſo prevailed on Tondeman to aſſiſt with all his people on this important occaſion. A large body of his Peons entered Trichinopoly to reinforce that garriſon, while a conſiderable party adapted for that ſervice, were employed to harraſs the enemy and intercept their ſupplies. For theſe, and his former ſervices, the Governor and Council thought proper to reward Captain Caillaud with a Major's commiſſion.

M. Lally finding that he did not advance his affairs by hoſtilities, and being in great want of proviſions, and other neceſſaries, attempted once more to perſuade the King of his ſincerity, by ſending him an officer of ſome rank and quality, and alſo a prieſt, who were at once appointed to conclude an agreement, and to remain as hoſtages. By this ſtep he prevailed ſo far, as to receive in hand fifty thouſand roupees, and a promiſe of four lack, as alſo of a ſupply of three hundred

hundred horſe, and one thouſand Colleries; and on his part he engaged immediately to remove the army from before the town. M. Lally making no motions towards the performance of this part of his agreement, the King of Tanjore refuſed to let the two hoſtages return; and declared they ſhould not leave the town till the French army broke up from before it. This produced ſeveral meſſages, and, at length, it was agreed that the King ſhould forthwith ſend him the three hundred horſe and Colleries; and for his own ſecurity he might detain the gentlemen till the army was moved three days march from the place. The advantages of this treaty were all overthrown by the haſty temper of M. Lally, who ſeeing only fifty of the three hundred horſemen arrive in camp, ordered them all into confinement; declaring aloud, that as the King had not kept his word in ſending the full number engaged for, he would keep thoſe he had priſoners till he ſhould receive the whole.

The king upon this confined the two hoſtages, and would not ſend any more men till his people were releaſed. On the other hand M. Lally, pleaſing himſelf with the thoughts of his having brought up all his heavy cannon, and erected batteries, while he was amuſing the king a negotiation, began to fire upon the town, and had even made a conſiderable breach, when the Tanjoreans, determined on a general ſally. This they executed on the 9th of Auguſt, with ſurpriſing ſucceſs: for it will appear ſurpriſing that a body of country troops, although their number in horſe, Sepoys and Colleries was exceeding large, ſhould make any impreſſion upon ſo ſtrong an army of Europeans, and diſciplined Sepoys, as M. Lally had under his command, ſupported by a large train of artillery. They attacked at once the French camp and batteries, killed about one hundred Europeans, took one gun, one tumbril of ammunition, two elephants, and ſome horſes; blew up four tumbrils of ammunition, and then returned into the town.

M. Lally quitting at once all his designs, retreated towards Carical, leaving his guns spiked upon the batteries. The Tanjoreans did not pursue him till the morning, when they came up with him upon his march, cut off fifty more of his men, and took two pieces of cannon and two mortars. The rest made their retreat to Trivalour, and from thence to Carical; and about the end of the month, the greatest part of the troops, and M. Lally himself, returned to Pondichery. M. Soupire arrived there a few days before, after making a march towards Wandewash, and back by the way of Alamparvey.

They moved again about the beginning of October, and took possession of Arcot; they then returned, and having taken Tripassore, continued some time at Conjeveram, collecting ammunition and stores, till they were joined by M. De Bussy, with a body of three or four hundred foot and as many horse, from Golconda. Having also retaken Trinomalay, they shewed by their motions a design upon Chengalaput; advancing towards that place with three or four hundred Europeans, five hundred Sepoys, and five pieces of cannon; but were prevented by the arrival of four companies of Sepoys. This reinforcement came came very opportunely for the preservation of a post of so much consequence, as it covered all the countries on this side the Pollar; and, when in possession of the enemy, would expose even our own limits to incursion, be a harbour for deserters from our own garrison, and prevent supplies of firewood, grain, and other provisions, from coming into the town. For these reasons it was resolved, that the present garrison of nine companies of Sepoys, with a serjeant, corporal, and twelve gunners, should be reinforced by a detachment of seventy Europeans. This was the more readily determined, as there would be no expence of transporting stores, the pay of the Sepoys would be no more there than at Madrass, and yet their force would be sufficient to resist any sudden assault. The enemy, if they resolved to take the place,

must

muſt have been under a neceſſity of bringing up their whole army, or at leaſt a conſiderable part of it, and alſo a train of battering cannon, with proportionable ſtores: all which would be attended with ſuch an expence and loſs of time as they would probably think more than equal to the benefits ariſing from the conqueſt of the place. The juſtneſs of theſe concluſions appeared in the end; for the enemy, influenced by the ſame reaſons, waved their deſigns upon the place, which, it is to be ſuppoſed, they heartily repented during the ſiege of Madraſs. Captain Preſton was ordered to take the command of the fort, and to repair the works: he ſoon put it into ſuch a ſtate as made it defenſible againſt a coup de main, and by that means ſecured it till ſuch time as M. Lally heard of the arrival of Colonel Draper's regiment on the Malabar coaſt, and then he haſtened every thing for the immediate attack of Madraſs.

Colonel Draper himſelf arrived in ſeptember, with part of his regiment; and about the middle of October it was determined that he ſhould march with a battalion of our troops as far as Wandelour, while Colonel Lawrence took poſt with another at the Mount, to be in readineſs to ſupport the former. This was done to make the enemy cautious of bringing a heavy train on this ſide of the river; and by the check it gave to their motions, ſecured an opportunity of ſupplying the garriſon of Chengalaput with the needful ſtores.

In the mean time Iſouf Cawn was ordered to march towards them from Trichinopoly; and he accordingly ſet out the 20th of November with two thouſand well diſciplined Sepoys, and two light field-pieces. In his way he took Ellavanaſore.

The Nabob having recommended to the Governor the engaging a party of Marattas, as the moſt effectual method of preventing the enemy from tranſporting their artillery by land for the ſiege of Fort St. George, a propoſal was ſent to Morarow ſoon after the loſs of St. David's; with which he complied, and engaged to ſend his Vakeel to Madraſs to ſettle the terms. According to their dilatory way of proceeding the Vakeel did not arrive till October; it was then agreed that Morarow ſhould ſend two thouſand horſe to our aſſiſtance; that five thouſand roupees ſhould be advanced at Royal Cherow, a place near Tripety, for the expence of five hundred horſe, which were to march upon the firſt notice, ſo as to arrive at Chengalaput in twenty-five days from the time the Vakeel ſhould leave Madraſs.

That ten thouſand roupees, for the expence of the other fifteen hundred horſe, ſhould be paid at Guttee, from which place they were to ſet out, and arrive at Chengalaput in forty-five days from the time the Vakeel ſhould leave Madraſs; and that ten thouſand roupees ſhould be paid on the arrival of the ſaid two thouſand horſe at Chengalaput. The twenty-five thouſand roupees advanced as above to be deducted out of the allowance to the troops of half a roupee per day each horſeman, which was to commence from the day of their arrival at Chengalaput.

The Vakeel further deſired an allowance might be ſettled to the Sardars (or Commanders of the troops) and alſo for each horſe which ſhould be killed in our ſervice in the time of action; and it was accordingly agreed that an allowance of thirty roupees per day ſhould be made for all the Sardars and Jemidars; and that for a Sardar's horſe killed in battle one thouſand roupees ſhould be allowed, and four hundred roupees for each horſe belonging to the reſt of the troops.

Intelligence being received that M. Lally had been reinforced by the daily junction of conſiderable parties, it was thought no longer adviſeable to truſt a part of our force at ſo great a diſtance as Wandelour; therefore Colonel Draper was deſired to return to the Mount, as ſoon as he ſhould hear that the ſtores, for the protection of which he remained till then in thoſe

thoſe parts, were ſafely arrived. Colonel Draper accordingly moved from Wandelour the 11th of November, and joined the other battalion at the Mount.

This place, of which mention has been already made, and which will hereafter frequently be ſpoken of, is an eminence, properly called St. Thomas's Mount, from an ancient tradition, that the Apoſtle St. Thomas had preached the goſpel to the Indians on that ſpot. He has always been conſidered as the tutelar ſaint of the place, and at this day a Portugueze prieſt officiates in a chapel dedicated to him, which ſtands on the top of the mount. It is juſtly eſteemed for the goodneſs of the air, and the pleaſantneſs of the ſituation, on which account a number of villas have been built by the gentlemen of Madraſs, with gardens all ſurrounded with brick walls breaſt high. In this ſtation, which is about nine miles from Fort St. George, the two battalions remained till the 6th of December; when Colonel Lawrence receiving intelligence of a great augmentation of the enemy's force at Wandelour, ſent his Aid de Camp to Fort St. George, to deſire he might be reinforced with as many more men as poſſible. Accordingly a party was ordered, and marched that afternoon at five o'clock; but at the ſame time the Governor was deſired to write to Colonel Lawrence, to remind him that the utmoſt caution was neceſſary at this important criſis; and that it would be too hazardous to venture an action, unleſs upon terms of the higheſt advantage.

Colonel Lawrence having received the Governor's letter, and at the ſame time hearing the enemy was in motion, and conſidering the weak ſtate of the garriſon, ordered three companies of infantry to march to the little Mount with the two twelve pounders, as if to reinforce the party cantoned there; but at the ſame time they were directed to march to Madraſs. Theſe motions were made the 7th, and now the danger of Chengalaput being removed, and that fort having received all its ſupplies, the reaſons for maintaining the poſt at the Mount no longer ſubſiſted: therefore it was determined to draw the whole force nearer to the garriſon; and accordingly the enemy having advanced within ſight of the Mount in the afternoon of the 9th, our army retired that evening to the Choultry-plain, and there encamped.

The French army under the command of M. Lally, encamped at the Mount, and their advanced guard took poſt at Marmelan.

The enemy having marched from the Mount, the 12th in the morning, appeared about day-break upon Choultry-plain. Our army after about two hours cannonading, retired into the garriſon, and the enemy encamped upon the ſpot which our troops abandoned, about a mile and a half to the ſouthward. At the ſame time their advanced guards took poſſeſſion of the Garden-houſe, and the neighbouring village, in order to inveſt the town. The whole force of the enemy was three thouſand five hundred Europeans, two thouſand Sepoys, and as many horſe.

Nothing of any conſequence paſſed the next day, which was chiefly ſpent in reconnoitring; this occaſioned a few ſhot to be fired, but without much effect.

Three poſts which we held in the Black Town were reinforced, not with a deſign to make an obſtinate reſiſtance, but to retard their progreſs as much as poſſible, and then retreat towards the Fort in ſuch a manner, as to run no riſque of being cut off.

Early in the morning of the 14th of December, M. Lally marched in two columns to attack, and take poſſeſſion of the Black Town, whoſe large extent made it impoſſible for our ſmall force to diſpute it with the enemy; there had been poſted only two or three picquets in ſuch parts as were neareſt to Fort St. George. Upon M. Lally's approach, they made a haſty retreat towards the Fort, and increaſed the general confuſion, which at firſt was but too viſible;

occaſioned

occaſioned by the numbers of black people, women and children, who came thronging towards the fort for protection. It appeared neceſſary to do ſomething immediately, to reſtore the ſpirits of the garriſon; and to convince the enemy that we were not to be taken ſo eaſily as they had been taught to believe. Colonel Draper imagining that the moſt probable means of producing this effect might be by making a ſally, and diſlodging the enemy, whilſt they were yet unſettled, and perhaps plundering; for indeed their apparent contempt of the garriſon, and known want of diſcipline, ſeemed to invite to the undertaking, reſolved to offer himſelf to command a party for that ſervice. He communicated his thoughts to the Governor and Colonel Laurence, to whoſe ſuperior authority, and great judgment, he paid the utmoſt deference. They were both of his opinion; and, according to his requeſt, gave him five hundred men and two field pieces. At the ſame time one hundred and fifty men under Major Brereton, marched at ſome diſtance upon Colonel Draper's right flank, to obſerve Lally's brigade, and prevent their coming upon them from the north part of the Black Town, by which they had entered.

The men marched out of the garriſon with great reſolution; and had their regularity and obedience to orders been equal to their ſpirits, much might have been done; for the French ſuffered our people to form upon their left flank, miſtaking them for Lally's brigade. The fire of our artillery loaded with grape, ſoon convinced them of their error; they immediately fell into the greateſt confuſion, abandoned their cannon, and thought of nothing but ſaving themſelves. Had a proper advantage been made of this critical moment, the conſequence might have been fatal to the enemy. Colonel Draper's exhortations to the ſoldiery, to ceaſe firing, and puſh the broken remains of the French with fixed bayonets, were quite ineffectual; though he himſelf advanced forwards to ſet them

the

the example. But as he was followed only by four grenadiers, being unſupported, he was obliged to retire; for of the four brave fellows who went on with him, two were killed, the other two dangerouſly wounded.

Colonel Draper's march, poſitions, and retreat, were as follows. The Colonel proceeded through the ſtreet till he came to where he perceived ſome of the enemy, and received a ſcattering fire. To check them he left two platoons, and marched on with the reſt to where he had a fair view of the Lorraine regiment and Indian battalions in the flank, for they expected him in another ſtreet a little higher up, and had pointed four guns in that direction. Our cannon began to play briſkly with grape, and with the muſketry made ſuch havock among the enemy, that they ſoon fell into confuſion, and ran a-croſs the ſtreet under cover of ſome huts.

Colonel Draper then advanced towards their guns (from which they had only fired three ſhot) and exchanged a piſtol with the officer, who offered to ſurrender them; and had there been any men to bring them off, they would have been taken: but our troops having, like the French, thrown themſelves in among ſome old walls, and under cover of houſes, gave the enemy time to rally; and confuſion became ſo viſible among our people, that Colonel Draper thought it moſt prudent to retreat, but unfortunately about eighty of his men not paying a due regard to the motions of the reſt, (which might be owing to the black drummers having run away, who ſhould have beat the retreat,) were ſhut up by the enemy in a ſquare, and taken priſoners. Colonel Draper being joined by Major Brereton, continued his retreat with little loſs to the Fort, notwithſtanding the regiment of Lally came from the Armenian church to the little bridge, and, with two pieces, fired grape at our troops paſſing along, but they moſtly fell ſhort.

Could

Could regularity and obedience to the officers orders have been preſerved among the men in this ſally, it might in all probability have prevented the ſiege of Madraſs, and have ended in the total overthrow of the Lorraine regiment, and the two battalions of India; as it was, they had thirty officers or more killed and wounded, and near three hundred men. The Count D'Eſtaing, a Brigadier General, was taken priſoner in the beginning of the action. Our loſs was Major Polier mortally wound d; Captain Paſcall ſhot through the body; Captain Hume mortally wounded and taken; Captain Lieutenant Bilhock killed; Lieutenant Elliot ſhot through the body; Lieutenant Smith wounded and taken; Lieutenant Blair wounded and taken; Enſign Cook wounded and taken; Enſign Chaſe mortally wounded and taken. Our loſs of men was one hundred and three taken, of which nineteen were wounded, about fifty were left dead on the ſpot, and the ſame number came in wounded; ſo that we ſuffered a diminution of more than two hundred men, and nine officers.

In the beginning of December Major Caillaud, from his known intereſt and influence with the country powers, was ſent with letters from the Preſidency to the King of Tanjore, Tondeman, and the other Polygars in that part of the country, in order to procure aſſiſtance from them, with which the Major was to join Captain Preſton and Iſouf Cawn, and take the command of that party.

The danger both from the enemy and the ſeaſon were no ſmall objections to this undertaking; for as it was extremely difficult to guard againſt the former, the danger of the latter was not leſs to be apprehended, ſince it was the very height of the Monſoon; and there was no way of going to the ſouthward but by ſea in an open boat, within reach of many garriſons which the enemy now poſſeſſed on the coaſt. The Preſidency having duly weighed all theſe difficul-

ties,

ties, were determined at length to hazard them on account of the uncertain ſtate of affairs at the court of Tanjore, and the danger of its falling under the abſolute influence of the French. Major Caillaud was therefore ordered to proceed, which he did in the manner aforementioned; and having overcome all the difficulties which of conſequence attended ſuch a voyage at that ſeaſon, he landed at the Daniſh Fort of Tranquebar; from whence as ſoon as the rains abated, which was about the middle of December, he reached Tanjore. He found, at his arrival, the face of that court ſtrangely altered. Monagee, the Prime Miniſter, and all his adherents had been turned out, and a new ſet placed at the head of affairs. When he ſpoke to the King, he found him ready to conſent to every thing he aſked; but as ſoon as his back was turned, the new council overſet it all, by perſuading the King it was better to wait and ſee the event, and then ſide with the ſtrongeſt, according to the policy of eaſtern courts. This did not abſolutely diſcourage the Major, who perſevered till he was promiſed a body of five hundred horſe, which were to be got ready as ſoon as poſſible. While this was in agitation, the Major received the firſt advices that the enemy had inveſted Madraſs, and were in poſſeſſion of the Black Town. The King had alſo received the account; and as it is natural to ſuppoſe, the example of Fort St. David, which had been ſo ſoon given up, and his fears for the fate of the only ſettlement we had left, created new doubts and new delays. Major Caillaud was put off from day to day, but at laſt he carried his point, though for no more than three hundred horſe, which the company was to pay. He had collected about the ſame number of Sepoys, all choſen men, well diſciplined and active, and ſo they proved; for in eleven days they marched two hundred and fifty miles, and got to Chengalaput. There he heard the party he was to command was at the Mount. Upon this

in-

intelligence, the Major, leaving his men who were too much fatigued to follow him at that time, took fresh horſes, and arrived at the Mount about two in the morning.

Here he found that Iſouf Cawn, (who after ſeveral encounters had ſtill fifteen hundred Sepoys, and two thouſand horſe) had been joined by Captain Preſton, with part of the garriſon of Chengalaput, conſiſting of about ſix hundred Sepoys, ſixty Europeans, and ſix three pounders. There were alſo added to this party, Captain Vaſſerot, with ten of his troopers. The occaſion of his coming was the immediate neceſſity of ſupplying this little army with money, which being indiſpenſibly urgent, Captain Vaſſerot offered himſelf to lead ten of his troopers, who ſhould each carry a bag of a thouſand pagodas to the camp, and this he moſt gallantly effected.

With this body of troops Captain Preſton had frequently cut off the enemy's ſupplies by land, and ſurprized one convoy with a number of ſpare arms and tents for three thouſand men, which he took. He kept M. Lally in conſtant alarms, by continually moving about, but ſtill keeping ſo near him, as greatly to diſturb and harraſs him. Captain Preſton had repulſed ſeveral detachments from the French army; and, in one action, which had been very ſevere, had the good fortune to diſperſe great part of the black forces, which obliged the enemy to move off towards Arcot to recruit; from whence they had returned with an augmentation of the country troops three days before Major Caillaud joined the army.

Captain Preſton's activity, as it merited all the acknowledgments which were beſtowed on it by the garriſon, was in effect, the greateſt interruption to the beſiegers. At length Mr. Lally, thoroughly ſenſible of the check this flying camp could at all times give to his deſigns, reſolved to ſend ſuch a force againſt them as would cruſh them effectually. He uſed to

ſay

ſay they were like the flies, no ſooner beat off from one part, but they came to another. For this purpoſe he ordered a detachment of ſix hundred Europeans, fifteen hundred Sepoys, all his cavalry, (which conſiſted of near three hundred European dragoons, and about one hundred Huſſars, with a thouſand Marattas,) and ten pieces of cannon, to attack them. Notice being received before day that a large body of the enemy were advancing, Major Caillaud prepared to receive them, by poſting his troops to the beſt advantage. It has already been ſaid, that round the bottom of the Mount, many incloſures had been made, and gardens laid out, ſurrounded with brick walls parapet high not to intercept the proſpect. On the Mount, and behind theſe garden walls, the Major had made the beſt diſpoſition he could of his infantry. His cavalry were all drawn up on the right, being the beſt ſpot where they could act. As the day broke the enemy appeared in ſight, and the cannonade began. Their cavalry was inclining very faſt to the right, about three hundred paces from the front of our left. It was moſtly their Europeans who puſhed on that ſide, while their Sepoys endeavoured to occupy all the banks and places on our left, for there they could be under cover. Their cavalry made a ſtand as ſoon as they came oppoſite to ours, to whom orders were immediately ſent to charge. They readily obeyed, and moved on with a good countenance for about one hundred yards; but finding the enemy were advancing upon them with the ſame intention, they were ſeized with a pannick, and fled with the utmoſt precipitation.

The French cavalry who were foremoſt, purſued a little too eagerly a large body that were preſſing through an interval, which is between the village and the foot of the Mount. They were ſoon ſtopped by a diſcharge from a party of foot, which had been poſted there. Upon this they retreated, not without

loſs.

loſs. Things went on a little better on the left. The village was well defended, and two or three times taken and re-taken, till at length, after three hours diſpute, it was loſt by the raſhneſs of the officer who commanded that poſt; who ſeeing the enemy retreat in ſome confuſion, indiſcreetly purſued, not obſerving a party that was ready to ſupport them. This party ſtopped him, and drove him out of the village which he never after could recover.

Thus ſtood affairs about ten o'clock in the morning, when the enemy, tired of attacking, contented themſelves with cannonading us ſeverely, in hopes, by that means, they might diſlodge us: but though our people ſuffered a good deal, they could not prevail; therefore about four they made another attack; but the garden walls were ſo lined with muſquetry, that it quite diſpirited them, and they began to think of a retreat. At the cloſe of the evening they moved off their artillery, and ſoon after their whole body, and left us maſters of the field of battle, where we remained about two hours, which was all the time that Major Cailland thought proper to ſtay, having no ammunition left for his artillery, and very little for the muſquetry: he therefore moved off in the night towards Chengalaput, the only place from whence he could be ſupplied. The loſs of the enemy in this affair was about one hundred and ſeventy Europeans killed and wounded, and near three hundred Sepoys.

In the beginning of the ſiege, M. Lally, who had made very free with the Dutch ever ſince his arrival in the country, was pleaſed to give them another proof of what little reſpect he paid to their neutrality, by ſeizing the Fort of Sadraſs, a ſettlement of theirs on the coaſt, equally diſtant from Pondichery and Madraſs. Being reſolved to make a magazine of this place, he turned out the Dutch ſoldiers and garriſoned it with French, giving for a reaſon, that he did it

to

to prevent our taking it, which he pretended was our design.

When it had passed into the hands of our enemy, Major Caillaud thought proper to lay a plan for surprizing it, and disposed his march so as to be there about four o'clock in the morning. The darkness of the night deceiving the guides, he could not reach Sadrass, which is twenty miles from Chengalaput till late next day, which effectually disappointed his scheme, as he was not strong enough to attempt it by open force. An accident, however, made him amends for his disappointment. At night his patroles brought him one of Mr. Lally's messengers, with a letter directed to the Governor of Pondichery; which is so extraordinary, that it would be unpardonable not to insert it with the other occurrences relative to the siege of Fort St. George; especially as it is a most authentic proof that the garrison owed their deliverance to their own bravery and conduct, and not to the arrival of the ships, since they did not appear till after the writing of this letter.

Au camp devant Madras le 14 Fevrier, 1759.

Monsieur,

"Il auroit un beau coup a faire ici, il y a un Vaisseau en cette rade de vingt pieces de canon chargè de toutes les richesses de Madras et qu'on dit y devoir rester jusqu'au vingtieme: l'Expedition vient d'arriver mais M. Gorlin n'est point homme a l'attaquer, puis qu'il l'a déja fait fuir une fois. Le Bristol d'un autre cotè a peine a paru a St. Thomé que sur la nouvelle vague des treize Vaisseaux de Portonove il a pris l'epouvante et aprês avoir debarqueê les munitions dont il étoit chargé, il n'a seulement pas voulu se donner le tems de reprendre douze pieces de son canon qu'il nous avoit preté pendant le siege; si j'etoit juge du point d'honneur des officiers de la compagnie, je le casserois comme un verre, ainsi que quelques autres: or la Fidelle

Fidelle ou ce même Briſtol, avec ſes douze canons de plus, ſuffiroit pour ſe rendre maître du batiment Anglois, s'il pouvoit parvenir a gagner le vent ſur luy dans l'obſcurité de la nuit. Maugendre et Tremillier ſont, dit on, trés bons et ne duſſent ils ſervir qu'au tranſport de deux cens bleſsés que nous avons ici, le ſervice ſeroit d'importance.

" Nous ſommes toujours dans la même poſition: la breche faite depuis quinze jours, toujours à quinze toizes du mur de la place, et jamais ne levant la tête pour la regarder. Je compte qu'en arrivant à Pondichery nous chercherons tous a apprendre quelqu'autre metier, car celuy de la guerre exige trop de patience.

" De quinze mille Cipayes dont l'armée eſt censée composée, j'en compte a peu près huit cens ſur la route de Pondichery, chargé de ſucre et de poivre et autres marchandiſes, quant aux Coulis, ils ſont tous employés pour le même objet depuis le jour que nous ſommes arrivé ici.

" Je prendrai mes meſures dés aujourd'huy pour embraſer la ville noire et faire ſauter la Poudriere, vous n'imaginerez jamais que ce ſont cinquante deſerteurs François et une centaine de Suiſſes qui tiennent en arret deux mille hommes des troupes du Roy et de la Compagnie qui ſont encore ici exiſtant, malgré les états ſurchargés que chacun fait ici a ſa guiſe de la boucherie qu'on en a fait, et vous ſerez encore plus ſurpris ſi je vous diſois, que ſans les deux combats et les quatres battailles que nous avons eſſuyé, et ſans les deux batteries qui ont eté manquées ou faites de travers, pour parler plus clairement, nous n'aurions pas perdu cinquantes hommes depuis le commencement du ſiege, juſques aujourd'huy. J'ay ecrit à M. de Larche, s'il perſiſte a ne point venir ici, tirera de l'argent qui voudra des Poleagáres, ce ne ſera pas moy, et je renonce, comme je vous en ai deja prevenu il y a plus d'un mois, a me meler directement ni indirectement de tout ce qui peut avoir raport a vôtre adminiſtration, ſoit civile ſoit militaire; I'irai plus tôt commander les Caffres de Madagaſcar que de reſter dans cette Sodome, qu'il néſt pas poſſible que le feu des Anglois ne detruiſe tôt ou tard au defaut de celuy du Ciel.

I'ay l'honneur d'être, &c.

LALLY."

"Je ſuis obligèr de vous prevenir que Mr. De Soupire ayant refusè de prendre le commandement de cette armée que je luy ai offert, et auquel il eſt autorisè par le double de mes expeditions que la cour luy avoit remis, il faudra que malgrè vous, avec le conſeil, vous vous en chargiez. Je m'engage ſeulement a vous la ramener ſoit a Arcatte, ſoit a Sadraſs, envoyez y vos ordres, ou portez vous y vous même pour la Commander, car je la quite en y arrivant."

Tranſlation of an intercepted letter from M. Lally to M. de Leyrit.

From the camp before Madraſs, the 14th of February 1759.

"A good blow might be ſtruck here: there is a ſhip in the road, of twenty guns, laden with all the riches of Madraſs, which it is ſaid will remain there till the 20th. The Expedition is juſt arrived, but M. Gorlin is not a man to attack her; for ſhe has made him run away once before. The Briſtol, on the other hand, did but juſt make her appearance before St. Thomas, and on the vague report of thirteen ſhips coming from Porto Novo, ſhe took fright; and after landing the proviſions with which ſhe was laden, ſhe would not ſtay long enough, even to take on board twelve of her own guns, which ſhe had lent us for the ſiege.

"If

" If I was the judge of the point of honour of the Company's officers, I would break him like glaſs, as well as ſome others of them.

" The Fidelle, or the Harlem, or even the aforeſaid Briſtol, with her twelve guns reſtored to her, would be ſufficient to make themſelves maſters of the Engliſh ſhip, if they could manage ſo as to get to windward of her in the night. Maugendre and Tremillier are ſaid to be good men; and were they employed only to tranſport two hundred wounded men, that we have here, their ſervice would be of importance.

" We remain ſtill in the ſame poſition: the breach made theſe fifteen days; all the time within fifteen toiſes of the wall of the place, and never holding up our heads to look at it.

" I reckon we ſhall, at our arrival at Pondichery, endeavour to learn ſome other trade; for this of war requires too much patience.

" Of fifteen hundred Sepoys which attended our army, I reckon near eight hundred are employed upon the road to Pondichery, laden with ſugar, pepper, and other goods; and as for the Coulis, they are all employed for the ſame purpoſe, from the firſt day we came here.

" I am taking my meaſures from this day to ſet fire to the Black-town, and to blow up the powder-mills.

" You will never imagine, that fifty French deſerters, and one hundred Swiſs, are actually ſtopping the progreſs of two thouſand men of the King's and Company's troops, which are ſtill here exiſting, notwithſtanding the exaggerated accounts that every one makes here, according to his own fancy, of the ſlaughter that has been made of them; and you will be ſtill more ſurprized, if I tell you, that, were it not for the two combats and four battles we ſuſtained, and for the batteries which failed, or, to ſpeak more properly, which were unſkilfully made, we ſhould not

 have

have loſt fifty men, from the commencement of the ſiege to this day.

"I have wrote to M. de Larche, that if he perſiſts in not coming here, let who will raiſe money upon the Polygars for me, I will not do it: and I renounce (as I informed you a month ago I would do) meddling, directly or indirectly, with any thing whatever that may have relation to your adminiſtration, whether civil or military. For I had rather go and command the Caffres of Madagaſcar, than remain in this Sodom; which it is impoſſible but the fire of the Engliſh muſt deſtroy, ſooner or later, even though that from Heaven ſhould not.

I have the honour to be, &c. &c.

Signed, LALLY.

P. S. I think it neceſſary to apprize you, that, as M. de Soupire has refuſed to take upon him the command of this army, which I have offered to him, and which he is impowered to accept, by having received from the court a duplicate of my commiſſion, you muſt of neceſſity, together with the council, take it upon you. For my part, I undertake only to bring it back, either to Arcot or Sadraſs. Send therefore, your orders, or come yourſelves to command it; for I ſhall quit it upon my arrival there.

Upon the receipt of this letter, which was immediately ſent to Madraſs, Major Caillaud marched back again, to be near the fort, and to be ready for what ſervice might be required of him. M. Lally had not time to execute his intentions of burning the Black-town, for on the 16th in the evening, at length arrived our long expected reinforcement: on their firſt appearance he got ready for his march, and the next morning he was near out of ſight. He left behind him all his heavy cannon, about forty pieces, and a large quantity of ſtores. And thus Madraſs was ſaved, after a ſiege of nine weeks, to the great honour of of all those who were concerned in its defence. Colonel Lawrence, who commanded, had the satisfaction to see all his services in the country crowned by a most honourable defence of the capital. His judgment and experience were nobly seconded by the spirited conduct and bravery of Colonel Draper and Major Brereton. The Governor, Mr. Pigot, contributed also greatly to their success, by his prudent management of the stores, and the regularity which he enforced: he frequently visited all the posts, and was very liberal to those who distinguished themselves upon the works.

The sum of fifty thousand roupees had been promised, as an encouragement and reward to the garrison for their good behaviour, in case they should, by their resistance, oblige the enemy to raise the siege. Immediately upon the going off of the French the money was issued, and two thirds distributed among the Europeans, and one third to the Sepoys and Lascars.

A siege which occasioned the exertion of so much judgment, skill, and indefatigable activity, as were shewn by the Governor and military officers, deserves to be recorded in the most circumstantial manner; especially as the minute operations for the defence of the works will be instructive to all who either practice or delight in the art of fortification. It is very fortunate that a particular detail of all the operations has been delivered, in a journal taken upon the spot by the principal engineer: such a curiosity must be the more acceptable, as it is certainly rare; there having been few instances, of late years, of any place which has been so seriously attacked, and so obstinately and successfully defended.

A JOURNAL OF THE Siege of Fort St. George,

Begun the 12th of December, 1758.

Ended the 17th of February, 1759.

By J. CALL, Chief Engineer.

Thurſday, Dec. 14. 1758.

DURING the ſally, the enemy fired ſeveral ſhot from ſome field-pieces into the fort, but did no damage; they were quiet the remaining part of the day, and we only fired a few cannon on thoſe places where we imagined they were at work. No Europeans, were to be had this day for a working party; but I luckily collected a few Cooleys, brick-layers, and other artificers, and ſet them to make a dam in the gut, to ſhut up the communication between the water in the river and ditch, leſt the enemy ſhould cut the dam, which kept up the water two feet or more, and thereby drain ſo much off. This was a piece of work on which much depended,

 and

and which, with difficulty, I got finiſhed before night. I alſo ſet up a palliſadoe in an opening under the ſouth flank of the royal baſtion, and removed ſome gabions, faſcines, and other materials, which were in the way on the ramparts.

Dec. 15.] Several deſerters have come in from the enemy this day and yeſterday; who all agree in their reports, that the enemy loſt many men and officers in yeſterday's action. The enemy fired not a ſhot this day from cannon or ſmall arms, nor have they been perceived any where at work; though we have many informations of their erecting batteries, and fire now and then at the ſuſpected places. By the enemy's reconnoitring and ſituation, it ſeems as if they intended to attack the north front by the north-eaſt angle; I therefore conſidered what was moſt neceſſary to be done to oppoſe them, and reſolved to compleat the blind which I intended before the old north-eaſt baſtion, and to erect a faſcine battery on the glacis, before the ſhoulder of the eaſt face of the north-eaſt baſtion; which battery is to reach quite down to the ſurf, and intended to ſweep under the bank of the glacis, which had been cut down by the ſea, and afforded good cover for an enemy. It was alſo determined to ſet up a palliſadoe before the ſea gate, and to cloſe up with ſtones the ſmall gate on each ſide the large one. A Captain, two ſubalterns, and one hundred men, beſides all the blacks I could collect, were ordered on the above ſervices, with Meſſ. Leigh, Eiſer, and Stevenſon, engineers.

16.] A party of forty volunteers, and forty Sepoys, were this night ordered out, about eleven o'clock, to give the enemy an alert, and, if poſſible, nail up ſome pieces of cannon which it was ſaid were in the Black-town; but they had not proceeded much beyond the glacis, before the enemy's advanced centinels gave their fire, and alarmed their whole force; ſo that our party, on hearing the drum beat to arms, retired.

retired. A party of one hundred ſoldiers, and ſixty-five Sepoys, were this morning paraded for working, and diſtributed chiefly to the woıks mentioned yeſterday, which were nearly finiſhed by night ; and the palliſadoe round the ſea gate Viranda entirely compleated. Faſcines were alſo laid round, to form a parapet on that part of the ſea gate battery which had none ; and ſome ſand bags laid for the ſame purpoſe in part of the barbet battery towards the ſea : earth was alſo laid on the arch over the magazine under the old weſt curtain, and over part of the hoſpital adjoining.

Dec. 17.] Laſt night, about eight o'clock, the enemy gave an alarm, by a few men coming near the glacis and giving their fire : nothing remarkable happened afterwards. This day one hundred men, two Serjeants and one corporal, were on a working party, but the weather being very rainy, little was done ; they, and about two hundred blacks, were chiefly employed on the two batteries mentioned the 15th, to the north-eaſt, in thickening the parapets of the old north-eaſt baſtion, compleating the barbet battery with ſand-bags, laying earth on the hoſpital arches, fixing a palliſadoe to cloſe the communication from the covered way on each ſide to the north ravelin, and repairing ſome cheeks of the embraſures on the demi-baſtion, beſides other trifling repairs. The enemy was not for certain perceived to be any where at work, though ſingle guns (by way of ſecurity in the night, I ſuppoſe) were perceived in ſome of the ſtreets. Very few ſhot were fired by us, and fewer ſhells, during this day. Several deſerters came in laſt night and this evening ; from whom we learnt the enemy had ſome mortars arrived at St. Thomé. The Governor this day gave it out publickly, that he would diſtribute fifty thouſand roupees among the garriſon five days after the ſiege was raiſed, or the French beat off.

Dec.

Dec. 18.] This morning it was perceived that the enemy had thrown up a breaſt-work from the houſes on the beach near the Old-town, to the ſea ſide; but whether intended for a battery, or to prevent any attempt of ours on their flank, cannot be ſaid, though I believe the latter; becauſe the trench from whence the ſand has been taken is on the ſide of the enemy, contrary to the method of making batteries; ſomething of the ſame kind was perceived in the ſtreets next the ſea, but no guns or mortars have yet been fired, or appeared ready for that purpoſe On our ſide, a very few ſhot or ſhells were thrown. The gentlemen of the ſquadron, and marines, who had been on board a Dutch ſnow the 12th, with an intent to go and take the French ſhip which is coming up with their ſtores, were this morning landed, being very unwilling to undertake the expedition; and having been detained by bad weather ſo long in the road, that it was ſuppoſed they were diſcovered. Captain Jaſper, who was to have commanded them, appeared much chagrined at his diſappointment; and indeed with reaſon, for had he ſucceeded (and I think he had great reaſon to expect ſucceſs) nothing could have done us more ſervice, or the enemy greater prejudice. A great many people were perceived to day moving from the Mount towards the Black-town, which we apprehended were bringing up the enemy's ſtores. It is very remarkable, that thirty-three deſerters have come in from the enemy ſince their arrival, and not one man has deſerted from the garriſon, or been ſeen in liquor.

A Peon came in and informed us, that Captain Preſton had ſent out a party, under Lieutenant Airy, from Chengalaput, which had intercepted a convoy of the enemies ſtores, conſiſting of tents ſufficient for the covering of three thouſand men, a large mortar, which he ſpiked up, and burnt the bed; two guns, which he alſo ſpiked, and burnt the carriages;

riages; and some ammunition, which he carried off, with all the bullocks. No deserters last night; which is owing, I suppose, to some extraordinary care or orders of M. Lally's. The working party was this day about one hundred men, without officers; they, and the black artificers, were chiefly employed in fixing a pallisadoe before the new battery by the sea side; opening another embrasure in that battery; cutting down the high bank which the surf had made by washing away the glacis; thickening the parapets of the old north-east bastion; repairing the embrasures with palmeiras, which had been blown away by our own guns; laying earth on the hospital; fixing a pallisadoe on the gorge of the north ravelin, and repairing a dam which had been made in the gut to the north-west to keep the water in the ditch; but the water had rose so high by the last four day's rain, that half the dam was destroyed, and the water considerably sunk.

Dec. 19.] This morning we perceived that the enemy had thrown up another breast-work, about sixty feet in length, and one hundred yards, or more, advanced before that thrown up the preceding night; both these retrenchments terminate on the surf, the latter at the distance of about five hundred yards from the north-east saliant angle of the covered way, and seem rather intended to cover a guard posted there to prevent a surprize, or desertion, than for any annoyance to the fort; however, from the proceeding of the enemy it appears as if they intended to advance along the beach, and attack the demi and north-east bastions; it is therefore resolved that platforms should be raised in the covered way, sufficiently high for field-pieces, on covered way carriages, to fire over the parapet. It is further resolved to raise a parapet of the demi bastion, near the saliant angle, two or three feet higher than the rest, and to erect a traverse on the east wing, to prevent an enfilade; to raise the blind

blind before the north eaſt baſtion, ſo high as will juſt admit the guns to fire over it at the enemy's works; that the paſſage between the upper and lower flank of the demi-baſtion ſhould be cloſed in the ſecureſt manner; and that the north ravelin ſhould be put in the beſt condition of defence we might have time or workmen to do. The working party, of about one hundred men, with ſuch Cooleys, Pallankeen boys and others, as I could collect, were ſet about the ſeveral articles above mentioned. The firing on our ſide was little to-day, except from wall pieces; and not even a muſket ſhot came from the enemy. Five Chelingas were ſeen this morning going out of St. Thomè bar, and ſailed to the ſouthward, as we apprehended for ſtores.

Dec. 20.] Laſt night the ſubaltern on duty in the north eaſt angle of the covered way, with twenty-one men and ſome Sepoys, was ordered to ſally on the retrenchment and works, which we ſuppoſed the enemy was carrying on; but it being rather too light they were diſcovered, and the Sepoys taking a pannick at a party of ſix horſe which appeared, ran away, which intimidated the Europeans, and they, after giving their fire, retreated alſo. We had one European killed and two dangerouſly wounded: the Sepoys ſuffered in the ſame manner. The Commandant of Sepoys, Jemaul Saib, being deſirous of attacking St. Thomé laſt night, was ſent out with ten companies of Sepoys; but taking the direct road over the Long-bridge, he was diſcovered by a few French Sepoys, at Mr. Powney's houſe, who gave him their fire; upon which moſt of his people threw down their arms, which induced him to return. The enemy, we could perceive this morning, had been at work laſt night, and to appearance, had drawn about fifty yards of a parallel weſtward from their moſt advanced breaſt-work. They alſo had got a gun behind their firſt breaſt-work, and from

from thence fired ſeveral ſhot at the ſnow which lay in the road under dutch colours: the ſhot moſtly fell ſhort, one or two entered and killed a Laſcar; the veſſel therefore weighed and ſtood a little farther off, as well to avoid any annoyance from thence, as to prevent a ſurprize. A boat appearing off St. Thomè, a party of marines was ſent in three moſſulas to fetch her in, which they effected, and found her to be a boat going from Sadraſs to Pulliacat. The working party was this day one hundred men, and employed as yeſterday, except on the old north-eaſt baſtion, the parapets of which were finiſhed. This afternoon the artillery ſerjeant on the north-eaſt baſtion, intending to fire a diſcharge of grape at ſome of the enemy which appeared at their breaſt-works, unfortunately ſome ſcattering ſhot fell into the covered way, and miſerably wounded three Cooleys who were rolling gabions upon the work there carrying on.

Dec. 21.] Laſt night we fired ſhot or ſhells every eight or ten minutes, on the place where we ſuſpected the enemy would work, and by that means prevented them from doing any thing more than throwing up an imperfect communication from the firſt to the ſecond breaſt-work. Advice being brought in laſt night, that the enemy had two guns at Trivelcane, and very few troops at St. Thomè; about ten o'clock in the morning near one thouſand Sepoys, with twenty Europeans, commanded by Town-Major Bannatyne and Enſign Crawley, went along the beach to the ſouthward, croſſed the bar, and marched through the village beyond the Governor's gardens, where they ſurprized two or three ſmall Sepoy guards, intercepted ſome letters, took a trooper's horſe and arms, and one ſoldier priſoner; but on advancing down the road towards Mr. Turing's Houſe, they perceived a body of Europeans and blacks which they were not a match for, and therefore returned by the way they went.

went. From the fort-houſe we perceived, in the mean time, two guns perhaps eighteen or twenty-four pounders, the one drawn by bullocks, fifteen or eighteen yoke, and the other by bullocks and Cooleys, paſſing from Chindadree pagoda acroſs the plain towards the Potters village; but being near enough for our great guns to reach them, ſome ſhot were immediately fired from the Nabob's baſtion, and Lawrence's, which ſoon made the Cooleys and bullocks halt, and one of the guns ſinking almoſt to the axletree at the ſame time, it was propoſed to ſend a party of three hundred Sepoys, with a promiſe of a great reward, to nail up the cannon; they were accordingly ſent out at the weſtern gate, on the ſight of which, and our firing, the bullocks were caſt off from the guns, and the Cooleys ran away, leaving the guns alone. Our firing, and the motions of the Sepoys, alarmed the enemy in the Black-town, ſo that about two hundred European horſe were ſent in all haſte towards the guns, and their foot marched to the weſt ſide of the Black-town to ſupport them; this we perceived, and fearing the Sepoys might be cut to pieces, ſent orders for them not to advance beyond the little bridge leading from the iſland to Egmore. The enemy, by theſe motions, were entirely alarmed, and we had an opportunity of firing many ſhot at their horſe and foot, but the execution was uncertain. About four or five in the evening more Cooleys and bullocks were ſent to fetch their guns, and, in ſpite of our fire carried them off towards Mr. Turner's garden-houſe; where, I believe they were left for that night. The working party the ſame number, and employ, as yeſterday. Mr. Lally, by a letter to Count D'Eſtaing yeſterday, complained that Iſouf Cawn was committing great devaſtations to the ſouthward, near Pondichery; and that he ſhould in conſequence, be obliged to make repriſals round Madraſs.

drafs. As to that, he cannot well depopulate the county more than he has; for, though he may be obliged to retreat, it will be long e'er Madrafs recovers its inhabitants, and becomes a place of trade.

The Nabob and his family were laft night fent on board the fnow in the road, with Mr. Norris, a counfellor, and failed this morning for Negapatam, where it is propofed the Nabob fhall land, and proceed to Trichinopoly, from whence he may have an opportunity of difturbing the enemy.

Dec. 22.] Laft night the fire of fhot and fhells on the enemy was as the preceding nights; the working party was one hundred men, and employed, in general, as before, except thofe on the demi baftion, where the traverfe being finifhed, they were fet to repair fome part of the face and front of two merlons, which had fallen down in the late rains.

23.] The cannon or mortars fired laft night every ten minutes on the enemy, in order to difturb their workmen, who by morning had deepened and lengthened their parallel a few feet; they had alfo been at work on their line of communication between Mutall Pettah and Peda Naigues; but had not finifhed either that, or the work they had been on elfewhere. About eight or nine in the morning a fail appeared to the northward, and anchored about eleven o'clock; fhe faluted with nine guns, which we anfwered with nine fhot into the Black-town. This fhip was the Thames, from Vizagapatam in four days; and brings us advice of Colonel Forde having given the Marquis de Conflans, and the French forces under him, an entire defeat; the further particulars of which muft be deferred till the letters are landed, the wind blew fo frefh, and the furf ran fo high, that no boat could get off. However, that the enemy might not wait fo long, we had all the troops in the covered way, and gave

gave them a Feu de Joye from our muſketry, and three times ſeven twenty-four pounders with ſhot into the Black-town. The working party conſiſted of one hundred men, and were employed on the blind before the old north-eaſt baſtion, and on raiſing the faces of the royal to the diſtance of forty feet on each ſide the ſaliant angle, to prevent the effect of ſhot en ricochet; for which purpoſe the firſt embraſures on each ſide were cloſed. The black artificers and Cooleys were employed on the north lunette, raiſing the parapets, lining the embraſures with Palmeira trees, and cloſing the communication with the covered way by a traverſe an each ſide.

Dec. 24] The wind blowing very hard laſt night, it was apprehended the Thames, which had only one anchor and cable, and drove, would have been obliged to quit the road, however, ſhe rode it out; but on ſeeing the veſſel to the northward weigh, and ſtand towards the road, ſhe weighed alſo, and ſtretched off to ſea; in the afternoon ſhe attempted to fetch in again, but by the evening was out of ſight to the ſouthward. The French veſſel came oppoſite the north end of the Black-town and anchored. The fire of ſhot and ſhells laſt night, on ſuch places as the enemy was ſuſpected to be working at, was ſomewhat more frequent than the preceding evening: and, by what we could diſcover, they had only enlarged their parallel a little, and placed a few timbers within to keep up the earth. The working party was about one hundred men, and was employed on the blind before the old north-eaſt baſtion, and in raiſing the parapets of the royal baſtion. The blacks, in facing the embraſures of the northern works, and finiſhing the traverſes of the north ravelin. This evening a ſoldier was executed for attempting or threatening to ſhoot his ſerjeant. Finding that the ſoldiers on the working parties were ſomewhat unruly, the Governor gave out immediate orders, that all people ſo em-

ployed

ployed ſhould ſtrictly obey my own, or aſſiſtant's orders; and, in caſe of neglect, be ſeverely puniſhed. Mr. Catsford, a Company's ſervant, was appointed a practitioner, and to rank as Enſign.

Dec. 25.] The fire from our cannon and mortars was kept up laſt night as in the preceding. The enemy, as far as we could perceive, had done very little work, and that only in deepening and thickening their parallel. Our working party was one hundred men, beſides ſome few Laſcars, about thirty Coolees, and fifty or ſixty Sepoys: they were in general employed as yeſterday, except in removing the faſcine parapet on the ſea gate redoubt, and making another of gabions. The traverſes of the north lunette were this day finiſhed, and the platforms of the demi baſtion were lengthened eight feet with ſleepers and plank. The Governor, Colonel Lawrence, and the principal officers having aſſembled this evening, and conſidered ſome intelligence they had received of the enemy's erecting batteries, agreed that the moſt neceſſary work at preſent was finiſhing the traverſes on the royal baſtion, and then cloſing the opening between the north-weſt curtain and the blind before the Mint ſally-port; alſo erecting a traverſe in the covered way, before the north face of the royal baſtion. Laſt night, as a Corporal was patroling on the glacis to the northward, a Sepoy fired at him, and ſhot him dead. In the forenoon a ſloop appeared to the northward, ſtanding this way; but the French ſhip hoiſting her colours when the ſloop came a-breaſt, and firing two guns, the ſloop anchored, and ſoon after ſtood in under the ſhips's ſtern; ſhe had white colours, but appeared to be a Moors ſloop.

26.] The fire of our artillery and mortars was laſt night pretty ſmart, and we could not perceive that the enemy had done any thing on the north-eaſt; on the weſt, in the ſtreet near the old hoſpital, we perceived they had placed ſome green gabions, and made a

 work;

work; but it appeared to be rather a retrenchment a-crofs the ftreet than a battery. The working party was one hundred foldiers and about three hundred Sepoys, who, with the Lafcars and Cooleys, were employed on the works determined on yefterday, and on thofe in hand before.

Dec. 27.] Laft night a pretty brifk fire was made from the cannon and mortars on the north front, on fuch places as it was imagined the enemy were at work in. The working party was one hundred Europeans and two hundred and fifty Sepoys, employed as yefterday.

28.] In the morning we difcovered that they had thrown up fome earth among the ruins of the houfes a little to the north of the old hofpital, and that they had thickened and heightened their work to the north fo much, that it had more the appearance of a battery than a parallel. The working party, of one hundred Europeans and three hundred Sepoys, was employed on the works already mentioned.

29.] The fire of fhot and fhells, to the north and weft, was pretty brifk in the night; however the enemy had been hard at work, for in the morning we perceived they had formed a ftout parapet to the weftward, and, to appearance, had three embrafures in it, though they were not opened; the intent feems to be to fire on St. George's lunette, the bridge of communication to it, and on the bridge leading to the ifland. Their work to the northward appeared now very plainly to be intended for a battery, in which I obferved five rows of pickets, placed at equal diftances as centers of embrafures, and by the length of the work there might be room for four more; the direction feems to be againft the north face of the old north-eaft baftion, and the north face of the demi baftion. About ten in the morning we perceived a red flag on the Mount, inftead of the white there before; fo that we concluded Captain

Captain Preston had possession of that post. The enemy this afternoon appeared to be working on their battery to the northward, and several pieces of timber and plank were seen carrying thither for platforms towards the evening; I also discovered a large mortar placed in the communication between the two breast-works first begun by the enemy near the sea-side, from which it is to be supposed they will soon salute us. About sun-set a deserter came in from the enemy's works to the northward. The working party of Europeans was one hundred men, and about three hundred Sepoys, employed as yesterday.

Dec. 30.] The fire of our artillery and mortars was last night pretty brisk, and, I believe, prevented the enemy from working much; for I could not perceive any great addition to the northern battery. To the westward I observed they had thrown up a good deal of earth behind some old walls, which seems to be intended as a battery to enfilade the north face of the royal bastion, and the covered way before it; but the form is as yet very incompleat. In the night a boat came from Sadrass, and brought some letters of the 18th from the French army to Pondichery, which Captain Preston had intercepted. From these we learn, that the enemy lost by our sally on the 14th two hundred and twenty men and thirty officers, killed or wounded. In short, they acknowledge themselves to have been thrown into the greatest confusion, and that they must have been entirely ruined had our party advanced more regularly on them, and been supported by another body to the northward. A letter from one of M. Lally's Aid de Camps to the council of Pondichery, complains much for want of money, and desires they would supply him with some, if it be but one hundred roupees, and that too chearfully; for their affairs were in a fair way, and the conquest of Madrass certain. In the morning we perceived a great ſmoke at the Mount, from whence we concluded Captain Preſton and Iſouf Cawn, with their whole force, were there. This was confirmed by an Hircar coming in at noon, with advice that there had been a skirmiſh, and ſome French troopers taken. A great number of black troops, horſe and foot, with large herds of cattle, were obſerved to come from the Mount and St. Thomè to Egmore, and two guns were ſent from the Black-town thither. Another deſerter came in this afternoon, and in the evening a flag of truce with a letter from M. Lally, complaining of our firing at his head quarters, and threatening to burn the Black-town in return: but of this he had no right to complain, becauſe he is the firſt General, perhaps, that fixed his head quarters within point-blank ſhot of the fort, and lodged a regiment, and his ammunition at the ſame place. The working party, of one hundred men and three hundred Sepoys, employed as before, except on the blind before the old north-eaſt baſtion, which was finiſhed yeſterday.

Dec. 31.] Laſt night, and towards the morning particularly, the fire from the cannon and mortars was rather ſmarter than before. At day-break a large body of Sepoys, the firſt company of grenadiers, and the troop of horſe, went over the bar to the ſouthward, and into Trivelcane village, where they ſurprized a ſmall guard or two of Sepoys, and intercepted ſeveral letters; from which we learn, that a frigate was arrived from the iſlands to Pondichery, and had brought about two hundred thouſand dollars; but no mention was made of any forces. The going out of our Sepoys gave M. Lally the alarm, ſo that three or four piquets of Europeans, and ſome European horſe, with guns, were ſeen marching from the Black-town to Egmore. A party of forty Europeans and as many Sepoys, in eight boats, were

were ſent off in the night to ſtretch a chain out to the eaſtward, leſt the boats to the ſouthward, which had brought the enemy ammunition, ſhould ſlip by and land it to the northward. Letters came in, about ten o'clock in the evening, from Captain Preſton, acquainting us, that in the morning the enemy, in number about one thouſand, black and white, under Colonel Kenelly, had about day-break advanced four guns near the Mount, and cannonaded him, which our people anſwered ſo briskly that the French retreated; afterwards they came on with two guns, which our people made a puſh at and took, killing fifteen of the French on the ſpot, and wounding Colonel Kenelly, one Captain, and twenty five men.

An artillery man and huſſar came in laſt night. In the afternoon a large ſhip appeared to the north-eaſt, and by ſun-ſet was near eaſt of the fort, with her hull juſt appearing. The French ſhip hoiſted firſt Engliſh colours, then French, and fired two guns; but the other ſhip ſtood on to the ſouthward, and ſhewed ſome colours which had a white field, perhaps Portugueſe. The enemy's works to the northward appeared to have received no addition this morning, but that to the weſtward plainly appeared to be deſigned for two batteries; one, in which three or four embraſures were formed, apparently to fire in the north-weſt lunette, and the other, of five or ſix embraſures, not yet traced, to enfilade the face of the royal baſtion, and covered way before it. The working party conſiſted of one hundred Europeans, about forty Cooleys, thirty Laſcars, ten Peons, the Meſtry bricklayers, and about ſixty Sepoys; who were all employed on the ſeveral works before-mentioned.

January 1. 1759] Laſt night, about ten o'clock, came in two deſerters, and informed us that Mr. Lally propoſed to uſher in the new year by a bombardment; however the night and morning paſſed without any fire but what was on our ſide. The enemy having made large detachments to oppoſe Captain Preſton and Iſouf Cawn, was the reaſon, I ſuppoſe, of their working very little laſt night; for I could not perceive in the morning any material alteration in their works to the north or weſt. Letters laſt night from Sadraſs inform us, that a Moors veſſel, from the Nicabars to Porto Novo, brought advice of twelve Engliſh ſhips being at thoſe iſlands, and ready to ſail for this place. The ſhip which appeared in the offing was from Macao, had touched at Maſſulipatam, where a ſhip of ours (the Hardwick) had prevented her from ſelling any thing; ſo that ſhe intends to break bulk at Negapatam, and come up the coaſt. Iſouf Cawn, we hear, has left the Mount, and is gone to Trevambore, about a league ſouth of St. Thomé; and the French, apprehenſive of that poſt, have ſent all their black troops from Egmore, and a ſtrong body of Europeans to ſupport them. The working party was one hundred Europeans, one hundred Sepoys, and the ſame Cooleys and Laſcars as mentioned yeſterday: they were employed as before, except in making traverſes before the magazine doors of the Nabob's baſtion.

Jan. 2.] Our fire of artillery and mortars was laſt night very briſk; but as ſoon as the light appeared, the enemy began to fire from four or five pieces of cannon on their weſtern battery, and one mortar; they alſo threw twelve inch ſhells from four or five large mortars placed near the weſt end of their battery to the northward. This early ſalute ſurprized us, but as we had ten or twelve heavy cannon which bore on the enemy's battery to the weſtward, two of their guns were ſoon knocked to pieces, and their merlons ſo much damaged that they withdrew their guns before eight o'clock. From their mortars they threw

threw ſhells till paſt ſeven at night, commonly four in a flight, which were in general aimed at the fort-houſe, and ſo well thrown, that two fell on the top and pierced the firſt and ſecond roof; many others fell within the ſquare, and ruined ſome of the rooms; other houſes were alſo much damaged: but, what is moſt remarkable, not one European or Sepoy was wounded by ſhot or ſhell, nor any other perſon hurt but a Dubaſh and a child or two. By letters from Captain Preſton, and alſo by five deſerters which came into us in the evening, we learnt, that early in the morning, M. Soupire, Major-general, who commanded at St Thomè, had marched a ſtrong body and attacked him and Iſouf Cawn, who lay near Trevambore, in three diviſions; that the enemy had put our firſt diviſion in ſome diſorder, taken their two guns, and ſome priſoners; but that the broken troops, having joined the ſecond diviſion, fell on the enemy in their turn, and put them to flight, killing about fifty Europeans on the ſpot, with two officers, and, if we may believe the deſerters, the troop of M. Aumont was very roughly handled, a troop of huſſars cut to pieces, and three companies of grenadiers greatly diſordered: our guns and priſoners were retaken. It was to favour this attack of M. Soupire that the enemy began their fire earlier by ſome days than they would otherwiſe have done, to withdraw our attention from what paſſed to the ſouthward. We had advice to-day that M. La Tour, under pretence of a viſit in marching from Pondichery this way, had ſeized on * Sadraſs, and put a garriſon therein; and that M. Lally had given orders for the ſame fineſſe to be practiſed on * Pouliacat. His deſign on theſe places was the reaſon, we ſuppoſe, that, in a paſſport granted ſome of our ladies, he

* Both belonging to the Dutch.

excepted their going no Pouliacat or Sadraſs; however, three boats, with ſeveral ladies in them, were ſent off to Sa iraſs without paſſports before this news arrived; ſo that we fear they will all be ſeized.

Jan. 3.] Laſt night we threw many ſhells, and fired many ſhot at the enemy's works, but they ceaſed firing after eight o'clock. In the morning we obſerved they had cloſed up the embraſures of their weſtern battery, which was much diſordered by our cannon; they had alſo added ſomething in height and thickneſs to their northern battery, but did not fire from either cannon or mortars. We obſerved this day about ſixty or ſeventy European horſe returning in a ſtraggling manner from the ſouthward towards the Black-town, and among them thirty or forty led horſes, which we imagine loſt their riders in the action yeſterday againſt Captain Preſton and Iſouf Cawn. The working party was one hundred men and about two hundred Sepoys, who were employed in finiſhing the work acroſs the gut to the northward, in making traverſes before the doors of the Nabob's baſtion, and a-croſs the ſtreets leading to the ſouth curtain, where the guards are in future to parade.

4.] Our artillery and mortars made a briſk fire laſt night on the enemy's batteries, but neither ſhell nor ſhot was returned from them; however, in the morning I obſerved they had opened the epaulment of their northern battery, and let in faſcines for the facing of the embraſures; they alſo had repaired part of the weſtern battery, where we diſcovered two guns in the morning; but on our firing a few ſhot they were withdrawn, and the embraſures choaked with faſcines. Yeſterday I drew out the following inſtructions for my aſſiſtants, dividing them into two reliefs; and this morning Meſſ. Leigh and Cotsford went on duty, to be relieved by Lieutenants

tenants Eiſer and Stevenſon to-morrow. The working party was one hundred men and two hundred and fifty Sepoys, employed as yeſterday.

"That the buſineſs dependant on the engineers may be conducted with greater regularity and care it is ordered,

"That Captain-Lieutenant Lee, Engineer in ordinary, and Enſign Cotsford, practitioner, do attend on the front attacked, together; and Lieutenant Eiſer, of his Majeſty's ſixty-fourth regiment, engineer extraordinary, and Lieutenant Stevenſon, Sub-engineer, do alſo attend the front attacked, together; and that theſe four gentlemen do relieve each other, two and two, every twenty-four hours, at the ſame time as the guard is relieved.

"That the ſenior Engineer on duty, every twenty-four hours, do make a report to me if any very extraordinary occurrence happens; that he acquaint the ſenior Engineer who relieves him, with ſuch obſervations as he has made while on duty, and with the nature of the work carrying on; and alſo reports to me, by writing, in general terms, what has been executed during his tour of duty.

"That the ſenior Engineer going on duty every evening or morning, do attend the parade, and receive the working party, which he is to diſtribute according to the orders he has received; or, if he has none in particular, in ſuch a manner as he thinks the ſervice may require.

"That the ſenior Engineer on duty, on application being made to him by any military or artillery officer, for the repairing or ſecurity of any work, do give them all the aſſiſtance he can; and he is to take care that the parapets, embraſures, platforms, and the works in general, are kept in the beſt condition poſſible. The maſter bricklayer, and maſter carpenter, have orders to follow the directions of the

the Engineers on duty, and give all the aſſiſtance they can in their branches."

Jan. 5.] Our artillery and mortars fired pretty briſkly laſt night on the enemy's batteries, but they neither fired ſhot nor ſhell, in the night or to-day; they were not idle, however, having finiſhed the facing and almoſt opened ſeven embraſures in their northern battery, where I perceived three guns in the evening, and in the morning three in the weſt battery, which were ſoon maſked or removed. To-day I again propoſed to the Governor and Colonel Lawrence erecting a battery behind the covered way in the ſaliant place of arms before the demi baſtion, and had permiſſion about ſix in the evening, and a working party of one hundred freſh men; which I immediately ſet to work under Lieutenants Eiſer and Stevenſon. This battery, of at leaſt five guns, I thought abſolutely neceſſary to render our fire equal to the enemy's; for their battery of ſeven or eight guns, fronting directly the face of the old north eaſt baſtion, will fire on the north face of the demi obliquely. To oppoſe this fire we have only three guns on the old north-eaſt baſtion, which bear direct; two in the north ravelin, fire in an oblique line; and three or four from the royal baſtion, which alſo fire obliquely, and therefore have no great chance of ruining the enemy's guns. Now the new battery I propoſe will be a direct grazing fire, and can neither be enfiladed nor beaten down, becauſe the glacis is the parapet, and the embraſures will be cut through it. The working party was one hundred men, beſides two hundred Sepoys, employed as before.

6.] Our fire from the cannon and mortars was not laſt night very briſk. The enemy, in the morning, as ſoon as they could well ſee, threw five ſhells into the town, as a ſignal for their other batteries

teries to begin; and about ſeven began to fire from ſix guns and as many mortars from their north battery, and from their weſt battery, with three guns pointed on Pigot's baſtion; and four with an howitz firing on the flank of the demy baſtion, and enfilading the covered way before the north face of the royal baſtion; from theſe batteries they continued to fire till about five in the evening, and threw near one hundred and fifty ſhells, beſides ſhot, chiefly into and over the town. The damage done the works is very trifling; but the houſes in the town, where ſhells or ſhot fell, have ſuffered much. Our fire of artillery and mortars was much ſuperior to the enemies, and, to appearance, greatly diſordered their merlons. We alſo learn by a deſerter from the enemy's artillery, that our ſhells diſmounted one of their mortars, and killed three men in the north battery. The working party was one hundred men, and chiefly employed in forwarding the battery in the north-eaſt angle: as to Sepoys or blacks, we had little or no work from them.

Jan. 7.] Laſt night the enemy threw but few ſhells, and we only a ſhot or ſhell now and then. About four in the morning we were ſurprized with the arrival of three boats, with a Frenchman in each: they were the boats which had been ſent the third inſtant with the ladies to Sadraſs. The French having ſeized that place, alſo ſeized the boats, and loading them with one hundred and fifty ſhot of twenty-four pounds, one thouſand empty cartridges, fifty ſteel caps, fifty barrels of powder, and fifteen hundred ſand-bags, ſent them back with a ſoldier in each, to the Black-town. The boatfellows, towards the morning, being oppoſite Madraſs, ſeiz'd the arms of the ſleeping ſoldiers, poured water on the locks, then tied the men, and landed the boats at our ſea gate.

The

The enemy's fire was very brisk, till five in the eveing, from their cannon and mortars, and then they were silent; in order, I suppose, to repair their works. Our works, though not much damaged, bear, however, a rough aspect, and the demi bastion, as well as Pigot's, is stuck pretty full of shot. The shells the enemy threw have greatly damaged the houses in the town, but have not hurt many people; three Europeans only being killed this day. Our working party could do nothing in the day; a few indeed attempted to work in the north-east saliant angle of the covered way; but the enemy having discovered them, fired so briskly, that Lieutenant Stevenson, who directed them, was knocked down by the wind of a shot, but only slightly hurt on the cheek; so the party returned. The enemy opened a new battery near the burying ground.

Jan. 8.] As I found the soldiers, unused to such duty, were in general extremely aukward in repairing the damaged works, I conceived that the service would be much better carried on by appointing a Pioneer company, composed of volunteers drawn from the several corps, and to do no other duty but repair the works; so that by constantly employing the same people, they might more readily execute the service they were set about. I accordingly made application, and succeeded. The company to consist of two officers, Lieutenant Meyers, and Ensign West, six serjeants, six corporals, and eighty-eight private. Two companies of Sepoys were also formed, with proper officers, on the same plan. The working party was this evening one hundred soldiers and as many Sepoys; employed in repairing the embrasures, platforms, and forwarding the battery in the covered way before the demi bastion.

9.] This morning the enemy opened two embrasures more from their battery near the burying-ground, and some earth appeared to be cast up near a little upper room houſe beyond the Pettah bridge. In the night they threw a good many ſhot and ſhells after eleven o'clock. During the day their fire was very briſk from their cannon, tho' but few ſhells were thrown by them. Ten grenadiers were poſted in the north-eaſt angle of the covered way, to fire into the enemy's embraſures; and two twelve-pounders were fired from the new battery. The working party, of one hundred men and one hundred Sepoys, with ſix artificers, were employed in repairing the embraſures, platforms, and other damages done the ſeveral works; alſo in cutting up a damaged ſtone platform on the old north-eaſt baſtion, and laying one of wood: a blind of twelve feet thick and ſeven feet and a half high, was begun thirty-five feet behind the flank of the demi-baſtion, to cover the people on that work from the enemy's ſhot which might come in at the embraſures of the flank, or en-ricochet over it; the merlon next the ſhoulder was roſe for the ſame purpoſe. In the evening two ſail appeared to the ſouthward, and anchored near St. Thomé, with white colours, being both of them ſhips.

Jan. 10.] Laſt night the enemy threw very few ſhells, and fired not many ſhot: on our ſide we were almoſt as ſilent. The two ſhips which appeared to the ſouthward ſtill remain at an anchor near St. Thomé, and, as far as we can diſcover, are French ſhips from Pondichery. Our working party was laſt night one hundred pioneers, and ſixty grenadiers, beſides one hundred and ſixty Sepoys. They were employed in compleating the covered way battery to four pieces of cannon, which were mounted before morning; in filling bags of earth at the foot of the demi-baſtion, and clearing what the enemy had beat down; in repairing the parapets of the demi, north-eaſt, royal, and Pigot's baſtions, and laying two wooden

wooden platforms on the firſt baſtion, in the room of two ſtone ones, damaged. In the night the enemy carried on part of a zig-zag about one hundred feet long, nearly weſtward from their northern battery, and taking a turn, carried another two hundred feet long, back towards the ſea ſide. They alſo drew part of a trench from the little houſe in the Pettah towards the bridge; and repaired their ſhattered merlons with ſand bags.

Jan. 11.] Laſt night the enemy were almoſt wholly ſilent with their artillery and mortars, but were not idle with their ſhovels; for in the morning we diſcovered that they had deepened their zig zags begun the preceding night to the northward, and lengthened that which ſtretched towards the ſea almoſt to the beach: they had alſo drawn their trench from the houſe, quite to the Pettah bridge, and opened a battery of two guns from the kitchen of the new hoſpital, which fired on the north-weſt curtain and the blind before the mint ſally port; but I ſuppoſe were intended to plunge into the royal baſtion, and batter the eaſt flank in reverſe. Our working party was ninety men of the pioneer company, and ſixty voluntiers, grenadiers, beſides one hundred and ſixty Sepoys employed in repairing the damaged merlons, and platforms of the north-front; diſmounting ſome diſabled guns, and making blinds before the doors and windows of the arched hoſpital under the old weſt curtain: alſo in filling ſand bags at the foot of the demi baſtion, and clearing the earth beat down. This afternoon I examined the works, as to their ſtate, and obſerved that the parapets of the north face of the demi-baſtion are a good deal ſhattered; that the brick parapet of the north face of the old north-eaſt baſtion is wholly ruined; but the wall being well covered by the blind of gabions made before it, is not much hurt. The weſt face of the royal baſtion is but little hurt below the cordon, and the right-hand face of Pigot's baſtion being built to

a

a great ſlope, the enemy's fire has had no other effect than beating the earth to its natural ſlope, which is from the extremity of the berm to the top of the parapet. The old curtain wall to the northward is a good deal ſhattered about the parapets, and moſt of the palliſadoes of the caponniere broke, by the plunging ſhot from the enemy's weſt battery.

Jan. 12.] The enemy having yeſterday brought a field piece or two near the bar, and fired a few ſhot on the people and bullocks which had taken ſhelter to the ſouthward of the fort; and there appearing to be a breaſt-work and guard of the enemy near the ſea ſide, it was determined to attack that poſt early this morning, accordingly, as ſoon as the moon was gone down, the grenadiers of the third battalion under Captain Campbell, and near one hundred men more, with three hundred Sepoys, all under Major Brereton, marched by the ſea ſide to the bar, and there received the fire of the enemy's advanced poſt; by which we had one of the grenadiers killed, and two wounded. Our people, without firing, marched on to the Governor's garden-houſe, and in a ſmall lane or ſtreet on the ſouth ſide of it found the enemy drawn up with two ſmall field-pieces, and about fifty men. The enemy fired two diſcharges of grape on our party within fifty paces; but the gunners being killed they made no other uſe of their guns: on the contrary, the piquet broke, and ran each his own way. The guns were taken and brought in, one officer and ſix men were alſo taken priſoners, and about ten or fifteen killed or left wounded on the ſpot. On our ſide we had one killed, one officer (Lieutenant Robiſon, of the grenadiers) mortally wounded, and nine men. This little affair has doubtleſs given our people great ſpirits, and damped thoſe of the enemy. A party, with an officer, was alſo ſent out in the night at St. George's gate, which advanced on the bridge leading to the Pettah

Pettah, and fired into the enemy's trench, but could not perceive any people at work. About ſeven in the evening a party of the enemy advanced towards our north-eaſt ſaliant angle of the covered way, and gave a fire thereon. In the night alſo a party of our men, with an officer, was ſent out to diſturb the workmen of the enemy's zig-zags to the northward, who advanced to their work, fired on and killed their centinel, and took a ſtand or two of arms, without any loſs. The fire of the enemy's cannon was pretty briſk yeſterday, but they threw very few ſhells, and thoſe not large. I could not perceive that they had done much to their approaches laſt night; but the merlons of their batteries ſeemed to be tolerably well repaired with ſand bags. The working party was the pioneer company, and about one hundred and ſeventy Sepoys, who were employed in making a traverſe on the north face of the demi-baſtion; carrying off the earth at the foot of it; fetching pallisadoes to ſet up in the dry ditch before the north face, and repairing the damaged platforms and parapets. On the royal baſtion old north-eaſt, and covered way battery, the parapet, the platforms and embraſures were repaired.

Jan. 13.] Laſt night about ſeven o'clock, the enemy advanced pretty near the covered way on the north-eaſt, and gave a fire of muſquetry on our people there at work. They alſo fired in the night, from their approaches, on a ſmall party of ours, poſted on the ſaliant angle under cover of a boat, and wounded three men. From the covered way and north lunette, we could plainly perceive the enemy at work near the ſea-ſide, which we endeavoured to prevent by frequent diſcharges of grape, muſquetry, and ſhells. Our working party was ſeventy-eight men of the pioneer company, and one hundred eighty Sepoys, who were chiefly employed in removing the earth at the foot of the demi baſtion, on, and the rubbiſh before the old north-eaſt baſtion, which works I was determined to repair, and ſecure as much as poſſible, ſince the enemy ſeemed to bend moſt of their fire againſt them, and direct their attack that way. I therefore raiſed, and thickened the blind before the north-eaſt baſtion, whoſe parapet was much ſhattered, and begun a palliſado at the foot of the demi baſtion ſix feet within the lunette, which I propoſe to carry quite round the flank and north face, I alſo propoſe another, between the blind and north face of the old north-eaſt baſtion. The enemy, in the night, had covered the head of their zig-zag near the ſea, by a ſmall return or crotchet beginning near the beach, and ſtretching weſtward parallel to the north front. To the weſtward, the enemy fired with four guns from the new hoſpital, but did nothing to their trench near the Pettah bridge. Their Sepoys, to the ſouthward of the bar, were at work all day in raiſing a breaſtwork for their defence, in caſe we ſhould make another attempt on that ſide.

Jan. 14.] Laſt night, as we imagined the enemy would be at work again at the crochet before their zig-zag, we began a pretty ſmart fire of muſquetry from our covered way, and frequently gave them diſcharges of grape from the north lunette and covered way battery. From the royal and demi baſtions we threw ſmall and large ſhells into their approaches and batteries, ſo that they were prevented from doing much work. By the morning, however, they had run on their return about twenty yards, and compleated what they had roughly traced the night before. Our working party, beſides ſeventy-five men of the pioneer company, was aſſiſted by one hundred and twenty men, out of the two battalions, and one hundred ſeventy Sepoys. The earth, near the ſhoulder of the demi baſtion, having formed an aſcent almoſt practicable, about an hundred Europeans, and as

 many

many Sepoys, were ſet to carry it off in baſkets or ſand bags, to repair the parapet of the baſtion above. The palliſado, begun at the foot of the baſtion, was continued near an hundred feet more. The parapet of the north-eaſt baſtion being quite deſtroyed, and that work being of the greateſt conſequence to be kept in good repair, about one hundred ſixty Europeans, and the reſt of the Sepoys under Lieut. Stevenſon, were ſet to clear away the ruined parapets, and erect others with ſand bags, gabions, and faſcines, two merlons of which were finiſhed before the morning. An old ſally port in the eaſt curtain, near the ſouth flank of the old north-eaſt baſtion, was opened for the more ready communication with the north-eaſt part of the covered way, and a door placed in it.

Jan. 15.] Laſt night a briſk fire of muſquetry, cannon and mortars was kept up from our covered way and the works of the north front, on the enemy's approaches, and prevented them from doing more than lengthening their crochet a little, and opening it in the middle, from whence they placed fifteen or twenty gabions in an oblique direction towards the ſea ſide. Our working party conſiſted of the pioneer company, the firſt company of grenadiers, and ninety men of the two battalions, beſides two companies of Sepoys. They were employed in finiſhing the parapet of the old north-eaſt baſtion, which was put in very good condition, and three guns mounted thereon; in clearing the earth from the face of the demy-baſtion, repairing the parapet, and fixing palliſadoes at the foot of it. On the royal baſtion a blind was begun to cover the three guns in the eaſt flank next the curtain from the fire of the enemy's battery near the new hoſpital, which takes it in reverſe. The embraſures of St. George's, and the north-weſt lunette, being much out of repair, a party of twenty men, and a ſerjeant, was

was ſet to repair them. The fire of the enemy's cannon was this day very briſk, and their north battery was augmented to ten pieces of cannon, with which they fired in ſalvos on the old north-eaſt baſtion, and ſoon diſmounted two of the three guns.

Jan. 16.] Laſt night a piquet of the enemy's advanced to the boats, and drove an advanced party of ours from thence. The fire of the muſquetry from the covert way, and the cannon and mortars from the baſtions and north lunette, was well kept up on the enemy's approaches. They, in return, threw a few ſhells, and fired a few ſhot into the town and works, by which one of the working party was wounded. Our working party, of ſixty four pioneers, ſixty grenadiers of the ſecond battalion, and one hundred and thirty Sepoys, were employed in repairing the parapet of the old north-eaſt baſtion, which was again compleated for three guns. In repairing, and covering by ſome gabions, the palliſado before the faſcine battery near the ſea; in clearing the earth from the foot of the demi-baſtion, and therewith thickening the blind before the old north-eaſt baſtion; repairing the parapets and embraſures above, and carrying on the palliſado below. This day the enemy threw a great many ſhells into the town, particularly the north end, and killed or wounded us more men than in any preceding day; among the reſt, two of the pioneer company were killed at their barrack door. The enemy laſt night had augmented their north battery to twelve embraſures, and fired from thence very briſkly on the old north-eaſt and demi-baſtion. They alſo filled the gabions they had left empty the night before, and advanced their work in the ſame direction about twenty yards. About ten in the morning a ſnow appeared to the north-eaſt, and anchored, on which the French frigate chaſed, and all their ſhips threw out Engliſh colours.

Jan. 17.] Laſt night an inceſſant fire was kept up with muſquetry from the covered way, and about twelve o'clock, an officer with twelve men were ſent out to fall on the enemy's workmen, which he fired on ſeveral times, but a large body advancing, he was killed himſelf, and three of his men wounded. Notwithſtanding the interruption we gave them, the enemy carried on the remaining part of their zig-zag, and covered it by a crotchet or boyau. Our working party was ſeventy ſix of the pioneer company, the firſt company of grenadiers, and twenty-four ſerjeants and corporals off duty, beſides one hundred thirty Sepoys. They were employed in repairing the parapet of the old north-eaſt baſtion, which was put in order, and a platform lengthened for three guns, the ſame number as at firſt. The blind below was thickened, and the rampart of it enlarged. The covered way battery being deemed no longer uſeful, the guns were drawn off in the afternoon, and the platforms taken up. In the night we cloſed the embraſures, and lowered the merlons into a regular ſlope. Many of the palliſadoes which were fixed in the dry ditch, having been deſtroyed by the enemy's ſhot and ſhells, were replaced, and others fixed round the flanks of the demi-baſtion; the embraſures of the demi-baſtion next the ſaliant angle were filled up, the merlons of the the three embraſures next the ſhoulder were repaired, and the parapet ſtrengthened. The earth at the foot of the face was entirely carried away.

Jan. 18.] Laſt night the enemy brought two guns down to the bar, and fired a few ſhot at ſome Sepoys of ours poſted on the oppoſite ſide. Yeſterday and this night the enemy threw a great many ſhells into the town, and ſome into the works, which did us more damage than any they threw before. The enemy, yeſterday in the afternoon, worked at thickening the ſand-bank to the right of their battery ry close to the sea, and this morning they opened three embrasures through it, which in the afternoon fired on the north-east face of the north lunette; so that their north battery now consists of fifteen embrasures. The enemy extended their parallel or crotchet at the foot of the glacis westward about fifteen yards, but in a rough unfinished manner, as indeed their whole work appears to be. Our working party last night consisted of seventy-six pioneers, the second company of grenadiers, and one hundred and thirty Sepoys, who were employed in clearing the earth at the foot of the demi bastion, finishing the pallisadoes in the dry ditch, levelling the earth in the north-east angle of the covered way, raising and thickening the blind before the old north-east bastion, and giving the parapets of that bastion an entire repair. To day the enemy did not fire from their battery near the old hospital, and the embrasures appeared closed up.

Jan. 19.] Notwithstanding the fire which we kept up last night from our musquetry, cannon and mortars, the enemy advanced by a third zig-zag across the saliant angle of the glacis. In the forenoon, the enemy fired pretty smartly from their musquetry behind their first crotchet. They also brought two heavy guns to the south of the Bar, and threw some shot into the town. Our working party last night was one officer, three serjeants, and fifty six pioneers, the first company of grenadiers, and thirty-two serjeants and corporals, who were employed in levelling the earth raised for the guns in the north-east angle of the covered way, clearing the earth from the foot of the demi bastion, carrying a pallisadoe across the dry ditch before the east wing, thickening and raising the blind, and repairing the embrasures of the north-east bastion. The enemy's shells this day set fire to the sorting warehouse, to a warehouse in Gloucester-lane, and to some salt-petre in Middlegate ſtreet, ſo that the town was on fire in three places at once.

Jan. 20.] Laſt night the enemy threw very few ſhells or ſhot into the works or town; nor did they advance their works more than by producing the third zig-zag from the ridge of the glacis obliquely to the ſea-ſide, where they crowned it by a ſmall return of four or five gabions. In the afternoon, I obſerved a few Europeans working at a barbet parapet near the fiſhers huts to the ſouthward of the bar, where the enemy had brought two large cannon, or one cannon and one mortar; for ſuch they appeared to me. Our working party was the pioneer company and one hundred and twenty Sepoys, employed in the ſame manner as yeſterday, except driving rows of picquets in front of the faſcine battery, and making a breaſt-work before the palliſadoe which ſeparates the demi baſtion from the ſecond curtain.

21.] Laſt night the enemy threw few or no ſhells, and fired leſs than in any night of the ſiege; nor did they make any apparent approach in their works. They thickened their ſecond zig-zag and crotchet, and laid ſome ſand bags for their muſquetry. Our working party conſiſted of the pioneer company, and one hundred and twenty Sepoys, who were employed in repairing the parapets and embraſures of the old north-eaſt baſtion; in finiſhing the blind for muſquetry; in clearing the face of the demi baſtions, and driving pickets in the front of, and laying faſcines on the faſcine battery; repairing the parapet and embraſures of the left face of the north baſtion, and in clearing the ſea gate of rubbiſh, and making a traverſe before the gate of the redoubt. The enemy's batteries were this day very ſilent; but they fired pretty briſkly from their trenches on ſuch of our people as appeared at the embraſures or over the parapets. The enemy's method

method of proceeding, by ſimple ſap, in ſo confined and unſupported a manner as their approaches are formed, giving great room to believe a ſally might eaſily drive them from their works, and overſet ſome of the gabions, it was determined to ſend out thirty ſoldiers and forty pioneers, to try what could be done. A little paſt five in the evening ten men and a ſerjeant went out by the ſea ſide, and an officer and twenty men went out by the barrier in the north-eaſt angle of the covered way; an engineer, with the Captain of pioneers and forty men, followed. The ſoldiers were to poſſeſs the enemy's ſecond crotchet, and cover the pioneers while they deſtroyed the lodgment forming on the ridge of the glacis. Every thing ſucceeded as we could wiſh; the enemy ran out of their ſap in an inſtant, and our pioneers, for about eight minutes, worked hard at deſtroying gabions, and ſuch things as the found. The enemy then began to collect in their firſt crotchet, and a ſignal was made for the return of our party. We loſt two Serjeants killed, and three or four pioneers wounded: what the enemy (who had moſtly Sepoys in their works) loſt, we can't gueſs; but as our cannon, mortars, and ſmall arms played briſkly upon them, before and after the ſally, they no doubt ſuffered. It was apprehended they were carrying a gallery under the glacis, in order to open the covered way by a mine; but nothing of that kind was diſcovered.

Jan. 22.] Laſt night the enemy did not advance their approaches, but worked at thickening their ſecond crotchet, third zig-zag, and raiſing the head of their ſap on the ridge of the glacis. They fired few ſhells, and thoſe chiefly into the works. During the day the enemy fired very few cannon, particularly from their northern battery, where moſt of the embraſures ſeem to be blinded. Our pioneer company having been out on a ſally we could only get a Serjeant and twelve men to work in the night, who were employed in repairing the parapets of the old north-east bastion, and one hundred Sepoys, who worked at the traverse before the pallisadoe which serves as a barrier between the royal bastion and low curtain; they also carried pallisadoes down to the fascine battery.

Jan. 23.] Last night a brisk fire of musquetry was kept up on the enemy's approaches; however, they advanced a few gabions on the glacis, almost parallel to the east face of the covered way; and they opened a battery of four embrasures in their third zig-zag, with an intent to fire on the right face of the north ravelin; but it did not answer their expectations in bearing well on that work. Our working party, of sixty-three pioneers and one hundred Sepoys, were employed in repairing the north-east bastion, in making a traverse before the gate leading into the caponniere from the low curtain; another before each of the gates which close the communication to the royal and demi bastions; also in filling sand-bags in the north east angle of the covered way, and carrying them to the several works. Two embrasures were repaired, and one platform on the demi bastion; and one platform on the north ravelin.

24.] Last night the enemy attempted to push their gabions close to our covered way, but some of our men posted there overset many, which rolled into the sea, and pulled others in between the pallisadoe. A smart fire of musquetry commenced on this occasion, and continued two or three hours, in which we lost ten or twelve men, killed or wounded. From the north-east bastion and fascine battery the field-pieces fired grape in such plenty, that seventy discharges were made out of one gun; the enemy's loss, from such a fire, must doubtless have been great, and their work appeared this morning rough and

and incompleat. Our working party was ſixty pioneers and one hundred Sepoys, who were employed in repairing the old north-eaſt baſtion; the embraſures of the north ravelin, and making a blind behind the flank of the royal baſtion; but the pioneers being ſent for to go and overſet the enemy's gabions, little work was done. We loſt of that party one killed and two wounded.

Jan. 25.] Laſt night the enemy puſhed on their approaches in a line parallel to the eaſt face of the covered way, as far as the Palmeira palliſadoe, which runs quite into the ſea; parallel to which they made a return. In the night a ſmall party of our pioneers went and pulled ſeveral of the enemy's gabions into the covered way, and a ſmall party of grenadiers alarmed them in their trenches. Our working party conſiſted of fifty-three pioneers and one hundred Sepoys, who were employed in repairing the embraſures of the old north-eaſt baſtion, in repairing the parapets and embraſures of the north ravelin; filling in the ſhell holes in the caponniere, and making a banquet behind the traverſe leading to it. About two o'clock in the afternoon it was determined to make a ſally, with twenty men of the guard behind the blind, and twenty of the pioneer company, with an intent to deſtroy the work the enemy had done the preceding night: they accordingly went out and drove the enemy from their approach behind the ſtockadoe, and our pioneers endeavoured to demoliſh their work by overſetting the gabions, and throwing the tools they found into the ſea, or our covered way. After maintaining their ground near fifteen minutes, the enemy began to grow very numerous in their crotchet on the ridge of the glacis; on which our people were ordered to retire. We had Captain Black, who commanded the twenty men, wounded through the leg, and Lieutenant Fitzpatrick of the grenadiers (of whom

twenty

twenty went out) through both his arms, two or three men and one Serjeant killed. The enemy muſt have ſuffered conſiderably from our fire, which was kept up very briſkly from the works above an hour.

Jan. 26.] Laſt night the enemy puſhed on their approaches in a line almoſt parallel to the north face of the covered way before the demy baſtion, and made a return at the end of it, to cover their flank; ſo that by the work of this and the preceding night they wholly embraced the ſaliant angle of our covered way, and conſequently made it too hazardous for us to keep troops therein. Our working party laſt night conſiſted of fifty-three pioneers and eighty-eight Sepoys, who were employed in repairing the north-eaſt baſtion, the parapet and embraſures; in repairing the embraſures and parapets of the faſcine battery, and lengthening it towards the ſea; and at the ſea gate redoubt, in ſhutting up the great gate which was damaged and very difficult to paſs, by the falling of the viranda; and opening the ſmall gate on the ſouth ſide; alſo in clearing the rubbiſh from the north flank of the battery, and filling the gabions placed on the face. To-day the enemy fired moſt of their ſhot from their ſeveral batteries into the town; but threw their ſhells chiefly towards the works on the north front.

27.] The enemy, laſt night, did nothing but widen and raiſe the work of the preceding night; which we in ſome degree impute to the detachments they made to oppoſe Captain Preſton and Iſouf Cawn, who we heard were at Ponamallé. Our working party conſiſted of forty-ſeven pioneers and ninety Sepoys, who were employed in repairing the north-eaſt baſtion; in repairing the embraſures of the flank of the royal baſtion; and in repairing the parapets and embraſures of the north lunette; they alſo worked, during the day, at the ſea gate redoubt

doubt, when the north flank was entirely repaired, and embrafures formed for four guns. In the afternoon Captain Prefton's fignal, of a great fmoke, was feen weft of Egmore, and an Hircar came in, with a report that the French had been entirely routed by our troops.

Jan. 28.] The enemy did not laft night, to appearance, work much at their approaches, owing, I fuppofe, to the extraordinary guards they were obliged to keep, on account of Ifouf Cawn, whofe horfe were yefterday very near Egmore. This morning, the French black horfe, foot, and their European cavalry, were drawn up in a line, between Egmore and Capt. Mafkelyne's gardens, and by their motions to the right and left, we expected that Ifouf Cawn was near them, efpecially as feveral fmokes were feen that way; however, nothing appeared. In the forenoon, we obferved that the enemy, with feveral yoke of oxen, intended to draw off the guns they had to the fouthward of the bar; but on our firing a few fhot, the bullock drivers and bullocks difappeared. The enemy having now furrounded out north-eaft faliant angle, and probably intending to make a battery on the glacis, it was determined to try laft night if we could pufh a mine from the counterfcarp that way. An engineer and eight men were accordingly fet to open an arch, which had been turned in the counterfcarp for that purpofe. The reft of the working party, being thirty-two pioneers and eighty Sepoys, were employed in repairing the parapet, and embrafures of the right face of the north lunette, and making a ditch before the fouth flank of the fea gate battery, in which a pallifadoe was fixed.

29.] Laft night the enemy drew off one of their guns to the fouthward, but we could not perceive that they had worked any thing at their approaches 'till two o'clock in the afternoon, when they were difcodiscovered throwing up earth through a small hole just within the banquet in the covered way opposite the stockadoe, which was placed on the eastern glacis; which makes me imagine they were working by covered sap, with an intent to open the counterscarp under cover of the saliant angle of the demi bastion, where they could not be seen from the flank of the royal, but having come too near the surface, the earth fell in, and they were discovered. Some grenadiers were immediately sent out to fire into the hole, and throw granades, which they did, and thereby stopped the enemy's working. Our working party was last night thirty-seven pioneers and sixty Sepoys, who were employed in carrying on the gallery, and in raising the right side of the caponniere, to cover our people passing and repassing to the north ravelin. Twelve men and a serjeant, with some boatmen, worked in the day at the sea gate, in raising the south flank of the battery, and filling up the useless embrasures.

Jan. 30.] The enemy were last night quite silent in their trenches, but threw plenty of shells into the town, and at the north ravelin. By their silence, and other appearances, we concluded they were making a battery some where on the face of the covered way, or carrying on a gallery towards the blind. Our working party consisted of forty five pioneers, and about seventy-five Sepoys, who were employed in pushing on the mine, compleating the right side of the caponniere, and in repairing the parapet and embrasures of the right face of the north ravelin. A sail, which had been in sight to the southward all day, came into the road towards the evening, under English colours, and proved to be the Shaftsbury, from Bombay, having been left by the other four India-men, and two twenty-gun ships, which came as a convoy, the seventh instant off Ceilon, and expected to have found them here.

This

This ſhip, being the worſt ſailor, had been an hoſpital-ſhip, and therefore brought us only the ſick, and thereby added to our diſtreſs for room.

Jan. 31.] The French frigate, laſt night, came near and received a broadſide from the Shaftſbury, and then ſailed to the ſouthward, and to-day in the afternoon returned into the road again. A little before her return, ſeveral boats were ſeen going with men to the Haarlem, a Dutch Indiaman ſeized by the French, which ſhip immediately weighed and ſtood towards the Shaftſbury, who ſlipped her cable and ſtood quite under our guns. The Haarlem fired ſeveral ſhot at our ſhip, and followed her ſo cloſe, that we tryed to reach her with our guns from the ſea line, but ſhe was at too great a range to fire with any certainty. The enemy, from their battery of two guns to the ſouthward, and one from the northward, ſtruck the Shaftſbury ſeveral times, but night coming on, ſaved her from the damage ſhe muſt otherwiſe have received. Early in the morning, the enemy opened four embraſures on the north face of the covered way before the demi baſtion, and began to fire with three guns, but the earth in the cells of their embraſures was ſo high, and the battery ſo ill conſtructed, that, after firing twenty or thirty ſhot, none of which came within ſeveral feet of the top of our parapets, the battery was ſilent, not only from its inutility, but, I imagine, ſome of the guns were diſmounted by the fire from our north-eaſt baſtion. The working party laſt night was forty-eight pioneers, twelve of which were employed in puſhing on the mine, the reſt in clearing the earth from the demi baſtion, and repairing the faſcine battery. It being alſo imagined that the enemy were puſhing on a gallery behind the counterſcarp under the narrow covered way to the eaſtward, with an intent to deſtroy our blind, or blow up the covered way, it was determined to open another gal-

lery

lery from the covered paſſage under the blind, and carry it on to meet the enemy, in caſe they ſhould advance that way.

Feb. 1.] The enemy laſt night repaired the damaged merlons of their battery, and endeavoured to lower the cells of their embraſures, from whence in the morning they fired three guns, but with little effect, and were ſoon obliged to cloſe their embraſures, as in the preceding day. The Haarlem, the enemy's battery to the ſouthward, and one gun to the northward, fired on the Shaftſbury, at intervals, all day, and have ſent ſeveral ſhot through her; we, in return, fired at the ſhip, and the enemy's ſouthern guns; in the evening, a twenty four pounder burſt on St. Thomé baſtion, and wounded ſix men, of which four were mortally hurt. The Governor being there, very narrowly eſcaped with a ſlight ſcratch. The Cuddalore ſchooner came near the road in the evening, and then ſtood away to the northward again. Our working party laſt night was fifty-four pioneers and thirty-five Sepoys, who were employed as follows: twenty-four pioneers, puſhing on our gallery, relieved each other every ſix hours, the reſt, with the Sepoys, were repairing the palliſadoe in the gorge of the north lunette, repairing the embraſures in the eaſt flank of the royal baſtion, and levelling the earth beat down on the banquets of the lower curtain. The enemy threw but few ſhells laſt night or in this day.

2.] Laſt night the enemy worked at repairing the parapet, and lowered the embraſures of their battery on the creſt of the glacis, in which they opened again this morning five embraſures, and fired with two guns on the angle of the demi baſtion, which rarely ſtruck the top of the parapet. Our working party was fifty one pioneers, and a hundred Sepoys, who were employed in repairing the faſcine battery, in ſetting up palliſadoes in the gorge of the north ravelin,

velin, and in repairing the parapets of the north-eaſt baſtion; twenty-ſeven men were employed in puſhing the gallery under the north covered way, and under the covered way near the blind. The enemy's battery, which fired a ſhot now and then from one gun, was ſilent before noon. About three in the afternoon, Captain Preſton, Iſouf Cawn, and the enemy, ſeemed to be engagad in ſome topes four or five miles north-weſt, and continued firing till five o'clock. The Haarlem and the French frigate drew off laſt night, and anchored to the northward, ſo that the Shaftſbury had only two guns from the ſouthward and one from the northward to fire on her.

Feb. 3.] This morning, about day-break, the enemy ſprung a mine behind the counterſcarp of the ditch, oppoſite the eaſt-end of the cuvette, and opened the wall about twenty or twenty-five feet, but did no other damage than wounding three or four men and an officer in the demi baſtion with bricks. The intent of this opening is not very clear, becauſe if it was deſigned as a deſcent into the ditch, it is ſo injudiciouſly made, that four guns from the flank of the royal baſtion fire directly into it; but Colonel Lawrence is rather of opinion, it was intended to deſtroy the entrance to our mine, which was but twenty feet from theirs, or that they ſprung it, thinking we were at work on the outſide; for the engineer and people at work on our mine heard the enemy very diſtinctly at work within the counterſcarp about two o'clock in the morning, and alarmed them by knocking, and calling out to bring the match that we might ſpring our mine. Our working party, of fifty-four pioneers and forty or fifty Sepoys was employed on the mine and countermine, and thickening the parapet of the demi baſtion near the ſaliant angle, which part the enemy's battery ſeems to be intended againſt.

Feb.

Feb. 4.] Laſt night, the enemy endeavoured to make their guns on the glacis bear on the demi and north-eaſt baſtions, by lowering the embraſures; but after firing a few ſhot in the morning, they cloſed them as before. In ſhort, the fire from the flank of the royal baſtion oblique, and three guns in the north-eaſt direct, is ſo ſuperior to the enemy's, that they cannot poſſibly ſtand that and our ſhells above an hour or two every morning. Our working party conſiſted laſt night of fifty-three pioneers and fifty or ſixty Sepoys, who were employed in thickening the parapet of the demi baſtion, and carrying on the two galleries. The enemy's large ſhells being all expended, is the reaſon, we imagine, that they only throw from time to time thoſe of eight or ten inch from two mortars in the crotchet at the foot of the glacis. The fire of their artillery from the ſeveral batteries, except that at the burying-ground of four guns, was alſo very ſlow. The two large guns at the bar were this morning withdrawn, and a field-piece brought thither.

5.] This morning early we were ſurprized with the ſight of ſix or ſeven veſſels under ſail, and concluded them at once to be our ſhips from Bombay, but the advance of the day ſoon diſcovered to our view the enemy's two ſhips, and five ſmall veſſels, going out of the road, and ſtanding eaſtward, and as ſoon as the ſea wind came in, they ſtood to the ſouthward. This extraordinary motion we can no ways account for, but by ſuppoſing the enemy have had advice of our ſhips being ſomewhere on the coaſt, and fearful of theirs falling into our hands, have ſent them to take ſhelter under Pondichery. A red flag was ſeen at the great mount in the morning, and a great ſmoke, ſo that we conclude Captain Preſton and Iſouf Cawn are got thither, and hope they will ſoon get nearer to us. The enemy, laſt night, fired a good deal of Muſquetry, and this morning

morning fired three or four rounds from two guns on their breaching battery, but were obliged to cloſe it immediately, and ſcarce fired a muſquet ſhot all day. The four guns at the new hoſpital were ſilent or withdrawn, and only two fired ſlowly at the old hoſpital. our working party, of fifty-three pioneers and forty Sepoys, were employed on the demy baſtion, north ravelin and galleries: yeſterday that under the north covered way fell in, and had like to have diſcovered us to the enemy, but being no further advanced than the banquet of our covered way, we turned to the right till we got into the center of the old town wall, and then advanced forward towards the enemy's battery. Indeed we imagined the gallery to have been under the parapet, and were ſurprized to ſee, by the face of the covered way, that we were not ſo far.

Feb. 6.] This morning ſix embraſures of the enemy's battery to the northward appeared to be repaired; and by their withdrawing the guns from the new hoſpital, it is ſuppoſed they intend to reſtore their firſt grand battery. Nothing elſe appeared to have been done as to their works, and their battery on the glacis was ſilent. Our working party, conſiſting of fifty pioneers and as many Sepoys, was employed in repairing the parapets of the demi baſtion, and carrying on our two galleries; thirty ſailors were landed from the Shaftſbury to aſſiſt the artillery; and the ſhip, no longer apprehenſive of the enemy, went out into deeper water.

7.] Early this morning the enemy ſaluted us with four guns and one mortar from their old grand battery, which cannot be much to the credit of the attack, thus to retreat, after having had four guns in battery five days on the glacis, The old north-eaſt baſtion, which with three guns has been maintained the whole ſiege, ſeems to be the object of their old (but once more new) battery. The angle of the demi baſtion is alſo battered from theſe four guns, and as many from the burying-ground fire on the face: ſo that the enemy have now, as it were, gone back to the ſixth of January, and have on us the following batteries; at the old hoſpital two guns plunging into and enfilading the whole north front; at the burying-ground four guns battering the face of the demi baſtion; at the grand battery four guns, firing on the ſaliant angle of the demi, and on the old north-eaſt baſtion, and one mortar, throwing ſhells of ten inches into the town. On the zig-zag which croſſes the ridge of the glacis, three mortars, throwing eight and ten inch ſhells into the demi and north-eaſt baſtions, the blind and faſcine battery. Our working party, of fifty pioneers and as many Sepoys, were employed in raiſing and repairing the left face of the north ravelin, repairing two embraſures on the north face of the royal baſtion, and in carrying on the galleries.

Feb. 8.] The enemy this morning fired with four guns from their grand battery; but the greateſt part of the ſhot from thence and the burying-ground go over our parapets. Nothing new appeared in their approaches. Captain Barker and myſelf this morning went off in a Moſſula boat on board the Europe ſhip, and rowed from thence a little to the northward, with an intent to come back along ſhore, and take a view of the enemy's works in reverſe. We got ſo far north, and ſo near, as to ſee plainly behind their grand battery, which at firſt appeared very ill manned; but in an inſtant it was filled, and a gun or two turned againſt us, with which they fired five rounds at the boat. This obliged us to make an haſty retreat, and prevented us from ſeeing ſo much of their works as we propoſed. A deſerter who had formerly been in our ſervice came in from the enemy this evening; and informs us, that the reaſon they abandoned their battery on the glacis, was,

becauſe

becauſe they loſt many men from the ſuperiority of our fire, had ſeveral guns diſabled, and were conſtantly apprehenſive of being blown up by our mine, which they heard we were making under it. He alſo aſſures us, that they are not making any mines on their part, as we apprehended. Our working party, of fifty pioneers and twenty-ſeven Sepoys, were employed in repairing the embraſures on the north face of the royal, which fire on the enemy's grand battery; and thoſe of the old north-eaſt baſtion; alſo in puſhing on our galleries, one of which is now under the enemy's battery, and the other ſo far advanced as to prevent any poſſibility of deſtroying the blind by a mine. We had certain advice this afternoon of Major Caillaud's arrival at the Mount, but no account of the forces with him. One of the enemy's ſhips anchored this afternoon in St. Thomé road, which it was determined the Europe ſhip ſhould attack; for if ſhe is loaded with heavy ſhells, as we apprehend, we ought to hazard greatly rather than let them be landed; becauſe the damage they will do the works, now the enemy is ſo near, will be irreparable, and give them an opportunity of effectually eſtabliſhing the battery on the glacis.

Feb. 9.] Early this morning we heard a ſmart cannonading towards the Mount, which continued at intervals all day, and was renewed very briſkly towards the evening. The action was, no doubt, between a ſtrong party of M. Lally's European forces, with his black army, and our troops under the command of Major Caillaud, who had juſt joined Captain Preſton and Iſouf Cawn, from Tanjore; how it ended is hard to ſay, but we hope, from the repeated reinforcements which the enemy ſent out, that our people had the advantage. In the afternoon two companies of Sepoys were ſent out to the bar, and from thence proceeded to the garden-houſe, which posts the enemy had abandoned; they found some ammunition, sand-bags, &c. which they brought away, and set fire to the enemy's gabions. It was intended that our Europe ship should make an attempt in the night on the ship which anchored off St. Thomé yesterday; however it was not done, and to-day many stores was unloaded and carried to the Black-town. The enemy's fire was not very brisk to-day, and most of their shot flew over the town. Nothing appeared to have been done at their approaches. Our working party was last night fifty-one pioneers and twenty-seven Sepoys, employed in repairing the demy and north-east bastions, and carrying on the galleries.

Feb. 10.] The enemy last night did nothing apparently to their approaches, and were pretty silent in their batteries. During the day they fired smartly from their northern battery, but most of the shot seemed to be directed for the houses in the town, among which they made great havock; they also threw all their shells into the town, so that the siege seems to be begun a-fresh, and the attack intended against the houses rather than the works. Our working party, of pioneers and forty-eight Sepoys, were employed in repairing the old north-east bastion, the demi bastion, clearing the earth below, and in carrying on the galleries. The enemy's ship went off in the night.

11.] The enemy last night fired little musquetry, and did not, that we could discover, make any addition to their approaches. Our working party, of fifty-six pioneers and one hundred and thirty-three Sepoys, were employed in repairing two embrasures and thickening a traverse on the demi bastion; in clearing the rubbish from the mint bastion, in laying a platform and making another embrasure near the beach at the fascine battery. The gallery under the counterscarp being advanced about ninety-five feet,

two

two chambers were made, and loaded with two hundred and fifty pounds of powder each; that before the blind, was opened by a pit up through the glacis, and a branch carried on a parallel to the covered way, towards the enemy at the ſtockadoe.

Feb. 12.] Laſt night the enemy advanced, or rather repaired, a ſmall breaſt-work they had at the end of the ſtockadoe, near the ſea-ſide; but made no other alteration in their approaches. Our working party, of fifty-ſeven pioneers and thirty-three Sepoys, were employed in repairing the north-eaſt baſtion and the demi, and in lengthening out the faſcine battery quite into the ſurf, by means of caſks filled with ſand; placing a barricade of palliſadoes, cheveaux de frize, and trees in front, and raiſing the parapet. The pioneers employed under the north counterſcarp continued to ſtop the mine, and the Blacks to advance the new ſhaft. A deſerter came in this afternoon over the enemy's lodgement on the glacis, and aſſures us, that the enemy are making no mines, but are much afraid of ours. The fire of the beſiegers artillery and mortars has not been ſo briſk to-day as it was yeſterday.

13.] This morning, between two and three o'clock, we were alarmed by an attempt of the enemy, with thirty Europeans and fifty Coffrees, to nail up our guns at the faſcine battery: they advanced along the ſea ſide from the ſtockadoe, to within thirty yards of our work; when being diſcovered, they made an halt, and after receiving a fire or two from a ſix-pounder placed near the beach, they went to the right about in ſome confuſion, and returned within their works. The drums having beat to arms, the whole garriſon repaired to their poſts, and plenty of ſhells and grape ſhot were thrown into the ememy's approaches. We had a Captain and one ſoldier wounded, and the enemy left five or ſix men dead on the beach; and in the morning a ſerjeant of the Lorraine regiment, being mortally wounded, crawled into our covered way, and died ſoon after: from him we learnt the force and intention of the enemy. Our working party conſiſted of fifty-ſeven pioneers and forty-eight Sepoys, who were employed in repairing the north-eaſt baſtion, and the demi-baſtion; clearing the rubbiſh from the north curtain, and clearing the earth from the right face of the north ravelin, with which banquets were made above. The ſtopping of the mine under the north counterſcarp was compleated to-day, and intended to deſtroy the enemy's battery, if ever they attempted to re-eſtabliſh it. The fire of the enemy's north battery was to-day very briſk, and that at the old hoſpital ſilent.

Feb. 14.] Having obſerved that the enemy, before the riſing of the moon laſt night, had placed ſome gabions near the ſea ſide, a little advanced beyond the ſtockadoe, a briſk fire was kept thereon from the faſcine battery, and a ſally reſolved to be made in the morning. Accordingly, about ſix o'clock, a ſubaltern and fifteen men were ſent along the covered way till they got on the flank of the ſtockadoe; forty more, with two Captains, went directly in front of the ſtockadoe; and twenty, with an Engineer, went without arms. The enemy ran from their poſt immediately, and our people took poſſeſſion, which they maintained till the gabions by the ſea ſide were overturned and thrown into the ſurf, the earth levelled, and the enemy's tools gathered up; our party then returned, having only two men ſlightly wounded. The enemy being fired on by the north ravelin, royal baſtion, demi-baſtion, and faſcine battery, with grape, beſides all the works with muſketry, muſt have loſt many men. We could have kept poſſeſſion

poſſeſſion of the ſtockadoe if we pleaſed; but it was not thought neceſſary. The intent of the enemy advancing by the ſea ſide, muſt be with a view to bring cannon againſt our faſcine battery; or under cover of the beach, which is ſteep, to advance, by means of traverſes, till they got beyond our place of arms, and then make an attempt on that and the faſcine battery together. The enemy were remarkably quiet all night in their trenches and batteries, the only diſturbance they gave us being by a ſhell or two now and then; thus they generally act when they are carrying on any work. Our working party conſiſted of twenty-four pioneers and thirty Sepoys, who were employed in clearing and repairing the embraſures of the north-eaſt baſtion, repairing the embraſures on the demi, and repairing the caponniere before the blind.

Feb. 15.] Laſt night, before the riſing of the moon, the enemy replaced the gabions which had been overſet yeſterday morning, and endeavoured to compleat the traverſe; but the fire of a twelve pounder from the faſcine battery, and the ſhells from the demi-baſtion, made ſuch deſtruction among their gabions, that they advanced their work but little. Our working party, of thirty-five pioneers and forty Sepoys, were employed in repairing the north-eaſt baſtion, the embraſures of the demi, one embraſure on the royal, the demi caponniere before the blind, and driving the pickets in front of the faſcine battery. The mine being loaded, three pioneers attended it by turns, and were covered at night by ten grenadiers. The enemy's fire to-day was very briſk in the morning from ſix guns on their grand battery, three at the burying-ground, and two at the old hoſpital; but at five in the evening they only fired from three at the grand battery and two at the burying ground; a great quantity of artillery indeed to deſtroy defences! The French ſrigate having returned the 14th at night, and anchored in St. Thomé, road, the ſailors which we had on ſhore, and thirty marines, were ſent on board the Shafteſbury, which ſailed to attack her about eleven at night; but the frigate was gone out of ſight by the morning.

Feb. 16.] Though the enemy laſt night did not again attempt to puſh on their ſap by the ſea ſide, we kept a briſk fire till moon-light, and by their ſilence ſuſpected them to be ſomewhere at work. Our people were employed in laying large timbers and ſand-bags on the beach, to make a platform at the faſcine battery for a ſhort iron twelve-pounder of a new make, weighing eleven hundred weight, of which two came on board the Shaftſbury; in driving pickets in the front, and ſecuring the flank of the faſcine battery by trees laid in the ſurf. A party of Sepoys were ſent to level the earth at the foot of the demi-baſtion; but, the moon riſing early they were diſcovered and fired on by the enemy, who killed one man, and the reſt thereon abandoned the work. The embraſures of the north-eaſt and demi-baſtions were repaired. The enemy's fire to-day was very briſk from their artillery, but they threw very few ſhells. We got the platform ready on the beach for the iron twelve pounder by noon; ſo that we had two twelve and one ſix pounder to prevent the enemy's approach. About noon a ſmall ſloop anchored in the road, and acquainted us, that our ſhips were ſeen by her a few days before in the latitude of fourteen north, and about five in the evening we perceived ſix ſail to the north ward, which we concluded to be ours; and apprehending the enemy, on ſight thereof, might attempt ſomething, the whole garriſon was ordered to lay on their arms at the ſeveral poſts during the night.

17.] The whole garriſon being at their poſts laſt night, a briſk fire of muſketry was kept up againſt the enemy's works. About ten o'clock the ſix ſhips ſeen in in the evening anchored in our road, and were known to be thoſe we expected from Bombay. A few pioneers only were employed to lay plank, with nails drove through them, in front of the faſcine battery. About two in the morning the enemy fired pretty ſmartly from musketry, but their ſhot flew high; fires appeared at the ſame time in their trenches, and, by morning, we diſcovered that the approaches were evacuated, and the enemy were quitting the Black-town, having nailed up all the guns they could fire from, and deſtroyed the carriages which they thought ſerviceable. The troops, about ſix hundred in number, were landed this morning.

Thus terminated the ſiege of Fort St. George, after the garriſon had been ſhut up ſixty-ſeven days, and the enemy's batteries had been open forty-ſix. The arrival of the ſhips from Bombay with ſuccours, doubtleſs, haſtened the enemy retreat, and ſaved the Black-town.

As nothing very different from what is met with in all ſieges, or laid down as general maxims, was practiſed in our defence, it will be unneceſſary to enter into a particular recapitulation; but I cannot with juſtice omit the following circumſtances. To the credit of our artillery let it be remarked, that two twelve-pounders from the north ravelin diſmounted four twenty-four pounders oppoſed to them; and that, of thirty-two pieces of cannon found on the enemy's batteries, thirty-one were diſabled by our ſhot, which are many more than we had hurt by the enemy, notwithſtanding our works were enfiladed, plunged into, and taken in reverſe. I muſt alſo mention, as a thing not common in ſieges, that the works, by a few men, were kept in extraordinary good repair, and three guns, with a ſtout parapet, were maintained on the north-eaſt baſtion from the firſt to the laſt day of the ſiege. An addition was alſo made of a battery by the ſea ſide, and two and two pieces more were fired the 16th of February than the 14th of December. Nor muſt I forget to obſerve, that a few raw men, taken from the pioneer company, greatly out-did the much boaſted miners of the French, who were to blow whole baſtions into the air: for, after the breaching battery was erected, thoſe men, without having ſeen any thing of the kind before, and without any previous preparation of ſtantions or tools, were ſent to open the counterſcarp, and, by continued hard labour, carried a ſhaft ninety five feet in length under the enemy's battery, where two chambers were made, and loaded with two hundred and fifty pounds of powder each. This work was executed within a few feet of the enemy, and in ſight of their lodgment on the glacis. They ſaw, and dreaded, but could not interrupt it, though we loſt many men. Whoever conſiders the nature of the ſoil, and that the ſhaft was carried on under the exploſion of the enemy's guns, which every day made the earth fall in, muſt allow this to have been a moſt laborious and hazardous undertaking.

I will now proceed to a particular view of the enemy's approaches and batteries, as they were the day the ſiege was raiſed; beginning with that on the creſt of the glacis.

This battery opened with five embraſures; three of which were intended to breach the ſaliant angle of the demy baſtion, and two to fire againſt the blind and north-eaſt; but the conſtruction and poſition was ſo ill contrived, that the enemy were obliged to cloſe the embraſures every day, after firing a few ſhot, which in general flew over. The havock made in this battery by our ſhells and ſhot, muſt certainly have been very great; for ſeven guns, eighteen and twenty-four pounders, with their carriages, lay diſabled.

The

The lodgment on the eaſt ſide of the covered way, and behind the ſtockadoe, inſtead of being raiſed with a thick parapet well faced with faſcines, and banquets made below, was nothing more than a little looſe earth, thrown up into ſome gabions placed without order. Nor were the crotchets or demi parallels, which ought to have been capacious and well made works, formed in any other manner than the common zig-zags, which were a kind of flying ſap about four feet broad; ſo that, undoubtedly, had it ever been neceſſary to reſolve on attacking the enemy's trenches with a body of four or five hundred men, we could not have failed to drive them from their grand battery, and nail up all their guns.

Near the foot of the glacis, on the face of a zig-zag, was a battery of four embraſures, intended to ruin the parapet and diſmount the guns of the right face of our north ravelin; but the alligment of the parapet was ſo far from parallel to its object, that it was hardly poſſible to twiſt the embraſures into an opening that the guns might ſee our work. Here lay four twenty-four pounders diſabled.

On that part of the ſecond crotchet to the right of the zig-zag, the enemy had fired three eight and ten inch mortars, and left behind them two diſabled beds.

In the grand battery, which opened fifteen embraſures (of which three were directed to the north ravelin, and twelve on the demi and north eaſt baſtions) were ſix guns mounted on their carriages; and though the enemy had fired from four of them the 16th in the evening, yet all but one had received conſiderable damage on the muzzles, and might, in fact, be reckoned diſabled; there were, beſides, five guns with their carriages, and ſome ſpare ones diſmounted and ruined. Behind the right wing of this battery the enemy had ſix mortars of twelve French inches,

inches, but removed them to make room for guns, leaving two diſabled beds.

In the battery a little to the left of the burying-ground, which was tolerably well built, and opened four embraſures, were three guns mounted on their carriages, which had been fired the preceding evening, but were all damaged on their muzzles. Five guns in the battery, and one more, near, lay diſmounted, and three carriages by them ruined. This battery, to appearance, was built with a deſign to enfilade the right face of the north ravelin and the covered way before it; but it was placed a conſiderable diſtance to the left of the face produced, and conſequently could not anſwer that purpoſe; its greateſt execution was on the face of the demi baſtion, near the ſhoulder, againſt which two guns conſtantly played.

On the ſide of the old townditch, behind a ſteep bank oppoſite the Portugueze church, were the remains of four mortar platforms and two diſabled beds; and from hence the enemy threw their heavy ſhells after they had made their lodgment on the creſt of the glacis.

On the battery to the left of the old hoſpital, I could not diſcover any guns; but imagine ſome muſt have been diſabled and buried, as that battery was ſilent ſeveral days before the enemy's retreat. It was built among the ruins of houſes, and had ſix embraſures, from two of which the enemy for ſome days battered the left face of the royal; but afterwards with four only enfiladed the right face and the covered way before it, took the right flank in reverſe, and plunged into the demi baſtion. Adjoining to this battery on the left was another in a different direction, which opened four embraſures, and from whence three guns were fired on the right face of Pigot's baſtion for a few days, after which it was ſilent; but with what view the enemy directed any fire

fire on that work, no one ever could conceive, because that baſtion could neither be attacked nor offend them.

The battery built in the front of the new hoſpital, near the place where the Company's garden-houſe formerly ſtood, had four embraſures, and as many guns were conſtantly fired from thence, till a few days before the ſiege was raiſed. It was intended, I ſuppoſe, to ricochet and plunge into all the works of the north front; and indeed it might have proved the moſt troubleſome battery to us of all which the enemy erected: but I do not think they had cannon enough on it, nor that thoſe they had were managed with the greateſt addreſs. There were neither guns nor carriages found on this battery, and perhaps none were diſabled on it; becauſe, as the guns always fired en ricochet, the embraſures were choaked in front, and the guns not to be ſeen.

WAR

WAR

ON THE

Coaſt of Coromandel.

1759.

THE enemy when they raiſed the ſiege the 17th of February, marched off with ſo much precipitation that the Black-town eſcaped the deſtruction with which it had been threatned by M. Lally. He marched directly to the Mount, where he left marks of his reſentment unworthy of a ſoldier. Among the reſt of his devaſtations, he ordered three barrels of gunpowder to be lodged in Colonel Lawrence's country houſe, and blew it up.

The

The next morning he reached Conjeveram, and immediately began to fortify it againſt a ſudden attack; but the want of bullocks, Cooleys and other neceſſaries, made it impracticable for our army to take the field till the beginning of March. We had then repoſſeſſed Poonomallay and Trepaſſore, having about thirteen or fourteen hundred Europeans, for the reinforcement which arrived the ſeventeenth of February, amounted to ſix hundred men compleat, and with theſe were the Black army of Iſouf Cawn and the Nabob's brother.

Colonel Lawrence who commanded, being deſirous of bringing on an action, marched towards Conjeveram, and moved round it, expoſing his flank; but as he found nothing could provoke the enemy to ſtir, and being in a very bad ſtate of health, he prudently reſolved to quit the command rather than ſubject himſelf to certain fatigue (which he could not bear) without a proſpect of performing the ſervice he was deſirous to accompliſh, he therefore returned to England, leaving the command to Major Brereton, a gallant officer, and next in rank to Colonel Draper, whoſe ill ſtate of health obliged him likewiſe to leave a climate which was ſo prejudicial to him, that he found it neceſſary to take the firſt opportunity of withdrawing himſelf from the bad effect of it. He accordingly took his paſſage in a China ſhip, and left the garriſon full of regret for the loſs of a brave officer who had endeared himſelf to them by every other part of his conduct and behaviour.

Major Brereton, to draw out the enemy if poſſible to an engagement, made a motion towards Wandewaſh, and opened ground before that place. The French marched to relieve it, and came with-

within nine miles of our army, who advanced between three or four miles towards them, where they remained two days under arms. Major Brereton finding the enemy had taken a poſt which from its ſtrength, it was not prudent for him to attack, and being informed that they had left but a ſmall force in Conjeveram, made a forced march in the night of the 12th of April, and the day after entered the town. It was garriſoned by five hundred black troops commanded by Muſtapha Beg, an enterprizing partizan, who left our ſervice, withdrawing himſelf from Captain Preſton, during the ſiege of Madraſs. Muſtapha Beg retired with his party to the Pagoda, where he made an obſtinate reſiſtance till he was killed, with the greateſt part of his followers; but not till they had made the beſiegers ſuffer in their turn, by the loſs of four officers, though ſcarce any men in proportion. Major Monſon, as he was reconnoitring, received a wound which entered near his ear, paſſed through his cheek, and came out near his noſe, but he never found any great inconvenience from it. Major Brereton, in the attack, received, a contuſion on his knee which laid him up for ſome time, and Major Caillaud was wounded in the cheek.

Theſe accidents loſt them the critical time of action, for the enemy were never in a worſe condition; being ready for a general mutiny for want of cloathing and pay. The deſertion of the infantry was very great, and fifty Huſſars coming over to us were an addition of a very uſeful corps, and of moſt particular benefit at this juncture, as they helped to overcome a very falſe prejudice which our people had hitherto entertained, that ſuch troops were uſeleſs; whereas in fact though exceedingly expenſive, they are abſolutely neceſſary for ſome

ſome particular ſervices, and the Sepoys are always in the greateſt dread of them. Upon theſe conſiderations it was at length reſolved to raiſe a body of between two and three hundred Huſſars.

Being in poſſeſſion of Conjeveram we remained there a month, as did M. Lally at Cauvery-pauk, till having contrived to cloath his men, and perſuading himſelf that they would be inclined for action, upon intelligence that Iſouf Cawn was returned to Trichinopoly, and that the Nabob's brother had alſo left the army, he moved towards Conjeveram. About this time the regiment grew very ſickly, and it being thought that a change might be of ſervice to them, Major Brereton marched them towards the enemy at the ſame time that the French alſo had juſt put themſelves in motion, ſo that the two armies unexpectedly found themſelves near each other. Many of Draper's battalion being recruits unuſed to ſervice, and ſtrange to the climate, were ſo affected by it, that in a march of eight miles, ſix of them fell down dead, and ninety were taken ill, and by the inclement heat, rendered unfit for ſervice.

THERE was no heſitating in a caſe of this nature, for M. Lally being informed of theſe extraordinary accidents, was in full march; therefore a retreat was immediately made to Conjeveram. M. Lally advanced within three miles of the place, and the Engliſh could not reconcile it to their ſenſe of honour to be ſhut up within walls. Major Brereton being greatly affected by the climate, they marched out under Major Monſon, who though he was prevailed on not to riſque a general action againſt eighteen hundred Europeans, had the good fortune to be ſucceſsful in ſeveral ſkirmiſhes, ſuſtained two ſmall attacks which M. Lally made on him, in both which he repulſed the enemy; and having killed a Captain, a ſubaltern, and eighteen grenadiers, rendered his ſmall force ſo reſpectable to the enemy that M. Lally, convinced that there was no real diſpoſition in his army for an engagement, prudently decamped and marched in the night to Trivatoor, which is twenty miles diſtant. He then ſent his army into cantonments and went himſelf to Pondichery, heartily tired of his command and of the country, as he would not ſcruple frequently to declare. The ſame complaints were univerſally made by all his officers, and moſt ſurprizing it is that they could ſo long keep together, unpaid, a body of troops continually clamouring for their arrears. At length the whole regiment of Lorraine mutinied to a man, and taking poſſeſſion of four guns, marched out of the garriſon with their colours to a conſiderable diſtance, where they declared their reſolution to ſupport themſelves, and put the neighbouring country under contribution for their maintenance. The officers followed them and by entreaty and promiſes endeavoured to prevail with them to return to their duty. The intention of the ſoldiers was not to deſert to the Engliſh; but only to declare off from ſerving without pay; therefore the officers were never able to get from them any other anſwer but that they would agree to return, provided their arrears were paid in three days, otherwiſe they would, from that moment, begin to ſubſiſt themſelves in the country. Advice of this being diſpatched to Pondichery, a ſupply of money was immediately ſent out, and diſpatched on the third day, with a promiſe that the remainder of their arrears ſhould be paid in a week. Upon this the regiment returned to their quarters, and it is remarkable, that not a man of them deſerted.

Colonel

Colonel FORDE's Expedition TO GOLCONDA.

[1758.] THE events which preceded, and which immediately followed the ſiege of Fort St. George, being thus continued to the preſent ſtate of inaction, the great and glorious undertakings, and providential ſucceſs which bleſt the Engliſh arms in other parts of the country, may here find a place without impropriety or interruption.

M. Lally, as ſoon as he reſolved on the ſiege of Fort St. George, ſent orders to Golconda for M. De Buſſy and M. Moracin to join him with part of their forces, leaving the command of the army at Maſulipatam, with the Marquis De Conflans. Soon after the departure of M. De Buſſy, the country powers, heartily tired of the French yoke, embraced this opportunity to throw it off. The Raja of Viſanapore collected an army of about three thouſand men, marched to Vizagapatam, impriſoned the French chief, plucked down their colours, and hoiſted Engliſh in their ſtead, and at the ſame time plundered the factory. The Marquis De Conflans, in order to puniſh this inſult, marched his army from Maſulipatam, purpoſing to reduce the Raja, and take his capital Viſanapore. The Raja not being able to make head againſt the French army, applied to Colonel Clive at Calcutta, acquainting him with what he had done at Vizagapatam, and repreſenting that M. De Buſſy had taken moſt of the European forces out of the country. He aſſured him, that all the country powers were unanimous in deſiring to be freed from the tyranny of the French; and that with a ſmall aſſiſtance of Europeans, he would engage to drive them entirely out of those parts. Colonel Clive weighed every part of this precarious enterprize with that coolness and sound judgment, which few men possess in the deliberation on great and perilous undertakings. The council, to whom he communicated his plan, considered it in no other light than as hazardous in the execution, and subject to the most fatal consequences in case of ill success. These did not escape the attention of Colonel Clive, but he was at the same time justly prepossessed with the idea of what had been so familiar to him on the coast of Coromandel, where he had so often seen an army of French flying before an handful of English; and he knew that such an event, which he considered as more than probable, would greatly contribute to the preservation of Madrass. Animated by the expectation which he with reason entertained, and confiding in his own experience, he took upon himself to influence the council in an affair of so great difficulty, and preferring the security of Madrass to any honours or advantages he might acquire to himself by a larger command, chose rather to weaken his own army by detaching two-thirds of his force, than not prevent the Marquis De Conflans from reinforcing M. Lally at so critical a conjuncture..

If the dangers incident to the prosecution of this enterprize were so alarming, those also merited attention which threatened Calcutta, if this expedition had not been undertaken. For it should be remarked, that at this very time the Shaw Zadah was preparing to march against the Soubah, our ally; and it was necessary, for the preservation of all our settlements in those parts, to lead an European force to repulse him. Therefore it should be explained, that had M. Lally succeeded against Madrass, the superiority of our fleet would have been no security to Bengal, and our victorious troops at Patna might have experienced a fatal reverse of fortune, by finding themselves cut off from all possibility of a return, it being nearer

nearer by land to Calcutta, from thoſe parts of Golconda, which were poſſeſt by the French, than it is from Patna to that Settlement.

Preparations were made with the greateſt expedition, and Colonel Forde was ordered for the command of the army, conſiſting of five hundred Europeans, including a company of artillery, and ſixteen hundred Sepoys, with ſix ſhort ſix-pounders, and a howitzer for the field artillery; four twenty-four pounders, four eighteen-pounders, one eight inch mortar, and two royal mortars, as a battering train.

The troops embarked the 12th of October, and on the 20th arrived at Vizagapatam. Mr. Johnſtone who was ſent before to the Raja, to inform him of their ſailing, and prepare for their reception, waited on Colonel Forde, to acquaint him that the Raja's army, conſiſting of between three or four thouſand men, were encamped about thirty miles diſtant, but that the French were much ſtronger than they were repreſented, and that the M. de Conflans, with his army, was on this ſide Rajamundry river, diſtant from Vizagapatam about one hundred and twenty miles; and that by the beſt intelligence he could procure, they amounted to near ſix hundred Europeans, five or ſix thouſand Sepoys, and many country forces, who had joined them on their march.

The remainder of this month was taken up in landing the troops, and providing bullocks, cooleys, and other requiſites for their march; and on the firſt of November they moved from Vizagapatam towards the Raja's army, which they joined the third, and marched together for ſome days.

Mr. Andrews, who was ſent from Madraſs with orders from the governor and council to take charge of the factory at Vizagapatam, together with Captain Callinder, and ſome of the company's ſervants, joined the army the fifteenth. They paid their court to the Raja in form, introduced by Colonel Forde.

 Here

Here the Colonel (while Mr. Andrews was preſent) ſettled articles of agreement between the company and the Raja.

I. The Raja to pay the extra expence of our army during the time they ſhould act together, allowing the officers double batty, which was to be paid when we ſhould put him in poſſeſſion of Rajamundry, (a large town and fort then in poſſeſſion of the French.)

II. The Raja to poſſeſs all the inland country that belongs to the country powers in the French intereſt, and at preſent in arms.

III. The company to poſſeſs all the conquered ſea coaſt from Vizagapatam to Maſulipatam, *&c.*

Theſe articles being agreed to and ſigned, Mr. Andrews took his leave of the Colonel, and returned to his ſettlement at Vizagapatam: Captain Callinder, as ſenior officer, commanded as ſecond in camp.

The army marched for ſeveral days till they came within ſight of the enemy's camp the third of December, which was near the village of Tallapool, ſtrongly ſituated about forty miles on this ſide Rajamundry; they had upwards of five hundred Europeans, thirty-ſix pieces of cannon, and ſome mortars, eight thouſand Sepoys, and a great many of the country powers. On the ſixth, Colonel Forde marched nearer the enemy, and gained an eminence at about three miles diſtance from their camp. The French ſeemed not inclined to quit their ſtation, and the Colonel did not approve of attacking them to ſo great a diſadvantage, therefore determined either to draw them from their preſent ſituation, or march round them and get between their army and Rajamundry. About ſix o'clock in the evening the Colonel waited on the Raja to inform him of his intentions, and orders were given out late for the army to march at half an hour after four in the morning, no morning-gun to fire, and no beating of drums, but the greateſt ſilence to be obſerved. The M. de

Conflans

Conflans expecting the Colonel would wait at his ground, and being informed by one of our deserters, that the troops were all raw, and unexperienced in discipline, determined to cannonade our camp, and the deserter undertook to shew the enemy where they might most annoy our people. Their whole troops were under arms at one o'clock in the morning, and a large party was detached with six pieces of cannon conducted by the deserter.

Our army struck their tents, and marched at the hour appointed, not knowing of the enemy's intentions. The Raja's army being not so alert, was left on their ground. A little before day-break, the French began their cannonade, not being informed of our march; this greatly disconcerted the Raja, who dispatched a messenger after the Colonel, acquainting him with his distress. Our men were ordered to halt, and the Colonel returned and brought up the Raja's army. They then marched on together till they came to the village of Golapool, and there they halted on a small plain, about three miles from their encampment: In the mean time the M. de Conflans observing our army had moved, and perceiving our intentions of stealing a march round him, ordered his troops immediately in line of march, and proceeded towards us, keeping between our army and his own camp. We had not halted above half an hour before we discovered the enemy's Sepoys, and presently after their whole line, about ten or twelve hundred yards distant on our left flank: In a few minutes after they closed, and moved down towards us in good order.

About nine our line was formed, but the Indian army not recovered of their morning fright, were all in confusion. The Raja, conscious of the ill behaviour of his troops, and also of his own neglect, upon Colonel Forde's remonstrances, submitted the disposal of them for the future entirely to him; upon which the Colonel ordered all the Indians, with fire arms, to form upon the right and left of our Sepoys on each wing, as the enemy's line extended much further than ours. Captain Briſtol, a European in the Raja's ſervice, commanding a ſmall body of European deſerters, with four pieces of cannon, was ordered to join our artillery on the left of the battalion.

The enemy began a cannonade about ten o'clock, which was continued by a ſharp fire from both armies for upwards of forty minutes, at which time we obſerved the enemy's battalion, and their right wing of Sepoys, with a body of horſe moving up, in order to fall upon our left flank, for they miſtook our battalion of Sepoys on the left wing for Europeans, being cloathed in red cloth jackets The French drawing near, poured in their whole fire upon them, which was returned by our Sepoys pretty ſmartly, though they were in ſome confuſion, giving way at the ſame time, while the enemy kept advancing. On ſeeing this, Colonel Forde ordered the European battalion to make a quarter wheel as quick as poſſible. They had but juſt time to make their proper front, before the enemy's European battalion were advanced very cloſe. Our people gave them their whole fire, which made a great ſlaughter, and giving two or three huzzas at the ſame time, advanced briſkly in order to puſh bayonets. This motion being ſo ſudden on the enemy, they had not time to recover their miſtake; at the ſame time our cannon galled them greatly with grape ſhot.

As our troops advanced, their men gave way, and ſoon fell into diſorder, going to the right about. Our Sepoys on the left wing, that had before given way, renewed their charge; and thoſe on the right wing behaved with uncommon reſolution, and ſoon made the enemy's Black forces on the left give ground, by which means about eleven o'clock the retreat became general. The Raja's troops, except the

the few Europeans commanded by Captain Briſtol, all this time were idle ſpectators, only firing a few rockets. Had the Raja's horſe, which were at moſt five hundred, purſued at this juncture, few or none of the French could have eſcaped; but there was no poſſibility of getting them to charge, or even advance beyond our European battalion. The other part of his army were more intent upon plunder than fighting. The enemy attempted to rally again at their camp, but were ſo cloſely purſued, that they were obliged to diſperſe in ſmall bodies, making the beſt of their way for Rajamundry. We took poſſeſſion of their camp, with all their ordnance, ammunition, ſtores, tents, and camp equipage; the enemy not having time to carry off any thing but four ſmall field-pieces, and two camels loaded with money and papers, which the Marquis de Conflans had ordered away on the firſt diſorder of their army to Rajamundry, there to wait his further orders. The Marquis, with the commandant of artillery, and their attendants, on finding we had got poſſeſſion of their camp, made off without waiting for any of their ſcattered troops, and getting to Rajamundry that night, proceeded the next day to Maſſulipatam.

Our army being much fatigued, the Colonel halted in the French camp for the remainder of the day. After placing the proper guards of the camp, and ſecuring our priſoners, all the pallankeens belonging to the officers, and the covered chairs (which they call dooleys) were ſent back to the field of battle to bring the wounded of both armies. The French officers taken priſoners had their paroles given, and leave to go along with our ſick and wounded to Cockanara, a Dutch ſettlement about twenty miles from the field of battle.

We had forty-four Europeans killed and wounded, among which were two Captains and three Lieutenants; and the French, one hundred and fifty-ſix, officers

officers included. Great numbers of the Black forces fell on both ſides.

It was a moſt compleat victory, for the enemy loſt their whole camp, baggage, ammunition, and all their artillery, except the four field-pieces above mentioned. Our people took thirty-two pieces of cannon, and the Indian army alſo took ſome guns. Though the enemy had ſuch a number of guns, they were ill manned, by which means, when their line advanced, the artillery became uſeleſs, being all left in the rear, while our guns moving with the battalion, were conſtantly in play.

Captain Knox, with the firſt battalion of Sepoys, was ordered that evening to purſue the enemy as far as Rajamundry, and there wait the arrival of the army; and the next day, upon receiving intelligence that the French were very ſtrong at Rajamundry, having collected together moſt of the ſcattered parties of Europeans, and ſome Black forces, the Colonel detached Captain Maclean, with two battalions of Sepoys, to reinforce Captain Knox; being joined, they marched, and came upon the enemy in the duſk of the evening, while they were croſſing the river in boats. They killed ſome Europeans, and took fifteen priſoners; as for the Sepoys, they threw down their arms and diſperſed. Captain Knox took poſſeſſion of the fort of Rajamundry, and from thence cannonaded the enemy acroſs the river, which obliged them to abandon the four field-pieces left in the boats on the oppoſite ſide.

Rajamundry is a barrier and key to the Vizagapatam country; the French held it as their own property, and always kept a governor, and a ſmall body of troops to garriſon it.

In this fort were taken more artillery, ammunition, and ſtores, with about five hundred draught and carriage bullocks, ſome horſes and camels, and a good deal of rich furniture. The Colonel reſerved all

all the military ſtores for the company, and the remainder of the effects were ſold by auction, and divided as a reward to the troops for their good behaviour. The army encamped without the town by the river's ſide; one company of Sepoys doing duty in the fort, and another in the town, to prevent any diſturbance.

Colonel Forde now called upon the Raja to fulfil the terms of agreement, and pay the extra expences; but the Indian Chief, like all his countrymen, could not bear the thoughts of parting with money, and pleaded, as uſual, the impoſſibility of doing it without going about the country to collect the revenues. As it was impracticable to carry on any military operations without money to pay the troops, and provide for their march, the Colonel was obliged to inſiſt upon the Raja's complying with the articles which were ſo ſolemnly agreed to by him, who after many frivolous excuſes, and even endeavouring to lay the blame on the interpreter, convinced at length by the juſtice, neceſſity, and intereſt he had in enabling the troops to take the field about the middle of January, he paid the money, and at the ſame time Colonel Forde delivered up the fort of Rajamundry. The Raja appointed Captain Briſtol, a European in his ſervice, governor of this fortreſs; and under his care were left the ſick and wounded, and alſo the ſpare artillery, and ſome baggage. Both armies now marched towards Maſſulipatam, Colonel Forde taking the direct road, arrived at Elore the ſixth of February, where he waited for the Raja, who went out of the line of march to raiſe contributions.

The French had a factory at Narſipore, about twenty miles from Elore, at which place there were a hundred Europeans, and ſome Sepoys; and M. Panneau the Chief ſeemed determined to defend it. Captain Knox with the firſt battalion of Sepoys, was detached againſt him, and letters were ſent by the Colonel's orders to the Raja of Narſipore and his brother,

brother, that in caſe they offered to moleſt Captain Knox's party, or give the French the leaſt aſſiſtance, they might expect to ſee their whole country ruined; at the ſame time offering him proper encouragement to induce him to enter into our alliance. The Raja of Narſipore having received the Colonel's letter, met Captain Knox on the march, offering him aſſiſtance, and promiſing to join the army in a few days with what forces he could raiſe. On the approach of our party, M. Panneau ſent away all the company's goods in boats to Maſſulipatam, and carried the garriſon to join the army of obſervation, which was encamped about forty miles in our front, conſiſting of two hundred and fifty Europeans, two thouſand Sepoys, and four pieces of cannon. This flying army always kept a day or two's march before us, obſerving our motions, and haraſſing the country in order to diſtreſs us, and retard our march.

There were found in Narſipore two four and twenty pounders, three twelve pounders, and ſome ſmall guns, with ſeveral veſſels, boats, and marine ſtores. All the ammunition M. Panneau had ſunk in the river.

The Raja's army coming up the eighteenth, and being joined the next day by the Raja of Narſipore, marched together with Colonel Forde, and encamped near a ſmall fort, called Concale, on the twenty-ſixth. Here the French had placed a ſerjeant, with thirteen Europeans, and two companies of Sepoys, giving him ſtrict orders to maintain the place to the laſt extremity. Captain Maclean, with ſix companies of the ſecond battalion of Sepoys, was detached againſt it. The French commandant of the army of obſervation had ſent the ſerjeant word, that if he could maintain the fort till the following day, he would ſend him a large reinforcement. On the approach of our detachment the enemy fired ſmartly upon them from the cannon of the fort, however, by the help of a riſing ground, and the adjacent

adjacent houſes of a village, our Sepoys inveſted it cloſe round. Captain Maclean attempted to force the gate, but was twice repulſed with loſs, having ſeveral of his men killed and wounded; and finding it impoſſible to gain an entrance without cannon, he wrote to the Colonel, acquainting him with what had been done, and requeſting a ſmall reinforcement, and two guns, which were immediately ſent, with an officer of artillery, who advanced his guns cloſe up to the gates, and blew them open. Our Sepoys entered, and made a great ſlaughter among the enemy's Sepoys: as for the Europeans, they hid themſelves till our people ceaſed firing.

Some few hours after we had been in poſſeſſion of the fort, a country fellow brought intelligence of a party of forty Europeans, and ſome Sepoys, advancing to the relief of the place, upon which Captain Maclean marched his detachment out of the fort, on a ſmall plain to the weſt of them; but the French party hearing that the fort was taken, returned back to their own army.

The Marquis de Conflans was encamped in the Pettah, or village, diſtant about two miles from the walls of Maſſulipatam. Here the army was ſupplied with water, for it is to be obſerved that there are no freſh ſprings in the garriſon, and here they were poſted to ſo great advantage, that it is ſurpriſing the Marquis de Conflans did not chuſe to keep poſſeſſion of that ground, from whence, if he had been obliged to retire, his retreat would have been covered by the guns in the garriſon. However, he did not chuſe to hazard an action at any rate; but when Colonel Forde appeared on the ſixth of March, he moved into the fort, and our army encamped on the ground he quitted the ſame afternoon.

The French had an army of obſervation, conſiſting of about two hundred and fifty Europeans, and two thouſand Sepoys, who lay for ſome time between our army and Rajamundry, to cut off our ſupplies from

from thence: at length they ſummoned Captain Briſtol, who was obliged to ſurrender, having firſt conveyed away by ſea to Cockanara all the money which was ſent him by Mr. Andrews from Vizagapatam, for the uſe of the army, and alſo the ſick and wounded. The advantage which the enemy reaped from the taking of Rajamundry was the diſappointing our army of the money, the ſeizing ſuch baggage and effects of the officers as were left there, and making priſoners twenty Europeans, and forty Sepoys.

Maſſulipatam was inveſted the ſeventh o March, the ſame day on which the news arrived that M Lally had raiſed the ſiege of Fort St. George.

From the ſeventh of March, to the ſeventh of April, the beſiegers were conſtantly employed in carrying on the uſual and neceſſary approaches. They bombarded the town, and deſtroyed a great many houſes: they battered and made ſeveral breaches in the baſtions, which the beſieged, by their numbers, very eaſily repaired. On the ſixth of April, breaches being made in two baſtions, great hopes were entertained of our being able to attack the next day, but notwithſtanding our continual fire all night, by the morning of the ſeventh, the enemy had repaired them; and now the commander of artillery repreſented to the Colonel, that there was only two days ammunition remaining, having expended upwards of four hundred barrels of powder, with ſhot and ſhells in proportion, that with briſk firing all day, the breaches might be opened again as before, but that was all that could be done further by the batteries. Upon this report, Colonel Forde knowing the conſequence which muſt unavoidably attend the raiſing the ſiege, determined to attempt it by ſtorm the ſame evening. Accordingly the diſpoſition was fixed, and the army ordered to be under arms at ten o'clock at night. Depending wholly upon his Europeans, he deſtined them for the

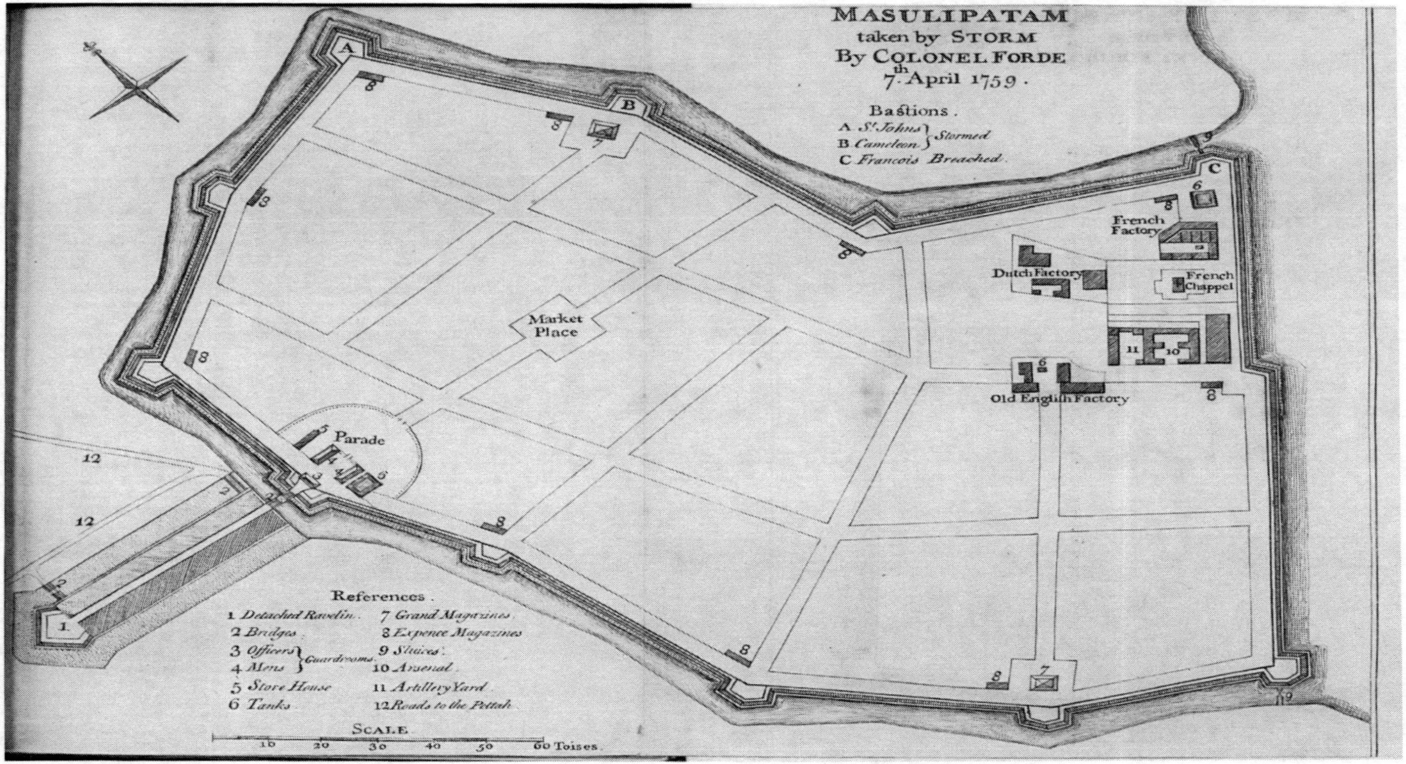

MASULIPATAM
taken by STORM
By COLONEL FORDE
7th April 1759.
Bastions.
A St. Johns } Stormed
B Cameleon }
C Francois Breached.
French Factory
French Chappel
Dutch Factory
Old English Factory
Market Place
Parade
References.
1 Detached Ravelin.
2 Bridges
3 Officers } Guardrooms.
4 Mens }
5 Store House
6 Tanks
7 Grand Magazines
8 Expence Magazines
9 Sluices.
10 Arsenal.
11 Artillery Yard.
12 Roads to the Pettah.
SCALE.
10 20 30 40 50 60 Toises.

the effectual ſervice : and to amuſe the enemy with two falſe attacks, he ordered Captain Knox, with the firſt battalion of Sepoys, to march at duſk of the evening, round the town to the weſtward, with directions to draw as near the walls as poſſible, and begin his fire exactly at twelve o'clock. At the ſame time the Raja of Viſanapore was to make another falſe attack by the gate way, and front of the detached ravelin, with orders to follow Captain Knox's fire, making as much noiſe as poſſible by firing of cannon, ſmall arms, and rockets, and uſing every other means to alarm and perplex the garriſon. The European battalion, with part of the gunnery taken from the batteries, and ſome ſeamen from the Hardwicke, and the ſecond battalion of Sepoys, with two field-pieces, formed the main attack for the baſtions, where the breaches had been made. The firſt battalion of Sepoys began their fire exactly at twelve o'clock, the hour appointed, which was followed by the army of the Raja according to his inſtructions.

In the mean time the party for the grand attack croſſed the Moraſs which ſurrounds the whole city, and came to the ditch before they were diſcovered. The grenadiers and two battalions of Sepoys, puſhed for one of the baſtions where the breach had been made, and the battalion of Europeans with the gunners and ſeamen made for the other. While the men were croſſing the ditch, the enemy poured in upon them their ſmall arms and grapeſhot from the flanks of the baſtions, which was ſoon returned by our muſquetry. The enemy were driven from the breaches, but ſtill kept up a ſmart fire from the other works. As the two field pieces could not be got over the main ditch, the officer, and men belonging to the artillery, left them, and entered the town with the reſt of the troops, where they were of great ſervice by turning the enemy's own guns againſt them. In this manner they fought the

ememy,

enemy, gaining baſtion after baſtion, till they approached the gateway, and cut off their communication from the detached ravelin.

At this time a French officer came to the Colonel, from the Marquis de Conflans, aſking quarter for the Garriſon. The Colonel ſent a Captain with the French officer to the Marquis, with the following meſſage, That he could not give quarter while reſiſtance was made in any part, and that unleſs the beſieged would immediately ceaſe firing, and ſurrender themſelves, he ſhould be obliged for his own ſafety, to put the whole garriſon to the ſword.

The Marquis De Conflans diſpatched his orders for the troops to quit their arms, and repair to the Arſenal, and ſent the ſame meſſage to the outpoſts. The firing ceaſed in about half an hour after, and the main body of our troops repaired to the Eſplanade. A detachment of one hundred Europeans, two companies of Sepoys, and two guns, were poſted over the priſoners that night: the next day the gentlemen gave their paroles, and had liberty to walk about the town, and the Colonel ſhewed them great lenity in granting all their effects, except private trade, which was ſecured for the captors.

The enemy ſuffered greatly, but it was never known exactly what numbers they loſt, but by comparing their muſter rolls, with our number of priſoners, which were four hundred and nine, they muſt have had above a hundred Europeans killed during the ſiege, their wounded being included amongſt the priſoners.

The ſtrength of the Engliſh in the grand attack was three hundred and twelve in battalion, thirty gunners, as many ſeamen, and ſeven hundred Sepoys. On the falſe attack of the gateway four thouſand of the Raja's forces, and ſeven hundred on the other, but neither of theſe entered the town. The ſtrength of the enemy in garriſon according to their muſter rolls

rolls the 6th of March, was five hundred and twenty-two Europeans, and two thouſand and thirty nine Coffrees, Topaſſes, and Sepoys. There were taken above one hundred and fifty pieces of cannon, one thirty-two, and five twenty-four pounders, and a great quantity of ammunition.

Salabatzing advanced with his army within about forty miles of Maſulipatam, ſome days before it was taken, and there waited like a true Eaſtern Politician the event of the ſiege. Our ſucceſs both there and at Madraſs, freed him from the ſlaviſh dread of the French, which had too long influenced his councils.

About the ſame time his brother Nizam Allee, who had ſet up a ſeparate intereſt, marched from Aurengabad, and arrived at Hyderabad. This was another circumſtance that induced Salabatzing to wiſh for the Alliance of the Engliſh, and perhaps diſpoſed him the more readily to ſign the following treaty.

Treaty with Salabatzing, Souba or Viceroy of the Deckan.

The ſeal of Salabatzing.

The whole of the Circar of Maſſulipatam, with eight diſtricts as well as the Circar of Nizampatam, and the diſtricts of Codaver and Wacalmanner, ſhall be given to the Engliſh Company, as an Enam (or free Gift) and the Saneds granted to them in the ſame manner as was done to the French.

Salabatzing will oblige the French troops which are in this country, to paſs the river Ganges within fifteen days, or ſend them to Pondichery, or to any other place out of Deckan country on the other ſide of the river Kriſtna. In future he will not ſuffer them to have a ſettlement in this country

U on

on any account whatſoever, nor keep them in his ſervice, nor aſſiſt them, nor call them to his aſſiſtance.

The Souba will not demand or call * Gauzapetty-rauze to an account for what he has collected out of the Circars belonging to the French, nor for the computation of the revenues of his own country, in the preſent year, but let him remain peaceably in it in future, and according to the computation of revenues of his country, before the time of the French, agreeable to the cuſtom of his grand-father and father, and as was then paid to the Circar, ſo he will now act and pay accordingly to the Circar, and if he (the Raja) does not agree to it, then the Souba may do what he pleaſes. In all caſes the Souba will not aſſiſt the enemies of the Engliſh, nor give them protection

The Engliſh on their part will not aſſiſt the Souba's enemies, or give them Protection.

Dated Moon Ramadan, 16th Hegira, 1172, which is the 14th of May, 1759.

In the Souba's own hand.

I ſwear by God and his Prophet, and upon the Holy Alcoran, that I with pleaſure agree to the requeſts ſpecified in this paper, and ſhall not deviate from it even an hair's breadth.

The French ſhewed how greatly they valued this country, by detaching from Pondicherry four hundred men to reinforce an army which before was almoſt double the number of Colonel Forde's. They ſent this reinforcement on board the Harlem, which they took from the Dutch, and the Briſtol. Theſe ſhips arrived in the road of Maſſulipatam the 15th of April, a very few days after the town was in the hands of the Engliſh.

The Hardwicke Indiaman, which was there at anchor when ſhe firſt ſaw the French colours, got

* The name of the Raja of Viſanapore.

under-

under-way, and made ready for an Engagement, which continued about an hour, during which time Mr. Samſon, the firſt mate (the Captain his brother being aſhore) had the addreſs to get to the windward of the French, and came to an anchor. One of them alſo came to an anchor, but the other continued beating up to windward about three hours, by which time Captain Samſon came on board. He was determined to fight his way through them and make for Bengal, where he was to have carried a large number of priſoners, but had then only forty on board. The enemy's largeſt ſhip got under ſail at the ſame time as the Hardwicke, and together with the other exchanged broadſides, till finding they were not able to come up with the Hardwicke, they returned and came to an anchor, and Mr. Moracin, who commanded the troops, not having heard the fate of the place, ſent a boat aſhore about midnight, with a letter to the Marquis de Conflans, to acquaint him that he had brought him ſuccours, and that he ſhould not diſembark the men till he received his orders. The next morning diſcovering his miſtake, he ſailed for Ganjam, where he ſtaid till the beginning of November, as it was not poſſible for them to return to Pondichery againſt the Monſoon. There he loſt forty men in an attack made on him by Narraindu, a Raja of thoſe parts, who projected every ſcheme he could deviſe to cut them off by the ſword, by famine, or poiſon. Their numbers were greatly diminiſhed by the above-mentioned diſtreſſes, and alſo by deſertion, and when all their proviſions and money were gone, the country people left them to the diſtance of a league all round.

Mr. Moracin then came away in a boat with his nephew and ſecretary, and arrived about the middle of December at Pouliacat, in his way to Pondichery. There were about two hundred men left, who went to Cockanara, where ſome of them landed, and were endeavouring to get the people of the country to join them, but were attacked by Captain Fischer, who took ten officers with one of the Rajas who had joined them, and sixteen Europeans, and killed several more, on which those that were in the vessels sailed for Pondichery, and many of these were drowned.

SURAT.

[1759.] IT being the design of this work to treat of such events as have been brought about by the military expeditions of the English in India; the last revolution in the government of Surat, must be considered as a necessary part of this undertaking.

To give the history of the former state of this great commercial city, farther than it concerns the present change of government, would be here unnecessary, but without a representation of such alterations in the jurisdiction of the city and castle as have not only preceded, but conduced to bring about this revolution; neither the causes nor conduct of the transactions can be understood.

Surat has for so many years been one of the most frequented cities in the East, that, from the concourse of Mahometan pilgrims, who make it their road from India to visit the tomb of their Prophet, it has been called the gate of Mecca. The castle has always been held by a governor, appointed by the Mogul, to keep the city under proper subjection, but not to interfere with the government of it.

The Indian seas having been infested to an intolerable degree by pirates, the Mogul appointed the Siddee, who was chief of a colony of Coffrees to be his Admiral. It was a colony which, having been settled at Dundee Rajapore, carried on a consideraa conſiderable trade there, and had likewiſe many veſſels of force.

The Mogul, being equally moved by zeal for the Mahometan religion, and a concern for the intereſts of commerce, in order to keep the ſeas open between Surat, and the Perſian and Arabian gulphs, had been at the annual expence of a large ſhip, purpoſely fitted out to carry pilgrims to Judda, which is no great diſtance from Mecca. For the ſecurity of this veſſel, as well as to protect the trade of Surat, which was then very flouriſhing, he granted his Admiral, the Siddee, a revenue called the Tanka, to the yearly value of three lack of roupees, at the time it was firſt ſettled; ariſing partly from ſome adjacent land, and partly from the revenues of Surat, which were paid him annually by the governor, while his officers were allowed to collect his rents; but he had not the leaſt title to any power independent of the marine.

The uſual endeavours of all Mahometan chiefs to defraud or circumvent each other, are continually producing revolutions. The government of Surat had for ſome time been backward in their payments, and with-held great part of the ſum ſtipulated from the Siddee, who to make himſelf amends, took occaſion to ſend ſome of his cruiſers into the river of Surat, at a time when the Monſoon was ſetting in, and then made a pretence of the ſeaſon for remaining there. Siddee Muſſoot, the commander of that ſquadron, made uſe of this opportunity to get ſome kind of footing in the government, and to ſeize on the caſtle, which he held till his death, when he was ſucceeded by his ſon, in the year 1756.

Muſſoot not only retained the government of the caſtle, but greatly encroached on that of the town, and appropriated to himſelf one third of its revenues; another third has long ſince been annually paid to the Marattas, and by them farmed out to an officer who resides in Surat. The walls of the town, with the assistance of the Europeans who have factories there, are a sufficient defence against these plunderers; but as they are at all times masters of the whole country up to the very gates, it has been thought expedient to pay them duly their allotment, rather than subject the inland trade to the many delays and difficulties with which it is in the power of the Marattas to clog and interupt it. They are continually hovering about the place, and watching for invitations which through the inconstancy and fluctuation of the governing powers of the city and castle, they frequently receive, and though they know that their admission into the town would be the absolute loss of their revenue for the future, (for their government, wherever established is fatal to trade) yet from their habitual passion for plunder, they are ever feeding themselves with hopes that some governor in the decline of his power will open the gates and invite them to a present booty, which no arguments of reason or policy can restrain them from seizing.

Meah Atchund, had applied to them for their assistance, to turn out Novas Allee Cawn from the government, who himself also entertained a secret correspondence with some of the Maratta chiefs. Meah Atchund, was brought by a party of Marattas from Poona, to the walls of the town; having so far availed himself of their assistance, he discarded them, for the Siddee preferring him to Novas Allee Cawn, whom he thought to be more dangerously connected with them, agreed to join Meah Atchund, and establish him in the city, upon condition that he would absolutely renounce their alliance: but as the government was continually weakened by the incroachments of the castle upon the town, it was daily expected that the Marattas, would take advantage of this state of of anarchy, to which it was in a manner reduced, for the lawleſs behaviour of the Siddee's ſon filled the city with riot and murders, while new exactions and additional burthens upon trade grew to be intolerable.

In the year 1758, earneſt application was made to Mr. Ellis the Engliſh chief, by the principal merchants and inhabitants, deſiring him to recommend it to the preſidency of Bombay, to fit out an expedition for taking poſſeſſion of the Caſtle and Tanka. They enforced their ſolicitations by entering into an obligation to become reſponſible for five years for any deficiency in the revenues of the Caſtle and Tanka, which were rated at two lack of roupees per annum.

Pharras Cawn, who had been Naib or deputy governor to Meah Atchund, and properly ſpeaking the acting magiſtrate, had regulated the police to the ſatisfaction of the whole city; therefore it was propoſed to have him for Governor, ſince he had ſufficiently ſhewn how well he was qualified for it by his conduct and behaviour while he acted as Second. Theſe propoſals were the more readily approved and accepted, as the Engliſh had been often grievouſly oppreſt by frauds, extortions, and many impediments thrown purpoſely in the way of their buſineſs; as alſo by frequent inſults, violences, and even murders committed on their Servants, with a total diſregard to the protection of the company. It was alſo a conſideration of no ſmall weight, that the poſſeſſion of the caſtle would be a ſecurity againſt the apprehenſion of the Marattas. Theſe were arguments for undertaking ſuch an enterpriſe at any time, but what determined the preſidency of Bombay to a deciſive reſolution, and at laſt cauſed the expedition to take place, was the weight and influence of the ſquadron which was at Bombay, in the year 1759. Mr. Ellis, as it has been already obſerved, had taken great pains to obtain a thorough knowledge of the ſtate of affairs and intereſts of the ſeveral perſons concerned in the government of the city and caſtle during his reſidence there, and had with no leſs judgment concerted a plan for ſettling it upon a better eſtabliſhment.

Mr. Spencer, who ſucceeded Mr. Ellis, communicated to the governor and council of Bombay, the beſt information he could procure of the poſture of affairs in Surat, in the beginning of the year 1759.

He found Meah Atchund governor of the town, but with ſo little power that the Siddee did not ſo much as leave him the nomination of the officers properly belonging to him; and thoſe of the Siddee's party, who had been moſt inſtrumental in lowering the authority of Atchund, were apprehenſive of his entertaining a correſpondence with the Marattas. The dread of thoſe ravagers, and the frequent murders, which were committed with impunity, ſince the government of the city ceaſed to be reſpectable, had intimidated the inhabitants to ſo great a degree, that many conſiderable traders and people of ſubſtance had left the place, through apprehenſions of being plundered in the conteſt between the two parties; and thoſe who ſtaid there were ſincerely deſirous that the caſtle ſhould be in the hands of the Company, from the confidence they had in the Engliſh, and the opinion they entertained of the humanity and juſtice of their government, truſting that ſo long as they poſſeſt the caſtle, they would have influence enough in the town to prevent the violence and oppreſſions which had too long raged without controul.

Beſides the invitation from the whole mercantile intereſt, overtures were made to Mr. Spencer from two of the principal men in the government, Siddee Jaffier and Velley Ullah, who engaged to contribute all in their power towards ſecuring the Caſtle and

Tanka

Tanka for the Company, on condition that they ſhould agree to make Pharraſs Cawn governor of the town, or in caſe it ſhould be found too great a difficulty to ſet Atchund aſide, it ſhould be determined for the Company to bring Pharraſs Cawn to Surat with their forces, and place him in the government, by agreement, as Naib to Atchund. This was meant for a ſatisfaction to all parties, there being ſeveral who would be leſs jealous of Atchund while Pharraſs Cawn was thus placed as a check upon him.

The principal motive of Siddee Jaffier, was the preſervation of his large property, which he could not but apprehend to be in great danger under ſuch a government, notwithſtanding his influence with both parties. As for Velley Ullah, he acted upon very different principles. He had formerly been a dependant on Novas Allee Cawn, and had ſacrificed him to Meah Atchund, with whom he held the ſame place, but with a greater degree of influence; and this he was ſuppoſed to uſe without any ſcruple, for the betraying his new maſter to the Siddee. Conſcious of this, and aware of the diſtruſt which Atchund muſt naturally have of him, from his known inſincerity, he was for embracing any opportunity of ſecuring himſelf by overthrowing or weakening that power which he had too juſt reaſon to fear.

From the character of theſe people, there was very little reliance to be had on their profeſſions of friendſhip and promiſes of aſſiſtance, therefore it was of much greater conſequence to the ſucceſs of the deſign to examine into the force that was to oppoſe it, than to be vainly looking after that which was too precarious to be depended on for ſupport.

It was ſoon diſcovered that the Siddee had about two thouſand men in pay, from which, after deducting ſuch as were employed in domeſtic ſervices, or kept merely for parade, there might remain a body of ſeventeen hundred, compoſed of various people, Moors,

Moors, Gentoos, Arabs, Pattans, and others; but they were allowed to be a better corps than Atchund's Sepoys, which amounted to four thousand. To this body were to be added such a number, as they could be expected to raise upon the news of the preparations at Bombay for an intended attack. At the same time it was considered that a body of men so raised, could be no great addition of real strength, since they were not likely to behave themselves as soldiers, on the meer consideration of a few days pay, well knowing that they should be discharged as soon as ever the affair was decided. There seemed therefore to be but one thing to be apprehended, which was least Atchund, or even the Siddee, should in distrust of their own strength, fly to the desperate resource of calling in the Marattas.

The presidency of Bombay, now fully apprized of all particulars, and being principally upon their guard against the last mentioned fatality, in order to secure themselves from any danger of that kind by sea, and in other respects to give weight to the enterprize, desired Admiral Pocock to accompany it with two ships of his squadron. The Admiral consenting to their request, gave orders for the Sunderland and Newcastle to countenance the expedition, for it is to be observed, that the Siddee who enjoyed the Tanka on condition of keeping up a Fleet for the Mogul, had so far fallen off in the performance of that condition that his marine was by no means capable of opposing the ships of the Company.

Captain Maitland, of the royal regiment of artillery, being appointed to take the command of eight hundred and fifty men, artillery and infantry, and fifteen hundred Sepoys, was sent on board the company's armed vessels, commanded by Captain Watson, who sailed on the ninth of February, and landed them the fifteenth.

When

When Captain Maitland approached the town, he found ſome of the Siddee's people had taken poſt in the French garden, from whence he diſlodged them after a hot diſpute of four hours, in which he loſt twenty men. He then directed the engineer, to look out for a proper place for a battery, which was erected in the night and the next day, and alſo the three following, a briſk fire was kept up from two four and twenty pounders, and a thirteen inch mortar. The enemy had taken poſſeſſion of the Engliſh garden and Siddees * Bunder, and had ſecured them with works and ſtrong paliſadoes. After this continued firing without any apparent effect, Captain Maitland, called a council of war, compoſed of military and marine officers, when they concerted a plan for a general attack, and reſolved to carry it into execution the next morning. In purſuance of this plan the Company's grabs and bomb ketches warpt up the river in the night, and anchored oppoſite the Bunder early in the morning, and then a general attack began from the veſſels and a battery, with a deſign to drive the enemy from their batteries, and ſo facilitate the landing of the infantry, who were embarked on board the boats. The firing laſted till after eight, when upon a ſignal made, the boats put off, and landed under cover of the veſſels, the military being greatly aſſiſted by the conduct and gallant behaviour of Captain Watſon. They ſoon put the enemy to flight, and took poſſeſſion of all the outer town. There ſtill remained the inner town and the caſtle. In order to attack them both at once, three mortars were planted at the diſtance of about ſeven hundred yards from the caſtle, and five hundred from the inner town.

About ſix in the morning, the mortars began to play very briſkly, and continued to do ſo till two the next morning. The cannonading and bombardment

* Cuſtom-houſe.

put

put the beſieged into ſuch a conſternation that they never returned one gun.

Several meſſages paſt during the attack between the principal perſons in the town, and Mr. Spencer, who uſed his utmoſt endeavours to place Pharraſs Cawn in the government; but it appeared that his friends, notwithſtanding the hopes they had given, made not the leaſt effort in his behalf, even after the Engliſh had been two days in poſſeſſion of the outer town, but ſignified to Mr. Spencer, that they choſe Pharraſs Cawn ſhould be Naib, and that the government ſhould be continued to Atchund. Theſe conſiderations, the expence of ſtores, and loſs of men by the caſualties of war and deſertion, made it imprudent to perſiſt in bringing in Pharraſs Cawn againſt the inclination of his former partizans, and the intereſt of Atchund, who, ſhould he be thereby provoked to unite with the Siddee, might fruſtrate the whole deſign. It was therefore agreed to propoſe this plan to Atchund and his party, offering to ſecure the government to him, on condition of making Pharraſs Cawn, Naib, and eſtabliſhing the Engliſh in the poſſeſſion of the Caſtle and Tanka. Mr. Spencer accordingly ſet on foot a treaty with Atchund, and the following agreement was ratified on both ſides.

Agreeable to your deſire, I ſent a perſon to you, by whom you adviſed me verbally of your demands, and with ſinceriry of heart, I now write the particulars I can agree to, which are as follow.

(Atchund's Seal.)	(Cootbodeen's Seal.)
Article I. That Pharraſs Cawn ſhall be appointed to the office of Naib, in its greateit extent, as in the time of	Article I. Agreeable to this article, I fully conſent to Pharraſs Cawn's appointment.

Suffdair,

Suffdair Cawn, and no body but himſelf ſhall interfere in the ſaid poſt.

II. That whatever articles Pharraſs Cawn has given in writing, or promiſed to the honourable Company (the particulars of which cannot be drawn out at preſent, and muſt be deferred till we can meet) ſhall be fully complied with, without the leaſt diminution.

II. Whatever Pharraſs Cawn has wrote or promiſed to do for the honourable company, I will ſtand to without the leaſt alterations.

III. That the Mecca gate ſhall be opened, and our troops admitted, and we ſhall join our forces to drive our enemy out of the town.

III. The Mecca gate ſhall be opened, your troops admitted, and joined by mine to drive out the enemy.

IV. The above articles a perſon in your behalf demanded, all which I agree to and will comply with, and the government ſhall be continued to me in full authority, and to the above I have put my own ſeal, and Meer Cootbodeen will ſign and ſeal the ſame, after which you muſt ſend a counterpart of this writing with the honourable Company's ſeal affixed.

IV. Agreed to, and that we ſhall act jointly in turning the enemy out of the town. Whatever the honourable Company have demanded I agree to.

A counterpart of the above articles were ſealed with the honourable Company's ſeal, and ſent to Atchund the fourth of March, 1759.

As

As ſoon as theſe articles were executed, Atchund immediately opened the inner town gate, and ordered a party of men to aſſiſt in bringing the Siddee to terms, who being acquainted with this junction, was convinced that it muſt be impoſſible for him to hold out againſt their combined force, and the general voice of the people. After many repeated meſſages, with a variety of propoſals, it was at laſt granted, that the Siddee's people ſhould have liberty to march out with their arms and accoutrements, and alſo be permitted to take away all their valuable effects, and even the common furniture of their houſes. This was done with the greateſt regularity, and the Engliſh were peaceably put in poſſeſſion of the Caſtle and Tanka.

The guns and ammunition found in the caſtle were ſecured for the company, as alſo the veſſels and naval ſtores, till ſuch time as the Mogul's pleaſure was known. As ſoon as the grants arrived from Delli, appointing the Company Admiral to the Mogul, the ſhips and ſtores belonged to them of courſe as part of the Tanka. It ſhould be remarked, that the above-mentioned grants, and all Phirmaunds hereafter inſerted, were ſolicited and obtained before the murder of the Mogul, and the revolution at Delli; and arrived ſome time after the reduction of the caſtle.

The number of killed and wounded did not amount to a hundred Europeans, but the loſs by deſertion was greater. Thus was accompliſhed a revolution of general benefit: peace and good government was reſtored to the city, and the Engliſh acquired a valuable and moſt neceſſary poſſeſſion, to the univerſal ſatisfaction of the inhabitants, and alſo with the concurrence of the people in power. As the authentic papers hereunto annexed, will prove that this eſtabliſhment had the ſanction of the Mogul, that which immediately follows will ſhew that proper care was taken to have the aſſent alſo of the Marattas.

PROPOSALS

PROPOSALS from the NANNA PUNDIT PRADEN, Chief of the MARATTAS.

I. As the Siddee at Surat has not only become troublesome for many years to the honourable Company, the * Circar, merchants, &c. but has possessed himself of the castle, and usurped the government of the place, to the entire ruin of trade and the city of Surat. It is therefore agreed, between the Circar and honourable Company, to turn him out of Surat, that every body may be easy there, to pursue his own advantage, and for the general benefit of the place.

II. That the English shall have the sole power and authority to make any man † Nabob there, and the Circar shall approve such election without hesitation; and they (the English) shall have the same power and authority to turn him out, by informing the Circar, (who will not have any objection to it) should he prove a bad man, in any respect, towards the merchants, or any body else.

III. That the Nabob, *&c.* shall make no alterations in the customs on goods, *&c.* but let that article, and every thing else remain as at present.

IV. That the castle when taken, shall be possessed by the English, and they shall have the sole command of it for the safety of the place, and benefit of the government, and for which they shall receive the usual allowance.

V. That when the Siddee at Surat is turned out, the Tanka which he had for maintaining a fleet, shall be divided yearly in three shares, *viz.* The Circar, the Company, and the Nabob, each one-third.

VI. That the Circar, shall receive, as usual, from the government, what is justly due to them, and

* The Marattas's officers.

† The Governor of the Town is called Nabob.

pay

pay out of it what is due to Damojee, but both the Circar's and Damojee's officers and people are to give aſſiſtance for the greater import and export of goods, *&c.* to and from Surat.

VII. That the Nabob or government of Surat ſhall receive, as uſual what is due to him from the Circar and Damojee, for the country without Surat gates.

VIII. That ſhould there be any quarrel or diſturbance within the town, and there be an occaſion for putting a ſtop to any thing any where out of the gates of Surat, the Circar's people are to do or deſiſt from the ſame conformable to the deſire of the Engliſh, and not otherwiſe, and thoſe officers and people are not to offer to meddle in any affairs of the Surat government, or ſhew any moleſtation to the ſame.

After theſe propoſals it was extremely difficult to manage the Marattas, who were continually interfering. During the ſiege a body of their troops ap proached Surat, and deſired to be admitted to act in concert with the Engliſh, but as ſuch an affair would have diſguſted the Moors in the town, Mr. Spencer managed ſo as to wave it without offence, uſing at the ſame time all poſſible precautions to prevent their having any intercourſe with the Siddee or Atchund, with both of whom they had been tampering notwithſtanding their profeſſions to the Company. At laſt he found it neceſſary to declare that he would not allow of any force appearing before the place, while the Engliſh were carrying on their operations againſt it.

PER-

PERWANNA, under the seal of Nabob Vizier Ulma Malech, Asof Shaw Nizamel Muluck, Bahadour, dated the ninth of Shuval, in the sixth year of the reign of his present Majesty, (seventh of June, 1759.)*

BE peace and happiness with the renowned Mr. John Spencer, Captain of the factory in the city of Surat, by the hands of your vakeel, your present and arzee (or request) have been received, and the purport and particular thereof are understood, and your arzee (or request) to his Majesty, has been delivered. The pains you have taken, and the success you have met with in keeping open the Door of Mecca, and delivering our subjects from oppression, we are pleased and satisfied with. As to the Phirmaund for the government of the castle and saned for the fleet, which are requested in the name of the English company, I have given your Vakeel an answer, who will particularly advise you thereof. Let the Piscah on this account be quickly remitted, that it may be presented to his Majesty, and your request thereby granted. In the mean time it behoves you to carry on affairs with alacrity, and be assured that herein nothing on my part shall be wanting to countenance you.

A REPRESENTATION made to the Mogul by John Spencer, in behalf of the Honourable English East-India Company.

THAT by virtue of Royal Phirmaunds of your Majesty's Predecessors, the English hitherto

* A grant given, or paper signed by the Mogul, is called a Phirmaund.
By the Mogul's Son, a Nushawn.
By the Nabob, a Perwanna.
By the Vizier, a Housbul-hookum.

enjoyed ſavour at Surat, and carried on their buſineſs in a reputable manner, till in theſe days that the Siddees uſurping an undue authority in the town, uſed it to the ruin of the city in general, the lives and properties of your Majeſty's ſubjects being made light of by them, and they even proceeded ſo far, as to take away the lives of our people, in direct breach of your Majeſty's Phirmaund; and in ſhort, inſtead of being the Protectors of the place, became the oppreſſors of it to ſuch a degree, that the juſt orders of your Majeſty, were no ways regarded in this city by their means, and things were come to this paſs, that though in conſideration of the Tanka, the Siddee was to protect the bar, yet ſo far was he from doing that, that for many months paſt, a large fleet of Sancrajee Punt's, Ballajee Row's Naib, entirely ſhut up the bar, as did a large land force by land, to the infinite detriment of the place, and inhabitants in general, without the Siddee's interfering therein, and there was the greateſt reaſon to believe, that unleſs ſome ſpeedy and rigorous meaſures had ſoon been purſued, your Majeſty's famous city of Surat, the only port of good Muſſellmen to the tomb of your Prophet, would have been brought to ſhame. In ſuch circumſtances, the eyes of the whole town were caſt on us, as the only perſons of force ſufficient to ſave the city from the calamities that it then felt, and was ſtill further threatened with, and in conſequence of their ſolicitations to me, though our buſineſs in thoſe parts of the world is only to trade and merchandize, and we are not deſirous of taking, or governing cities or countries, yet as all the inhabitants of this place great and ſmall, were earneſtly deſirous of it, and I ſaw it was for the good of the place, I wrote to the General of Bombay on the ſubject, in ſuch manner, that at an immenſe expence, he ſent hither in our King's ſhips, a great force of good and experienced men, with a large quantity of artillery, and other warlike ſtores, of all ſorts, with

with which I have had the happineſs to procure ſafety to the city, and eaſe to the inhabitants, and have procured an entire currency to your Majeſty's orders in the place; and your Majeſty's authority, by all ways in our power will be preſerved in the place, as it uſed to be, and you will conſider the Engliſh as deſirous of receiving your orders, ſuch being the intention of the Governor of Bombay and myſelf, whoſe whole power will be uſed to maintain the caſtle, that we have poſſeſſed ourſelves of, for your Majeſty, and to preſerve the bar and ſea open againſt all oppoſers, on your behalf, for we ſhall not apply the Tanka you have granted for this purpoſe to others, as has hitherto been the caſe; and ſince our having done this, the enemies that ſurrounded the place both by ſea and land, to its great prejudice, have been removed, we are always ready for the ſafety of the caſtle and city, with its inhabitants; and therefore hope for your Majeſty's favour, in behalf of the Honourable Engliſh Company, for whoſe good ſervices on this occaſion I muſt refer your Majeſty to the repreſentation of the inhabitants of the place.

N. B. There accompanied this a letter to the Vizier, much to the ſame purpoſe, requeſting his countenance; letters went alſo in the name of the Governor of Bombay on the occaſion, to the King and Vizier, referring in general to the above, and the whole was attended with a repreſentation of the town in general on our behalf, under the ſeals of the Nabob, Naib, the head Siads, and Officers, and the Heads of the Merchants in general.

*PERWANNA under the Vizer's ſeal for * Sciad Moynodeen Caun to act as Governor of Surat.*

BY the advices received here from Surat, it has been made known unto his Majeſty, that you with the conſent, and at the deſire of the inhabitants, are arrived there, and that afterwards the Honourable Mr. Spencer, Captain of the Factory at Surat, with the renowned Pharraſs Caun, came and turned out Siddee Amed, who had poſſeſſed himſelf of his Majeſty's Caſtle, and greatly oppreſſed our ſubjects, and that thereby the city is now at eaſe, and the inhabitants ſatisfied. Therefore it behoves you to act as may be moſt conducive to the good of the city and his Majeſty's affairs, that every body may follow their calling without fear, and the city flouriſh. Let this be implicitly obeyed, on the ſecond of Shaban, and the ſixth year of the reign of his preſent Majeſty.

HOOKUM or ORDER, under the Vizier's ſeal, to Mr. Spencer, to aſſiſt and adviſe with Sciad Moynodeen Caun, in the Government of Surat.

BE it known unto the Honourable Mr. Spencer, Captain of the Factory in Surat, that in theſe days advice has been received that with the conſent, and at the deſire of the inhabitants of the Bunder of Surat, the renowned and brave Sciad Moynodeen Caun Bahadour came into the place, and that afterwards you, with the renowned Pharraſs Caun, came, and turning out the Siddee from the King's Caſtle, which he had poſſeſſed himſelf of, and given much trouble to the ſubjects by oppreſſion and otherwiſe, gave eaſe and ſatisfaction

* Another Name for Atchund.

to

to the inhabitants of the place. with which we are well satisfied, and it now behoves you to advise with, and in conjunction with the above renowned, so to carry on matters, as may be most conducive to the good of the place, and the honour of his Majesty, by assisting one another. Let this be done on the second of Shaban, in the sixth year of the reign of his present Majesty.

HOOKUM or ORDER, under the Vizier's seal, to the subjects and inhabitants of Surat, to acknowledge and assist Sciad Moynodeen Caun as Governor of Surat.

BE it known unto all the principal Sciads, Shaiks, and otherwise, and old men of understanding, as also to all the merchants, and others our subjects, inhabitants of Surat, that his Majesty is made acquainted by advices from thence, that by your consent, and at your desire, the brave and renowned Sciad Moynodeen Caun, is come there, and after him Mr. Spencer, Captain of the Factory at Surat, with the renowned Pharrass Caun, came and turned out Siddee Amed, who possessed himself of his Majesty's castle, and greatly oppressed our subjects, and that thereby the city is now at ease, and the inhabitants satisfied. Therefore it behoves you, in all respects, to assist and advise the said Moynodeen Caun, and with one accord to concur in every thing for the good of the place, which I would have implicitly obeyed on the second of Shaban, and the sixth year of the reign of his present Majesty.

HOUSBUL-HOOKUM, under the great seal of the Nabob Vizier, Ulmah Maleck, Nirzam al Muluck Bahadour.

BE peace unto the high and renowned Mr. John Spencer. The courage and conduct you have

 shewn

ſhewn in his Majeſty's ſervice, for the good of our ſubjects the inhabitants of Surat, are made known to his Majeſty, and their letter expreſſing their ſatisfaction therewith, has alſo been ſhewn, with which his Majeſty is well ſatisfied, and praiſes you therefore upon this account. He has been pleaſed to order this Houſbul-Hookum to be ſent to you, that you may take care of his Majeſty's caſtle, and take the preſervation of the trade of theſe ſeas particularly upon you, ſo that the inhabitants of Surat may carry on their buſineſs, and live in eaſe and quiet, and the ſhips and veſſels going to and coming from the moſt remarkable ports, as well as others, be in no fear from rovers and pirates. The Phirmaund for the government of the caſtle, and Perwannah for the fleet, being given in charge to the Engliſh Company, ſhall be ſent you from Court, on the firſt of the month of Zickat, and the ſixth year of the reign of his preſent Majeſty, (the 24th of June, 1759.)

N. B. The Houſbul-Hookum to the Governor, is in the ſame words as the above.

PERWANNA, under the Coochuck, (or the ſmall ſeal) of the Nabob Vizier Ulma Maleck, Nizam al Muluck Bahadour, to Mr. John Spencer.

THE Arzee of the high and renowned, with the preſent, and letter expreſſing the merchant's ſatisfaction, have been received by the hands of Hadee Caun. The conduct and courage you have ſhewn for the good of the inhabitants of Surat, and his Majeſty's ſervice, have been in a particular manner made known to him, with which he is well pleaſed, and praiſes you therefore. It now behoves you with a ſatisfied mind particularly to look to the peace of the inhabitants, and the preſervation of his Majeſty's caſtle, and to take care that the trade of the ſeas is kept open and ſafe

ſafe, that the Hadjees (or Pilgrims) and merchants meet with no trouble or impediment, and that the ſhips to and from the renowned and other ports, may be ſafe from any fear of violation from rovers and pirates. The Phirmaund for the government, and Perwannah for the fleets, being given in charge to the Engliſh Company, ſhall be ſent you from Court.

PERWANNA, under the Coochuck, (or the ſmall ſeal) of the Nabob Vizier Ulma Maleck, Nizam al Muluck Bahadour, to Mr. John Spencer.

HIGH and renowned, the ſums uſually remitted from Surat, are now much wanted at Court, and his Majeſty is preſſing for them. As yet what money the renowned Moynodeen Caun may have ſent, is not yet received, therefore Perwannah's have been wrote to haſten him in that reſpect; but it likewiſe behoves you to preſs him on this head, and procure the remittance of the Tohod by bills, as ſoon as poſſible. Look upon this as abſolutely neceſſary.

PHIRMAUND or ORDER, under the great Mogul's ſeal, and under ſealed by his Vizier, for the Honourable Company's holding the government of the caſtle of Surat.

Verſes from the Koran, in Arabick.	The Great Seal of the King's Names in Perſian.

LET the renowned among the people, the Engliſh Company hope for his Majeſty's favour, and be it known unto them, that in theſe

 happy

happy and victorious times, his Majesty has been pleased, out of his great grace and favour, to grant unto them, the Killidaree, or government of the Castle of Surat, on its being taken from Mussoot Achmed Caun, it therefore is requisite, that they should be very grateful for this his Majesty's favour, and look particularly to the welfare of the castle, keeping proper order and discipline among the troops, and having provisions, stores, and ammunition always in readiness, as has been usual, which is strictly and especially required of them by his Majesty.

Given on the eleventh day of Mohoram, and in the sixth year of his Majesty's reign, (or 4th of September, 1759.)

At the back of the Phirmaund is the Grand Vizier's Seal, and all his titles wrote at length.

DUSTUCK or ORDER, under the Chan Sumaun, or Steward's seal for the Honourable Company's holding the King's fleet.

THE Dustuck in the name of the noble and renowned English Company, is as follows. By his Majesty's Housbul-Hookum, the office of Deroga of the great fleet, belonging to the Bunder of Surat, vacant by the dismission of Siddee Yacood Caun, is now delivered into your charge; therefore it behoves you, to execute the said office, with great care and circumspection, and carry on the business of it justly, and with moderation. Look on this as absolutely required of you. Dated the second day of Mohoram, in the sixth year of his Majesty's reign, (the 26th of August 1759.)

At the back of this is the seal of Zecah al Doulat Tidaudin Caun Bahadour, who is Caun Samaun or Steward to his Majesty, whose prerogative it is to grant this Order.

Tran-

Translation of an ORDER, under the Vizier's seal, to Sciad Moynodeen Caun, Governor of Surat, regarding the payment of the Tanka on account of the fleet to the Honourable Company, &c.

TO the brave, noble, renowned, and careful Sciad Moynodeen Caun Bahadour, on whom is his Majesty's favour. The Vakeel of the English Company having represented, that as the Deroga, or post of the great fleet, belonging to the Bunder of Surat, under the Subah of Amedabad, on the dismission of Siddee Yacood Caun, Killidar of Dunde Rajahpore, from the said post, had been granted his constituents, he hoped that a Perwannah or order for the Tanka, and account of the troops of the fleet, as has been usual since the time of him, who is now in Heaven (meaning Aurungzebe) among the other charges of Surat, exclusive of what is sent to Court, might be given him, in your name, from the Archieves of the Kingdom, it appears, that this office was in the hands of Siddee Yacood Caun, and that in the twenty-third year of the reign of Mamud Shaw, he procured an Order on Teg Beg Caun then Governor, for the annual payment of two lack, according to custom, besides what was sent to Court. Now in these days the office of Deroga of this fleet, on the dismission of Siddee Yacood Caun, has been granted to the said Company, as has been usual, under the Dustuck, or Order of the Caun Samaun (or steward) and dated the second of Mohoram, and the sixth year of the present reign, therefore I now write to you that you may pay unto them, account charges, for the forces of the fleet, the usual Tanka, of two lack every year, agreeable to the hereafter Order, among the other charges, exclusive of what is sent to Court, and let the accounts and papers relative thereto be transmitted hither

hither. Dated the twenty-fifth of Mohoram, and the ſixth year of the reign of his preſent Majeſty, (or 18th of September, 1759.)

On the back of this Perwanna, is the Vizier's ſeal, and the zimra or certificate from the ſeveral officers and regiſters at court, ſetting forth, as is above related in the Perwannah, and that the Vizier had given orders for regiſtering the ſeveral grants.

HOUSBUL HOOKUM, under the ſeal of the Nabob Vizier, Ulma Maleck Bahadour, to the Engliſh company accompanying the Phirmaund.

MAY his Majeſty's favour ever remain upon the brave and noble Engliſh company. It has pleaſed his Majeſty to grant unto you the office of Killedar (or caſtle governor) of the Bunder of Surat, vacant by the diſmiſſion of Hoffis Amud Cawn; as alſo the office of Deroga of the great fleet of the Vaid Bunder, vacant by the diſmiſſion of Siddee Yacood Cawn. Therefore, agreeable to his order, you are now directed to take particular care of the proper execution of the above offices, by looking well to the welfare of the caſtle, and preſervation of the merchants, &c. on the high ſeas, keeping them clear of pirates and rovers, who may infeſt them. This is poſitively required of you.

HOUSBUL HOOKUM, from the Vizier to Governor Bourchier.

IT has pleaſed his Majeſty, to grant unto the brave and noble Engliſh Company, the office of Killedar of the Bunder of Surat, vacant by the diſmiſſion of Hoffis Amud Cawn; as alſo the office of Deroga, of the great fleet of the ſaid Bunder, vacant by the diſmiſſion of Siddee Yacood Cawn; there-

therefore agreeable to his order this is wrote to you, to direct, that according to the directions and advice of the said Company, you take all the care in your power for the proper execution of the said offices, by looking well to the welfare of the castle, and preservation of the trade and merchants on the high seas, from pirates, and other rovers.—Of this you are desired to be very careful.

HOUSBUL HOOKUM, to Mr. Spencer, the same as above, except two or three words which are almost synonimous.

To Atchund the same, directing him to give the company all the assistance he can in the execution of these offices.

GOMBROON.

[1759.] ABOUT fifteen degrees west of Surat, the East-India company have a small settlement, called Gombroon, which being remote from the rest, and what is more, unfortified, could never have had a place in the account of the war in India, had not the French thought proper to beset this defenceless factory with all the parade of a siege, and to crown their hostilities with the pompous form of a capitulation.

The articles in this capitulation, which relate to the Count d'Estaing, have so greatly surprized the military gentlemen, before whom he gave his parole, that it is evident they will be new to all those who come from the coast of Coromandel: therefore to satisfy them of the truth of so extraordinary a proceeding, the capitulation is here published, together with an account of the whole transaction.

Gom-

Gombroon is an European name for the famous Bunder-Abaſſi, which was built by Shaw Abbas when he ruined Ormus. Ormus, that jewel of the world, as it was called, is at this preſent time a rocky iſland ſo entirely covered with ſalt, that there is ſcarce any part of it but what is cruſted over with it, at leaſt two inches thick. In all places where they dig, is to be found rock ſalt, and conſequently there are no pools, neither are there any ſprings of freſh water; notwithſtanding which, the Portugueſe, from its advantageous ſituation for trade, built a very elegant city there, with a ſtrong fortification: but near two hundred years ago, the Perſians, with the aſſiſtance of the Engliſh, expelled the Portugueſe from it, The great Shaw Abbas Sophi of Perſia, when he removed the trade to Gombroon, on the oppoſite ſhore, granted the Engliſh great privileges in commerce, and a proportion of the cuſtoms of that port, which amounted to near 4000*l. per annum*; but theſe advantages they have loſt by the unhappy ſtate of the country, which has long been in confuſion and anarchy.

The Engliſh eſtabliſhed a factory here on account of the great demand for woollen goods from Perſia, before that country was impoveriſhed by the troubles. The air of Gombroon is ſo unhealthy from the hot winds, that even the natives themſelves fly from it in the bad ſeaſon, but knowing the time when the ſhips are to be expected; they come down with caravans, and carry off their lading. As there was therefore no occaſion for large warehouſes, the company never erected any fortifications, but only ſecured the houſe in which their Agent, or Chief, and his clerks lived, with a very ſmall party of ſoldiers, ſcarcely ſufficient to ſerve as a defence againſt robbers.

The Mooriſh governor of this place, is Moolah Allee Shaw, who ought to be ſubordinate to the governor

governor of Lhor, as the governor of Lhor ſhould himſelf be ſubject to the Sophi of Perſia: but the troubles and total want of government throughout all Perſia, have made them both in a manner independent. The remains of ſome ſtrong fortifications at Ormus afford a ſecure retreat for the governor of Gombroon, when the adjacent part of the continent is diſturbed; and when it is quiet he comes to Gombroon, collects the cuſtoms, and very often endeavours to extort loans from the Europeans, by laying difficulties in the way of their trade, and terrifying them with his Arabs. It was by ſuch means that Moolah Allee Shaw very lately prevailed with the Dutch to comply with his requeſt of a loan which they had at firſt refuſed. Theſe Arabs are very ungovernable and inſolent, and when they have been taken in the act of plundering, ſeveral of their tribe have run out of the fort and wounded our people who were carrying the delinquents before the governor; and though application has been made for redreſs to Moolah Allee Shaw, he never could be prevailed on to chaſtiſe them, but always excuſed himſelf, by alledging that they were a tribe which no body dared to puniſh but Sheik Rama. Such inſtruments had Moolah Allee Shaw, to employ for the gratification of his avarice; and from his own diſpoſition he was glad of every opportunity to make uſe of them.

On the 15th of October, 1759, the French, with four ſhips under Dutch colours, one of which was a veſſel of ſixty-four guns, and one of twenty-two, landed to the weſtward of Gombroon. They advanced with two mortars and four pieces of cannon, and began to batter the factory, which was not a fortification, but only a ſtrong houſe. The Agent and his clerks, together with the crew of the Speedwell, which was burnt by the French, did not exceed the number of ſixteen men, againſt whom

whom the French brought at leaſt a hundred and fifty Europeans, and as many Coffres. The ſmall number of Engliſh who were there, did what they could to defend it; as to the Topaſſes and Sepoys, few of them would ſtand to the guns.

About eleven o'clock, being high water, the twenty-two gun ſhip hauled within about a quarter of a mile of the factory, and began to fire: at the ſame time thoſe who were aſhore played upon it with their mortars and guns from the weſtward. At about three in the afternoon a ſummons was ſent from the French camp. Upon a conſultation held in the factory, the military gentlemen were of opinion that the houſe was not tenable; it was therefore unanimouſly agreed to ſurrender upon the beſt terms that could be procured, and thereupon the following capitulation was ſigned.

Articles of capitulation for the Eaſt-India company's factory of Gombroon, between Alexander Douglas Eſquire, chief of the ſaid ſettlement and council, and Monſieur Des Eſſars, captain of his moſt Chriſtian Majeſty's ſhip Condè, and commander in chief of the preſent expedition, and Monſieur Charnyau, captain, commander of the land forces.

ARTICLE I. So ſoon as the preſent capitulation is ſigned, a detachment of French troops are to take poſſeſſion of the factory; the keys are to be delivered to the commanding officer, and no perſon is to come in, or go out, without his permiſſion, as he will take care to prevent diſorders and thefts.

II. All effects of what kind ſoever contained in the factory, are to belong to the beſiegers, and are to be delivered to the French commiſſary, with all books and papers in poſſeſſion of the beſieged; the beſiegers are to be ſhewn the warehouſes,

houſes, that they may place the neceſſary centinels over them. The artillery, arms, ammunition, proviſions, money, merchandize and ſlaves, in general every thing contained within the factory, are comprehended in this article.

III. The Chief, the Garriſon-factors, writers, and all Europeans in the ſervice of the Engliſh East-India company, in general all the ſubjects of his Britannick Majeſty in the factory are to be priſoners of war, under the following clauſes only.

IV. Whereas Monſieur d'Eſtaing, brigadier of foot, and formerly a priſoner of his Britannick Majeſty, is now on board the ſhip Condè in his way to Europe, by the way of Buſſorah, being deſirous of rendering more ſecure the intelligence received of an exchange having been made in his behalf, between Mr. Pigot, governor of Madraſs, and Monſieur Lally, lieutenant-general; it is now agreed between the beſiegers and beſieged, that Alexander Douglas, Eſquire, chief of the Engliſh Eaſt-India Company's factory at Gombroon, with William Naſh, Enſign Johnſton, Dymoke Lyſter, Lieutenant George Bembow, Lieutenant Richard Evans, and Richard Mainwaring, are lawfully exchanged for Monſieur d'Eſtaing; and they are at full liberty to go where and to what places they pleaſe, in conſequence of which, Monſieur d'Eſtaing, is under no other clauſe than what is ſpecified in the ſixth article.

V. Though the preſent exchange of priſoners is an unneceſſary precaution in behalf of Monſieur d'Eſtaing, yet all perſons mentioned in the preceding article are abſolutely free, but ſhould Monſieur d'Eſtaing have been already exchanged as he undoubtedly is in that caſe, for the ſeven perſons already mentioned who now enjoy their liberty, a like number, and of equal ſtation of his moſt Chriſtian Majeſty's ſubjects, are to be releaſed whenever a cartel is made.

VI.

VI. Monsieur d'Estaing, in order to fulfil with the greatest exactitude the promise he made governor Pigot, that he would not take up arms against the English on the Coromandel coast only, for the space of eighteen months, reckoning from the first of May, one thousand seven hundred and fifty-nine: desires it may be inserted in the present capitulation, that notwithstanding he is now exchanged, yet he will keep the promise he made governor Pigot, of not taking up arms against the English on the Coromandel coast only, for the space of eighteen months, but he is at free liberty in all other places to take arms.

VII. If it is possible to agree about the re-purchasing of Gombroon factory, it will be looked on as a part of the present capitulation, the besiegers reserving to themselves the liberty nevertheless to do therewith as they may think fit, should no agreement be concluded with the besieged.

VIII. In consideration of the exchange of Monsieur d'Estaing, and at his particular request to Monsieur Des Essars, Alexander Douglas, Esquire, chief of the English East-India Company's settlements of Gombroon, and all others mentioned in the fourth article, have liberty, and may carry away all their own effects of what kind or sort soever, excepting ammunition, provisions, marine, military, or warlike stores.

Dated at Gombroon the fourteenth day of October at six o'clock in the morning, and in the year of our Lord one thousand seven hundred and fifty nine.

Des Essars
Charnyau.

Alexander Douglas,
William Nash,
Richard Johnston.

As it must appear very extraordinary that the Count d'Estaing should chuse to have his name so often mentioned in the capitulation, the impossibility

ſibility of his having had the intelligence he pretends to have received, will make it ſtill more ſurprizing: for it is a certain fact, that there had not been even an attempt made towards his exchange. The parole he gave was in the uſual form not to ſerve directly or indirectly againſt the Engliſh, during the preſent war, or till he ſhould be regularly exchanged.

On the twelfth, while the French were ſtanding into the road, Moolah Allee Shaw came to the factory, and gave the agent all imaginable aſſurances of his affording him aſſiſtance, and that if the French attempted to land, he would do what was in his power to prevent it; but when the agent ſent to him in the morning, acquainting him, that they were approaching the ſhore in order to land, inſtead of performing his promiſe he remained quiet in his fort, and though about ten o'clock, he was deſired to ſend a few men to our aſſiſtance, he abſolutely refuſed. The reaſon he aſſigned for not fulfilling his offers was, that one of his ſhips (then at anchor in the road) was in the power of the French, and that if he aſſiſted us with any men, they would carry her away. His fear and preſent intereſt governed him at that time, and ſoon after the French landed, he ſent them ſuch refreſhments of greens and fruits as the ſeaſon afforded, offering to ſupply them with whatever was in his power.

The French during their ſtay paid little regard to the articles of capitulation. On the 30th of October, at about twelve o'clock at night, they went on board their ſhips, having firſt ſet fire to the factory. They dug mines in ſeveral parts thereof, ſome of which took effect; they had likewiſe fixed combuſtibles to the beams of the apartments and warehouſes. The greateſt part of the wall of the eaſt-ſide of the factory was blown up, and the cieling and floor of the apartments of the weft fide were burnt. Moolah Allee Shaw's people took away the beams, planks, and window-frames, and fet fire to all the doors and other wood-work, for the fake of the iron that was in them.

Had Moolah Allee Shaw acted a becoming part, many valuables might have been faved, after the French evacuated the factory; for they left upwards of thirty thoufand maunds of copper, with feveral other goods, which they could neither carry away nor deftroy: but notwithftanding all the applications that were made to him, inftead of placing people to prevent thefts, and fecure what remained, or even to extinguifh the fire, he gave the factory up to a general pillage; and in a vifit he made the agent, he had the affurance publickly to confefs, he believed there was not a man in the town but had his fhare of plunder. What with the copper, and other goods the French gave Moolah Allee Shaw before their departure, and the copper which he clandeftinely carried to Ormus, he was fuppofed to have got in the whole to the amount of fixty thoufand roupees, (not reckoning the guns which the French left behind) and his whole gang of Arabs enriched themfelves proportionably. As for fuch of the lower clafs of inhabitants as had got any booty of copper, Moolah Allee Shaw obliged them to fell it to him, at the rate of two roupees the maund: but the Arabs had the precaution to fend their plunder to their different habitations.

The French and Moolah Allee Shaw, entered into articles of alliance, wherein it was agreed that there fhould be an everlafting friendfhip between them, that his ports and veffels fhould be fecure, and that whofoever were Moolah Allee Shaw's enemies, fhould likewife be enemies of the French nation. The writing given by them was in the French language, figned by Monf. D'Eftaing, the counter-

counterpart given by Moolah Allee Shaw was in the Persian language.

REVOLUTIONS at DELLI.

[1757.] IT has already been related by what means the Revolution at Delli was brought about in the year * 1754.

In the beginning of the year 1757, Ahmed Abdalla, the Pattan Chief, marched to Delli, and took Allum Geer, and all the Omrahs prisoners.

After having kept possession of the capital for some time, he at length on the sixth of June, sent for the Mogul to his tent, where he received him with great honour, and replaced him on the throne, having first secured to himself as large a treasure as could be expected from the low state of the finances of the Empire. He then proceeded to Agra, and seizing the revenues of that district, marched to Lahore, from whence he issued his orders to all the neighbouring Nabobs, and Rajas, that they should acknowledge themselves in subjection to his son Timur, whom he then proclaimed King of Lahore. Having thus invested his son with the dominion of a Country from whence he proposed that he should also superintend the affairs of Indostan, he returned to his own Country, recommending to Timur to treat the Mogul with continued marks of regard and friendship.

Shaw Abadin Cawn, the son of Gauzedy Cawn, and consequently the true Vice-Roy of the Deckan, chose rather to suffer his right to be usurped by Salabatzing than relinquish the office of Vizier,

* See Page 110.

 which

which gave him ſo great an aſcendency over the Mogul, and conſequently an unbounded power in the Empire. But as all power is precarious, the ſons of the Emperor became daily more formidable to the Vizier, and created him continual trouble and jealouſy. At length about the end of the year 1759, to free himſelf from all ſolicitude of that kind, he reſolved on the murder of his maſter, in order that he might place in his ſtead a more inconſiderable repreſentative of the Royal Family, who ſhould be leſs reſpectable in himſelf, and not ſo formidable by the ſupport of his children or other relations. As theſe were the great obſtacles to the ambition of the Vizier, they were no leſs ſo to the execution of his preſent deſign: therefore to remove them from the capital, he propoſed a hunting-match, and took with him the ſons of the Mogul, and the greateſt part of his friends to a great diſtance from Delli. The next difficulty was to overcome the ſuſpicions of the Mogul, and the ſuperſtitious principles of the Moors, who though they are ready to execute any kind of villainy, can never be brought to murder their Sovereign in the ſanctuary of his own palace.

It was well known that Allum Geer had a moſt particular veneration for the Fakeers; and the Vizier was ſenſible that unleſs the Emperor could be prevailed on, by a motive of devotion, to come from under his roof, no other inducement could ever engage him to abandon what he would conſider as his only protection in the abſence of his friends. Every thing being concerted accordingly, before the departure of Shaw Abadin Cawn, the creatures of that Miniſter came to the Mogul, and informed him that a Fakeer of moſt eminent ſanctity was in the garden, and though it was with great reluctance that the Emperor yielded to the dictates of his zeal, he was at length

by

by their persuasions, prevailed on to go out and meet this holy person, whom he had long exprest a desire to see. He had not advanced many steps in the garden, when too Moors in the habit of Fakeers, came suddenly behind him, put a noose about his neck, and then stabbed him with spears till he died on the spot.

As soon as the Vizier was informed of the death of his master, he immediately confined his sons, and all the friends of Allum Geer, who were then with him, and placing on the throne one of the Royal Family, whom he thought the most convenient for his purposes, went himself directly to join an army of Marattas, who were waiting for him about thirty miles from Delli.

It was not long before the Pattans, equally displeased with the Vizier for his conduct, and the Marattas for interfering in the government of Delli, marched a considerable force against them, and coming up with them at a place called Paniput, near a hundred miles from Delli, they killed the Maratta General, and put the army to flight, which retreated till they were joined by another body of their own troops. They were pursued by the Pattans, and routed again in another engagement.

Ahamed Abdalla then entered Delli, and placed his son Timur upon the throne; and orders were issued out to all the Rajas and Governors in the neighbourhood, to exert their utmost endeavours to prevent the Marattas from approaching the city.

NAVAL OPERATIONS.

[1759.] NOtwithstanding the attention of the reader has been long suspended from the Coast of Coromandel, the principal object of this work; it is expedient here to give an account of the

 engage-

engagement at ſea in 1759, and here conclude the Naval Operations. This will afford an opportunity of purſuing afterwards the affairs of the Coaſt without interruption, as far as they can be aſcertained by the lateſt accounts.

Vice Admiral Pocock having refitted his ſquadron at Bombay, and made it ready for the ſea by the ſeventh of April, 1759, ſailed on that day for the Coaſt of Coromandel, uſing his utmoſt endeavours to get round Ceylon before the French fleet, which were expected ſoon to ſail from the Iſlands of Mauritius and Bourbon.

Having gained this neceſſary point, he continued in the proper ſtations to intercept the Enemy, or protect our own trade, till the third of Auguſt, and then, as the ſeaſon advanced, proceeded to cruize off Pondichery, in hourly expectation of the Enemy. The whole month being paſt without any advice of the French ſquadron, which had ſo long been expected, proviſions and water grew ſhort, and the Admiral was obliged while he continued to cruize for the Enemy, to proceed to Trincomalay the firſt of September to water the ſhips, as he found it very difficult to water them at Negapatam. He had diſpatched the Company's frigate Revenge a few days before, with orders to proceed off Ceylon, and look out for the Enemy. The ſecond, at ten in the forenoon, they ſaw from the maſt-head fifteen ſail in the S. E. quarter, ſtanding to the N. E. which proved to be the Enemy's fleet, and ſoon after perceived the Revenge chaced by one of their frigates, which fired ſeveral ſhot at her. Upon this the Admiral made the ſignal for a general chace, and ſtood towards them with all the ſail he could make, which obliged the Enemy's frigate to give over chace, and rejoin her own ſquadron. The abatement of the wind prevented our getting near them when the day cloſed.

The

The French line consisted of eleven sail of large ships. Le Zodiaque, M. D'Aché, Lieutenant-General, seventy-four guns, and six hundred and sixty men. The Minotaur, M. L'Aguille, Chef D'Escadre, seventy-four guns, six hundred and sixty men. Le Comte de Provence, M. La Chaise, seventy-four guns, six hundred and sixty men. Le Centaur, M. Surville, seventy guns, six hundred and sixty men. L'Actif, M. Beauchaine, L'Illustre, M. De Ruis, and La Fortune, M. Lobry, all of sixty-four guns, and six hundred men. Le Vengeur, M. Palliere, sixty-four guns, and five hundred men. Le Duc D'Orleans, M. Surville le Cadet, Le St. Louis, M. Johannes, Le Duc de Bourgogne, M. Benvet, all of sixty guns, and five hundred men. They had two frigates, and two store-ships.

This extraordinary force, like which none had ever yet been seen in the Indian seas, was chased, invited, and in vain provoked to fight, by a much inferior strength; for the English squadron were no more than nine ships of the line, of which two were only fifty-gun ships, and the largest carried no more than sixty-eight guns. They were the Yarmouth, Vice-Admiral Pocock, Captain Harrison, sixty-six guns, five hundred and forty men. The Grafton, Rear-Admiral Stevens, Captain Kempenfelt, sixty-eight guns, five hundred and thirty eight men. The Elizabeth, Captain Tiddeman, sixty-four guns, four hundred and eighty men. The Tyger, Captain Brereton, the Sunderland, Honourable Captain Colville, the Weymouth, Sir William Baird, Baronet; all of sixty guns, four hundred and twenty men. The * Cumberland, Captain Somerset, fifty-eight guns, five hundred and twenty men. The Newcastle, Captain Michie, and the Salisbury, Captain Dent, each of fifty guns, three hundred and fifty

* The Cumberland being weak and disabled was reduced from 66 guns to 58.

men. There were alſo three frigates and a fireſhip From hence will appear, the diſproportion of the two ſquadrons, which was ſo great that the French had a ſuperiority of one hundred and ninety two guns, and two thouſand, three hundred and ſixty five men, beſides the great advantage in the ſize of their ſhips.

Notwithſtanding ſo apparent an inequality, the French endeavoured by taking the opportunity of the duſk, and falling off of the wind, to ſteal away undiſcovered, but were fruſtrated in this deſign by the Revenge, who having orders to make ſail to the S. E. and try to keep in ſight of them, about eleven at night, made a ſignal for diſcovering the enemy, and then the whole fleet bore down towards them.

About one in the morning of the third, a heavy ſquall coming on, which continued till three, obliged us to bring to, and clew up our top-ſails. At day-light we ſaw the Enemy's fleet bearing N. E. by N. about five or ſix leagues diſtant. The Admiral then made the ſignal for a general chace to the N. E. Point Pedro on the Iſland of Ceylon bearing Weſt, diſtant ſix or ſeven leagues. At nine, the Enemy's fleet bore N. E. by E. and were formed in a line of battle, a-head on the ſtarboard-tack, with the wind about W. N. W. A little after nine, the Admiral made the ſignal for the line of battle a-breaſt, and ſtood for the center of the Enemy's fleet, which kept under-way, and appeared to go from the wind; by which means we altered their bearings greatly, for by noon they bore S. E. by E. diſtant ſix or ſeven miles. The wind decreaſing as the day advanced, we were not able to form our line till near Sun-ſet, two of our ſquadron the Tyger and Newcaſtle ſailing very ill, though they made all the ſail they could croud.

About a quarter after five our ſquadron being nearly a-breaſt of the Enemy, they wore and came to the wind on the other tack, upon which our ſhips tackt, the rear firſt, and ſteered with the Enemy's

ſqua-

ſquadron. We were now about four miles diſtant with very little wind, had ſcarcely ſteerage-way, and continued ſo till near ten, when a freſh breeze ſprung up from the S. S. W. on which we hauled cloſe to the wind under our topſails, and formed the line a-head. This ſhift of wind, brought the Enemy a-ſtern, and a little upon the weather quarter of our line, but ſoon after, it proving hazy, we loſt ſight of them. It is remarkable they made no ſignal in this or the preceding night, either with guns or lights. The Revenge was ſent to look out a-ſtern, but not being able to diſcover them, was ordered to keep a-head, with better ſucceſs; for about eight next morning, the Revenge made the ſignal for ſeeing four ſail to the N. E. A general chace was begun by the whole ſquadron, and continued till near two in the afternoon, at which time ſeeing no more than two ſhips, and finding he could not come up with thoſe, the Admiral made the ſignal for the Revenge to come into the ſquadron, then ſtood to the northward, and made all the ſail he could to get off Pondichery, juſtly concluding the French ſquadron was bound thither.

The Admiral arrived off Pondichery on the eighth early in the morning and ſaw no ſhips in the road, but at one o'clock in the afternoon diſcovered the enemy to the S. E. and by three, counted thirteen ſail, he was then ſtanding to the ſouthward with the ſea breeze, and to prevent their paſſing him kept a good look out the following night. At half an hour paſt ſix in the morning of the ninth, he ſaw part of the Enemy's ſquadron to the S. W. and by nine counted ſixteen ſail. At two in the afternoon, the wind ſpringing up, the Admiral made the ſignal for a general chace, and at four, the Enemy appeared to be formed in a line of battle a-breaſt, and ſteered right down upon him. The Revenge was ordered to keep (during the night) between our ſquadron and the Enemy, to obſerve their motions.

The

The tenth, at ſix in the morning, the body of the French ſquadron bore S. E. by S. diſtant eight or nine miles, and was formed in a line of battle a-head, on the ſtarboard tack. We continued bearing down on them in a line of battle a-breaſt, with the wind about N. W. by W. At ten the Enemy wore and formed the line a-head upon the larboard tack. At eleven we did the ſame, and kept edging down upon them. At two in the afternoon, the Yarmouth being nearly a-breaſt of the French Admiral's ſecond in the rear, and within muſquet ſhot, M. D'Aché, made the ſignal for battle. The Admiral immediately did the ſame, on which both ſquadrons began to cannonade each other with great fury, and continued hotly engaged till four, when the Enemy's rear, and ſoon after their center, began to give way; the Sunderland having got up ſome time before, and engaged their ſtern-moſt ſhip. Their van made ſail, ſtood on, and with their whole ſquadron bore away, and ſteered to the S. S. E. with all the ſail they could make.

As four of our ſhips in the van had ſuſtained a hot fire from ſix of the Enemy's largeſt ſhips during two hours: after ſo great a diſadvantage, we were in no condition to purſue; for the Tyger having her mizen-maſt and maintop-maſt ſhot away, appeared in other reſpects to be greatly diſabled: The Newcaſtle was much damaged in her maſts, yards, and rigging; and the Cumberland and Saliſbury in the rear, were not in a condition to make ſail. The Yarmouth had her foretop-ſail-yard ſhot away in the ſlings; and the Grafton and Elizabeth were greatly diſabled in their maſts, yards, and rigging. The Weymouth and Sunderland, the only ſhips that had not ſuffered, could not get properly into action, as M. D'Aché began to engage before they could cloſe, and by that means thoſe two were precluded from their ſhare in the engagement, ſo that only ſeven of of our ſhips received the whole fire of the Enemy's fleet till near the concluſion, and then only eight.

The Enemy continued retreating to the ſouthward till dark, at which time the Admiral, ordering the Revenge, as uſual, to keep between him and the Enemy, lay to, with the ſquadron, on the larboard-tack; in order for the diſabled ſhips to repair their damages. At day-light in the morning, we ſaw the Enemy to the S. S. E. lying to alſo on the larboard-tack about four leagues diſtant; the wind being about weſt. The Enemy upon ſeeing our ſquadron, immediately wore and brought to on the other tack, and continued ſo till the evening, when their diſtance was ſo much increaſed that we could ſcarcely diſcern them from the main-top. At this time the wind coming to the eaſtward, the Admiral wore and ſtood under an eaſy ſail to the N. W. the Sunderland having the Newcaſtle in tow, the Weymouth the Tyger, and the Elizabeth the Cumberland.

The French having received leſs damage in their rigging (though they were very much ſhattered in their hulls, and ſuffered a loſs of near fifteen hundred men killed and wounded) were enabled now to gain the only point they ſeemed to be ſolicitous of obtaining. They ſailed directly for Pondichery, and landed four hundred European ſeamen, (for they brought no troops) two hundred Coffrees, about two or three lack of roupees, and the diamonds which they found in the Grantham Indiaman, for that ſhip had been taken by the French near the Cape, in her paſſage home. The value of the diamonds might be about two lack more.

Our loſs was very conſiderable, though greatly inferior to that of the Enemy. We had one hundred and eighteen men ſlain in action, and ſixty-ſix died of their wounds. Beſides theſe, a hundred and twenty-two were dangerouſly wounded, and two hundred and ſixty-three ſlightly, ſo that our whole number killed and wounded, amounted to five hun-

dred

dred and ſixty nine men. Amongſt the ſlain was Captain Michie, who commanded the Newcaſtle, Captain Gore of the Marines, and Lieutenant Redſhaw, both of the Newcaſtle. Lieutenant Elliot, and the Gunner of the Tyger, the Maſter of the Yarmouth, and Boatſwain of the Elizabeth. Captain Somerſet, who commanded the Cumberland, was wounded in one of his ankles, and Captain Burton received a contuſion on his head. All the officers and ſeamen in general behaved with the greateſt bravery and ſpirit during the action, and by the vigour and conſtancy of their fire obliged the Enemy to retreat, notwithſtanding their great ſuperiority.

The Admiral having loſt all hopes of renewing the engagement, on the fifteenth ſtood into the road of Negapatam. There he anchored and continued repairing his damages, and refitting the ſquadron till the twenty-ſixth, when having put the ſhips in as good condition for ſervice (as the time permitted) he weighed and ſtood to the northward. He was joined by the Revenge, which he had ſent with diſpatches to Madraſs, who brought him ſixty-three men belonging to the Bridgewater and Triton, who were taken in Fort St. David, and had been exchanged at Pondichery. Theſe he ordered on board the Tyger and Newcaſtle, as thoſe were the ſhips which had loſt the greateſt number of men in the late engagement.

By this frigate the Governor and Council ſent a letter to the Admiral, of which the following is an extract.

SIR,

THE Revenge anchored here in the night of the fourteenth inſtant, and the next morning we received the honour of your letters, dated the eighth and twelfth inſtant, containing advice of your diſcovering the enemy's fleet on the ſecond, and after much fatigue, bringing them to action the tenth.

The

The warm fire you ſuſtained for two hours with ſeven ſhips againſt eleven, and obliging them at laſt to make their retreat, will do immortal honour to you and Mr. Stevens, and all the brave officers who have the happineſs to ſerve under you; and we feel much for the commanders of the Weymouth and Sunderland, who were deprived by the nature of the enemy's diſpoſition, from coming in for an equal ſhare of the glory of the day. We look upon this as the laſt effort of the enemy, and well might they boaſt of their ſuperiority; but the check they have met will ſhew them that they are diſappointed of the mighty effects they expected from this armament. It is fortunate that you found means to force them to an engagement before they reached Pondichery, as the troops they may have brought for landing, have, no doubt, had a ſhare in the loſs. As yet we have not heard of their arrival at Pondichery, but we ſuppoſe them there by this time, as the winds have been ſtrong ſoutherly. After they have landed their troops and ſtores, no great advantage can be hoped by engaging them again, and we would rather take the liberty to recommend the waiting until joined by the reinforcement expected from England, *&c. &c.*

Fort St. George,
16 *Sept.* 1759.

The French by their having been ſome time at Pondichery, muſt have had it in their power to come out from thence well prepared for action: but the Admiral, as he was obliged to paſs them in his way from Negapatam to Madraſs, judged that his doing it in the night would be liable to miſinterpretation, and that it would certainly give the enemy reaſon to conclude, that we had ſuffered ſo much in the late action as to be deſirous of avoiding another engagement; therefore he determined not to paſs the enemy's port without looking into it by day-light.

The

The twenty-ſeventh at day-break our fleet were got cloſe in with Pondichery road, where the French ſquadron was lying at anchor in a line of battle. The ſquadron was not in a condition to withſtand the fire of both the ſhips and fort at once, therefore the Admiral drew into a line of battle a-head upon the ſtarboard tack, and was then very near within random ſhot of their neareſt ſhip. The wind being off ſhore, and about W. S. W. our ſhips lay with their main-top-ſails to the maſt, juſt keeping a proper ſteerage-way for the line to continue well formed. While our ſhips continued in this ſituation, the French Admiral made the ſignal at ſix o'clock to heave a peak, and an hour after to weigh, and by the time all their ſquadron, which conſiſted of eleven ſail of the line, and two frigates, was under ſail, it was near ten o'clock, at which time, as the wind was off ſhore, our ſhips were conſequently driven to leeward of them, and lying as before-mentioned, expecting they would bear down directly and engage; but M. D'Aché made the ſignal for his ſquadron to keep cloſe to the wind, and alſo to make ſail, and ſtretched away to the ſouthward in a line of battle a-head, by which manœuvre they increaſed their diſtance from about random ſhot at day-light, to near four leagues to windward at ſun-ſet. Had they cut or ſlipped their cables on firſt diſcovering us, we muſt have come to action by ſeven o'clock, and after they got under ſail, had they bore directly down, we might have been cloſe along ſide by eleven.

The Admiral was now convinced that the Enemy had no inclination to come to a ſecond action; and as their whole conduct manifeſted an intention to get off and make good their retreat to the Iſlands, he conſulted the Rear-Admiral and Captains on their preſent ſituation, and the probable conſequence of a further purſuit. They all agreed in opinion that the French officers being reſolved to ſatisfy themſelves with

with the very trifling ſervice they had done the Company by ſtealing in thoſe inſufficient ſupplies to Pondichery, were now determined to avoid any farther engagement; and that if we purſued with any view of coming up with them, they would lead our ſhattered ſquadron quite to their iſlands. But beſides, that the condition of our ſhips would not permit us to follow them at all to the ſouthward, upon ſo little proſpect of ſervice, there was a more cogent reaſon for their immediate return to Madraſs, for at that time there was not above two days bread on board the ſquadron, and but very little water.

It was expedient to repair to that port as ſoon as poſſible, in order to get a ſupply of proviſions and water, for the voyage to Bombay, before the change of the * Monſoon, which was near at hand, at which ſeaſon it is dangerous to remain on the coaſt. Therefore the whole ſquadron anchored in Madraſs road on the twenty-eighth, and ſuch expedition was uſed in victualling the ſhips, and adminiſtring to the recovery of the ſick and wounded, that they were enabled to ſail again the ſeventeenth of October; and the next day they met Rear-Admiral Corniſh with four ſhips of the line, and the Ajax, Stormont, and Houghton Indiamen, on board of which was Colonel Coote with the greateſt part of his battalion.

* On the Coaſt of Coromandel the wind changes from South to North-Eaſt moſt commonly between the fifteenth and thirtieth of October. It is beſt to leave the Coaſt between the fifteenth and twentieth, but it is full late to ſtay till the end of the month. In order to effect ſome very important ſervice, it may be not altogether imprudent to riſque the wintering a fleet in theſe ſeas, becauſe in India, as in all other places, ſome winters are more, and ſome leſs tempeſtuous than others. In 1741 M. de la Bourdonnais remained on the Coaſt without any danger till the twenty-ſecond of October, but in 1746 he was ſurpriſed with a ſtorm, which ſunk and damaged his whole ſquadron. In 1747, and 1748, the Engliſh fleets kept the Coaſt, and met with no violent winds during the whole ſeaſon. And on the twenty-fourth of April, 1749, there was a tempeſt which deſtroyed fifty or ſixty veſſels of different nations. All that one can infer from hence is, that it is prudent to leave the Coaſt in the middle of October. *Memoire M. de la Bourdonnais. See Appendix, page* 9.

Admiral

Admiral Pocock ordered all the troops which were brought out in the ſhips of war to be put on board the Queenborough, and diſpatched her, with the three Indiamen for Madraſs, where they arrived the twenty-ſeventh. The whole ſquadron now ſailed for the coaſt of Malabar, and in going round Ceylon, they met with ſuch hard gales of wind, that the Cumberland and Saliſbury made the ſignal to ſpeak with the Admiral, being in great diſtreſs from leaks, which they could not keep under with all their pumps. The Saliſbury's diſtreſs being the greateſt, the Admiral ordered her to be aſſiſted with eleven men and an officer from each ſhip, for their own people were over fatigued by being kept conſtantly to the pump; and notwithſtanding this ſupply of freſh men, and their having thrown overboard thirty of their guns, at the end of two days they found the water ſtill gain upon them, and were obliged again to make the ſignal of diſtreſs. Upon this, the Admiral ordered all the boats in the fleet to ſtay by the Saliſbury to ſave the crew, in caſe of the ſhip's foundering; and ſent Admiral Corniſh and Captain Harriſon on board, to examine into her ſituation before he would too haſtily take the people out of her. They immediately ordered freſh men to the pumps, beginning with their own barge-crews, and by this means they ſoon cleared her, and by the help of a thrummed-ſail put under her bottom where the principal leak was, they made it practicable to keep her free with half her pumps; and now judging her to be no longer in danger, they returned to their own ſhips, and the Saliſbury made ſail the next morning.

The Admiral being deſirous of ſending Rear-Admiral Corniſh to the Coaſt of Coromandel as ſoon as the ſeaſon would permit, diſpatched him with the Lenox, Duke of Aquitain, York, Falmouth, Weymouth and Sunderland, for the Telichery, which was the general rendezvous. The weather becoming

coming exceeding fine, and the Monſoon appearing to be ſet in, the Admiral ſuffered every ſhip to make the beſt of her way for the intended port, knowing that a ſingle ſhip will always make a ſpeedier paſſage than a fleet, and as they arrived they might begin to take in their water, and put their ſick on ſhore. The twentieth of November the Yarmouth arrived at Telichery, as did the Elizabeth and York, and by the thirty-firſt the whole ſquadron came in.

That no time might be loſt for refitting the ſhips at Bombay, and preparing them for their return to the coaſt of Coromandel, the Admiral gave orders to Rear-Admiral Stevens on the twenty-ſixth, to proceed directly for Bombay, with the Grafton, Elizabeth, Tyger, and Saliſbury, and followed himſelf the twenty-ninth, leaving orders with Admiral Corniſh to ſail with the ſix ſhips under his command to the Coaſt of Coromandel on the fifteenth of December, as it was to be hoped the ſeaſon would then be favourable, and the ſick and wounded recovered.

Admiral Pocock had received orders to return to England, nevertheleſs upon the news of freſh diſturbances in Bengal, he determined to remain with the Yarmouth ſome time longer, and acted in purſuance of this reſolution, till ſuch time as advice was received of the entire re-eſtabliſhment of the affairs of Bengal, and the ſignal victory obtained over the French on the Coaſt of Coromandel.

[1760.] Upon ſo happy a turn in the affairs of the company, the Admiral thought it now adviſeable to comply with the orders for his return, eſpecially as he had the ſatisfaction to ſee the command devolve on ſo brave and experienced an officer as Rear-Admiral Stevens, whoſe worth had been proved by his behaviour in the three engagements, as well as by the conſtant harmony which had always ſubſiſted between them, and his alacrity to concur in any ſervice for the honour of his country.

The Admiral had himſelf received from the three Preſidencies the ſtrongeſt expreſſions of their ſenſe of the zeal which he had at all times ſhewn, and the actual ſervices which he had ſo often performed for the benefit of the Eaſt-India Company, and the honour of the Britiſh flag. Having at length reſumed his intention of returning to Europe, he diſpatched Rear-Admiral Stevens for the coaſt of Coromandel on the twenty-firſt of March, with the Grafton, Elizabeth, Tyger, and Newcaſtle, and ſailed himſelf the ſeventh of April in the Yarmouth, leaving at Bombay the Saliſbury which had had a thorough repair, and was then almoſt ready to ſail, and the Cumberland, which was to be taken into the dock the firſt high tide.

Admiral Pocock anchored at Anjengo the ſeventeenth of April, and ſailed from thence the twenty-firſt. He there received a letter from Admiral Stevens, dated the eleventh, on which day he ſailed from that port, acquainting him with his proceedings, and that he had retaken three ſmall Engliſh veſſels off the Vingorla Rocks, from the Malwans, a ſet of pirates who had taken them but a few hours before. There had been no account of the French ſquadron ſince the time of their departure from Pondichery on the ſecond of October, 1759.

On the eighteenth of June, Admiral Pocock arrived at St. Helena, where he found the Colcheſter and Rippon waiting to convoy ſeventeen of the Company's ſhips, three of which were of extraordinary great value, having on board a large quantity of rich goods and diamonds from Bengal. For the ſecurity of ſo conſiderable an object, the Admiral thought proper to delay his voyage till the ſeventh of July, on which day the whole fleet being ready to ſail, he took them under his command and anchored in the Downs the twenty-ſecond of September, with the richeſt convoy that ever arrived at one time in England.

WAR

W A R
ON THE
Coaſt of COROMANDEL.

[1759.] THE China ſhips being arrived at Madraſs with three hundred of Colonel Coote's battalion, in the beginning of September, Major Brereton, now Commander in chief, being very ſanguine for action upon the ſtrength of this reinforcement, prevailed on the Governor and Council, though with difficulty, to conſent to an attempt upon Wandewaſh. Both armies had lain ſome time inactive; the French in Gingee, Wandewaſh, Arcot and Chitteput, and our troops at Conjeveram. At Wandewaſh was a party of four or five hundred French, which Colonel Brereton, by a ſudden march, propoſed to ſhut up or drive from thence, and then take the place before the enemy could collect their force. Every thing was to be ready with great ſecrecy by the tenth, and all neceſſaries were accordingly prepared. The rains which fell about this time cauſed a delay till the ſixteenth, when the news arriving of the engagement between the fleets, the Governor and Council wrote to Major Brereton, that they thought it would be better to make no motion till it was certain whether the enemy had received any reinforcements.

Major Brereton being unwilling to be with-held from a favourite project, by a ſuppoſition, to which he did not give any weight, marched and took Trivitore the twenty-ſixth, where he made priſoners one Captain and twenty-two men of the Lorrain Regiment, and eight Huſſars. He then proceeded to Wandewaſh, and endeavoured, but in vain, to draw the enemy to an action out of the Pettah, (the town or village belonging to and commonly ſurrounding every Indian fort.) The French having ſome intelligence of our preparations, by the delay from the tenth to the twenty-fifth, diſcovered our intentions, and had made themſelves almoſt equal to our force, which was far ſhort of ſeventeen hundred men, the number that had been at firſt propoſed. Major Brereton gave out orders for an attack to be made upon Wandewaſh-Pettah at three o'clock in the morning of the firſt of October, by Majors Monſon and Caillaud, with five hundred men at one end of it, and Major Gordon, with two hundred men between the fort and Pettah. Major Monſon meeting with little reſiſtance, entered without loſs, and ſoon after Major Gordon attacked, but received ſo warm a fire from the fort and the Pettah, that his party broke, and only twenty men got in with him: however he joined Major Monſon, and they advanced to the head of the Pettah, having driven the enemy quite out of it. But as our people were expoſed to a great fire, and every ſtreet was enfiladed from the fort they retreated towards the center of the Pettah, and there took poſt, detaching ſome pickets in the ſtreet to the right and left, which was all that could be done till day-light.

The French having made a diſpoſition for that purpoſe, at day-break attacked our parties on all ſides, who after near two hours warm diſpute, were obliged to abandon the Pettah, (leaving four guns behind them) with the loſs of two hundred and two men in the action and retreat. The enemy ſuffered no leſs in point of numbers, but we had a moſt eſſential diſadvantage in the loſs of eleven officers of approved worth and bravery. The army was ſtill in a condition to have undertaken ſomething of conſequence, but the advanced ſeaſon, the ſcarcity of proviſions, and the diſcouragement of an unſucceſsful attack, were reaſons that juſtly determined them to go into cantonment at Conjeveram.

In

In the neighbourhood of Trichinopoly, near Ellavanasore, is a strong place called Tagada, held by Kistnarauze, an ally to the Nabob, who had been very troublesome to the French, and frequently, with the assistance of the garrison of Trichinopoly, beat several of their parties. His little fort was by situation almost impregnable, but wanted ammunition to hold out against such a force as the French were now resolved to send against it.

Captain Smith apprized of their designs, and having intelligence that a considerable party of the enemy were actually marching against it, consisting of one hundred European Infantry, forty Hussars, five hundred Black Horse, fourteen hundred Sepoys and matchlocks, and five pieces of cannon. Captain Smith had the precaution to throw into the place three companies of Sepoys, under the command of Serjeant-Major Hunterman. Afterwards he detached Lieutenant Raillard with forty Europeans, six companies of Sepoys, three small guns, and a large supply of ammunition, with orders to proceed within a night's march of Tadaga, and then to forward the ammunition with one company of Sepoys: and from the particular situation of Tagada, he had great hopes of throwing in this supply with safety. Before the party reached Volconda, the Nabob's horse, in number one thousand, marched and joined them.

The Enemy having collected all their forces, made four several attacks on the town of Tagada. They brought two guns to each gate, and ordered two parties to escalade the walls. The attack continued a considerable time, till at length a party forced a passage at one of the gates, and brought four guns into the town, so that it was with great difficulty the garrison could gain the rock, where there were some provisions, ammunition, and water. They sent word to Lieutenant Raillard that they would hold out till he came to their relief, which they desired

ſired he would do as ſpeedily as poſſible, as they had loſt near one third of their people in the late attack. The Enemy ſuffered much more, having thirty Europeans, and two hundred Sepoys killed and wounded. Kiſtnarauze, with all his Horſe, and ſome Sepoys, marched in the night from Tagada, and the next day joined Lieut. Raillard, by whoſe advice it was determined the next morning early to attempt the relief of Tagada. They marched accordingly, till they came within two miles of the fort, where, upon the appearance of the enemy, they halted and began to cannonade. This gave time to the French to bring up their artillery. Upon the firſt diſcharge of the field-pieces, the Nabob's Horſe fled with the utmoſt precipitation, nor could all the entreaties of Lieutenant Raillard and Kiſtnarauze bring them back. This happened before the Enemy's Infantry appeared. Soon after our Sepoys ſeeing themſelves abandoned by the horſe, took a pannic and fled likewiſe. About two hundred, chiefly Officers, remained with the Europeans and Topaſſes, who guarded the guns, and were endeavouring to make good their retreat to a village about a mile in their rear; theſe being in ſome diſorder, were hard puſhed by the Enemy's European Cavalry and ſome Infantry, who having taken poſſeſſion of the guns, our whole party was entirely routed, the Europeans and Topaſſes either killed or taken priſoners. Many of the Sepoys cut to pieces, and almoſt all diſarmed. Lieutenant Raillard, who was on horſeback during the engagement, eſcaped being made priſoner, but did not long ſurvive the diſgrace of his defeat, for it made ſuch an impreſſion on him as doubtleſs produced his unfortunate end. Having no cartridges to load his arms for his fatal deſign, he bruiſed himſelf ſo much with repeated ſtrokes on the breaſt and head with his piſtols, that he fell off his horſe and expired about five miles from the ſcene of action. As he was found there with no other marks of violence, it is is evident he destroyed himself in the manner abovementioned.

The miscarriage of this brave man was owing to his impatience at the cowardice of the Nabob's horse: for as soon as they broke, he left his own troops, who were in need of his presence and might have profited by it, and rode among the broken cavalry, vainly attempting to rally those who were alike insensible to his exhortations or reproaches. Soon after Serjeant Hunterman surrendered the Fort of Tagada upon honourable terms.

The French to make a diversion to the southward, and also to have at hand a sufficient force to surprize Trichinopoly upon the first favourable occasion, marched a large body of men towards Seringam. An advanced party of them were discovered from the Golden Rock, near Trichinopoly, and a sally was made from that garrison with some Europeans, Sepoys, and the Nabob's horse, who came upon them in the night and took one officer, thirty Europeans, forty Coffrees, and Sepoys, and killed or dispersed the remainder of the corps, taking also their arms, baggage and ammunition, with two field-pieces. The main body of the French army, consisting of above a thousand Europeans, continuing their march to Seringam, attacked and carried it, there being only two companies of Sepoys to defend it. As this small body made a gallant resistance, the French, in resentment, most shamefully turned them out of the place, and then sent their horse after them to cut and mangle them, and fired grape shot on some that were then got to the Glacis, by which means above a hundred were killed. The French left two hundred Europeans at Seringam, and returned with the rest to join their army, since which, one of their convoys going to Seringam was surprized by Captain Smith who commanded at Trichinopoly.

On advice of an escort being at Utatore, Captain Smith detached a party of fifty Europeans and some

Sepoys to intercept it. The French marched an equal force from Seringam for the protection of their convoy. Captain Smith, as ſoon as he found they had weakened their force at the Pagoda, attacked it with the remainder of his garriſon from Trichinopoly. As he received a wound in the attempt, it had no other conſequence than that of bringing back the French detachment. Our party in the mean time attacked the convoy in Utatore, took two officers, with thirty Grenadiers, and diſarmed three hundred Sepoys, carrying off or deſtroying all the ammunition and proviſions.

After this, Captain Smith, with the aſſiſtance of the King of Tanjore and Tondeman, retook ſeveral poſts, and interrupted the communication with Seringam, till at length M. Lally, thinking the place in danger, reinforced it with a body of horſe, and two hundred European infantry.

It has been already related that three hundred of Colonel Coote's battalion were brought by the China ſhips in September, and that he arrived himſelf with the remainder of his corps in the Queenborough, and the three Indiamen on the twenty-ſeventh of October. As ſoon as Colonel Coote landed, the neceſſary preparations were ſet about for his regiment to take the field. It was in this interval that the enemy ſent the large detachment afore-mentioned to the ſouthward, and poſſeſſed themſelves of Seringam. The Preſidency apprehending they might extend their deſigns againſt Trichinopoly, recommended to Colonel Coote to proceed with all expedition to join the army at Conjeveram, and to form an attack upon ſome of the Enemy's poſſeſſions in that neighbourhood, in order to draw their troops from the ſouthward. The army accordingly marched from Conjeveram the twenty-fifth of November, and the next day a detachment under Major Brereton inveſted Wandewaſh. Two batteries were erected with great expedition, they were opened

opened the twenty-ninth, and a ſummons was then ſent by Colonel Coote to Lieutenant Mahony, who commanded in the garriſon, to ſurrender. He very properly returned for anſwer, that he would defend the fort to the laſt extremity.

On the thirtieth, a breach being made, the Killedar, or Mooriſh Governor, ſent to treat with the Colonel, offering to pay a ſum of money, and deliver up the French garriſon, upon condition of his being continued in the government of the Fort; but before any agreement was perfected, the French ſoldiers, fearing the intrigues of the Killedar, got upon the walls and calling out to our people, declared they would deliver up the garriſon. Five officers and ſixty-three private men were made priſoners on this occaſion, and a place of great note in this Country, which had been often threatened by our army, was at length taken without any loſs on our ſide. There were five hundred Sepoys in the fort beſides the European garriſon.

From thence the army marched immediately to Carangoly, and on the ſixth of December opened a battery againſt that Fort, which was defended by Colonel O'Kennely, and one hundred Europeans, and five hundred Sepoys. The breach was made the eighth, but there being yet a ditch, the paſſing of which might have been attended with loſs of men, Colonel Coote thought it better to grant the garriſon the terms of capitulation they demanded, which were, that the Europeans ſhould not be made priſoners, but have leave to march to Pondichery, and accordingly the Fort was ſurrendered.

The French troops which were aſſembled at Arcot, being joined by the detachment from the ſouthward, the ſon of Chunda Saib, and the ſon of the Killedar of Wandewaſh, were ſent with other emiſſaries to bring over a party of Morarow's

Marat-

Marattas. They had already a great number of Country troops brought in by M. De Buſſy, who went with a few troopers as far as Cadapa, to pay a viſit to Baſaletzing on his return to Golconda, and not being able to perſuade that Prince to return with him, engaged one of his chiefs with a conſiderable number of Country horſe and Sepoys, and brought him with great ſtate to Arcot. Theſe were joined the ninth of January by Innis Cawn, Morarow's chief officer, with three thouſand Maratta horſe, beſides a number of foot, who followed them for plunder. The French force at Arcot conſiſted (according to the beſt intelligence) of near two thouſand five hundred Europeans, and M. Lally himſelf reſumed the command of the army upon this occaſion.

Colonel Coote having poſted his forces in a ſtrong ſituation between Cauverypauk and Arcot, not more than three miles from the advanced guards of the Enemy, remained there in order to cover our diſtricts in the beſt manner he could againſt the ravages of the Marattas, who were diſperſed on all ſides in ſmall parties on purpoſe to drive off the cattle, plunder the inhabitants, and deſtroy the produce of the Country. The army with Colonel Coote conſiſted of two thouſand one hundred Europeans, (including the artillery, the cavalry, and officers of all denominations) about four thouſand Sepoys, and fifteen hundred Country horſe. The great number of cavalry on the ſide of the Enemy, rendered it indiſpenſably neceſſary for us to take into the ſervice as many of the beſt as could be procured, notwithſtanding the immenſe expence, for without them the army would have been abſolutely unable to keep the field, as it would have been impoſſible to have ſupplied it with proviſions.

The day after the junction of the Marattas, M. Lally moved with his whole force from Arcot by the road of Wandewaſh, but on the ſecond day, a party a party turned towards Conjeveram, who ransacked the town, but could not get possession of the fort, being repulsed in the attempt, by an officer with two companies of Sepoys. Colonel Coote, upon this intelligence, marched with all expedition from Cauverypauk to Conjeveram. Upon his approach, all the Enemy's parties retired from that neighbourhood, and joined their main body at Papatangel, a town upon the road from Conjeveram to Wandewash.

The Enemy's designs proved to be against the latter place, where Captain Sherlock commanded with one hundred and fifty Europeans, and eight companies of Sepoys. The sixteenth in the morning, the Enemy attacked the Pettah adjoining to the fort, and after a stout resistance from three companies of Sepoys, commanded by an Ensign of the Sepoy establishment, lodged themselves there, and set about erecting a battery. The twentieth they began to fire against the walls from one twenty-four pounder and three eighteen pounders.

Wandewash was thought a place of too much consequence to be suffered to fall without making some attempt to relieve it: therefore, though the Enemy might have some superiority in Europeans, besides their multitude of Blacks, it was determined to march the army towards them.

It had long been debated at Madrass, and was always matter of doubt with many members of the Council whether it would be expedient to hazard an action at so critical a time, for till the arrival of the good news from Bengal, the affairs of the Coast bore a melancholy aspect. The Enemy had greatly the superiority in European horse, which would have led on the Marattas to destroy our army totally in case of a defeat. They had already plundered and destroyed the country, and encreased the scarcity of provisions to so great a degree, that the cry for rice both at Madrass and in in the army, was exceedingly alarming. The army alſo made continual demands for their pay when the Country was entirely exhauſted of caſh. At length a veſſel arrived from Bengal, with the welcome news of the eſtabliſhment of peace and tranquillity in that Province, and the long expected ſupply of money.

This was a great relief to the preſent anxiety, and gave ſpirit to our Counſels, as well as to the army and our allies, and muſt be ſuppoſed to have had ſome effect on an Enemy that was naturally preſumptuous. But theſe circumſtances did not cauſe the Governor and Council to act with leſs precaution. Still dubious of the event, they approved of Colonel Coote's march towards the Enemy, but at the ſame time ſtrongly recommended to him to keep Chengalaput and Carangoly in his rear, that he might be ſupplied with proviſions, and have his retreat to Madraſs ſecured, in caſe of any unfavourable event.

Colonel Coote being determined to march the army towards the French, took poſt at Outremaloor the ſeventeenth, and judging by his advice from Captain Sherlock, that the breach in the fort might be practicable the twenty-ſecond, he reſolved to make an effort to raiſe the ſiege that morning; for this purpoſe he marched with the whole army the twenty-firſt in the evening, and encamped at Trinborough, about ten miles from the Enemy, where he gave out the following orders.

Trinborough Village, January 21, 1750, ſeven o'Clock in the Evening.

The army to march to-morrow at ſix o'Clock by the left upon the Taps beating, which is to be looked upon the ſame as the Generals beating, it is to form and be ready to march off immediately after. All the cavalry and five companies of Sepoys to form the van of the army, except two hundred Black horſe, who together with three com-

companies of Sepoys are to cover the baggage in the rear. The army to obſerve the orders given out the twenty-ſeventh of December, which were, that the firſt line conſiſt of Colonel Draper's regiment on the right, Colonel Coote's on the left, and the Company's in the centre; the artillery to be divided as follows; four pieces on the right, four on the left, and two pieces between each interval, making in all twelve in the firſt line. The ſecond line to conſiſt of the grenadiers of Colonel Draper's, Colonel Coote's, and the Company's, with one piece of cannon upon each flank, who are to form two hundred paces in the rear of the firſt line: An eight inch Howitz to be between the two lines. Major Brereton to command the right of the firſt line, Major William Gordon the left, and Major Robert Gordon the centre. Major Monſon to command the ſecond line. The cavalry to be divided into five ſquadrons, the Europeans to make the center ſquadron.

The names of the Jemidars who are appointed to command, to be given into the commanders in chief to-night. When the line forms, the cavalry will have orders to form about fifty paces in the rear of the ſecond line, having a proper interval between each ſquadron: at the ſame time the five companies of Sepoys who ſupported the cavalry are to form upon the right of Colonel Draper's regiment, and the five companies of Sepoys that were in the rear of the line of march, to form on the left of Colonel Coote's regiment, five companies who were on the left flank of the line of march, are to form in the following manner; two on the right of the ſecond line, and two on the left, and one on the rear with the cavalry, The whole army, as well Europeans as Blacks, are to have a green branch of Tamarind Tree fixed on their hats and turbans, likewiſe on the tops of the colours, in order to diſtinguiſh them from the Enemy.

Enemy. The commanding officers of corps are to take particular care that their reſpective corps are properly told off, and that the men know their right and left hand men and file leaders. They are to be cautioned not to give their fire till they are ordered by their reſpective officers, *&c. &c.*

The army marched at ſix o'Clock in the morning of the twenty-ſecond, agreeable to the orders that had been given out the day before for that purpoſe. About ſeven o'Clock our advanced guard of horſe and that of the Enemy began to fire at each other, upon which Captain Baron de Vaſſerot who commanded the cavalry, was ordered to form them in order of battle; he was ſupported by five companies of Sepoys and two pieces of cannon, and Col. Coote advancing himſelf with two companies of Sepoys, obliged the Enemy to retire to their main body of horſe, which conſiſted of two hundred Europeans and three thouſand Marattas on their left. As the whole of our cavalry advanced, that of the enemy retreated in pretty good order till our cannon, which was extremely well ſerved, obliged them to retire precipitately. The Major of the brigade was then ſent to the army, which was about three quarters of a mile in the rear, with orders for them to form the line of battle, but not to advance till the Colonel had joined them, who ſoon after having taken poſſeſſion of a Tank, which the Enemy's cavalry had occupied, returned to the line, which by that time was formed. After reviewing the whole, and finding the men alert and eager to engage, he ordered the army to move forwards. About nine o'Clock they arrived at the poſt they had driven the Enemy from, which was about two miles from their camp, and halted in their view near half an hour, during which time Colonel Coote went very near to them and reconnoitred their ſituation.

ation. Upon finding they were ſtrongly poſted, and his flanks expoſed to the Enemy's cavalry, which was greatly ſuperior to his own, he ordered the army to march by the right in order to gain the advantage of a hill about three miles diſtant, and near two miles from Wandewaſh fort, and the horſe which was then in the front, to wheel to the right and left and form behind the ſecond line, in order to make the rear guard. Thus he covered his right flank with the hill, and had ſome Villages in his rear, to which he ſent his baggage, and this motion obliged the Enemy to alter their diſpoſition. During all this time they cannonaded each other, and ſkirmiſhed with their advanced poſts and Maratta horſe, but the latter ſoon diſappeared and returned no more. The Enemy after making their ſecond diſpoſition, moved forwards under the cover of a bank. The cannonading then began to be ſmart on both ſides, and the two armies advanced briſkly towards each other.

At twelve o'Clock the Enemy's European cavalry puſhed with a great deal of reſolution in order to force our left, and come round upon our rear. The Colonel immediately ordered up ſome companies of Sepoys and two pieces of cannon to ſuſtain our cavalry, who had orders when the Enemy approached to open to the right and left, which gave room to pour in grape ſhot upon the Enemy's horſe from the two pieces of cannon, the muſquetry alſo galling their flank, while our cavalry wheeled and charged them in front. They were immediately thrown into confuſion, and puſhed back above a mile from our left, upon the rear of their own people. Our army now advanced upon the Enemy who kept their flank well covered by a Tank, till we approached near enough to perceive the diſpoſition of their army, which was formed in the following manner. The regiment

ment of Lorraine on the right in line of battle, the regiment of Lally on the left with the marine formed into a column, and the brigade de L'Inde formed into another in the centre, with two Tanks covering their right and left, and ſome broken ground in front. By this time it was near one o'Clock, and both armies continued advancing till they came within the reach of muſquetry when a ſhot from our guns ſtriking one of their tumbrils, it blew up, by which accident, five of their guns became uſeleſs to them: upon this Major Brereton wheeled Colonel Draper's regiment to the left, and charged their left flank, which was executed with great order and reſolution, and much to the honour of that corps, and their Commander; Colonel Coote ſeeing that regiment likely to ſuffer from a body of Black troops, together with their marines who were under cover, and fired very briſkly upon them, and at the ſame time finding the Enemy had reinforced their left with a piquet from Lally's regiment, ordered the Grenadier Company of Draper's, which was on the right of the ſecond line, to ſupport their own regiment, and having likewiſe two pieces of cannon playing upon the Enemy's flank, compleated the rout of that wing, who abandoned their cannon and fell upon their own centre, which was by this time, together with their right, cloſely engaged with our left. He then ordered up Major Monſon with the reſt of the ſecond line, and placed him ſo as to be able to ſupport any part of our line, at the ſame time flanking the Enemy. About two o'Clock their whole army gave way, and ran towards their own camp, but finding that we purſued them, they quitted it, and left us entire maſters of the field, together with all their artillery, except three ſmall pieces which they carried off. There were taken twenty pieces of cannon, three of which were twenty

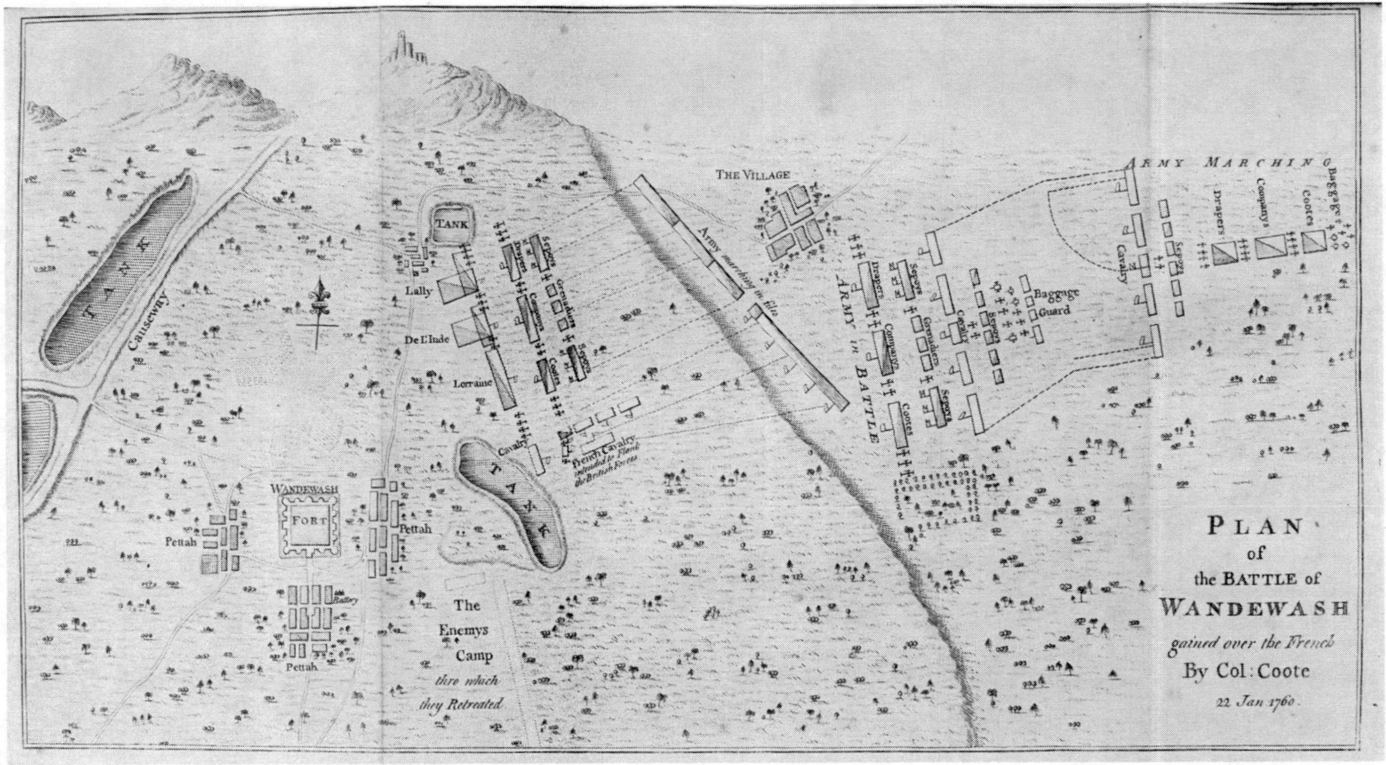

PLAN
of
the BATTLE of
WANDEWASH
gained over the French
By Col: Coote
22 Jan 1760.
ARMY MARCHING
Baggage
Cootes
Companys
Drapers
Sepoys
Cavalry
Baggage Guard
Grenadiers
ARMY in BATTLE
THE VILLAGE
Army marching in files
TANK
Lally
De L'Inde
Lorraine
French Cavalry intended to Flank the British Forces
TANK
Causeway
WANDEWASH
FORT
Pettah
Battery
The Enemys Camp thro which they Retreated

twenty pounders, one twenty four, and one thirty-two pounder.

The French had eight hundred killed and wounded, two hundred of which we buried in the field, and we took two hundred and forty prisoners, of which number two hundred were wounded. We lost only fifty-two Europeans, officers included, in the field of battle: there were besides one hundred and forty-one wounded, of which some died of their wounds: and among these was the gallant Major Brereton, who had the honour to have so great a share in the success of that glorious day.

The French army consisted of two thousand two hundred Europeans, including artillery and cavalry; three hundred Coffrees, and between nine and ten thousand Black troops. They had twenty pieces of cannon in the field, and five in their batteries against the fort, where they blew up a large magazine of powder upon their retreat. Our army amounted to seventeen hundred Europeans, including artillery and cavalry, three thousand five hundred Black troops; and all our artillery were fourteen pieces of cannon and one howitz.

The principal persons among the prisoners who were taken were Brigadier General de Bussy, Le Chevalier Godeville, Quarter-master General. Of Lally's regiment, Lieutenant-Colonel Murphy, two Captains and two Lieutenants. Of the Lorrain regiment, one Captain and one Lieutenant. Of the India Battalion, two Lieutenants and two Ensigns. Of the Marines, Le Chevalier de Poete, Knight of Malta, who died of his wounds. All the above-mentioned were wounded, except M. de Bussy, and an Ensign of the India battalion. Colonel Coote indulged these gentlemen together with M. Godeville, with leave to go to Pondichery on their parole:

but when he learnt that ſeveral officers on parole had been in the action, he wrote to M. de Buſſy and the other two officers, to repair to Madraſs according to the tenor of their parole. In anſwer to which, M. Lally ſent to offer him their ranſom in money.

So compleat a victory over a ſuperior force could not have been obtained, but by the maſterly conduct of Colonel Coote, and the univerſal good behaviour of all the officers and men, and it would be great injuſtice to paſs over in ſilence the extraordinary diligence and ſkill of the officers of the artillery.

The Enemy retreated as faſt as poſſible to Chetteput, which is eighteen miles from the field of battle, and the next day aſſembled the remains of their broken army at Gingee; but the twenty-ſixth, M. Lally thought proper to retire within the walls of Pondichery. Our cavalry being fatigued were not able to purſue them the evening of their defeat, but the next day Colonel Coote ſent out two detachments to haraſs the Enemy; and upon advice of M. Lally's retreat, he ſent freſh orders to Captain de Vaſſerot, who commanded the horſe, to deſtroy the French country round Pondichery, as M. Lally had done by the environs of Madraſs. To prevent his being interrupted in this expedition by the Marattas, who were then between Arcot and Chetteput, the Colonel wrote to Innis Cawn, to advertiſe him that, ſince he had ſhewn by his behaviour in the late action, as well as by the whole tenor of his conduct, that he came not into the country as a ſoldier, but only as a plunderer and marauder, he muſt now immediately quit the country, or he ſhould be compelled to it, and if intercepted he muſt expect no quarter for himſelf or his troops.

The

The Maratta General, ſenſible of the ſmall benefit he reaped from his alliance with the French, who were in no capacity to pay him, decamped without heſitation, and went off to his own country; and Captain de Vaſſerot proceeded without interruption to lay waſte the bounds of Pondichery. This was not done as a mere act of retaliation, but as a very neceſſary ſtep towards the reduction of that place, as it ſtruck a terror into the inhabitants, promoted the diſpoſition to deſert, and alarming the Black people with the dread of a ſiege, cauſed them to move off, and deprived the garriſon of the neceſſary aſſiſtance of the Cooleys. Beſides this, Captain De Vaſſerot took four thouſand head of cattle.

On the twenty-eighth, Colonel Coote marched to Chetteput, and began to erect batteries, at the ſame time ſummoning the Chevalier De Tilly, who commanded there, to ſurrender, which he refuſed. The next day, after a breach was made, the garriſon flung out a flag of truce, and ſurrendered priſoners of war. Here were four officers, fifty-four Europeans, beſides ſeventy-three who had been wounded in the battle of Wandewaſh, and were at that time in the hoſpital; and three hundred Sepoys. In the fort were taken nine guns, and a large quantity of ammunition.

Captain Smith having been detached after a ſmall party of French and ſepoys, with two braſs eight pounders, returned with them the thirtieth, and alſo brought in a Captain of the Lorrain regiment and three French Commiſſaries. And Major Monſon having thrown a few ſhells into the fort of Timmery, it ſoon ſurrendered, and twenty Europeans were made priſoners.

Colonel Coote immediately after the battle of Wandewaſh, ſent orders to Captain Wood to inveſt Arcot. He ſoon got poſſeſſion of the Pettah, having routed Zulapherzing's forces, and taken his whole camp. On the ſecond of February he was joined by Colonel Coote, who marched with the whole army, and encamped within two miles of the place. The ſame day he began to erect batteries againſt the Fort. Two of five eighteen pounders againſt the curtain between the North-Weſt corner tower and the gateway, one of two eighteen and one twenty-four pounder, againſt the tower and curtain Weſt of the South-Weſt corner tower, and one of a twelve pounder, againſt the North gate, to enfilade the Weſt front.

The next day the Enemy threw a number of ſhells from the garriſon without any effect. The batteries were opened on the fifth, and the next day two of our guns were diſabled, and two men killed and four wounded.

On the eighth, Colonel Coote having carried on his approaches to the South Weſt, within two hundred and ſixty yards of the creſt of the Glacis, and thoſe to the Weſt within two hundred and fifty, ſummoned the garriſon to ſurrender. He received for anſwer from Captain Huſſey who commanded there, that in caſe he was not relieved in ſix days he would then deliver up the garriſon, on being allowed the honours of war.

Upon this hoſtilities were re-commenced, and ſome of our men were wounded at the batteries and in the trenches, by the Enemy's ſhells and fire-balls. Our whole loſs amounted to no more than ſeven men killed and ſixteen wounded: for the next day, the approaches being carried on within ſixty yards of the creſt of the glacis, the garriſon ſurrendered priſoners of war.

Colonel Coote took poſſeſſion of the fort of Arcot the tenth of February, and thereby not only reſtored to the Nabob the Capital of his Dominions, but greatly weakened the French force in India, by a capture of two hundred and thirty-ſix European ſoldiers, three Captains, and eight Subalterns.

This

This was not only a real and a preſent loſs to the French, but a great blow to their credit, and operated no leſs on the minds of their own people, than it affected them in the opinion of the country powers. The very day that Arcot ſurrendered, ſeven and twenty Huſſars, with their horſes and arms, deſerted and came over to us, and by the laſt advices from the Coaſt, it is ſaid that the whole body of their European cavalry has ſince ſollowed their example, and are now in our ſervice. This is an earneſt of the general diſcontent at Pondichery, occaſioned by their want of pay and the ſcarcity of proviſions, with a diffidence of one another, a ſenſe of their miſconduct, and in conſequence thereof, their calamitous proſpect from this ſudden reverſe of fortune.

M. Lally, immediately after his defeat, ſent orders to recal his troops from Seringam; by which means he augmented his army with a great reinforcement of Europeans (near five hundred horſe and foot) but at the ſame time being obliged to abandon that part of the country, all thoſe valuable diſtricts, from whence the Nabob draws ſo conſiderable a part of his revenue, and, without which Trichinopoly does not produce enough to defray the ordinary expences of the garriſon, were now left to be viſited by his ſeveral renters and collectors without moleſtation.

Rear-Admiral Corniſh arrived at Madraſs the twenty-third of February. As the French had no fleet upon that Coaſt, he had no object but to co-operate with the land forces; however the Falmouth meeting with the Haerlem in her way from Merguy, obliged her to run a-ſhore two leagues to the Northward of Pondichery. The garriſon of Permacoil and Allamparva having ſurrendered priſoners of war, there remained only Carical of all the ſubordinate ſettlements on that Coaſt.

Carical is a very ſmall but exceeding ſtrong Fort, being a pentagon, built exactly on the plan of Lisle. It being of great importance to reduce the Enemy to the possession of one single port, both the land and sea officers under Rear-Admiral Cornish and Major Monson, were employed in the attack of Carical, and on the fifth of April it was surrendered.

By the loss of this place, the French have not a single man in the Peninsula, except a small garrison at Mahé on the Malabar Coast, another at Gingee, and those which are blocked up within the walls of Pondichery.

THE END.

THE FOLLOWING

ACCOUNT

Of the Progreſs and Effects of one of thoſe violent

HURRICANES

Which ſo often attend the Change of the

MONSOON,

Is the more curious, as few People have ever ſurvived ſuch a Diſaſter, who have been capable of giving ſo clear and diſtinct an Account.

A JOURNAL of the

Loſs of the PEMBROKE,

Which was wrecked in St. DAVID's road the 13th of April, 1749.

By the MASTER of the PEMBROKE.

ABOUT ten o'clock in the morning it blew Single
freſh, the wind at N. E. by E. and a great ſea Anchor.
began to come in. We then having a cable out, the Captain ordered half a cable more to be veered away. At noon I deſired the Captain would pleaſe Noon.
to order more cable to be veered away, he replied, he was afraid if we ſhould veere more cable it would bring home the anchor, but that a new foreſail and a mizen ſhould be bent, which was immediately done. At one in the afternoon it blew very hard, the wind One
at N. E. his Majeſty's ſhip Namur lying about a ca- o'clock.
ble's length within us and abaſt our beam; I went to the Captain, as did likewiſe the Lieutenants, and deſired him to go to ſea. He replied, he could not

Apr. 13, 1749. answer to go to ſea, unleſs the Namur did, (on board which Rear Admiral Boſcawen's flag was flying) but ordered all our ports to be barred in and well ſecured, and the tarpawlings down without battening, which made them blow up again after we put to ſea.

Three o'clock. At three o'clock I went again to the Captain who was ſick and in his cabin, and again deſired him to go to ſea, he ſeemed very angry, and ſaid he could not, giving the ſame reaſon as above; nor would he ſuffer any more cable to be veered away: at the ſame time the ſhip rode hard, ſtrained much, and made water.

Four. At four the ſea increaſing, we expected the cable

Five. to part every minute, at five our cable parted and we caſt our head off to the ſea, otherwiſe we ſhould have fallen on board the Namur; we immediately ſet the foreſail and mizen, got on board the main tack, and ſet our mainſail and fore and mizen ſtay-ſails, at the ſame time ſome of our people were employed in heaving in the cable, for the Captain would not have it cut, which took up ſome time. I found it to be parted about three fathoms without the ſervice of the outer cable. It blew ſo very hard that the ſhip would not bear any more ſail.

Six. At ſix we ſounded and found fourteen fathoms water, at the ſame time there being a great head ſea, we made but very little way, and found the ſhip gained more water than one of the chain pumps could poſſibly diſcharge, which obliged us to ſet both pumps to work. The weather continuing very bad with a great ſea and ſtrong gales; at half paſt ſix our mainſail ſplit in pieces, we got down the yard in order to bend a new ſail, but it blowing ſo hard and the ſhip lying down very much, we could not

Seven. get the ſail to the yard. At ſeven we ſounded eighteen fathom water. An half paſt ſeven ſounded twenty fathoms, the wind at N. E. the firſt and ſecond Lieutenants at the pumps encouraging the men.

Eight. At eight the carpenter ſent word to the Captain that the

the ſhip gained upon them much, four foot water in the hold, at the ſame time, depth of water twenty-two fathoms; half paſt eight, our tiller rope broke ſhort off at the rudder head, and we likewiſe found one of the rudder chains broke. The ſails we had now ſet were our foreſail, mizen, and fore ſtay-ſails. At nine ſounded twenty-four fathoms water. The ſea now made a free paſſage over us, and the ſhip being water-logged, we hauled up our foreſail to eaſe her, but expected to go down every minute. In hauling down our foreſtay-ſail it ſplit, and as I looked aft from the fore-caſtle I ſaw the main and mizen maſt gone, but never heard them go. By this time the ſhip righted much, and in about ſeven minutes the foremaſt went by the board, but the bowſprit held faſt, depth of water about twenty-five fathoms. Our pumps continually working. The third Lieutenant being on the quarter deck ſent forward to me to clear and let go the ſmall bower anchor, which was immediately done. We veered the cable out to the ſervice and ſtoppered the cable, the wind at N. E. by E. we found the ſhip drive to ſhore very faſt, depth of water ſeventeen fathoms. Half paſt ten we had eight feet water in the ſhip's hold, kept the pumps working. About eleven o'clock we found the ſhip ſettle, depth of water twelve or fourteen fathoms, and then the anchor brought the ſhip up, but the cable parted in a few minutes, then we let the ſheet anchor go which was all we had. The ſea now made a free paſſage over us again, which broke and tore away our boats and booms. The ſheet cable tore out with ſuch violence that no man could venture near it, 'till the clench brought up the ſhip. Depth of water about ſeven fathoms. The cable held ſome time, but the ſea came in with ſuch force and ſo very high, that in the hollow of the ſea the ſhip ſtruck, and the cable im-

Apr. 13, 1749.

Nine.

Eleven o'clock.

Apr. 14, 1749. immediately parted. It was now near twelve o'clock, the ſhip ſtruck fore and aft but abaft very hard. The third Lieutenant was near me when the ſhip

Twelve. o'clock. firſt ſtruck, but I ſaw no more of him afterwards. I kept the fore caſtle accompanied by the boatſwain, cook, and about eight men more, I got myſelf laſhed to the bitts before the ſhip took heel, but ſhifted myſelf over to windward when ſhe began to heel, and laſhed myſelf as before, the

Morning. ſea continually beating over us. About two ſaw the Captain's cabbin waſhed away, and the ſhip almoſt on her broad ſide. When daylight came, we were ſixteen men on the forecaſtle, and four hanging abaft to the timber heads, but three of the the laſt got on a piece of the wreck, which was looſe and drove away, the other was drowned; all this time the ſea came over us in a dreadful manner ſo that we could ſcarce take breath. About eight o'clock nine men were waſhed off the forecaſtle. We could now ſee the trees aſhore between the ſeas. About nine o'clock the boatſwain and cook were waſhed away from each ſide of me, then I removed myſelf to the cathead as did another man alſo. About ten o'clock all our men were waſhed away except we that were laſhed to the cathead; we judged we were near two miles off the ſhore; we continued there all the day, the ſea beating over us continually ſo that we had little time to fetch breath or ſpeak to

Apr. 15. one another. At noon we found the ſea to come every way upon us, and could perceive the wind was ſhifted which was the cauſe thereof. This part of the wreck kept faſt, but night coming on we had a diſmal proſpect before us, having no hopes of relief. About midnight the ſea a little abated, ſo that we could ſpeak to one another for the ſpace of two or three minutes together; but I found myſelf ſo weak having been ſick ever ſince we arrived in the country, that when

when the ſea waſhed me on one ſide in my laſh- Apr. 15,
ing I was not able to help myſelf up, but was 1749.
obliged to get my companion to aſſiſt me. At day light I found myſelf much weaker and very thirſty. The ſea at this time came over us once in a quarter of an hour: we found the wreck much nearer the ſhore than yeſterday. Some time after day light my companion told me he ſaw a flag to the northward, which we judged to be at Porto-Novo, a Dutch ſettlement, which gave us great hopes that we ſhould ſoon have ſome aſſiſtance. About noon we found the ſea much abated, ſo that it ſeldom came over us, and the weather began to be fine, but I found myſelf very faint. About two or three o'clock we ſaw two Three
paddy boats coming along ſhore about a mile o'clock.
without us; we ſpread abroad a handkerchief which I had about my neck that the boats might ſee us; one of them ſeemed to edge towards us for ſome minutes but hauled off again. Then we ſaw ſeveral Catamarans near the ſhore which we judged to be fiſhing, we ſpread abroad the handkerchief again, but none of them approached us. Soon after we ſaw ſeveral people gather together aſhore, the ſun began to grow low, ſo that we judged it to be about five o'clock. At laſt we ſaw two of the Catamarans above mentioned coming towards us with three black men on each. They took us off the wreck and carried us aſhore. As ſoon as we were landed, we found ourſelves ſurrounded by about three hundred armed men. My companion told me we were fallen into the hands of the Marattas who were at this time in arms againſt the Engliſh; they ordered us to come off the Catamarans: I ſtrove to riſe, but found myſelf ſo very weak, and my legs ſo terribly bruiſed, that I could not get up; upon which ſome of them came and lifted me off, and laid me upon the ſand, for I could not ſtand. I made a ſign

to

Apr. 15, 1749. them that I wanted ſome water to drink, but they gave me none, and only laughed at our condition. Their commander ordered ſome of them to ſtrip us, which they did quite naked ; but before they ſtripped me, they took a pair of gold buttons out of my ſleeves, two half crowns, my keys and a knife out of my pockets, and having metal buttons on my breeches, they cut them off alſo. When they had ſtripped me they made a kind of clout of my ſhirt to hide my nakedneſs. During this time, we were in the utmoſt want of ſomething to quench our thirſt. As I was not able to walk, they led us part of the way to Davecotta (a fort belonging to them) and there put us into a canoe and carried us up a river to the fort walls. About ten this night they put us within the walls and laid us on the ground, where we had nothing to cover us but the heavens, and about eleven
16. they brought us a little rice and ſome water. Great numbers of people gathered round us, laughing at us, and expreſſing great contempt and deriſion. We got little ſleep that night, being extreamly cold, and not without apprehenſions for our lives, as they had threatened to cut us to pieces with their cutlaſſes. When day light appeared the gates being opened, I found myſelf very ſick, and ſeized with the flux, and my legs extreamly bad, ſo that I concluded I could not ſurvive much longer, if deſtitute of better relief. I told my companion I could not live long, and deſired, that if ever he got home, he would give my friends the hiſtory of my death. Some days they gave us a little rice, and ſome days none at all. About the ſeventh day they gave me ſome lamp oil, with which I bathed my legs, and found ſome eaſe by it.

The country people flocked daily to the fort to ſee us ; but none of them ſhewed us the leaſt pity, but on the contrary laughed at, and threatned us with death. Our lodging-place was between the gate-ways, and when we had been there fourteen or fifteen days they carried us into the country. Tho' my my legs were much better, yet ſtill I could not walk, and my companion was likewiſe extreme weak, which I believe was chiefly owing to our want of more victuals; ſo they put us into dooleys, or cradles, faſtened together with ropes, which they got from the wreck. About four o'clock on the fifteenth day they carried us about twelve miles to their King, who was encamped againſt our Company's troops. By him we were examined, and he queſtioned us if either of us was an officer; this I judged ſafeſt to deny, as the contrary would render our eſcape the more difficult. The King was deſirous we ſhould enter into their ſervice; but we told him (by the interpreters who were three Dutchmen) that we could not conſent to it. He ſaid, we ſhould want for nothing if we would ſerve him; we replied, we were very ill and not fit for any ſervice. However we were ordered a good meals victuals, which was the only one we had had ſince our being amongſt them. The linguiſts aſked us, if it was not better to enter into their ſervice than be ſent to priſon; we told them we could not anſwer to fight againſt our own Countrymen. With that they travelled us till midnight (it being near ſun ſet when we ſet out) and then reſted till near three in the morning, at which time they ſet out with us again, and kept on till noon, when they reſted about two hours to eat, and then proceeded about S. W. till it was night, and we came to a fort, and were immediately put into a dungeon. There were two more priſoners, one of them our ſhip-mate, the other a deſerter from the India company's troops. Our new comrades told us they had been there three days. At ſun riſing the next morning the door of the dungeon was opened, and ſigns were made to us to come out, which my comrades did; but for my part I kept in, being very ill and weak, and my legs exceeding painful and full of running ulcers. I begged they would get me ſome lamp oil to bathe them with, which

1749.

1749. which they accordingly did. They fed us as before with rice, water, and a little gee, viz. a quart of rice a day for four, and a noggen of gee instead of butter. I bathed my legs with the gee and oil, and in four or five days they were greatly mended, which gave me some spirits. For we had liberty in the day time to walk before the dungeon.

In about three weeks time my legs were almost well, so that I was able to walk. We now began to entertain some hopes of making our escape. And taking an opportunity, I with some difficulty got high enough upon the wall to look over it, and found it was very high, and surrounded with a wide mote or ditch; but there was a path between the wall and the ditch, so that we might chuse our place to swim over if it proved deep. We got at several times some strands of rope of the dooleys which they had carried us in, as they happened to be left within the bounds of our liberty. And in a few days we got so many pieces, as when knotted together made seven fathoms and an half. After some consultation we resolved to undermine the foundation of the dungeon at the farthest part from the guards, and on the twenty-seventh of May began to work. On the first of June we came to the foundation, being six feet deep; and the wall thirty inches through. In two days time we had worked upwards on the other side so far, that the light began to appear through the surface, so that we let every thing remain till night. At seven it beginning to grow dark, they put us into the dungeon as usual; and soon after, we worked ourselves quite out, and without being discovered, got over the wall by the help of our rope, and in less than half an hour, had all crossed the mote, though very deep and wide. We travelled all night we judged about sixteen miles, and in the day time hid ourselves among the bushes: the second night we travelled as before to the S. E. and day coming or, we concealed

ed ourſelves among ſome ruſhes. About three in 1749.
the afternoon we were diſcovered, which obliged us to go on, but we were not moleſted. We proceeded till about midnight, and then ſlept till the dawning of the day. I now had a very ſtrong fever on me, and was extremely weak for want of ſomething to eat. This day, being the third, we agreed to travei till noon and plunder the firſt ſingle houſe we could meet with. But providence was more favourable to us than we expected; for about ten o'clock we met a Cooley, who told us he would ſhew us to Carikal, which was a ſettlement belonging to the French. We thanked the Almighty for this joyful news, and gladly accepted the offer. About noon we arrived there, and were received with great humanity and kindneſs, but my fever was not at all abated. The next morning the governor ſent to Mr. Boſcawen to let him know we were there, and by the return of the meſſenger the Admiral deſired we might be furniſhed with what money we wanted. In twelve days time we found ourſelves well recovered, and went to Trinkabar, a place belonging to the Danes, where we ſtayed three days, and then got a paſſage to fort St. David's where I arrived with my two ſhipmates (the deſerter having left us at Carikal) the twenty-third of June, and immediately waited on our Admiral.

THE END.

PROCEEDINGS of the COMMISSARIES at SADRASS.

ARTICLES proposed on the 23d Jan. 1754, by Messrs. Robert Palk and Henry Vansittart, as a basis to the conferences they are appointed by the president and council of Fort St. George to hold at Sadrass, with the reverend father Lavaur and Messrs. De Beauset and De Kerjean, deputies on the part of the marquis Dupleix, governor of Pondichery, for terminating the present troubles in the Carnateck.

ARTICLE I.

Nabob Anaverdy Cawn Behauder shall be acknowledged as Souba of the Carnateck in as full and ample a manner as his father or any other Soubas have enjoyed the province.

II. The king of Tanjore shall also be comprehended in this treaty, and the peaceable possession of his kingdom guaranteed to him by the contracting parties.

To the Honourable Thomas Saunders, *Esq;*

Honourable Sir,

We met the French deputies early this morning according to appointment. They produced a paper of which the inclosed is a translation, and some Persian writings, which they called original grants, desiring we might examine them. We answered, that as they had already been communicated to you, it would be only losing time; that we could not take upon us to say whether these grants were genuine or not, nor whether those that gave them had a power so to do; that Salabatzing was well known to be in a situation not to refuse any thing to the French; and that it was a great doubt whether the Mogul knew what grants Salabatzing had given, though he is said to have approved of his acts. That Gauzedey Cawn's being sent to depose him was no strong argument on his side; that in short, all these points had been so often contested between you and Mr. Dupleix, that it was unnecessary to enter on a further discussion; that the marquis was well acquainted with your sentiments, and that it would be needless and vain for us to attempt to explain them better. We thought therefore that it would be employing our time much more to the purpose, if we proceeded to the proposals; and that we would begin by communicating our preliminaries; upon which we delivered them the paper of which we sent you a copy yesterday, assuring them at the same time, that if they were admitted, a speedy satisfaction might easily be found for all parties. They entered into a long detail to invalidate Anarverdy Cawn's title, which we supported by arguments founded on Nazirzing's Phirmaunds, confirmed by Gauzedey Cawn, and even by the Mogul. This ended in a declaration from them that they could not consent

A to

to our proposals, but that they would transmit them to Pondichery and wait for an answer. They then retired, with a promise of sending us what they intended as preliminaries on their part; and two hours afterwards we received the extraordinary propositions which come inclosed, but not without representing that such an unreasonable demand would rather help to inflame than accommodate the differences, however that we would transmit it to Mr. Saunders, who no doubt would be full of *resonnoissance* for the independancy of Madrass.

On the receipt of our preliminaries it is not improbable but Mr. Dupleix may send orders to his deputies to return: in that case we shall be glad of the same liberty from you. We are only sorry there is no inclination on their side towards a reasonable accommodation. They would have it believed, that the marquis's right of government from the river Krisnah to the sea is incontestible.

We are, with great respect,
Honourable Sir,
Your most obedient humble Servants,

Sadrass, 23d Jan. 1754. ROBERT PALK.
HENRY VANSITTART.

First Memorial presented to the deputies of the English nation by those of the French nation, in the conferences held at Sadrass to consult on means to terminate the troubles of the country.

It being first agreed that we should begin by communicating reciprocally the pieces that are to serve as a basis to the present negotiation, the French deputies communicated the following pieces.

I. A Perwana of Muzapharzing, viceroy of Decan, which appoints the marquis Dupleix, intitled Zupherzing in the Persian language, commander of all the territories in his dependance from the river Krisnah to the sea.

II. Another Perwana of Salabatzing, successor to Muzapherzing, confirming the foregoing.

III. A saned granted by the abovesaid Muzapherzing to Chunda Saib, otherwise called Hussan Dost Cawn, for the Carnateck country.

IV. Another saned granted to the same by Salabatzing after the death of Muzaphering.

V. A Perwana of Salabatzing to give the countries of Arcot and Trichinopoly to the marquis Dupleix after the death of Chunda Saib.

VI. Two Perwana's of the same, confirming the foregoing, and nominating Mootis Ally Cawn, governor of the citadel of Velour, lieutenant under the marquis Dupleix in the Arcot and Trichinopoly countries. In one of these mention is made of a saned formerly granted to Raja Saib, son of Chunda Saib, for the Trichinopoly country.

VII.

VII. A most authentick Phirmaund from the Great Mogul, approving and confirming all that Salabatzing has done in favour of the marquis Dupleix.

Translated from the French original in our hands,
ROBERT PALK.
HENRY VANSITTART.

Signed FR. LAVAUR, superior general of the French jesuits in India.
BAUSSET.
DE KERJEAN.

The Answer and the Proposals of the French deputies to the English deputies assembled at Sadrass, the 23d of January, 1754.

Gentlemen.

The proposal that we cannot avoid making previously to all others, is the restitution of the French prisoners, which regularly ought to be the first preliminary, for the reasons which have been so often set forth to Mr. Saunders.

Coming next to the affairs of the Carnateck, and what you call your proposals we beg you will remark first, that they are only a demand by which you require that we shall give up all, before we have treated of any thing. Secondly, that such a demand does not appear to be founded on any title; you do not even communicate to us the title of Mahomed Allee Cawn, on which you pretend to justify the legality of your alliance with him, which would not appear lawful to us, considering the peace between the two nations, were Mahomed Allee Cawn even authorised. The saned of Nazerzing, which you quote in his favour, should be a paper to be examined; but supposing its existence, you cannot dispute that they are invalidated by the Saned granted afterwards to others, by those who have a right to appoint to the governments of the Carnateck. Thirdly and lastly, the marquis Dupleix has already absolutely declared to the honourable Mr. Saunders, that he looked upon it as a refusal to treat, to propose the aforesaid preliminary, that is to begin with acknowledging Mahomed Allee as legal and absolute master of the Carnateck; if it was resolved to persist in that, it was to no purpose to invite us here.

We have proved by authentick pieces the right of the chief of the French nation to take part in the affairs of the Carnateck, and to make proposals concerning the said country. The following therefore are what we have to make, with the sole motive of restoring peace to the country, and which cannot but appear advantageous to your nation.

ARTICLE I.

The town of Madrass, which has hitherto been possessed by the English nation only in dependance, and with the acknowledgment of a tribute of 4000 pagods a year to the Duan of Arcot, shall henceforth be independent, free from all tribute, and shall have no other master but the honourable English company; if there are any arrears due, they shall be forgiven.

II. The

II. The ſaid company ſhall be ſecured in the legitimate poſſeſſion of Pondemaly and its dependancies.

III. Some eſtabliſhment ſhall be ſecured to Mahomed Allee Cawn, which ſhall be agreed on if the preliminaries are received, and his differences with the Maiſſoreans about Trichinopoly ſhall be conciliated.

IV. In conſideration of the foregoing advantages, the Engliſh ſhall evacuate the places taken from the French, to whom they belonged, whether by right of conqueſt or conceſſion, as well as all other places in the Carnateck country, without oppoſing the diſpoſition and regulations made by Salabatzing, to whom this right belongs without any doubt.

Theſe propoſals comprehend the principal heads which are the object of the negotiation. If any queſtions ariſe which have been omitted, we will add to this memorial, in proportion as they appear.

With regard to Tanjour, the marquis Dupleix has already declared to the honourable Mr. Saunders, that it was in the breaſt of the Tanjoreans to be at peace with the French; and that he would give them aſſurances, free from equivocation, if they on their part would lay down their arms. We renew the ſame declaration, as far as can be neceſſary.

Tranſlated from the French original in our hands,
ROBERT PALK.
HENRY VANSITTART.

Signed FR. LAVAUR.
BAUSSET.
DE KERJEAN.

To Meſſrs. Palk *and* Vanſittart.

Gentlemen,

I have received your letters of the 22d and 23d, with the anſwer of the French deputies to yours, and their propoſals, on which you ſhall have full inſtructions to-morrow morning.

This is chiefly to deſire you will demand of the French deputies the dates of the ſeveral ſaneds to themſelves and Chundah; from theſe depends the confuting them.

Should any orders come to them from Pondichery before you receive ours, acquaint them you expect final ones from me; and then I ſuppoſe the conference will break up.

The following is a paragraph of a Letter, dated Bandarmalanka, 19th January.

"Since my laſt a report has been ſpread, that Mr. Buſſy has been cut off, and Salabatzing made priſoner, and Jaffir Ally "Cawn expects new phirmaunds for the country every day."—— Should this be true, it muſt be very ſoon confirmed.

I am, Gentlemen,
Your moſt obedient Servant,
THOMAS SAUNDERS.

Fort St. George, 24th Jan. 1754. 8 P. M.

To

To Messrs. Palk *and* Vansittart.

Gentlemen,

As on the validity of the several saneds Mr. Dupleix is said to be invested with, depends in a great measure the answer thereto, the translator (as you have none) will set out to morrow morning, when you will demand that he may see them, take their dates, nay a copy of them; by which we shall easily judge of their authenticknefs.

I am, Gentlmen,

Fort St. George, 24th Jan. 1754. 11 P. M.

Your most obedient Servant,

THOMAS SAUNDERS.

P. S. Please to return him with the copies express.

To the honourable Thomas Saunders, *Esq;*

Honourable Sir,

Your general letter of the 22d and 23d we received the 24th, and last night we were favoured with two from you of the 24th. Ours of the 23d will shew you that we have strictly adhered to your instructions in the first; and with regard to the latter, the French gentlemen are already acquainted with our intentions, and consent that the saneds shall be enquired into the moment the translator arrives. They hope that it may promote the conference, and give us to understand that by degrees it is not impossible but we may come to an agreement, though we do not find they are the least inclinable to our first article. If the news from Bandarmalanka should prove true, and Gauzedey Cawn's son have received the phirmaunds, it will be a very strong argument on our side, as they insist chiefly on the validity of theirs.

We are, with great respect,

Honourable Sir,

Sadrass, 26 Jan. 1754. ½ past 10 A. M.

Your most obedient humble Servants,

ROBERT PALK.

HENRY VANSITTART.

To the honourable Thomas Saunders, *Esq;*

Honourable Sir,

The translator arriving this morning, the French deputies met us, and we set about copying the saneds. On Moodo Kisnah's observing the seven first were only copies, we told them that we expected to have seen the originals; they answered, that Mr. Dupleix had them at Pondichery, and, if required, they should be sent hither; but that copies attested by the Caudy were esteemed of equal validity. This caused some dispute, but we agreed to proceed in the copying. On examination it appearing that the first had no date, the father Lavaur immediately objected, that unless we produced Nazirzing's saned to Anaverdy Cawn, they could not admit of theirs being copied; that an answer should first be given to their proposals, and the Nabob's powers produced, that the pieces on both sides might be examined at the same time. We replied, that as we had acted

from

from the beginning only as allies to the Circar, the ſaneds could not be in our hands, but in the Nabob's; that Nazirzing ſupporting him at the head of a numerous army, was a ſtrong ſaned in his favour; and that we did not join him but at the repeated inſtances of Nazirzing himſelf. Upon this they recalled the copies of three or four of the ſaneds that were already finiſhed, deſiring that we would acquaint you with what had happened; and farther, that if our preliminaries were to be inſiſted on, the treaty muſt drop; for that Mr. Dupleix was abſolutely and poſitively determined never to acknowledge Anaverdy Cawn for Souba of the province. Here the conference ended; however we had time to obſerve, that the ſaned from the Grand Mogul, which they declared to be the original, had no chop, only a ſeal of wax annexed to the cover in which it is ſaid to have come. Moodo Kiſtna took a copy of the inſcription which we incloſed to you. If the figures at bottom are the year of the Hegyra (and we know not what elſe it can ſignify) it is thirty-four years old; for this is the year of the Hegyra 1167.

Moodo Kiſtna will ſet out this evening, as you may probably want him at Madraſs. Should you find it neceſſary to return him to us, your orders will meet him on the road.

Sadraſs, 27 Jan. 1754.

We are, with great reſpect,
Honourable Sir,
Your moſt obedient
humble Servants,
ROBERT PALK.
HENRY VANSITTART.

The ſuperſcription.

A Phirmaund of high dignity in the name of governor general Behauder Zapher Jung.

On one ſide of the ſeal.

The Country belongs to God——3
1133.

On the other ſide.

Order belongs to God——3
1133.

To the honourable Thomas Saunders, *Eſq;*

Honourable Sir,

Incloſed is the copy of a letter which we have juſt received from the French deputies, with our anſwer. Unleſs our Interpreters are greatly miſtaken, the Mogul's ſaned is not original.

We beg your anſwer as ſoon as poſſible, as the gentlemen begin to grow impatient.

We are, with great reſpect,
Honourable Sir,
Your moſt obedient
Humble Servants,
ROBERT PALK.
HENRY VANSITTART.

Sadraſs, 27 Jan. 1754.
7 P. M.

Letter

Letter from the French, to the English deputies.

Gentlemen,

Be ſo good as to repreſent to Mr. Saunders, that if we require to ſee the original ſaneds that Mahomed Allee Cawn pretends to have from Nazirzing, it is only to convince yourſelves, gentlemen, that Mahomed Allee Cawn has impoſed upon you; but ſuppoſing even the reality of this ſaned, you are as well acquainted as we, of the little validity it could be of, after the ſaneds granted by the ſucceſſors of Nazarzing. It is therefore needleſs, gentlemen, to wait for this ſaned all the time it will take to ſend for it from Trichinopholy, where you told us it was, and to be ſo long idle. Beſides, as you have declared to us, that independant of all pieces, Mr. Saunders inſiſted on the preliminary propoſed; pleaſe to aſk him for his freſh intentions on that article, ſince they are deciſive for the continuation or the breaking up of the conferences; without them we could only at the end of fifteen days, which would be loſt, tell him what was expreſsly declared to him before we came here.

We beg you will alſo communicate to him all that we have had the honour to ſay to you, gentlemen, on the ſubject of ſecuring the moſt perfect liberty of commerce, ſuch as the Engliſh may deſire, as well on the means of eſtabliſhing in this country a perpetual and invariable peace between the two nations. We wiſh with all our heart that theſe two objects may make on Mr. Saunders the impreſſion they deſerve.

We are, with true reſpect,
Gentlemen,
Your moſt humble
And moſt obedient Servants,
FR. L. LAVAUR.
BAUSETT.
DE KERJEAN.

Tranſlated from the original
in our hands,
ROBERT PALK.
HENRY VANSITTART.

The Anſwer to the foregoing Letter.

To the reverend Father Lavaur *and Meſſrs.* De Bauſet *and* De Kerjean, *deputies of the French nation.*

Gentlemen,

We have received the Letter which you did us the honour to write to us; we have already communicated the contents to Mr. Saunders.

We are not a little ſurprized to find that Nazirzing's appointment of Anaverdy Cawn to the ſoubaſhip of the Carnateck is diſputed, ſince neither the marquis Dupleix nor you, gentlemen, can be ignorant, that this maſter of Deckan not only granted him the ſaneds, but ſupported him with a numerous army to put him in poſſeſſion of the government, which he would have enjoyed peaceably to this day, and the country have remained in perfect tranquillity, had it ſo pleaſed the marquis Dupleix.

The English entered into an alliance with Anaverdy Cawn in support of this title, which, to give it all possible force, has since been confirmed by Gauzedy Cawn and his son Shaw Abadin Cawn, the succeeding masters of Deckan; and it is for these substantial reasons, that his rights are made the basis of the present conferences: when this is settled, the equitable demands of all parties may be easily reconciled.

As to the saneds, it was your first proposal that yours would be enquired into; and we are at a loss to guess the reason of your declining it after some copies had been taken: pieces of so publick a nature might, we apprehend, be exposed to all the world. But we cannot help remarking to you, that the first of these saneds is without date; and the only original one you produced, said to come from the Great Mogul, wants what we are assured are the usual forms, which certainly should not have been neglected in a piece of so much consequence; for instance, it has no chop of the Mogul or his Visier, it has no sign manual, and under the superscription of the seal annexed to the cover are the figures 1133, the date no doubt of the Hegyra, according to the custom of the country; and if so, we need not tell you that it is thirty-four years old, this being the year of the Hegyra 1167.

With regard to the saneds of Anaverdy Cawn, we have had the honour to acquaint you, that as we are only allies, the originals he has from time to time received rest with him, and attested copies may be procured whenever it shall be thought necessary.

As Mr. Saunders has nothing more at heart than a just and equitable peace to the reciprocal advantage of both nations, we cannot but wish Mr. Dupleix would give proofs of the same sentiments.

We have the honour to be,
With the most perfect regard,
Gentlemen,
Your most obedient humble servants,
Robert Palk.
Henry Vansittart.

Sadrass, 27 January, 1754.

To the honourable Thomas Saunders, *Esq;*

Honourable Sir,

We have yet received no answer from the French deputies to our letter of the 27th. The father Lavaur took a translation of it that evening, as we explained the sense to him, for none of them understand any English; and when he came to our remarks, he confessed that things to be sure could not be decided by saneds; that we should proceed further in our proposals, and try if affairs could not be accommodated in that manner: however, he talked yesterday of sending us an answer; but as it is so long coming, we imagine they have wrote

wrote to Pondichery for one. It ſeems to be paſt all doubt, that Mr. Dupleix's friend at the court of Delhi has deceived him.

We are, with great reſpect,
Honourable Sir,
Your moſt obedient
Humble ſervants,
ROBERT PALK.
HENRY VANSITTART.

Sadraſs, 29 Jan. 1754.
½ paſt 8 A. M.

To Meſſrs. Palk *and* Vanſittart.

Gentlemen,

We annex hereto our inſtructions for your anſwer to the French deputies memorial, reply to their anſwer and propoſals, and our freſh propoſals. By what has already paſt, we are convinced Mr. Dupleix has no intentions of peace. You will receive an anſwer in writing to our propoſals, which we ſuppoſe will put an end to the conference.

We are, Gentlemen,
Your moſt obedient ſervants,
THOMAS SAUNDERS.
CHARLES BODDAM.
HENRY POWNEY.
ALEXANDER WYNCH.
JOHN SMITH.
CHARLES BOURCHIER.

Fort St. George,
30 Jan. 1754.

Anſwer to be preſented by the Engliſh Commiſſaries to the firſt memorial delivered by the French Deputies at Sadraſs.

Our firſt propoſal being, that Nabob Mahomed Allee Cawn ſhould be acknowledged Souba of the Carnateck; his right being founded on ſaneds granted by the ſeveral princes of the Deckan, it is matter of ſurpriſe to us, that the marquis Dupleix, who is only an ally of the country powers, ſhould aſſume to himſelf the authority and government, not only of this province, but of the whole country from Cape Comorin to the River Kriſtna, in direct oppoſition to the eſtabliſhed laws of the Mogul, and his officers legally appointed; to us, and to every one well known. Yet as Mr. Dupleix in his letters to Mr. Saunders advanced, that he had ſeveral ſaneds to ſupport this authority, preſſing repeatedly an examination of them; and the French commiſſaries preſenting the ſame, we agreed to it: upon the peruſal of ſome of them, the incoherencies appearing ſo very ſtrong, they then declined, and denied us any farther ſcrutiny. The reaſon aſſigned by Father Lavaur, that unleſs the Nabob's ſaned from Nazirzing was firſt produced, they would not admit of a farther ſcrutiny, we think unjuſt and groundleſs; becauſe on the validity of thoſe ſaneds certainly depends Mr. Dupleix's authority to judge of Nabob Anaverdy Cawn's right, and is therefore what ſhould be firſt ſettled. But we cannot help thinking that Father Lavaur was influenced by a more cogent reaſon; he knew too well they would not bear the teſt. The palpable defects found in thoſe we had the peruſal of, give us full liberty to make this concluſion.

As

As patents of ſo publick a nature are in their very intention granted to be publiſhed to the whole community, what can their ſuppreſſing an examination into them mean more than a conſciouſneſs of their illegality. To every candid reader it muſt certainly appear ſo; and as we are from undoubted facts convinced that they are of no force, we object to them, deny their validity, and declare that Mr. Dupleix has no more authority to govern this province than any private perſon whatſoever.

Reply to be made by the Engliſh Commiſſaries to the anſwer and propoſals of the French Deputies. Dated 23 January, 1754.

That it is very certain Mr. Dupleix has often wrote to Mr. Saunders concerning the French priſoners, and that he has uſed his influence with the Nabob for their relief; which has been returned with breach of honour, by ſeveral officers appearing in arms againſt him contrary to their parole; and though by this they were liable to immediate death, they have by his interceſſion been pardoned: that as Mr. Dupleix cannot be ignorant that priſoners are never releaſed till a peace is concluded, he will certainly think it reaſonable when we tell him, that when the articles on which the peace and ſecurities of the Nabob's government depends are ſettled, this will be immediately conſidered.

And as it appears evidently by the invalidity of theſe papers Mr. Dupleix is pleaſed to introduce under the name of ſaneds, that he has no authority to conteſt the commiſſions granted by the Mogul's legal officers; yet we are ready, if he deſires it, to remove all doubt he may have concerning Nabob Mahomed Allee's juſt title, and will ſend for copies atteſted of the ſaneds granted him by Nazirzing, Gauzedey Cawn, and confirmed by Gauzedey Cawn's ſon, for the peruſal of Mr. Dupleix or his commiſſaries.

Tho' our propoſal of Mahomed Allee's being Souba of the Carnateck is founded on juſtice and equity, as no Nabob but himſelf has been named to that government ſince his father Anaverdey Cawn's death, and is ſo far abſolute, that no peace can be concluded without it; yet in regard to Mr. Dupleix it is conditional, and he is deſired to give in his demands, which will be conſidered, and, if conſiſtent with the tranquillity of the country, granted; ſo that it cannot be ſaid that they ſhould give up every thing. And if Mr. Dupleix is not ſatisfied with the ſaned from Nazirzing, Gauzedey Cawn's cannot be diſputed; but ſhould this be the caſe, ſurely when it is confirmed by Gauzedey Cawn's ſon it will be deemed juſt to any others.

They are pleaſed to ſay they have proved by authentick pieces, that the French had a right to take a part in the affairs on the coaſt of Coromandel. We are of opinion thoſe very papers, the invalidity of which are as clear as the ſun at noon, manifeſt evidently that they had no juſt grounds for ſo doing; or that we may be convinced that we err, let Mr. Dupleix produce a ſaned from the Mogul, empowering him to take a part with Erat Mooden Cawn and Chunda

Saib,

Saib, in deposing and killing Anaverdey Cawn; let him produce a saned also for assisting the same rebels in the assassination of Nazirzing, who it is universally known governed the Deckan by orders from the Emperor; it will be necessary also to produce powers from Gauzedey Cawn, who was by the Mogul appointed successor to Nazirzing, to continue his support to Chundah Saib against Nabob Mahomed Allee Cawn. If he cannot produce these pieces, what title has he to assume the government of the coast of Coromandel? And as Nabob Mahomed Allee has saneds from these legal princes, by what authority can Mr. Dupleix dispute them?

When Mr. Saunders made proposals to Mr. Dupleix to treat, he told him it was by virtue of a power from Nabob Mahomed Allee. What then can he mean by his offer, that Madrass should be free from the tribute of 4000 pagodas per annum, paid to the circar of Arcot; and that Poonamalee should be secured to us? We can hardly surmise that he could be ignorant that the settlement of Madrass never has paid such tribute, and that the country of Poonamalee is ours by a legal grant; but supposing it was otherwise, it has in this conference sufficiently appeared that he has no power to secure to us either; therefore these two articles are certainly ridiculous and insolent.

Equally so is the third article, to make a prisoner of a prince who has beat his enemies in every battle; and who, not compelled by necessity, but through a humane disposition to put a stop to the calamities of war, would treat his enemies as friends.

The fourth is absurd and quite unintelligible; the English have not taken any one place from the French, nor are they at this day in possession of a single one belonging to either French or Moors.

In regard to the King of Tanjore, the offer is an equivocation; as it is known the King of Tanjore is in alliance with the Nabob, and cannot treat separately; if a peace is concluded with the Nabob, and Mr. Dupleix will engage not to molest the King or his country, he will lay down his arms.

To recapitulate the whole of the French deputies memorial, answer and proposals, they are, that Mr. Dupleix (the chief of the French nation) grasps at the government of the coast of Coromandel: that he produces several papers, which he terms saneds, to prove his authority, which he offers to examination, but when found defective, a further scrutiny is denied: that he repeatedly desires the Nabob's right may be enquired into; but when the deputies are told they shall be satisfied in this point, instead of entering into any enquiry, they declare absolutely that Mr. Dupleix never will consent to Nabob Mahomed Allee's being Subah of the Carnatick; and that if the Nabob will betray his master, and consent that he shall rob him of the whole coast of Coromandel, he offers to secure to the English what he would not with impunity attempt to take from them; and what if they had not, he has no power to bestow. To the Nabob, under whose protection he should live peaceably, and whose govern-

government he ſhould obey, he would give a penſion; and the King of Tanjore he would tempt to be a villain, in deſerting his allies. Theſe propoſals will ſufficiently ſhew to our ſuperiors his inclinations to peace; as they will at the ſame time convince the Mogul and his officers of his intention to plunder him of his dominions, and induce them to take ſuch meaſures as may convince him that the liberty of a nation will not eaſily become a prey to the ambition of a ſingle ſubject.

Propoſals to be made by the Engliſh Commiſſaries in behalf of Nabob Mahomed Allee to the French Deputies at Sadraſs.

As it is notoriouſly evident from what has paſſed in this conference, that by the examination of thoſe few papers which Mr. Dupleix calls ſaneds, and by the ſuppreſſion of any further ſcrutiny into the reſt, as well as by the orders from the Mogul to his ſeveral officers of the government of this province and the other part of the coaſt of Coromandel; that thoſe papers are of no force, ſhould Mr. Dupleix perſiſt in aſſuming to himſelf an unlawful power thus by acts of violence in ſupport of rebels to rob the Emperor of his country, and the people of their liberty, what can it be productive of but a continuance of the war? And as when it was offered that atteſted copies of the Nabob's ſaneds ſhould be laid before Mr. Dupleix or his Deputies, they, without alledging any thing to diſannul his right, or even waiting for a peruſal of thoſe pieces, contrary to all reaſon and juſtice, replied that Mr. Dupleix declared abſolutely, Nabob Mahomed Allee ſhould never be Subah of the province. A ſpeech ſo arbitrary that it amounts to a publick declaration, that in open violation of all laws, he is reſolved to uſurp the government. How different is this from his ſolemn proteſtation, that he reſerved no animoſity to the Nabob, or that he had nothing more ſincerely at heart than reſtoring peace to the country? We flatter ourſelves, upon mature conſideration Mr. Dupleix's good ſenſe will lead him to lay aſide a ſcheme ſo contrary to the eſtabliſhed laws of the country and ſo deſtructive to the people, and that he will ſeriouſly think of peace; to promote which, and that he may be convinced of our good intentions, we in behalf of Nabob Mahomed Allee Cawn make the following propoſals.

That the Nabob, as he is determined not to ſwerve from the rules of his government, but afford protection equally alike to the European nations ſettled on the coaſt, and to put an end to the animoſities the late unhappy troubles have occaſioned, will make no diſtinction between the French and Engliſh, will grant to the French, Jagueers to the full amount of what were poſſeſſed by the Engliſh; and that no diſpute may in future ariſe, thoſe Jagueers ſhall be ſo ſituated as not to be liable to any inconveniencies from the ſettlements or poſſeſſions of the Engliſh; and that in regard to commerce, both nations ſhould enjoy a free circulation through the province, without partiality to either; and that the goods paſſing or repaſſing through each

each others Jagueers ſhall not be liable to any cuſtom or moleſtation.

That the French ſhall evacuate all places poſſeſſed by them or by their order, excluſive of theſe Jagueers; ſhall not interfere in the Nabob's government, give protection to, or aſſiſt ſuch of his ſubjects who may endeavour to diſturb the peace or defraud him of his revenues.

That when the articles for ſecuring to the Nabob his government are adjuſted, the releaſe of the priſoners ſhall be ſettled in ſuch manner as may be conſiſtent with the ſafety of his government.

That the Nabob will give the Myſoreans a ſecurity for ſuch a ſum of money as may upon an equitable ſtate of the account appear to be due to them.

That a penſion for Ruzza Saib ſhall be agreed on and ſettled.

That in conſideration of the above, Mr. Dupleix ſhall, in behalf of the French nation, acknowledge and pay all lawful obedience to Nabob Mahomed Allee Cawn, as Nabob of the Carnateck, in as full and ample manner as his father Anaverdey Cawn poſſeſſed it.

That the King of Tanjore ſhall enjoy his country in peace, free from any moleſtation.

That this treaty be ſigned by Mr. Dupleix, as governor, &c. council of Pondichery, and Thomas Saunders, governor, &c. council of Fort St. George, with the ſeals of the reſpective companies affixed by Nabob Mahomed Allee, Subah of the Carnateck, with the ſeal of the Circar; by the King of Tanjore with his royal ſeal, and the King of Myſore with his. That the ſeveral articles contained in this treaty ſhall be guaranteed by each party to the reſt; and that whoſoever infringes it ſhall be deemed as a common enemy, and ſhall by the reſt be compelled to render ſatisfaction to the party aggrieved. That all animoſities ſhall ceaſe, what has paſt be buried in oblivion, and a perfect friendſhip and harmony ſubſiſt.

To be propoſed in a ſeparate Article.

That as the influence Mr. Dupleix, as governor of Pondichery, and Mr. Saunders, governor of Madraſs, have on the country powers is well known, Mr. Saunders is ready to concert meaſures with Mr. Dupleix for eſtabliſhing a perfect peace and friendſhip, not only in this province, but on the whole coaſt of Coromandel; not doubting but if they both ſincerely exert their endeavours, it may be with facility effected.

To the honourable Thomas Saunders, *Eſq;*

Honourable Sir,

The incloſed letter we received from the French deputies yeſterday, which we deferred anſwering till the Tappies came in, expecting your further inſtructions, as they might in ſome meaſure direct us in doing it; but as we have not yet been favoured with them, we

determined

determined to ſend the anſwer, of which a copy alſo comes incloſed.

We have confined ourſelves as ſtrictly as the ſubject will permit us to your former directions; and having the beſt of the argument, we thought it our duty to enforce it.

We are, with the greateſt reſpect,
Honourable Sir,
Your moſt obedient
Humble Servants,
ROBERT PALK.
HENRY VANSITTART.

Sadraſs, 30th January, 1754. 2 P. M.

To Meſſrs. Palk *and* Vanſittart, *Deputies of the Engliſh nation.*

Gentlemen,

It is very true that we propoſed to you to begin our conferences by the expoſition and examination of the pieces that might ſupport our reciprocal pretenſions: it is the natural method, if it is intended to proceed according to the rules of juſtice. To this end the marquis Dupleix deſired the honourable Mr. Saunders to furniſh you with the titles on which you pretend to juſtify the rights of Mahomed Allee. We came here in confidence that you had brought them; but we were miſtaken. That did not hinder us from producing and ſubmitting to your examination all our perwanas, in the hopes you gave us of procuring immediately from Madraſs whatever might exiſt in favour of Mahomed Allee. But after the time neceſſary, we ſaw nothing arrive but interpreters deſtined to examine our pieces; and you ſaid that your's or Mahomed Allee's (which is the ſame thing) were at Trichinopoly. Notwithſtanding this ſecond delay, which muſt be much longer than the former, on account of the diſtance of the places, we put ours into the hands of your interpreters. You required copies of them, and we conſented that they ſhould be taken. They were at work upon them when you ſpoke to us of a new ſaned of Shahabedy Cawn, ſon of Gauzedey Cawn, in favour of Mahomed Allee; and of another from the Mogul in favour of Shahabedey Cawn You had prepared us for theſe new pieces by diſtant hints in converſation, but you had not yet declared their exiſtence. We were alſo prepared for them by information that had been given to Nandi Raja of a pretended ſaned ſent by Shahabedey Cawn to Mahomed Allee, which falls of itſelf, as we ſhall make appear in proper time.

All that, gentlemen, (ſince we muſt declare it) gave us ſtrong ſuſpicions that our pieces, ſent by you to Mahomed Allee, might ſerve his people to direct or correct the work they were employed about, which had not been yet communicated to us, and of which they ſent you the firſt productions, as you are leſs intereſted to examine ſtrictly into them.

Further, you informed us that you did not propoſe to treat upon pieces, but on the propoſals which Mr. Saunders had made the invariable baſis of our negociation. Thereupon, gentlemen, we we represented to you, first, that our condescension to you might appear excessive, in that we submitted our pieces to you on the distant hopes of seeing yours. In reality, would it be decent that we should be subject to undergo an examination on the part of your interpreters, without having on our side the liberty of examining on what you carry on a war against us? It is true, that we might suppose the saned of Nazirzing, which is the only foundation of the pretensions of Mahomed Allee, without weakening ourselves in the least, as we have demonstrated several times; but having very justifiable occasion to doubt of its existence, why should we give up such a superabundance of right?

We had the honour, gentlemen, to tell you, in the second place, that the delivery of our pieces would only produce disputes and useless delays, if Mr. Saunders was inflexible on his first proposition, and that we must demand, previously to every other thing, a final declaration on his part on this article. These, gentlemen, are the reasons which made us recall our pieces. We had the honour to mention them to you; undoubtedly you did not understand us perfectly, which makes it necessary for us to repeat them.

We shall answer your remarks on our pieces when yours arrive and we enter upon this examination. Be not surprized, gentlemen, at our doubt of the existence of Nazirzing's saned; if you establish it on proofs like what you have mentioned to us, namely, the assistance he gave Mahomed Allee with a numerous army to put him in possession of the Carnateck; this motive of the war of Nazirzing has hitherto been a mystery undiscovered; unluckily it is refuted, because all the world is acquainted with interests which brought him here, and for which he acted, all of them very foreign to Mahomed Allee. It is moreover known in what light he looked upon him, or rather that he would not see him at all, after the unfortunate expedition which the said Mahomed Allee undertook with a view of meriting the saned in question. Nazirzing thought so little of him, or of his elder brother who was in the same army for the government of the Carnateck, that at the very time he offered the same government to many others, the French even not excepted, if they would abandon the engagements which they were in honour bound to keep. Mahomed Allee himself never mentioned this saned till the successes of the English, his protectors, inspired him with views on Arcot. The English themselves when they went to join him at Trichinopoly, assigned no other pretext but to get payment of five lacks which Mahomed Allee owed them. We do not advance this without proofs. At what time was the saned in question cited? when it was found necessary to justify a train of facts by colours of justice.

We must add, gentlemen, to these reasons, of which we know the insufficiency for forwarding an accommodation, the assurances which we give you afresh, that we are ready to retrench from our rights for the advantage of your nation, when it shall be no longer required

required that we muſt begin with abandoning them totally, by acknowledging Mahomed Allee ſole and lawful maſter of the Carnateck. We diſcovered this diſpoſition in the ſentiments of Mr. Dupleix, who ſent us. If you are willing to make uſe of them, tell us openly and frankly what you require; we will anſwer you in a manner ſatisfactory to your nation, in the judgment even of thoſe who command it, and who cannot but be acquainted with the advances we have at leaſt made towards a peace, if we have not the happineſs to conclude it.

We have the honour to be, with real reſpect,
Gentlemen,
Your moſt humble
And moſt obedient Servants,
Fr. L. Lavaur.
Bausett.
De Kerjean.

Pleaſe to communicate Mr. Saunders's anſwer, tranſlated from the original in our hands.
Robert Palk.
Henry Vansittart.
Not dated, but received the 29th Jan. at 12 A. M.

To the reverend Father Lavaur *and Meſſrs.* De Bauſſet *and* De Kerjean, *deputies of the French nation.*

Gentlemen,

If all the reaſons you are pleaſed to give for declining the examination of your pieces were mentioned at the conference, moſt aſſuredly we did not underſtand them, although we paid the ſtricteſt attention to all that you did us the honour to ſay; if we examined the Perwanas it was only at your requeſt, and to pay a proper regard to what, by your own confeſſion, was the foundation of your rights. We were willing, gentlemen, to put it in your power to juſtify your pretenſion to the utmoſt, that you might not have reaſon hereafter to ſay that we paid no regard to the powers you produced; not that we could conceive the marquis Dupleix had merited ſo much from the Mogul, or that the Mogul ſhould confer ſo much authority on him, who is known to be the cauſe of a calamitous war in his country for five years together, by which a large part of his revenues, not only in this province, but many others has been ſtopped, and his dominions laid waſte.

You have endeavoured, gentlemen, to give ſpecious reaſons for declining the examination, but you have omitted the only material one; the diſcovery you no doubt made as well as we, that your ſaneds were not of a nature to ſtand the teſt of the ſlighteſt examination, of which the ſuperſcription on the ſeal, not to mention any others, is an inconteſtable proof: truth wants no colourings to ſet it off, and falſhood is generally detected by affecting to lay on too many to diſguiſe it. If that which by way of eminence you intitle the moſt authentick, carries its own conviction along with it, what judgment

judgment can we form, gentlemen, of your other pieces? The highest compliment we can pay them must be only to place them in the same rank. Your silence on so material an article will be looked upon as a very strong proof, if we wanted others, of what we advanced. Our not having the saneds of Anaverdey Cawn to produce, could be no reason for your declining the examination of yours, which, had they been genuine, would not have suffered by being proclaimed to the whole world. The marquis Dupleix himself, in his letter to Mr. Saunders of the 25th December, speaking of the powers he was invested with to treat concerning the interests of the Carnateck, makes this proposal.

" If you do not give credit to what I have had the honour to " write to you very particularly on that subject, I am able and " ready to justify it: you may therefore commission your deputies " on this head, or send such person to me as you shall think fit, and " I will shew him the original writings." These writings we have seen, and given you unanswerable reasons why we cannot think them original; and you, gentlemen, have too much penetration not to perceive the force of them.

It is very true, that all the world is acquainted with the interest that brought Nazirzing into this province; it was to restore order, and to punish those that had been the disturbers of it. To this end he wrote to the English to assist the family of Anaverdey Cawn against all invaders; and it is for this reason confirmed by the authority derived from him to his son Mahomed Allee, afterwards named Anaverdy Cawn, that they have constantly supported him. That Nazirzing offered the government of this province to the French, contradicts all his other actions; and as to the article you advance about the five lacks, as the cause of our joining him at Trichinopoly, it serves only to convince us how little you are acquainted with what passed at that time.

You are very pressing, gentlemen, in your demand of our final declaration on our first article, but do not on your part make any proposals for the satisfaction of a prince who, both by his titles and successes, has a right not only to be first considered, but to be himself the source from whence all other parties should derive a just satisfaction, and which, we renew our assurances, he is ready and willing to give.

As soon as we receive Mr. Saunders's final answer, we shall make you acquainted with it; and we must request on our part also, that you will communicate the final resolution of Mr. Dupleix, which we sincerely wish may tend to promote a happy end to our negociation.

We have the honour to be, with perfect respect,

Gentlemen,

Sadrass, 30th Jan. 1754.

Your most obedient humble Servants,

ROBERT PALK.
HENRY VANSITTART.

To

To Messrs. Palk *and* Vansittart.

Gentlemen,

I have this minute received yours of the 30th, with a translate of one from the French deputies, and your reply, which I approve. This morning our instructions were forwarded to you, so that I have only to remark,

That an examination of Mr. Dupleix's Powers was what he earnestly insisted on; and that certainly those powers should be first proved authentick, as on them he founded his authority to the river Kistna, &c. is but reasonable.

The reason they give for declining the examination is trifling.

Mr. Dupleix has not sent the originals, but copies, and says that the former may be inspected by any person sent to him; and you certainly have the same liberty of replying, that the originals are with the Nabob, and may be inspected in the same manner.

Those gentlemen should suspend their judgment of Shahabedey Cawn's saned till it was examined; strong suspicions are what any one may suggest. They ought to be regarded as such, but will never be thought convincing proofs.

The gentlemen seem to acknowledge, at least not to deny, the saned from Nazirzing. This justifies the Nabob's conduct in supporting his right, as it condemns Chundah and his allies in invading it.

They saw our proposals, and afterwards delivered a memorial of saneds. Why should they retract them till by my answer they were assured that I was inflexible? and this they certainly could not know before they received it.

The motives of Nazirzing's coming into the province you have very justly explained: that the government was offered to the French, till now I never heard, and might venture to affirm in the negative. The Mysoreans made a fruitless interest for it. Mauphus Cawn, the Nabob's eldest brother, did not bid high enough. Mahomed Allee was always reputed the Subah. The reasons assigned for our joining him at Trichinopoly are notoriously false and scandalous, for at that time he was not indebted to us.

What do these gentlemen mean by we shall do so and so? Who gave them the power? Mr. Dupleix may talk thus in Pondichery amongst his slaves; I do not doubt but they know his disposition, and possibly may approve it as little as we do. Surely Mr. Dupleix does not think we are begging a peace, and will accept of any terms he pleases. I observe they are particularly fond of granting advantages to our nation; this is designed to appear plausible at home; but however, we shall take care to secure the peace of the country, and ever have before us his designs on the whole coast. I think it will not be amiss to ask them, as we are treating for the Nabob, whether by these offers they mean to offer us a bribe to be villains, and betray the trust reposed in us.

Their

Their saneds are so defective, we can by no means allow them. Without Mahomed Allee's enjoying the Subahship no peace can ensue; and when these articles are agreed on, that of the French prisoners, a knotty article, remains to be adjusted in a manner consistent with the security of the Nabob. Considering the disposition of Mr. Dupleix, little, I believe, inclined to drop so darling a scheme, I am of opinion the conference will terminate unsuccessfully. This advantage indeed we shall reap from it, that our reasonable inclinations for peace will be manifested to the publick, and his hostile disposition, with the falsity of the authority on which he founded it.

I am, Gentlemen,
Your most obedient Servant,
THOMAS SAUNDERS.

To the honourable Thomas Saunders, *Esq*;

Honourable Sir,

Inclosed is a letter we received last night, in answer to ours of yesterday, on which we must observe, first,

That as they communicated their pieces to us in a cursory way, we had not then time sufficient to examine them, but enough to remark, that the first was not dated, and you are already acquainted with our objections to the last, which can never, we apprehend, be confuted: indeed by their method of reasoning they give up what they would be thought to defend. Secondly,

The only original, now for the first time called a letter or saned, was represented to us to be of the strongest validity; and if they had it double, they never once hinted it when it was produced; even all their pieces at our first conference were represented as originals, and it was not till the copies were beginning that we found they were otherwise. It is true, Mr. Vansittart did peruse the paragraph from Mr. Dupleix, which was at the end of a very long letter, from whence we are inclined to think it was inserted there on purpose; but even here we believe the epochas will not agree: And as to their offering at the same time to shew him the original, they very well knew we had no interpreters, and if we had, we very much doubt if they would have submitted it to their examination. Mr. Vansittart declined it, because they might have asserted afterwards that he had seen it with his own eyes. We leave it to you to make the necessary remarks on their method of accounting for the mistake at Delhi. Thirdly,

No answer at all is it seems the best they can give to this article, as well as to some others contained in our letter. Fourthly,

An answer to their proposals you see is positively expected before they proceed any further: we shall wait till the tappies come in, and

 then,

then, if we have not the pleasure to hear from you, we shall give them a very short answer to their letter. We could multiply remarks to them, but we apprehend those we have already made will be thought sufficient.

We are, with the greatest respect,

Sadrass, 31st Jan. 1754. Honourable Sir,

9 A. M. Your most obedient humble Servants,

ROBERT PALK.

HENRY VANSITTART.

To Messrs. Palk *and* Vansittart, *deputies of the English nation.*

Gentlemen,

Not to multiply writings, we have the honour to reply as briefly as possible to the different articles of your last letter.

First, We did communicate our pieces to you, and gave you sufficient leisure to examine them. We only refused to let you have copies till you should communicate yours; when this is done, we will produce ours again with all confidence, and we will refute by them all the inferences you strive to draw for the present from our refusal. We will also produce the originals without fear, provided you do the same on your part.

Secondly, The only original that we have hitherto shewn you, is the letter or saned of the Great Mogul which we brought with us, having it double, as we told you when we produced it. As this is a decisive piece, it could not be sent without difficulty. We immediately advised the marquis Dupleix of what you remarked to us on the subject of the epoch marked at the bottom of the seal. The following is the answer he sent us immediately on the receipt of your letter: *As to the date of the seal, I can say nothing to you on that subject; it was the duplicate that I deliver'd you: but to dissipate all doubts on that subject, I send you now what was at first dispatched to me, which is dated the* 11*th of the month Rejub, the* 5*th year of his reign; and upon the chop is the year of the Hegyra** 1163. *This is what was delivered to me by Us Bachi Cawn, dispatched to bring it me.*

Such is the frankness with which Mr. Dupleix answers on this subject. Mr. Vansittart saw this paragraph of the letter with his own eyes, and we offered at the same time to shew him the original, which we had just received. It is impossible, gentlemen, to declare in a more polite manner than you have done, the suspicions you affect to form on this piece, and which you would extend to all the others. All of them, it is true, must be equally suspicious to you. But in reality, gentlemen, if we were capable of counterfeiting, do you think we should be so little upon our guard as to be mistaken in the date of the Hegyra, and to make use of two different Seals. The writers at Delhi might do the latter by making use of the seal of the reigning emperor for the first dispatch, and of the seal of his predecessor, which apparently came first to their hands, for

for the dispatch they afterwards made by way of duplicate; but such a piece of negligence, if it is one, is a proof of the truth of the piece. Make whom you will the judge, and he will tell you that the difficulty you make is at the very time a proof of the force with which this piece is invested.

Thirdly, The reproach you throw on the marquis Dupleix, as being the cause of the troubles of the country, might with more justice be applied to the chiefs of your nation; but whatever advantage we might be able to make by entering on this subject, we pass it slightly over as superfluous. In the same manner we say nothing of the motives that induced the Grand Mogul to recompense the marquis Dupleix; it would be easy to shew them, but the letter of this emperor subsists. That is the essential.

Fourthly, Laying aside for the present all allegations of which we have not yet got the proofs in writing, we will prove to you by a loyal letter from Mr. Saunders himself to Chundah Saib, that he interested himself at the beginning for Mahomed Allee, only on account of what this last owed, or was said to owe, to the English nation. We expect to be soon enabled to confirm this to you by other pieces of your chief's, and to make you also agree, if you will enter upon the proofs, that the English acknowledged Chundah Saib for governor of the Carnateck.

It is for us, gentlemen, to expect on your part an answer to the proposals we have made you; tell us if they are satisfactory or not? We do not allow, as you know of the precedency to be given to the interests of Mahomed Allee, but we have not neglected them in our proposals, and when ever you please we will settle the proper establishment which is to be procured for him.

Sadrass, 30th Jan. 1754. We have the honour to be,
Translated from the original Gentlemen,
in our hands, Your most obedient humble Servants,

ROBERT PALK. Fr. L. LAVAUR.
HENRY VANSITTART. BAUSETT.
DE KERJEAN.

To Messrs. Palk *and* Vansittart.

Gentlemen,

I had replied to your letter, of the 30th when I received that of the 31 with a translate of one to you from the French deputies.

When Mr. Dupleix pressed the examination, it was without limitation, and without any reference to those of the Nabob's.

So difficult is it to give to falsity even the appearance of truth, that the circumstances offered to support it often tend to the exploding it; and thus in regard to the paper called the Mogul's saned, a duplicate is something extraordinary; but that this duplicate should differ in so essential a point from what, after the falsity is exploded, is produced as an original, serves only to convince

 more

more ſtrongly of the invalidity, and to give us the greateſt reaſon to believe that what ever defects might be found in the reſt, as ſoon as noticed would be amended, without the loſs of time or trouble of ſending to Delhi; and therefore I think we may perſiſt in our objection to their validity, and wave all further enquiry, as it will only give them an opportunity to recover from their error, whereas it now turns much to our advantage.

The frankneſs with which Mr. Dupleix anſwers on the ſubject (*as to the date of the ſeal I can ſay nothing to you on that ſubject*) is a truth that ſerves to corroborate his weakneſs in offering to found his authority on a falſity, and his chicanery in having the Mogul's ſeal in ſuch readineſs to ſupply its defect. The excuſe afterwards framed is equally as abſurd.

The aſperſion that we engaged in the war on account of money, owed by Mahomed Allee to the Engliſh nation, is falſe and ſcandalous. Incloſed is a copy of that letter to Chundah Saib, dated 3d Auguſt, 1751, a long time after the war commenced. Trichinopoly was mortgaged, Mr. Dupleix was informed of it, and ſo great was the affront he offered us, as to anſwer that our colours ſhould be no ſanction to us. More will be ſaid on this occaſion to Mr. Dupleix when he poſſibly may not expect it.

By what I have wrote you, you will be able to return the proper anſwer. Do not preſs any farther examination of ſaneds, it will be of no effect, when they can ſo eaſily at Pondichery on every occaſion have in readineſs a proper ſeal for the Mogul, and without doubt for his officers.

I am, Gentlemen,

Fort St. George, the 1ſt Feb. 1754.

Your moſt obedient Servant,
THOMAS SAUNDERS.

To the honourable Thomas Saunders, *Eſq;*

Honourable Sir,

Yeſterday we were favoured with your letters of the 31ſt January and 1ſt inſtant, and in the afternoon we received the anſwer from the French deputies, of which we have juſt finiſhed the tranſlation we now incloſe you, with a copy of our letter to them of the 1ſt.

Their arguments are all founded on a ſuppoſition of the rights of the marquis Dupleix. We ſhall therefore make the proofs we have ſeen of the invalidity of theſe rights the principal object of our reply; and as they have at once rejected all our propoſals without even anſwering them, they are very evidently determined to come to no reaſonable accommodation. We ſhall therefore tell them it is to no purpoſe to wait for an anſwer from the marquis Dupleix, as his deſigns are plainly publiſhed in the letter; and that if they can give us no better hopes of a ſucceſsful congreſs, we are ready to ſet out for Madraſs; ſo we ſhall probably wait on you ourſelves with the copy of our anſwer.

We

We do not underſtand what they mean in their laſt paragraph by *the article which we call deciſive,* unleſs they have miſapplied the ſenſe of the firſt paragraph of our letter to them of the 31ſt, where we ſay, *as that muſt determine:* perhaps they have applied *that* to *the ſeparate article* inſtead of *their poſitive anſwer,* to which it refers ſo plainly, that we can hardly think it poſſible they ſhould miſunderſtand it without ſome deſign.

We are with the greateſt reſpect,
Honourable Sir,
Your moſt obedient humble
Servants,
ROBERT PALK.
HENRY VANSITTART.

Sadraſs, 4th Feb. 1754.
8 A. M.

To the reverend Father Lavaur *and Meſſrs.* De Bauſet *and* De Kerjean, *deputies of the French nation.*

Gentlemen,

We annex hereunto our general anſwer to your memorial, our reply to your anſwer and propoſals, and our freſh propoſals together with a ſeparate article; to which we deſire your poſitive anſwer, as that muſt determine the continuance or end of the congreſs.

With regard to your letter of the 30th of January, it is true, that you communicated your pieces to us in a curſory manner. We had not however, time to examine them all, but ſufficient to diſcover the defects we have already repreſented to you.

You cannot forget that the only original, now for the firſt time called a letter or ſaned, was repreſented to us to be of the ſtrogeſt validity; and if you had it double, you never once hinted it to us when it was produced; even at our firſt conference we underſtood that all your pieces were to be looked on as orginals, and it was not till the copies were beginning that we found they were otherwiſe. Nothing can be termed a duplicate that is not in every reſpect an exact copy of the original.

We could multiply remarks, but we apprehend thoſe we have already made, when impartially conſidered, will be thought ſufficient.

We have the honour to be, with real reſpect,
Gentlemen,
Your moſt obedient humble Servants,
ROBERT PALK.
HENRY VANSITTART.

Sadraſs, 1ſt February,
1754.

Anſwer to the three Memorials, accompanied with a Letter from the Engliſh Deputies, dated the 1ſt Febuary 1754.

Gentlemen,

The extract of the reaſons you have pretended to ſhew in your three memorials, accompanied with a letter, would ſoon be made, if if we were to leave out the vain allegations, some subtleties easy to be refuted, and the reproaches little becoming you and us; all is then reduced to a constant supposition, without proof or foundation of the rights of Mahomed Allee. Begin then with proving this right; this answer, gentlemen would suffice to refute all that you have hitherto said to us. But we are besides willing to justify the perplexity this question puts you in, and to manifest clearly that it is not your fault, if you cannot answer it but by endeavouring to make that pass for certain which you ought to prove.

First, You ought to prove, according to your allegations, that the government of the Carnateck was given to Mahomed Allee. We are waiting ready for this proof, supposing however that we were to receive it, it would not help your affairs much.

Secondly, You should further prove, that this pretended nomination of Mahomed Allee has not been revoked; here, gentlemen, is your stumbling block. The saneds granted to Chundah Saib by two immediate successors of Nazirzing, one of whom is now reigning, stops you beyond a possibilty of passing any further. You are obliged to apply to accusing us of falsity. Do you then look upon such a reproach to be so trifling as to be thrown so lightly on the chief of the deputies of the French nation; before you employed this resource in a desperate cause, you ought to have given a little more attention; for upon what would you found it? Upon our pretended refusal, which you ring out so loudly, to give you copies of our pieces, after having communicated them to you, and given you a list, at the same time that you evade the exhibition of yours, if you have any; it is not too much to treat upon an equality with you. We will submit our pieces again to your examination, when you shall produce to us those that you mention as your title; without shewing them, you may say as often as you will, that your remarks alarmed us; we will give you full liberty to continue them; those which you have made would insure us, if we had occasion for it, against those which you shall make; for to what do they amount? The saned, you say, or phirmaund of the Great Mogul, which we have once called a letter which according to you makes an article against it's validity, has not the sign manual of the emperor. Inform yourselves, gentlemen, of the custom of this court, before you hazard the answer you make us. It is besides, you add, without a seal, but it is on the seal you discover a proof of its falsity. The date at the bottom is superannuated. Do you pretend that the emperor must change his seal every year, and that he can never make use of that of his predecessor, although it be the same, except just the date of the time of its being made? Do you pretend too that a phirmaund sent by the emperor himself, and brought from Delly, to the knowledge of the whole world, by a considerable person named Us Bachi Cawn, should be of no credit; because the writers in the dispatch of the duplicate made use

of

of an older ſeal than that of the firſt diſpatch. We have replied in an inconteſtible manner to this chicanery; and we ſhall only add, that upon the arrival of this phirmaund, the marquis Dupleix not only communicated it by a copy ſent to Mr. Saunders, but alſo offered to ſend him the original by two counſellors, which Mr. Saunders refuſed. You it had not in your power, gentlemen, thus to evade the communication, but an accuſation of falſity was your reſource, as it has been before to the Engliſh upon ſome occaſions when they had no anſwer to make. This did not ſuffice to relieve you from your perplexities: the invalidating of the phirmaund being proved in the manner we have ſeen, muſt communicate itſelf by a kind of contagion to all the other pieces; upon which, however, you have with-held your remarks. Mr. Vanſittart only told us verbally, that they were nothing but copies, and that he thought we had produced them on the footing of originals. We told you however at that time, that we had brought only copies atteſted by the Caudy, and that we did not care, without neceſſity, to expoſe any more than the original, becauſe we had that double. Mr. Vanſittart thinks requiſite to contradict us alſo in that circumſtance: be that as it will, it has very little regard to the force of the thing, and we only mention it to ſhew the diſpoſition in which you came, gentlemen, or in which you were ſent; that is, to ſeize every ſtraw to keep you here, and not to forward the end to which we ought all to ſtrive. You are nevertheleſs very zealous for the publick good, and for the maintenance of the fundamental laws of the kingdom. You declare to us that theſe two points made you take up arms. Thereupon we aſk you in the firſt place, who gave you the neceſſary authority for that? Is it Mahomed Allee, Nabob by your favour? but you relapſe always into a circle of errors, ſuppoſing what is to be proved and what you cannot prove. In the ſecond place, we refer you yourſelves to the two great objects of juſtice, with which you defend your cauſe, which are, who troubled the publick repoſe, and who troubles it ſtill? We refer you to the letter in which the marquis Dupleix has detailed to Mr. Saunders himſelf the practices of your nation, and to which the laſt made no reply: [however, gentlemen, when we mention in this manner the Engliſh nation, we only mean ſuch as have had a part in the practices in queſtion, which many among you condemn:] remark in this detail what was the ſtate of affairs before you ſtirred up Mahomed Allee. Chundah Saib acknowledged, not only by the country, but by the Engliſh themſelves. Hogee Addee ſent by theſe laſt to compliment him, and offer him the Nazar [preſent] according to cuſtom, the ſame Vackeel who worked with him to obtain the town of St. Thome for you, but in vain. The ſame negotiation reſumed after you took poſſeſſion of it, but ſtill without effect. On the other ſide, Mahomed Allee fled to Trichinopoly to capitulate on the conſiderable arrears due by his father to the maſter of the Deckan; the

the same Mahomed Allee who had recourse to the marquis Dupleix to be his mediator: this last obtained a pardon and an establishment for him. This, gentlemen, is what preceded the time when the English worked with Mahomed Allee Cawn, to inspire him with other views corresponding with their designs. They nevertheless still wrote to Chundah Saib in the style of friends, while they were paving the way for Mahomed Allee to revolt. Proofs of all this have been furnished you: let it be judged from thence who began, continued, and fomented the war.

In vain you endeavour to turn this, by demanding that the marquis Dupleix should shew a saned authorising him to assist in killing Anaverdey Cawn and Nazirzing. The question is much out of place, as it is imprudent. Mr. Dupleix can easily justify himself on this head; and you expose yourselves to the same demand on the subject of the death of Chundah Saib, a much more horrid one, and the circumstances of which prove a crime on all that were the authors. But all this is but a digression to turn off the attention from the Perwanas, with which the marquis Dupleix was supported by the immediate successors of Nazirzing, and which have been confirmed by the Mogul. The mention of these Perwanas, as well as those appointing Salabatzing viceroy of the Deckan, leads us back to the second object of justice with which you affect to be touched.

What are, gentlemen, the fundamental laws of the country, as you call them, and what is the constitution of the government of this country? Is it to acknowledge the Grand Mogul for first sovereign, the governor general of the Deckan for the representative of this emperor in the country, and the particular governors appointed by the governor general as holding their authority from him? Do you conform to these laws in disputing the phirmaund of the emperor, and in declining the authority of Salabatzing? Leave him in the exercise of his authority, every thing will be in order in all respects, the constitution of the government in vigour, and the war at an end. If you refuse to acknowledge Salabatzing master of the Deckan by all the laws, who is the infringer of the laws, and the disturber of good order? You see very plainly, gentlemen, and it is for that reason that you bring the son of Gauzedey Cawn into play, or rather (for we are willing to be more considerate with regard to you, than you about us) you seize at a venture on the phantom Mahomed Allee presents to you, and which he is preparing to produce to us by opposing Shaw Abadin Cawn to Salabatzing; but on what title? Is it as having obtained the place of Salabatzing? This last has then been till now the true master, while you have been trifling with his authority. Besides, in the ill contrived pieces that Mahomed Allee has already transmitted to Nandi Raja, it is signified to Shaw Abadin Cawn, that the Carnateck for a long time has not been dependant on the government of the Deckan. By this it is rendered useless to you to invest this son of Gauzedey Cawn with the

the vice-royalty of the Deckan. Is it then, as Omir Buckshee, that Shaw Abadin Cawn shall dispose of the Carnateck? But yourselves have, hitherto, with all People acquainted in this matter, acknowledged that the Carnateck does depend on the Deckan. It is on this score, that you support the titles which Mahomed Allee Cawn pretends to have received from Nazirzing and Gauzedey Cawn.

What can be concluded from all that, except that Mahomed Allee had a mind to oppose us with two batteries, one of which should support the other; but he finds that one destroys the other. We shew ourselves before hand apprised of this job of work, to the end that Mahomed Allee may no longer be at liberty to finish it.

To continue, gentlemen, to proceed according to the established order; after acknowledging the viceroy of the Deckan, you should equally acknowledge him who is now invested by him with the power of governing the Carnateck. This is Mootis Allee Cawn of Velour, whose saned was notified to you in full form. It is true that he is so only by the authority of the marquis Dupleix, but still he is so by authority which you cannot contest; not by that of the marquis Dupleix, but of Salabatzing. Mr. Dupleix, you may say, got him appointed; confess in that, his moderation for you and consideration for you in consenting, although associated in the authority of Salabatzing, that this last should appoint to the government of the country a Moor's lord, who has always shewn at least as much regard for the English nation as for the French; to the end that you might take no umbrage. In this manner he paved a way to the peace he desires, and which you are not inclined to, without giving laws to all the legal masters of the country.

Still, to give a turn, you disclaim in favour of the rights of these, against the ambition of Mr. Dupleix, which is no more coherent than all the rest of your declamations. The ambition of the marquis Dupleix never has appeared, nor will appear, other than to answer the trust of those who have given him authority in this country, to preserve their rights, and to procure legal advantages to his nation, whilst the only end you propose is to dismember the country, to dispossess the lawful masters, and to deprive the French of what is lawfully due and acquired to them. How can you advance, that you have taken no place from these last; their flag torn down by your hands, notwithstanding the protests of the French commanders contradicts you. You say with the same sincerity, that you do not possess one place in the Carnateck, while you have commanders and garrisons in them. You advance too that there has been no other governor of the Carnateck since Anaverdy Cawn the father, but Mahomed Allee his son; whilst we shew you, and prove to you, that the said Mahomed Allee is not, that Chunda Saib was, and that Mootis Allee Cawn is at present. Did you intend, gentlemen, to make fools of us.

All that we have been exposing is a preparation, what judgment to form of your proposals: we shall not follow them in detail with all

all the reflections they offer, it will suffice us to say, first, that you will never put the change upon us so far as to engage us to build on such a foundation as the authority of Mahomed Allee, and that you only seek to establish this foundation; therefore all the rest of your proposals are vain and insignificant.

Secondly, You seem by them to be afraid to promise the release of the prisoners even after the peace is made; and you reserve some chicanery to employ on that occasion. However, whether peace be made, or war, we demand of you their immediate liberty in the name of the King our master, without admitting the usual shift, that Mahomed Allee does not consent to it. If Mr. Saunders does not pay regard to our demand, we shall continue to insist on this point in Europe, where perhaps it is already decided. There also will be manifested, if it is not already done, the force of the chimerical reasons that may have been alledged in justification of a war so contradictory on your side to the peace which reigns between the two nations. There, in the same manner, judgment will be formed on the violation of the law of nations, and of the rights of war, which may have happened in this country.

Thirdly, You seem, or you affect to have forgot the most sacred engagements, made by Mahomed Allee, and confirmed by yourselves, for the delivery of Trichinopoly to the Maissoreans.

Fourthly, The security which the marquis Dupleix will give, when serious proposals are entered upon, will be to get Salabatzing's consent, and procure from him the necessary perwanas, without which any disposal of the least part of the country would be unjust and unstable; all guarantees would be equally so, and he would not, from the same principle, acquiesce in the disposal of any country to the interested parties, but on the footing these countries have been on formerly, in relation both to the master of the Deckan and the governor of the Carnateck.

The evident necessity of the consent of the master of the Deckan for the alienation of any rights in his country, tells you, gentlemen, if nothing was offered you, when you was offered an immunity from all subjection, and acknowledgment for the town of Madrass; admitting even that Mahomed Allee Cawn was what you make him, such a concession on his part could at furthest only take place during his life. But Mahomed Allee having no right, to what is the immunity you told us you hold from him reduced? 'Tis nevertheless a point of more consequence than any other to a nation like the English. If you have never paid the tribute in question, as you say, the arrears are very considerable, and the offer merits the more regard. Be so kind to apply what we have said to Pondemaly and Trivendupuram also. We have proofs in writing which contain your confession that you applied in vain for the perwanas of these two territories in the life-time of Nazirzing. A time may come when some governor of Arcot may trouble you on those heads. If the offers made you do not suffice, we have desired

you

you to tell us what is wanting to your purpose. We offer you besides, to procure you on this very country the sum that Mahomed Allee may be indebted to you: this will save you the trouble and delay of a payment to be received on the country which shall be granted him, and which shall be loaded with many other mortgages.

Are such offers as these, gentlemen, what should appear insolent to you, or the proposal you make us of submitting to the laws of him whom you make a Prince in Europe and your slave in India, although invested with the name of Nabob. You ought not, nor cannot reasonably expect that the French will give up their rights and submit to this. You will not persuade them to it, neither by lending victories to Mahomed Allee, nor by alledging a right which possession, or rather force, gives you.

We will, however, communicate, according to the duty of our commission, your proposals to Mr. Dupleix; and we shall have the honour to communicate his answer, particularly on the article which you call decisive, and of which we yet comprehend nothing.

We have the honour to be, with real respect,

Gentlemen,

Your most obedient humble servants,

Fr. L. Lavaur.
Bausett.
De Kerjean.

To Messrs. Palk *and* Vansittart.

Gentlemen,

I have received your letter of the 4th February, with a copy of one to the French Deputies, and translate of their answer to your several pieces. Though this paper is very prolix, yet I can perceive nothing in it but what is easily confuted.

Mr. Dupleix earnestly pressed, and these gentlemen offered to examine the several papers called saneds; certainly these should be proceeded on first, not only for the above reasons, but as Mr. Dupleix places so great stress on them as thereon to found his authority for the government of the whole country; and this surely must be proved before it can be submitted to.

We have not refused to prove Mahomed Allee's rights; attested copies of the saneds have been wrote for, and will be sent for those gentlemen's perusal: those pieces, so far from having been revoked, have been confirmed.

If papers, produced as legal proofs, are upon examination found defective, and we as such reject them, 'tis reasonable and just, and no reflection on the French Nation; for they cannot expect an implicit submission to their papers, without they carry with them the necessary force: these do not, and that those gentlemen were sensible of it, sufficiently appeared by their suppressing any further enquiry. We are very well informed of the custom of the court, that on the decease of an Emperor his seal is totally laid aside, and the

seal

ſeal of the reigning Prince made uſe of: beſides, does it not appear very extraordinary, that upon this ſaned's proving defective, another ſhould ſpring up in ſo ſhort a time as a ſet of Peons could go from Sadraſs to Pondichery; is it not equally ſo, that in a patent of a publick nature, of ſuch conſequence as to transfer the right of kingdoms, the duplicate, and what is called the original, ſhould differ ſo much?

Our authority to ſupport Mahomed Allee is from Nazirzing, Gauzedey Cawn, and Gauzedey Cawn's ſon. This you have no occaſion to gratify them in mentioning, as his lawful right is a ſufficient authority for our ſupporting him.

Mr. Dupleix has wrote me many things, and I have anſwered them; nor is there any letter of his unreplied to. I have proved to him that he is the author of the war; but to what purpoſe? The refuſal of concurring in the reaſonable propoſals for peace ſufficiently demonſtrate it.

That Hodjee Addee was ſent to Chundah Saib is ſcandalouſly falſe; ſo far from it, that on the death of Nazirzing he was ſuſpended from his employ, and has never been truſted ſince.

The fortune of war throws down all diſtinction. If Mahomed Allee did apply to Mr. Dupleix, which is not certain, did not Mr. Dupleix alſo, when Seringham was on the point of ſurrender, apply to him and offer him Trichinopoly?

I do not apprehend the calling upon Mr. Dupleix to produce his authority for oppoſing a legal Prince is unreaſonable; if he cannot produce it, it will be concluded he has none: to ſay that he can eaſily juſtify himſelf, and to evade juſtifying himſelf (which he always does) will by all mankind be looked upon as a convincing proof that he is in the wrong.

We agree that the fundamental laws of the country are to acknowledge the Mogul for firſt ſovereign, the Viceroy of the Deckan for his repreſentative in that country, and the particular governors by him appointed as holding their authority from him. This is the rule we have always made the government of our conduct; the Mogul we acknowledge; Nazirzing as his Viceroy we obeyed; and Mahomed Allee as his governor, in diſtreſs we aſſiſted. On the death of Nazirzing we continued our aſſiſtance to Mahomed Allee, till a ſucceſſor, Gauzedey Cawn, was appointed; and agreeable to his directions, we perſevere in our alliance to the Circar. We could confute even the foundation of Mr. Dupleix's authority; for Salabatzing never had a ſaned for the Deckan; but as he is at the head of a large army, it is a prudent meaſure to avoid it. As Mr. Dupleix lays down this progreſſive rule for us, ought he not to obſerve it himſelf? Inſtead of ſaying he can eaſily juſtify himſelf, let him produce his authority for depoſing Anaverdey Cawn, and murdering Nazirzing; and as he cannot deny that Gauzedey Cawn was Viceroy of the Deckan, how comes it that this ſaned does not appear? Shaw Abadin Cawn derives his right to the Deckan from the

the Mogul. Of what force is the mentioning Mootis Allee Cawn, who has acknowledged the Nabob? However, we must wave the mentioning of this also, as I have only the copy of the agreement made by Mootis Allee Cawn with the Nabob. At the same time I have a letter from Mootis Allee Cawn, desiring a letter of indulgence, when we shall in a few days have the attested copies of Mootis Allee Cawn's agreement, it will plainly appear whether they intend to make fools of us, or we of them. We have not taken, nor are we in possession of, any places belonging to the French; wherever we have any force in the Circar's forts, they are under the orders of the Nabob.

We have no prisoners of the French King's; as a proof of this, all the officers have given their parole to Mahomed Allee, which is an acknowledgment they were his prisoners; and though several of our men and officers have been taken prisoners, we have never demanded them of Mr. Dupleix, except those that, contrary to the law of nations, Mr. Dupleix ordered to be seized as they were going to St. David from Madrass with regular passports; besides, we declared we treated in behalf of the Nabob; therefore this is a deviation, and foreign to the intention of the conference.

The fourth article is grounded on a supposition of the legal power of Salabatzing, and the illegal one of Mahomed Allee. The first has not been proved, nor the latter confuted.

There never was that tribute which the French deputies mentioned fixed on Madrass; therefore how ridiculous is it to make an offer of what does not exist; and as to the offer of procuring us the money, Nabob Mahomed Allee is indebted; 'tis but an offer, and not a certainty; and no dependency can be had on an offer from those who have not a power to fulfil it.

If the French have any rights they should be proved, and then will not be disputed, but acknowledged; but if such proofs are not produced, Nabob Mahomed Allee will conclude that the French are deaf to all reasonable proposals for an accommodation, and are determined to continue their alliance with rebels, which must compel him by real victories (which he has already had) to convince them he will defend his government against all unlawful usurpers.

If you can prolong the conference a few days, it will give us an opportunity to get copies of Mootis Allee Cawn's agreement, and be serviceable in other respects.

I know nothing that has passed in the conference of their side that carries with it the least weight, but that you have not Mahomed Allee's saneds on the spot; they are wrote for, and will be sent attested by the Caudee: you will therefore acquaint those gentlemen, that no exceptions may be taken, the saneds will be produced. That Mr. Dupleix will hearken to any measures for peace, I have not the least expectation, but that in rejecting them he may

appear

appear to act unjustly. Let your answer, which probably will be the last, be as full as possible.

I am, Gentlemen,

Fort St. George, Your most obedient Servant,
5th Feb. 1754. THOMAS SAUNDERS.

To the honourable Thomas Saunders, *Esq;*

Honourable Sir,

Inclosed we send you a copy of our answer to the last letter from the French deputies, which we hope you will approve. They have informed us that Mr. Dupleix is inflexible, which determines us to leave Sadrass in the morning, unless another letter, which they have been preparing all day, requires an answer.

We are, with the greatest respect,
Your most obedient humble Servants,

Sadrass, 5th Feb. ROBERT PALK.
1754. HENRY VANSITTART.

To the reverend Father Lavaur, *and Messrs* De Bausset *and* De Kerjean, *Deputies of the French nation.*

Gentlemen,

You accuse us of vain allegations and some subtilties, easily to be refuted, in your answer to our last memorial; but we do not find you have been able to prove them so. Reflections and reproaches are easily made, but when ill grounded, they return on those that make them.

You have begun with asserting the rights of the Marquis Dupleix. You have endeavoured to convince us of his authority, by producing what has sufficiently convinced us that he has none.

You say you are waiting ready for us to prove, that the government of the Carnateck was given to Mahomed Allee; but at the same time you give us to understand, that it will answer no end when it is proved. Is not this declaring before hand, that you are determined no laws shall restrain you?

You would have us further prove, that this nomination of Mahomed Allee has not been revoked; you say the saneds granted to Chunda Saib by two immediate successors of Nazirzing, one of whom is now reigning, stops us beyond a possibility of passing further. By the first you must mean Muzapherzing. Did he live long enough to be appointed by the Mogul, or did he get his commission at Pondichery? Perhaps the emperor by a spirit of divination foretold Nazirzing's cruel fate, and therefore appointed a successor in time; and what is almost extraordinary, a fomenter of divisions amongst his subjects, and an actual invader of his government. By the second, you mean Salabatzing, of whom you are confessedly the prop and support. Was this because his appointment of Chunda Saib was of more validity than that of Anaverdey Cawn by Gauzedey Cawn, who was sent by his master to depose him?

When

When Mr. Dupleix pressed the examination, it was without limitation, and without any reference to those of the Nabob. Our remarks, gentlemen, most certainly alarmed you; but you had a stronger reason suggested to you by your own eyes, as we have already had the honour to tell you, and to prove incontestably. We never advanced, that the piece said to come from the Mogul was without a seal. If you will take the trouble, gentlemen, to turn to our letter, or the Father Lavaur's translation of it, you will find that it was the want of a chop that we objected to. The most candid way we account for it is, that this considerable person, named Us Bachi Cawn, has imposed upon you. You may also recollect, gentlemen, that we had our doubts of the other pieces, one of them in particular was not dated, for which omission Mr. De Kerjean endeavoured to account, by blaming the incorrectness of these Eastern Princes in writings of the greatest consequence. If you told us at the first conference, that you had brought only copies attested by the Caudy, we declare to you again, gentlemen, that we did not hear it; and as to the plausible method you have found out of accounting for the defects in that said to come from the Mogul, by calling it a duplicate; even in your letter immediately in answer to our objections, you say nothing of it, no not till after you had received the marquis Dupleix's letter, in which he thinks it necessary to tell you that yours is a duplicate.

We were sent, and we came, gentlemen, with the best disposition in the world; it was with a strong disposition to do our utmost to restore peace to this unhappy country: it is true, if we will seize any thing, they are but straws to detain us here; for we have the misfortune to find that your commission will not permit you to forward the end which you affect so much to desire; and if you will not, gentlemen, our staying longer is to no purpose.

If you had made a just statement of the question, Who troubled the publick repose? you would have begun with giving us a view of the state of the province before you joined your troops to Chunda Saib: you would have shewn us Anaverdey Cawn in peaceable possession of his rightful government, and the country in a flourishing condition: you would then also have seen that the English did not take up arms till the disturbers of this tranquility, carrying desolation to the edge of our own limits, and there spreading your flags close to our presidency, by virtue of authority from Chunda Saib, obliged us to assist the lawful Nabob of the country for the restoration of order, and the repose of the people.

If Chunda Saib was acknowledged either by the country or the English, it is a secret, gentlemen, which never till now came to our knowledge, and which we would have been glad to have been acquainted with: we have heard, indeed, that the Phousdar of Vellour went through the ceremony of being made Nabob at Pondichery; but, if from his actions we may judge, he seems to have but an indifferent opinion of the rights you have given him, as little almost as we have of the good intended the English in the pretended appointment. We allow it, however, to be a great piece of condescension, moderation and consideration in the marquis Dupleix to consent that Salabatzing should appoint a Moorman to the Carnateck. Ambition is laudable when it only aims at answering the trust of those who have given authority, preserving their rights, and procuring legal advantage. Could you but prove that the marquis's ended here, we would be the first to commend it.

We are treating for Nabob Anaverdey Cawn, whose rights intitle him to be first considered, but they are found inconsistent with the pretended ones of the marquis Dupleix; and is it for this reason only that all our proposals are called *vain* and *insignificant*, or is it, gentlemen, because we will not betray the trust that is reposed in us? You gave us to understand, what we cannot apprehend, that Nazirzing offered the province to the French if they would have deserted Chunda Saib. Were we so firmly attached to a rebel? Then give us also leave, as we may do it with more justice, to support a lawful Nabob in his government.

Mr. Saunders, gentlemen, refers all his transactions to be judged of in Europe, where it will be done with less partiality; and if we may make any judgment from the reasons you, gentlemen, have given us, with more candour, there will be manifested the many affronts which have been continually offered to our nation, by laying waste our territories, and a declaration that our colours should be no sanction to us, together with the violence committed by seizing our forces on the open seas, in direct contradiction to the peace established between the two nations: there also it will be manifested, that the English are not the only nation whose rights have been invaded.

In Europe it will also appear, that the English never confirmed any engagements made by Mahomed Allee for the delivery of Trichinopoly, which would have been as unjust in them, as the laying it to their charge is rash and imprudent in you; and it will there be plainly seen, that the marquis Dupleix has usurped an authority which never was conferred upon him, and if we may judge from the regard he pays the emperor, never will. You could not have given your superiors and ours a clearer demonstration to whom the name of slave most properly belongs, Salabatzing or Anaverdey Cawn, than your own declaration, that the former, at the same time that you call him master of the Deckan, had need of the marquis Dupleix's consent to impower him to give a governor to the Carnateck, which is at the same time a conviction of the regard you pay to the fundamental laws you so justly describe.

The demand you make to us for the release of the French prisoners is ill placed: you should apply to the prince against whom you have been, and are carrying on an unjust war, and he he will release them whenever it is consistent with the safety of his government.

We do not understand what you mean by *the article we call decisive*, unless you misunderstand our letter of the 1st; when we desired your positive answer, it was to our general answer to your memorial, to our reply and new proposals; because by that we might be able to determine the continuance or end of the conference. You have rejected all these proposals with disdain; to what end then, gentlemen, shall we wait for an answer from Pondichery? It will be to little purpose, unless you can give us better hopes of the marquis's pacifick disposition, than we have hitherto been able to form.

The conference then terminates unsuccessfully. This advantage indeed we shall reap from it, that Mr. Saunders's reasonable inclinations for peace will be manifest to the publick, and also the marquis Dupleix's contrary disposition, with the invalidity of the authority on which he founds it.

We have the honour to be, with perfect respect,
Sadrass, 4th Feb. 1754. Your most obedient humble Servants,
ROBERT PALK.
HENRY VANSITTART.

To Messrs. Palk *and* Vansittart.

Gentlemen, The 5th of Feb. 1754.

We see with great regret an unsuccessful end to our conferences. The satisfaction we shall receive from your personal conduct, and your politeness with regard to us, will not be the less sincere. We will not even refuse you the justice you claim on the subject of your good disposition to conclude. We will add further, gentlemen, that we do not doubt of your uprightness in the allegation of the facts you have had occasion to advance. You have followed your instructions to a tittle.

It was recommended to you to insist firmly and strongly that Mahomed Allee is the only lawful master of the Carnateck; and you have done it, gentlemen, to your best. It would be superfluous to repeat the answers we have already made you on that subject.

You was told to deny boldly that the English confirmed any engagement made by Anaverdey Cawn for the delivery of Trichinopoly; and you have done it with so good a grace, that you proceed even to say, *that such an engagement would have been as unjust in the English, as the accusation is rash and imprudent in us.* We see evidently by that, gentlemen, that you have been left in ignorance of the pieces we shall offer to communicate to you before our parting: you will then see the strongest promises of Mahomed Allee, repeated, and confirmed by oath; a letter from Mr. Saunders himself to the Rajah of Maissore, wherein he tells him in express terms, *as to the act* or convention *concerning*

Trichinopoly, it is I that am anſwerable. As this affair, gentlemen, is one of thoſe which you refer to be examined in Europe, it will there undoubtedly be ſeen with pleaſure, with how much charity Mr. Saunders, in the above mentioned letter, warns the Maiſſoreans, *to be well on their guard againſt the French; that he is afraid leſt ſome misfortune ſhould happen to their Vackeel at Pondichery; and that if the enemies* (that is the French) *ſucceed, which God cannot permit*, they will go to Maiſſore. It is thus Mr. Saunders has piouſly watched after the ſafety of the princes of India, by ſpiriting them up againſt us by falſe alarms.

You were told, gentlemen, in the ſame manner to diſpute our rights obſtinately, to admit none of our titles, and to talk high of the neceſſity the Engliſh were in to take up arms, *after having ſeen the French flags cloſe to the preſidency under the authority of Chunda Saib.* You have done all that, gentlemen, and it has been often anſwered to. Give us leave, however, to ſay one word more to you on the ſubject of the laſt article, to beg you will diſtinguiſh the times. The only umbrage Chunda Saib and the French can have given you before you took up arms againſt them, was their encamping within five leagues of Cuddalore in his way to Tanjore. That was their road, and a country which acknowledged Chunda Saib for maſter. He never came nearer to your limits, and kept ſeveral days journey off in the march he made a long time after to go from Chelleput to Trichinopoly. Mr. Saunders at that time complained to him of nothing but his going into a country engaged by Mahomed Allee to the Engliſh. We ſhall offer you alſo, gentlemen, a ſight of this ſecond letter of Mr. Saunders's, where you may remark that he makes a plea of the *mutual friendſhip* which then ſubſiſted between Chunda Saib and the Engliſh. This letter may furniſh you with many reflections; we ſhall make but one at preſent, on the ſubject of the injuſtice it would have been on your part (as you ſay) if you had confirmed the engagement of Trichinopoly in favour of the Maiſſoreans. Was it more juſt that Mahomed Allee ſhould engage it to your nation, and you accept it? If a legitimate defence obliged us to join with the Maiſſoreans alienated from your party by the faithleſſneſs of Mahomed Allee, we do not pretend to procure him what he deſires, but with the conſent of Salabatzing, who only, as maſter of the Deckan, can legitimate any alienation of a country in his dependance.

If the above complaint, gentlemen, regards the time when you no longer obſerved any meaſures, when you ſeized upon the country and place of Arcot in the abſence of Chunda Saib, who was employed at Trichinopoly, we do not diſpute that Raja Saib, his ſon, was in the neighbourhood of Madraſs; with this circumſtance however, that the French who were in his army refuſed to follow him when he went towards your limits.

But

But a further detail would only lengthen this letter to no purpose; and we are charmed that you reserve this article for Europe, as well as the others mentioned in your letter.

The only one which admits of no delay, is that of the prisoners, whose deliverance we again demand of you; because we cannot see the subjects of our king perish in your prisons in a manner so little conformable to the mutual regard due from the two nations in peace, and particularly on a point wherein we have shewn you the example. The king depends on Mr. Saunders, and on him only. The shift he makes of referring us *to the prince Mahomed Allee*, is only proper, give us leave to say, to render his refusal more stinging.

You have then heard, gentlemen, that the Phousdar of Vellour was made at Pondichery, governor of the Carnateck; his appointment by Salabatzing was however notified to you, and this last even wrote you of it himself.

We did not say that Salabatzing could not have made this appointment without the consent of the marquis Dupleix, only that he did make it with the approbation of this last, for whom it is not surprising he should have some respect. If this Phousdar does not act accordingly, as in effect he did not push the advantage he once had over you, it is a consequence of the regard he has always had for your nation, and which is not unknown to us. This confirms what we said before of the good intentions of the marquis Dupleix, and shews plainly that you only refuse to acknowledge such a governor of the Carnateck; because you have a mind to remain masters of it under the name of Mahomed Allee. This, gentlemen, will always be a point of division as long as you insist on it.

Be so good to remind Mr. Saunders that we have made good the declaration the marquis Dupleix made him before we came here, namely, that it would be to no purpose to make us such a proposal.

If Mr. Saunders thinks proper to treat on the footing we have proposed, by acknowledging the titles of which we are bearers, we will endeavour, gentlemen, to give you all possible satisfaction.

It would be lost time, gentlemen, if our conference do not continue, to reply here to the other articles of your letter. Besides, the new strokes you strive to give to our pieces do not alarm us more than the others; if that to which you object the want of a date did not even exist, our rights would not be the less supported by all the others. But not to mention that the date is supplied by other circumstances, such an omission does not denote, as we have said before, a piece contrived to impose: remark, gentlemen, that the want of a date is not a sign of invalidity, that it can only affect particular points, of which the date must decide, and that is sufficient for us the piece exists. We ought to know better than any body what impressions such objections make upon us: be assured they do not frighten us.

We have the honour to be, with real respect,

Gentlemen,

Your most humble and most obedient Servants,

FR. L. LAVAUR.
DE BAUSETT.
DE KERJEAN.

To the reverend Father Lavaur *and Messrs* De Bauset *and* De Kerjean, *deputies of the French notion.*

Gentlemen,

After our commissaries had been disrespectfully made to wait twenty days, and spent a fortnight more, when nothing was offered to them but some few papers, by which the very name of saneds is obviously disgraced, when to their reasonable proposals only an arbitrary answer was given, contrary to that equity and justice which is the foundation of all lawful right and authority, plainly convinced that Mr. Dupleix had no sincere intention to adopt measures for the restoration of tranquility to the province; on the contrary, a violent resolution illegally to usurp an unjust authority, productive of the calamities of war, conscious to themselves they had done their duty, they took their leave; then, Gentlemen, you presented them with a letter of the 5th of February, which, as it contains new matter, I shall do myself the honour to reply to.

You are not ignorant we conferred, empowered by Nabob Mahomed Allee; and when we insisted on his being lawful master of the Carnateck, it was your part either to disprove or acknowledge his right. It is indeed superfluous to repeat your answer; for when, upon your asking for the saneds, you was told that attested copies should be sent for, it only produced a positive and arbitrary declaration from you, that Mr. Dupleix was resolved upon no account to acknowledge Nabob Mahomed Allee as Suba of the Carnateck. Those saneds are by this time on the road, you may send a person to inspect them.

I cannot but with surprise remark, gentlemen, that you are extremely over hasty in your conclusions, and too apt to assert for fact what you cannot have a clear knowledge of. In regard to the confirmation of the delivery of Trichinopoly, you make this quotation from a supposed letter of mine; "*As to* "*the act or convention of Trichinopoly, it is I that am an*"*swerable.*" You are imposed on, I never wrote to the Maissore King or Dalloway any such thing, nor they to me; nor had I a knowledge of any agreement between the Nabob and the Dalloway, till after Seringham was taken. Our records, where all letters are entered will prove it; nay the Maissore King's vacheel, now here, is convinced of it. I send you a copy

copy of the only letter that has any resemblance, and that very distant from what you mention: further, you forget, gentlemen, the letter to Chunda Saib, wherein I write him that Trichinopoly was mortgaged to the English. Mr. Dupleix also was advised of it, and his answer will always remain as a remarkable instance of his respect for his Britanick majesty's flag, which he says shall be no sanction to the English subject. I have used my mediation to accommodate matters between the Nabob and the Maissore Dalloway, and recommended to his vackeel to get a saned for it; his reply was, Salabatzing had no saned for, and was not legally invested with, the government of the Deckan; and therefore had no power to grant one. Now I am on this subject, I cannot avoid giving you the sentiments of that prince's vackeel in his letter to me, viz. " You are sensible of the pretended right of Chunda Saib, who " applied to Mustaphazing, and by the assistance of the French " proved a rebel, and is ruining the inhabitants of this province by " his wicked proceedings. If this man is punished according to " his deserts, the great Mogul will be vastly pleased, and you will " maintain a good name and reputation. As to Nabob Anaverdey " Cawn, he is of the family of the Omrahs, and was honoured " with a serpau by Nazirzing of the government of the Carnateck: " besides, he has lately received the Mogul's Phirmaund and Gauzedey Cawn's letter in confirmation of that government."

To what purpose is it, gentlemen, to say our commissaries were told to dispute your rights obstinately, and to admit none of your titles: I know of no rights but Pondichery and its district, nor any titles but the marquis Dupleix, the French East India company's governor; it is true, your vanity furnished you with chimerical ones, and the same excessive blind vanity hurried you on indiscreetly to press an examination of them: but when the principal one was exploded, and the spots began to appear in the others, you suppressed a further scrutiny; by this you meant to hide their defects. Thus gentlemen, you perfectly convinced us of their invalidity; so difficult is it to support a wrong cause, that the arguments made use of to corroborate, often expose it the more. I repeat we acknowledge no territories or titles but what are founded on lawful authority; and till the marquis has proved his, we reject them, and regard them as invalid. It is needless to repeat the many acts of violence done us by Chunda and his Allies; I could produce some pieces of the marquis and marchioness's, many more there are, I will give them their due weight, let the rabble, for whom they were designed, put them to the use they please; but when the officer of Mr. Dupleix's forces, whom Chunda's son writes that he had sent with a detachment to insult our colours at St. Thome, when the French also plundered and burnt our houses at the Mount; and the furniture was carried to Pondichery, when our officers at Conjeveram were ordered on the ramparts to be shot by their own countrymen. These facts carry with them a force not to be contradicted ; and when Mr. Dupleix writes me that his Britannick Majesty's flag shall be no sanction to his subjects ; when on the open seas he, contrary to treaty, piratically with armed vessels assaults and makes prisoners our men going with a regular passport from Madrass to Fort St. David : how chearfully do I submit it to his most Christian Majesty to judge and punish this breach of treaty, this affront to his Britannick Majesty. I have before told you, that Trichinopoly was mortgaged to us, the bond is now in our hands ; it is a legal one. I have related to you, that we never confirmed the agreement of Trichinopoly, and that Vencatrow, the Maissore Vackeel, is convinced of it, and acknowledges it ; and futher, that he says Salabatzing has no power to give a saned for it ; for that he has none himself.

By the date of my letter to Chunda Saib, it appears to have been written above a year after we had joined Nabob Mahomed Allee. The purport was to inform him that Trichinopoly was mortgaged to the English, and desire he would cease committing hostilities there ; so great, gentlemen, is your ignorance of real facts : and as groundless is your assertion that Chunda Saib was acknowledged by the whole province ; he was not by any one power in the country : as a proof of this, he was obliged immediately on his leaving Pondicherry, by the help of your forces to begin his assumed government by the besieging of forts ; for no officer paid him obedience. Please to remark the Maissore Vackeel s words : " You are sensible of the " pretended right of Chunda Saib, who applied to Mustaphaz-" ing. and by the assistance of the French proved a rebel, and is " ruining the inhabitants of the province by his wicked proceedings." You say that Hodjee Addee, our Vackeel, was sent to Chunda Saib to compliment him ; your knowledge of this affair, which I think may be doubted, is beyond mine : Hodjee Addee immediately on the death of Nazirzing was dismissed from his employs, and never since that time trusted. In regard to the second letter to Chunda Saib, it tells him, that after the treacherous assassination of Nazirzing, Nal ob Mahomed Allee was Subah of the Carnateck ; that he had since been confirmed by the Mogul and Gauzedy Cawn ; and that I would spport him offering terms to Chunda Saib if he desisted from his rebellion. Of all the pieces you have referred to, there is not a single assertion but what has been proved groundless, the supports of your pretended rights defective and null : they correspond indeed with a wicked cause, perpetrated with assassination, and rebellion.

It has been often repeated to you, that we never had, nor have any prisoners of yours : those in our settlements are there by the mutual agreement of your commandant and the Nabob. This act of ours was through a motive of compassion at your officers request. We are ready to surrender them when you and the Nabob agree on the terms : what others are in the Nabob's forts were made prisoners fighting against him in his own dominions, and are by him con-

confined. You are acquainted with this, a convincing proof is in Pondichery; please to ask your officers to whom they gave their parole.

You have been already informed, that we were not ignorant of the sham investiture of Mootis Allee Cawn at Pondichery; that sugar was distributed for the children, and the cannon discharged to awe old women. How tender, gentlemen, are you in protesting you did not say that Salabatzing could not make such an appointment; but yet so pleasing, so tickling it was to your vanity, that you could not avoid letting us know that he did it with the marquis's approbation, for whom it was not surprising that he had some respect. This is in French telling us what we have declared to you in English, that Salabatzing is not at liberty to do as he pleases, cannot make officers himself at Aurengabad, but must submit to Mr. Dupleix's approbation at Pondichery. From hence the murmurs and general dissatifaction that prevail among the omrahs and leading men from Aurengabad to the sea. The truth is, the rebellion at Delhi prevents the Mogul at present from putting an end to these irregularities. What acts of generosity has the Nabob ever experienced from the enemy? Surely you cannot call the killing of his father and depriving him of his government such. Mootis Allee Cawn may indeed be sensible of the friendship of our nation, in leaving his fort unmolested, when last year there was no force to oppose it, and in recommending a friendship between him and the Nabob; and if Mootis Allee Cawn did suspend taking any advantages that offered, it must be attributed to the sense he has of the illegality of the title you invested him with. That we aim at keeping the Carnateck is so absurd, that the very offers made in the conference immediately refute it.

I cannot concur with you that Mr. Dupleix has made good his declaration to me: he offered his pretentions to an examination, but it was suppressed: he assured me he dropped all animosity to Nabob Mahomed Allee; but without waiting for a scrutiny of his saneds, it was declared positively he would never upon any account acknowledge him as Nabob of the province.

I am very willing (and have already shewn myself so) to treat of measures for restoring tranquility; but to what purpose is it, when Mr. Dupleix will not co-operate with me; and insists on an acknowledgement of titles which have been already proved unjust and and illegal.

It is very evident that the dates of commissions cancel or prove their validity; for instance suppose a saned dated 1754, and another 1755, the former would of consequence be revoked and annulled by the latter; so that what you have advanced on that subject falls of itself.

Thus far in regard to subjects that have been introduced and discussed during the conference, it will not be foreign to the purpose, I conceive, to examine the proposals and answers of each party; as as both declare their sincere inclination to restore tranquility, let it appear why it has not succeeded.

Empowered by Nabob Mahomed Allee, we conferred, what regards the other parties is so dependant on this point, that it would of course be easily adjusted; therefore I shall proceed to say, we proposed Mahomed Allee should, agreeable to his legal saneds, be Nabob of the province; and that he would give the French Jageers to the same amount as the English; a free liberty of trade should be impartially granted to both, and both be considered as common friends to the Circar.

Can any thing be more reasonable, more equitable, than to propose that a prince invested with a legal authority should be acknowledged as such by those who as strangers live under his protection. If it is not acknowledged it certainly should be disproved, or the person disputing it without any legal authority, must be deemed acting contrary to the established laws of the country: What was the answer? Without waiting for an examination of these titles, it was, that Mr. Dupleix never would on any account acknowledge Nabob Mahomed Allee as Suba of the Carnateck.

When the Nabob offers to his enemies the same advantages as to his friends, and when these must appear beneficial to all that think themselves subject to the established government, what can a refusal of them mean, more than a firm resolution by power of arms to usurp? Let me add, that from these proposals the English have not endeavoured to gain to themselves any particular advantages, but are satisfied, in obedience to the government, to be concerned as common friends with the French; and that the liberty of trade should be mutual, without partiality to either. How unjust then is the reflection you make, gentlemen, that the English design to remain masters of the province under the name of Nabob Mahomed Allee: those very propasals refute it: and if you are resolved that this shall always be a point of division, we shall always retain our just sentiments and inclination for peace, and only defend when hostile invasion requires it. So moderate are the Nabob's proposals, that to persons unacquainted with facts, they would seem to come from a prince in distress, and not one whose army has never been repulsed; but wherever his standard has been displayed, the spoils of the enemy's arms have been constant marks of his victory.

The expression you used when our proposals were made you is remarkable; "That it would at once be giving up all." If your intentions are to usurp all, it may be so; though it may be asked at the same time what right you have to do it, or what reason to expect a tame submission to it, and this must appear to all mankind unreasonable; probably you may conclude that Nabob Mohamed Allee, sensible of our friendship to him will act partially in his favours to us; no doubt he will gratefully remember our steady alliance to the Circar, but so far as concerns what might be concluded and ratified

fied by treaty. The contracting parties, the King of Maissore, King of Tanjore and Morarow, would guarantee it; by this means the jealousy is removed

Now follow your proposals to exempt Madrass from a tribute of pagodas 4000 per annum, to secure to us Poonamallee, to see our debt paid, and to make a provision for Nabob Mahomed Allee in a private capacity. The marquis Dupleix's titles are to be acknowledged as prince of all the territories to the river Krisna.

By these concessions to us, and the divesting the Nabob of his government, at first view it would seem to be with a design to tempt us to be villains, in betraying the trust reposed in us by the Nabob, by whose powers we treated. If Mr. Dupleix's own actions are of so black a nature as to induce him to think so meanly of the rest of mankind, to them let him add this. But we have some reason to conclude that he well knows that our alliance with the Circar, and attachment to the Mogul's legal officer, is such as not to be shaken by any motives of self-interest, and rather think this is artfully designed to amuse his and our superiors; but by writing them, how beneficial to our interest his offers have been? This might be answered at once, that he would generously promise us what is not his to give. To invest him with a power, to take not only them, but every thing else away from us when he pleased: but I shall descend to particulars, and first, Madrass never has paid nor been taxed with such a tribute; next, we have a legal grant for Poonamallee; and as to the third, it must be done by a mortgage on other countries. Neither this nor the other two has Mr. Dupleix any power to do, or procure effectually; for when Monsr. Bussy extorted from Salabatzing an order for the rents of the Rajamundrum and Chickakole countries, the Nabob of those governments paid no regard to it, but dispersed the troops who were sent to collect the revenue. These, gentlemen, are not specious arguments, but facts which clearly prove the insufficiency of the power you assume.

Though you thought fit by no other means to set aside the Nabob's rights, than positively to declare it was not Mr. Dupleix's pleasure to ackowledge them; this did not lead our commissaries to make use of the like arbitrary weapons; when an examination of the marquis's pretensions was pressed, they judged it an improper rule for their conduct, and chearfully acceded to the proposal, with a resolution to acknowledge, if just, and if not, to object to them. Of the capital one from the Mogul, upon a slight view the defects appeared; it had the seal of the precedent emperor of so old a date as 1133 of the Hegyra: and when blots in some others also became obvious, you were staggered and immediately suppressed a further scrutiny; the reason you alledged was weak, for an examination of the Nabob's would have neither added to or diminished the force of your saneds; besides as these papers were produced by by you voluntarily, as the first and principal subject to be discussed, should not it have been finished before fresh matter was introduced? You were so sensible of their invalidity, that you declined the proposed examination of your saneds; but Mr. Dupleix soon furnished you with a salve, that it was a duplicate; that the original was in Pondichery; that the error in the seal was a mistake of the Mogul's secretary in affixing the old emperor's seal instead of the present. To these I answer, that it is unusual to send duplicates of saneds from the Mogul; that if this is admitted, as the duplicate is to supply the place of the original, common sense dictates that it should be in every respect the same as the original; and that in patents transferring the right of kingdoms, great accuracy and correctness is observed; and that the seal could not be the mistake of the secretary, as it is universally known, that after the decease of an emperor, his seal is never made use of. As the falsity of this saned has been palpably proved, and the arguments to supply its defects confuted; as it is a saned from Delly, and not from Pondichery, that will carry with it the proper weight; and as a total suppression has been made of an examination of the rest upon their defects appearing; for these reasons we do object to, and deny the rights which Mr. Dupleix may from these papers pretend to, and regard him with that politeness which one nation owes another, only as governor of Pondichery and its dependancies.

If, Gentlemen, this letter should appear spun out to a great length, impute it to a strong desire that no one subject you have advanced may be unreplied to. Our superiors may justly claim a right to be acquainted who commenced, continued, and still continue this calamitous war: you have very disingenuously said the English, but not supported your allegation. In treating this point, I will be governed by those very rules you have perscribed: that the fundamental laws of the country are to acknowledge the Grand Mogul for first sovereign; the govenor General of the Deckan for his representative in that country; and the particular Governors appointed by the Governor General of the Deckan, as holding their authority from him.

Should we trace these troubles so far back as the unhappy war between our two nations, we have the greatest reason to complain; for according to the established laws of nations, in a neutral prince's dominions peace should be preserved; such prince has a right to insist on it: and if after the loss of Madrass, Nabob Anever-dey Cawn, sensible of the injury to his country through our misfortune, endeavoured to prevent future mischiefs, from this you can take no umbrage, without contradicting those fundamental principles by which the rest of the world are governed. This war subsided, and some time after Mustaphazing, who had by his ill conduct undergone a reproof from his uncle Nazirzing, and disgusted retired to his small government of Adoni, where he was engaged in some disputes with his neighbours, when Chunda Saib, who

who had by stratagem made his escape from the Maratta's, entered into the service of Berma Remeadar of Cheatal Darga as a Jermidar over two or three hundred horse, and was defeated in a battle fought with the people of Bedanore or Savanore. He first instilled into Mustaphazing the seeds of rebellion; the scheme was laid for seizing the government of the Carnateck; certain people who had before assisted Chunda Saib in the reduction of Trichinopoly, came into an alliance with them; they collected what force they were able, and marched towards Arcot, a skirmish with the Circar's troops happened, when they were joined by the forces of their allies, a battle was fought wherein Nabob Anaverdey Cawn was slain, Arcot was taken and the usurpation commenced. From hence, gentlemen, those calamities which have so long prevailed took their rise: Had the English any concern in them? None: Why then do you unjustly cast the odium on them? Let Mr. Dupleix produce a saned from the Great Mogul or Nazirzing for destroying the legal governor of the province and fomenting a rebellion; I call upon him to do it, or his and our superiors must plainly be convinced that he has acted in open violence to the fundamental laws of the country in rebelling against Nabob Anaverdey Cawn, the legal governor of the province, holding his authority from Nazirzing, the Governor General of the Deckan, the representative of the great Mogul; an obedience to which, you have laid down as the fundamental laws of the country, and consequently ought to obey.

As every thing that has since happened is evidently the effect of that rebellion of which Chunda and his allies were the cause, it is but a reasonable assertion that they are the authors of the whole; and on the contrary, those who have withstood these rebels acting in opposition to the fundamental laws of the country, are justified. This you may urge is a conclusion very general, but it is a just one.

Rebellion can only be supported by acts of violence: such have appeared; the lives and property of the subject were invaded; Mahomed Allee, son to Nabob Anaverdey Cawn, invested with the Trichinopoly government, which was the principal one of the province, after Arcot was taken, faithful to his master, protected the rights of the Circar. Here, gentlemen, the English first made their appearance; from the Mogul and his officers they had received phirmaunds for their settlements and trade, and lived under the protection of his governors; and it was but gratitude to support his officers, it was just too. They joined Mahomed Allee, and acquainted Nazirzing with the state of the province, he approved of their conduct, wrote to Mahomed Allee to be firm in the government of the Carnateck, marched himself to settle the province, and then confirmed Mahomed Allee in it; Mustaphazing, sensible of his error, submitted; but Chunda and his allies continued rebellious, a conspiracy was formed with the Cuddapa and Condanore Nabobs, and Nazirzing the lawful prince of the Deckan was assassinated.

So

So true is what I have before ſaid, that rebellion muſt have recourſe to, and be ſupported by acts of violence; this commenced with the death of the lawful governor of the Carnateck, and was continued by the aſſaſſination of the Great Mogul's viceroy of the Deckan. Theſe are facts which clearly prove that Mr. Dupleix (not we) who commenced, ſtill continues this war, and as we have acted very conformable to, ſo has he in open violation of thoſe fundamental laws of the country, which he is ſubject to, and ought to obey. In your memorial of a ſaned, I do not obſerve, gentlemen, one for this authority; if you have any, pleaſe to produce it, or acknowledge you had no right to act thus, but have acted as an ally toa rebel.

After the aſſaſſination, Muſtaphazing was releaſed and ſet up as prince of the Deckan, who, with Chunda and Nazirzing's treaſure and jewels, were conducted to Pondichery. It was induſtriouſly ſpread about that a diviſion was made of thoſe jewels and treaſures. Some gratuities might be diſtributed to the villains who acted their parts in the betraying and aſſaſſination of Nazirzing; but the ſupporter of this rebellion, having the right of poſſeſſion, took for himſelf the greateſt part. Muſtaphazing had a ſmall matter generouſly beſtowed on him for his expences; greater honours were indeed allowed him, thoſe of prince of the Deckan, and to Chunda Saib the ſubaſhip of the Carnateck. It was a prudent meaſure firſt to appoint a prince of the Deckan, and ſubah of the Carnateck; for who will diſpute but a prince of the Deckan has a power to give jageers, and a ſubah of the Carnateck to govern the province. Nabob Mahomed Allee indeed might aſk whether all this was done by the Mogul's order, and if Mr. Dupleix cannot (as it is well known he cannot) produce any of the ſaneds; every thing from this mock authority proceeding, is defective, contrary to the eſtabliſhed laws of the country, and only the acts of rebels. To proceed, gentlemen, Muſtaphazing, thus according to the forms of Pondichery regularly inveſted, began his government, it is ſaid, by acts of generoſity for the aſſaſſination of his uncle; to Mr. Dupleix a large diſtrict, to madam Dupleix another, to the gentlemen of the ſuperior council each according to his rank, jageers to the officers according to their rank, the ſame to Mr. Dupleix's black miniſters likewiſe; though to do juſtice to the gentlemen of the ſuperior council, I never heard that they have had any ſhare in the management of theſe affairs, but ſilently condemn and deteſt them; the ſame I may ſay of the gentlemen officers. Theſe are what Mr. Dupleix calls his rights: it may be by ſome imagined that theſe gratuities were intended as a reward for the aſſaſſination of Nazirzing only; no, the rebellion was ſtill to be proſecuted. Muſtaphazing ſaw and heard the murmurs in the army, then awed by the guns of Pondichery; he dreaded their fury when they were removed from thence, knew the horrid murder was unanimouſly deteſted, and was ſenſible that a power uſurped muſt be ſupported by force, and that he could never eſtabliſh his government in the Deckan without it; the French troops were ne-

necessary, they accordingly joined him; but short-lived is power usurped by indirect means: after a few days march from Pondichery, the Nabobs of Cadaapah and Condanore, who had murdered Nazirzing, put an end to his life and usurpation. I accompanied this prince so far, that I might, as I begun with his rebellion, conclude with his fate, such as is generally the end of usurpers. I shall now return to the province: Chunda Saib and his allies, soon after the departure of Mustaphazing, took the field and begun their operations by plundering, besieging of forts, and by force garrisoning them. Nabob Mahomed Allee on the murder of Nazirzing had taken refuge in Trichinopoly, where the English sent a small detachment for his security; and on Chunda Saib's taking the field with his allies, the English detached a larger force to join the Nabob's army, which after taking Verdachilum, they did near Volconda; here a skirmish happened, and at Utatore another; the rebels being greatly superior, the Nabob's army crossed the Cauvery and Coleroon, and encamped under the cannon of Trichinopoly, the rebels followed; as a siege was impracticable, they formed a blockade for several months and raised works, but at such a distance as proved of no signification. At length the Maissoreans and Morarow joined the Nabob, when the Rebels to do them justice, made a good retreat with their cannon and baggage to Seringham, which in a short time capitulated; and the traitor Chunda Saib, who had formed a design of escaping by promises to Monagee, was in the fullness of his crimes executed. Please to remark, gentlemen, as the French continued their alliance with Chunda Saib, the English were firm in their attachment to Nabob Mahomed Allee, who had received a legal phirmaund from Nazirzing: the death of that prince did not cancel this phirmaund; he was killed by rebels; the government was by them usurped; the Nabob faithful to his sovereign, still continued to defend his rights. We wrote to the Mogul of the revolution, and our attachment to the Circar, and desired his orders, that we might act in obedience to them. He was graciously pleased to send Nabob Mahomed Allee a phirmaund for the Carnateck, to appoint Gauzedy Cawn viceroy of the Deckan who likewise granted Nabob Mahomed Allee a saned and gave us orders to support him: this phirmaund from the Mogul, this saned and these orders from Gauzedy Cawn have never been revoked; from which it is obvious, that Nabob Mahomed Allee Cawn's title is just, and that we have acted according to the fundamental laws of the country; and as Mustaphazing never could receive any saned from the Mogul, nor is it the least probable that any would ever have been granted to a publick disturber of the peace of the country; such rights as Mr. Dupleix may pretend to desire from him, such authority as Chunda Saib might have alledged for the Carnateck, are unjust, illegal, and of no force; and consequently Mr. Dupleix is proved by these facts to prolong the war, contrary to the established government.

As

As I have discussed the affairs of this province, which were transacted on your part by a pretended authority from Mustaphazing, I shall now return to the army, the command of which was given to Salabatzing, who was released from confinement; and your troops, very indifferent who it was, so as they had a specious pretence, continued their march with him to Hydrabad. As soon as the news of the assassination of Nazirzing reached Delly, Gauzedey Cawn received from the Mogul a saned for the Deckan. Some months were spent in settling this affair, when he marched at the head of his army towards his government, and arrived at Aurengabad, where he was poisoned by Salabatzing's mother. Here, gentlemen, is another horrid act to support that cause, the justness of which you take so much pains to defend; and when the mother was with the Omrah's, entreating her son Salabatzing to dismiss the French troops, bitter was his reply, that had she not poisoned his uncle, he might peaceably have enjoyed some small government under him, but now he detained the French as his security. Stung with remorse, she retired to her tent, setting fire to it with design to perish in the flames, but was prevented. In this appears a plain conviction, that Salabatzing acknowledged Gauzedey Cawn, and would have submitted to him. He remains at the head of his army at Aurengabad, environed by a French guard, and (as I have had the honour already to tell Mr. Dupleix) not at liberty to act as he pleases, in continual apprehensions from the Omrahs, who are in general dissatisfied. The Phirmaund from the Mogul to Nabob Mahomed Allee is still in force, and confirmed by his Visier Shecaubudy Cawn, son to Gauzedey Cawn, I have already told you, shall be forth-coming. By a train of facts closely connected, I am persuaded of the justness of the Nabob's title; and consequently our alliance with him, will to yours and our superiors appear, that you have ingeniously endeavoured to throw that odium on us, which a series of circumstances prove you the authors of; and that you commenced, continued, and still continue a calamitous war, contrary to the fundamental laws of the country, every one must be convinced of. I am sorry, gentlemen, proposals so reasonable, so moderate, so just, and so beneficial to your real interest, as those which our commissaries had the honour to make you, should meet with so cold a reception; I would, if there were any grounds, I would hope that Mr. Dupleix figuring to himself the idea, and as from a rising ground beholding the group of miseries springing from poisons, assassinations, breach of consanguinity, thousands by different deaths perishing, yet less miserable than thousands surviving, he would conclude, that the happiness of a whole people must be of more importance than the ambition of one subject satisfied by such crimes; and if he will still reflect further, that this scheme during a course of five years, supported by the perpetration of crimes shocking to relate, assisted by armies generally superior in number, yet always defeated, has been as yet frustrated; conscious of the wickedness of the design, he would prefer peace, and hearken to reason-pursue his plan, he must know, that the same firm measures which have already served to disconcert, will vigorously continue to oppose it.

Please, gentlemen, to acquaint Mr. Dupleix, that whatever pieces I receive from him are transmitted to my superiors; and I am persuaded he will do me the same justice in transmitting mine to his, as it will furnish them with the surest means to judge of the real state of affairs on this coast.

I have the honour to be,
Gentlemen,
Your most obedient humble servant,
THOMAS SAUNDERS.

Fort St. George, the
15th Feb. 1754.

To the honourable Thomas Saunders, *Esq; Governor of* Madrass.

SIR,

We have received the writing in form of a letter, which you did us the honour to address to us in the time when our last Europe ship was on the point of sailing. The French interpretation could not be finished soon enough to send it by that conveyance. We doubt not but you have supplied this want, and put it in the power of your superiors, to communicate, if they think proper, to ours, this last writing; of which we could give them but a slight knowledge. We did all in our power to fulfil what you recommended to us on this point; we are now going to reply a little more at leisure to the honour you have done us in prolonging our commission as deputies of our nation.

We shall begin, Sir, with confessing to you, that being at Pondichery, we at the utmost only flattered ourselves, that you would honour us with an answer on the subject of our prisoners at Trichinopoly, whose miserable situation induced us to intercede with you for them, before our departure from Sadrass: it was no longer their liberty that we demanded, only the preservation of their lives; and we acted in this, less as deputies than as members of the French nation. We were therefore doubly surprised at the reading of your letter; first, at your leaving us in the dark about the success of our request, and then, at your pleasing to continue with us the discussion of what had been treated in the conferences at Sadrass. With regard to this last point, we have requested of our governor to give his consent to our entering on one more act of our past dignity; and we made him sensible of our reasons; among which, give us leave to remark to you the desire we have of justifying ourselves, in your opinion, Sir, and in the opinion of all that may read your writing, from the reproaches you have there thrown on us. We desire no more than the strictest justice.

The first reproach is, *to have been wanting in respect and regard* towards your commissaries, in making them wait at Sadrass. We might complain, Sir, that you put us to this necessity, by not sending us the necessary passports. Their delay indeed was lucky

 for

for us; for if we had received them a fortnight sooner, we should have run a risque of meeting with some misfortune on the road, which, as it was, we did not pass without danger from the quantity of water we yet found.

If you would please to acknowledge on the side of the French commissaries, an equal right to complain of want of regard and respect, you would find them better founded. This does not point at the personal behaviour of your commissaries, at which we cannot but express our satisfaction, but at the manner in which they were obliged to act with us. When we produced our titles, the very next day after our arrival, the 22d of January, although you are pleased to say it was not till after a fortnight; they answered us, that they were not sent to treat upon titles, but to propose to us the preliminary you had prescribed as the basis of the whole negociation. This was to acknowledge Mahomed Allee, &c. Forced, however, by the sentiments of natural justice, they could not refuse to promise us, that they would immediately get his titles sent from Madrass. They wrote accordingly, and received for answer, that they were at Trichinopoly. We again demanded that they should be sent for; and while we were waiting for them, you recalled your commissaries, who declared to us the end of the conferences the 4th February, and actually set out the 6th.

Notwithstanding all this, Sir, you found a second reproach to make us, on *the impatience which hindered us waiting any longer for the arrival of those titles.* Where were we to wait for them? and how long? Vouchsafe to consider, that your deputies set out from Sadrass two days before us; for we did not begin our journey till the 8th in the morning; and that you tell us in your last letter, that the titles in question are yet on the road from Trichinopoly; you invite us nevertheless beforehand to come to Madrass to see them. We cannot guess how much it may take more for their arrival there: besides, what would be the effect? Judgment may be formed from what has already passed, and from the reflections which we have already sufficiently made on these titles, supposing even that you could actually produce them. Among these titles you speak of some, which, though of an old date, are nevertheless now mentioned for the first time. Such is the Mogul's Phirmaund in favour of Mahomed Allee. We shall see hereafter how you seek to contrive some probability for introducing this piece, which becomes necessary in order to oppose to the Phirmaund of that Emperor in favour of the marquis Dupleix.

You tax us in the third place with *precipitation and lightness, in believing and advancing as attested facts such as we cannot know with any certainty.* The utmost of our desire is however, Sir, that they will be pleased in Europe to pay regard, both in your writings and in ours, to such parts only as are supported with proofs. But to see if your reproach be well founded, let us take by way of example the very fact on which you attack us, and of which you are

are specially concerned to shew the falsity, as well as our precipitation in giving belief to it.

This is the promise of Trichinopoly, made by Mahomed Allee to the Maissoreans, and guaranteed by the English: we founded, and do found our belief of the first part on two authentick acts made by Mahomed Allee, and confirmed by oath. The second, which regards you, is clearly expressed in the letters of Messrs. Gingen, Cope, and yourself, Sir; those of the two former are addressed to Nanderauze, one of the ministers of the Raja, and yours to himself.

Is it believing lightly after such evidences? We know now that you pretend *never to have wrote such a thing either to the Raja or his ministers.* Let us see then whether the arguments you produce to persuade us of this, ought to work in us a change of that sentiment which the letter abovementioned had very justly given us.

In the first place, *the Maissore envoy* who is with you, *is convinced*, you say, Sir, *that you never took part in the engagement in question*; but his master, better acquainted with his own affairs, advances the contrary. He has put into our hands the pieces which justify his assertion; he empowered us to prosecute it, and to this end sent one of his envoys with us when we went to Sadrass. Which of these two authorities should prevail?

In the second place, you send us a copy of a letter which *may*, add you, *have some reference to what we believe, and the contents of which deceived us.* It is in reality very much like that which we produced. There is no difference, according to the translation we have got of it, except that the article, importing your engagement, is left out, and a phrase, with which we have no reason to be pleased, totally changed. What would you have us think of this difference? On one side, you tell us that it is registered at Madrass, the same as you communicate it, and it would look ill in us not to believe you: on the other side, it is in the hands of the Raja, such as we produce it. The conformity between the two shews that the draft produced by the Raja is not a made piece: the want of erazements and interlineations, which would appear in this draft, if the Raja had altered it, convinces us that he has not attempted it. This is the riddle, of which we leave the unravelling to different people from us, and proceed to your third argument; it is drawn from one of your letters to Chundah Saib, the which you would insinuate we omitted with design, although we mentioned it, and communicated it at the same time with that which makes the present question. The advantage you propose to draw from this letter, turns on the mention you there make of the engagement of Trichinopoly to the English, before that which was made to the Maissoreans, as if the first demonstrated the impossibility of the second. The marquis Dupleix has already shewed you, Sir, in his letter of the 18th February, 1752, that the engagement made to the English could not be brought so far back as the Epoch, you assign it; but ſuppoſing the fact to be as you ſay yourſelf; might not the neceſſity of affairs, which induced Mahomed Allee to make a ſecond engagement, have led him likewiſe to confirm it by ſacrificing the firſt to the want and the deſire you had of fixing the Maiſſoreans in your party? We dare not take upon us to ſay, as theſe people advance, that is, that your real deſign was not to abandon your views on Trichinopoly, even when you gave them your promiſe; and they juſtify their aſſertion by the conduct you have obſerved towards them.

For us, we ſhall be content with repreſenting to you, that, by your own confeſſion, you cannot produce the engagement you pretend to have been made to you, as a reaſon proper to prove, that you took no part in that which was made to the Maiſſoreans. You add, Sir, almoſt inſtantly, in your letter, that being become a mediator between Mahomed Allee, and Nandi Raja, the Maiſſore miniſter, *you adviſed the vackeel*, or envoy, *of the Raja to obtain a janed* from Salabatzing. How is it poſſible you ſhould have given him ſuch advice to ſecure Trichinopoly to him, if you had rights upon it; had you forgot theſe rights in making an advance ſo contrary to them? At leaſt, it appears that in writing this laſt article, you was crouded with ſo many objects, that they made you forget what you had ſaid to us a little before. You was in a hurry to produce this envoy again, to inſinuate through his means, and in his name, many things eſſential to your cauſe, which you would wiſh to be true, or at leaſt to be believed in Europe. Such are the uncertainty of the authority of Salabatzing, the invalidity of the rights of Chundah Saib, the nobility of Mahomed Allee, *a ſerpaw given* to him *by Nazirzing for the government of the Carnateck.* This inveſtiture confirmed by the Mogul, and by a letter from Gauzedey Cawn, if this envoy had read your own thoughts, Sir, he could not have better collected, under one point of view, all the different articles which you have at heart to confirm, among which the Phirmaund of the Mogul, in favour of Mahomed Allee, does not hold the laſt rank; for the reſt, he does not talk like a man of this country, in aſcribing ſo much honour to Mahomed Allee, for his having received a ſerpaw from Nazirzing, and in declaring him by this token governor of the Carnateck. The Moors and Indians all know that a ſerpaw, which commonly is only a preſent of ſome cloth, is not a diſtinction to build ſo much on, and much leſs a proof of an employ given. Perhaps this envoy ſpoke with a deſign to ſupport only on conjecture, a point which he knew not to be true: he ſhould have uſed the ſame circumſpection in mentioning the Mogul and Gauzedey Cawn. Before we leave this envoy, give us leave to remark of how much weight can be all that he has wrote, and all that he ſays. The letter which you quote of his, Sir, refers plainly to the time when the Maiſſoreans, leagued with you, had the ſame intereſts, and declaimed in the ſame tone againſt Salabatzing, againſt Chundah Saib, and againſt us, in favour of Mahomed Allee;

Allee; and as to what this envoy may ſay at preſent, if you have a mind to know his true ſentiments, give him leave to explain himſelf at twenty leagues diſtance from Madraſs; he will tell you, he was ſent by the miniſter Nandi Raja, to engage you to perform thoſe very promiſes, which you deny upon his own evidence. We have been aſſured from good hands, that you have detained him againſt his inclinations: certain people, who would be prying into all myſteries, pretend that you do it with a deſign to make it be believed in Europe, that the Maiſſoreans are not far from returning to your party, ſince they keep an envoy with you. But without detaining ourſelves on theſe kinds of politicks, we continue our juſtification.

The firſt reproach which preſents itſelf, after thoſe which we have already refuted, is that of *an exceſſive vanity, which blinded us to that degree, as to make us demand the moſt imprudently in the world, that our titles ſhould be examined.* Others than you, Sir, will ſee in our proceeding a difference quite oppoſite to vanity; and thoſe that ſhall read what was wrote on one ſide and the other on this ſubject by the deputies of the two nations, will remark, that in your letter you put in your own dreſs what paſſed in the conferences, to take an advantage which the truths of the facts, which we ſuppoſe you have not had leiſure to examine, would not give you. It will be ſeen in the authentick writings, which we refer to, that we only refuſed to give copies of our pieces till you had produced yours; and there alſo will appear the very well grounded reaſons we had to act in that manner. If you have a mind to know what was our deſign in advancing, that your commiſſaries had orders to diſpute our rights, it was only to deſcribe what had paſſed in our conferences, when, after the account that was given you of the firſt communication of our pieces, you ſent inſtead of titles, which we had been made to expect, interpreters to examine ours afreſh. Our pieces were ſo entruſted to them, that they were taking copies in a ſeparate chamber from that which we were in. It was upon certain words of your commiſſaries, thro' which we ſaw, that ſome ſecret piece of buſineſs was preparing at Trichinopoly; and upon the declaration which was repeated to us of the neceſſity of acknowledging Mahomed Allee, previouſly to every thing, that one of us went and withdrew as well the pieces as the copies, by this time almoſt finiſhed, ſaying, that we would again produce all of them, and even the originals (for we had brought only atteſted copies) as ſoon as you ſhould have in readineſs thoſe you ought to communicate, and have it in your power to produce them. For the reſt, your interpreters did not ſay a word againſt our pieces; and if we may aſſume a right of aſſerting any thing without proof, we could pronounce with truth, that they found them irreproachable. Your commiſſaries amuſed us to the end of the conferences in the chicanery, which may be ſeen in their writings, and of which we leave the judgment to thoſe to whom it ſhall belong.

 You

You had your reasons, Sir, for adding to all the other reproaches already pointed out, that of *our ignorance of the facts*; but you are not more lucky in the choice of the example by which you would convince us. It is on the subject of one of your letters to Chundah Saib, which we quoted to shew that you talked to him still as a friend, when he was on his way to Trichinopoly. This letter is of the month of August, 1751; it is mentioned in that of the marquis Dupleix of the 18th February, 1752, upon this your answer, to prove *our ignorance*, that *by the date of your letter* it must *have been wrote above a year after you had joined Mahomed Allee.* Does this prove that it was not of the time we referred to it? No, assuredly; nay, admit if you choose it, that it was even later than we make it, it will only be a stronger proof of what we advanced, as it will make it appear, that you kept up still longer with Chundah Saib the appearances of friendship, true or false; let our ignorance rest, Sir, on that, we place the declarations of friendship you made to Chundah Saib, in a time when you had already joined his enemy a whole year; this last circumstance does not render our assertion false: and if your conduct gives the lie to your letter, the contradiction falls rather on you than on us. It carries indeed an accusation of quite a different nature from *ignorance*, which you impute to us.

It is however after this so lucky an imputation, that you think you have a right to overset with one single word what we had advanced upon the justest grounds, and to advance on your part, what is contradicted by a crowd of witnesses. How can you say, Sir, that Chunda Saib never was ackowledged (at least you add by any one of authority) and that he was obliged on his leaving Pondichery, to besiege the strong places of the Province. Name one single siege that he made, except that of Chetteput, a place that had for many years belonged to his personal enemy, and which even he only invested to make him pay the money he owed to the Circar: he had then in his camp and in his attendance the greatest part of the lords of the country. We assert what we saw, and what we could get attested by thousands of witnesses, if it was necessary: but you know very well yourself, that if the whole country had not been in submission and peaceable, Chunda Saib would never have entered upon the siege of Trichinopoly, wherein, notwithstanding all your assurances of friendship, he could never doubt but you would oppose him. The truth of this is, that little do you concern yourself how much the invalidity of what you alledge appears here, provided the same evidence cannot be given in Europe.

You are contented with replying on the fact of Hodgee Addee, from which it appears plainly, that the English themselves did acknowledge Chunda Saib, that *what we know of this affair may be called in question, and is beyond your knowledge.* Only a few lines after this answer you conclude, *that in all our*

pieces

pieces there is not one true fact, or one that has not been refuted. You are in the right, Sir, if the method of refuting which we have been just observing appears to you sufficient, of which the very respect we have for you must make us doubt. It is however found convenient for the avoiding all perplexities; it would have been a great one in the plan of the history you proposed to exhibit, if in the course of it you had found Chunda Saib acknowledged and peaceable possessor, in tracing the rise that you would assign to the present war. You strive your utmost to prove that the French begun it, and to that end you advance, that before this the French had a quarrel with Anaverdey Cawn, which has been demonstrated to you to have been totally finished before the beginning of that now in question. But Mahomed Allee, you will say, is son of Anaverdey Cawn, dispossessed by Chunda Saib, and we only support his rights, which Chunda Saib had usurped. What, Sir, are the rights of Mahomed Allee derived from his father in a moveable government? Did Mahomed Allee himself pretend to have any till you forced him to suppose so? Was not all settled with him as he desired it, till you led him to revolt? This is not founded on simple allegations, the proofs exist and have often been shewn you.

In vain do you endeavour to make but one of these two different wars; you will find no connection between them but such as two succeeding events must necessarily have: the efforts you make to establish another, to justify you in the war you are now making, proves clearly that this last gives you no pretext to act in a manner as if the French did appear to be the authors.

The detail you have taken the trouble to go through, of what has passed since the Epocha, you have chose to fix, would furnish us with a fair field to take our revenge for the reproach you so frequently make us on the subject of facts; but it is with regret we see ourselves in a situation to contest on such a matter with the chief of a nation, and especially of yours; and we shall dispense with it as far as possible: we can do it on this occasion, without appearing to abandon either the interest of our nation or of the truth. The marquis Dupleix addressed to you, Sir, two years ago a recital of these same events, to which you have not yet given any answer. We refer to the memorial of the 18th February 1752, all such as would attain a true knowledge of the affairs in question. The difference they will find between your narrative and that which we speak of, is that the marquis Dupleix does not support what he advances on his sole authority, but that to every fact he annexes the proof.

We refer it in the same manner to the pieces and memorials of the marquis Dupleix, for the information of those who are to judge of the grievances of the two nations, and which you

 display

diſplay ſo pompouſly to the advantage of yours; we do not deny that they will have reaſon to be ſurpriſed in Europe at what has paſſed in India between Europeans, whoſe ſovereigns and the bodies of the nations are in peace; but the point is to ſee on which ſide the blame ſhould fall. You complain bitterly that our governor declared to you that your flag ſhould no longer be a ſecurity to you: ſuch an article merited that you ſhould have quoted the letter; and you will give us leave, at leaſt to doubt, from the ſtrong reaſons that we have to believe he never did write to you in this tone. He might however in ſome degree have been ſupported in it: Had he not a right to make repriſals after you had inſulted and torn down the French flag from the places where it was planted, and demoliſhed Covelong after a poſſeſſion of two years and a half; but the French went to St. Thome; ſuppoſing that true, does St. Thome belong to you? But the country houſes of the Engliſh were burnt! their furniture carried off, ſome of which was brought to Pondichery! It was in a Moor's country, that the Moors, lawfully enraged, made theſe expeditions, although ſome French might have been found in the croud at a time when the body of the French detachment refuſed to follow Rajah Saib on theſe kinds of expeditions, what would there be ſurpriſing in it? Without commending thoſe whom it may concern, we may venture to ſay, that their fault will be nothing to compare to that of your people, who carried fire even into our limits. But the governor of Pondichery ſtopped ſome Engliſh troops paſſing through the road of that town: was he to blame, ſince theſe troops were going to the camp of Mahomed Allee? that againſt all reaſon you keep our people priſoners at Cuddalore; and that he had reaſon to believe you would embark them to ſend them out of the country.

We do not, Sir, but the liſt of your grievances is well furniſhed to reply to all thoſe that can be oppoſed to you: there remains to make the compariſon and verification. This laſt point will be often embarraſſing; but a ſure rule to judge of the exceſs of the two nations would be this, let it be ſeen on which ſide appears moſt animoſity. The ſame ſpirit which has guided the ſword and the fire to act, guides alſo the pen to write. It may be ſeen in the writings of the two chiefs on which ſide harſh expreſſions, the ſevereſt reproaches, and the moſt offenſive invectives reign principally. We ſhall not think of anſwering thoſe which your laſt letter is filled with againſt our governor; if on one ſide we are touched with them, on the other we cannot be led to offend the leaſt in the world againſt that reſpect which we are willing always to ſhew to your poſt. The marquis Dupleix cannot but approve a modeſty of which we find the model in his writings: we ſee, in them that you reproach him continually with *the blackeſt of conduct*, *aſſaſſinations*, *poiſonings*, ſome

of

of which too have no foundation but fables which you have adopted, and which we never before heard of; such is that which concerns the mother of Salabatzing: you strive to make him appear as the author or the accomplice of all these crimes. Nothing more however is requisite for his full justification but to read your own narrative. On his side, he never speaks to you of the death of Chunda Saib, but on those occasions where yourselves oblige him to it, and then in the concisest manner, although nothing so shocking has passed, nor that can with more grounds be imputed to Europeans. It seems to us, Sir, (give us leave to tell you so) that it would better become the chief of a nation, such as you are, to let this crime rest with those that did it, than to justify it by giving room to believe that the whole nation approve it. You have endeavoured to disguise the affair by several means; at last you agree that Chunda Saib was executed as a criminal; so far is certain, that his head was cut off at the breaking up of a council, at which the chief of your army assisted; it is said that even this council was held in his tent. It is therefore of the English that it might be demanded with much more justice, than of us; whence derive their right to judge, and to put to death in an infamous manner Nabobs and governors? For all that you say, Sir, against Chunda Saib and his titles, does not disprove him to have been legitimate governor of the Carnateck. Vouchsafe not to be offended at this word, and to support for a moment our *temerity*, until it shall be dissipated by our justification. We have but one very plain question to ask you; Was not Salabatzing the master of Deckan, when Chunda Saib was put to death? and had not this last a saned from Salabatzing? You was not ignorant of it, and when we produced afresh this saned at the conferences, no objection was made to it. All that you say as yet against it yourself, amounts to no more than empty declamations against all our pieces in general; nothing decisive on this subject, only that one is without date, and that two draughts of another are sealed with two different seals. We have sufficiently replied to these two chicaneries, neither of which has any reference to the saned Chunda Saib was invested with. You will here produce Gauzedey Cawn, as having annulled the saned of Chunda Saib by that which he granted to Mahomed Allee. Shew us then this, Sir, for we deny it; and further, to satisfy you that we do not deny after your method, we will prove to you that we have authority for denying it, and this by a letter from Gauzedey Cawn himself to Chunda Saib. We spoke of this to your commissaries, and they may recollect it.

Suppose even there was a saned of Gauzedey Cawn in favour of Mahomed Allee; when Salabatzing became without the least doubt sole master, had not he a right to revoke it? If he did not do it expresly, it is because such a saned never appeared;

but he wrote to you expressly that Mahomed Allee was a rebel, and that he forbid you assisting him: this is proved by the very letter of Salabatzing. After this can one conceive how a man like you can persist obstinately in saying that Mahomed Allee is legitimate master of the Carnateck: still less can one conceive how you can hope to supply his want of right by inveighing against those that say he has none; it is nevertheless the method you adopt, and observe whither it leads you, to the disputing Salabatzing his authority, or the inventing to evade it, the vainest subtleties; to the refusing to acknowledge those that he has named for the government of the country, and to the denying or making a shew of ignorance of their titles, even after they have been notified to you; at the same time that you have said in another place, that you acted only by the orders of Salabatzing, in your letter to the marquis Dupleix, dated 21st Sept. 1753; and in your letter of the 18th October following, you admit of his right to substitute whom he should think proper to the government of the provinces in his subjection; and in that of the 18th December following, you say that the prince of Deckan, from whom you received letters to assist Mahomed Allee, would rejoice to the refusing to hearken to any conditions of peace, unless they are begun by submitting to Mahomed Allee in acknowledging invisible titles and chimerical rights: to the establishing on so slight a foundation, the advantages you would procure for your nation when it depends only on yourself to procure very solid ones. We offered you some, which do not deserve the contempt you hold them in; but it is plain to be seen by the manner in which you reject them, that there are none you would accept from any other hand but Mahomed Allee's, of whom you have made your idol, but an idol of the country fashion, which has no other movement but that which you give it.

If you are offered the independency and immunity of tribute for the town of Madrass (which is an inestimable advantage) you pretend that you have it already; for in denying the acknowledgment in question, you cannot, Sir, mean with regard to former times, when we knew very assuredly that it did exist: you have the proof in your books, and we in the demand that was made of it by the father of Mahomed Allee himself to the marquis Dupleix; it is therefore with regard to the present time by virtue of some concession; but from whom? it can be from no one but Mahomed Allee. If you are offered large sums on the footing of reimbursing your expences in the war, it is a snare, you say, to disengage you from Mahomed Allee; and you take the opportunity of bestowing the blackest epithets on the marquis Dupleix. If you are offered territories, you reply the grants are already given you.

We

We know very positively that they were not by Nazirzing; this then is again by Mahomed Allee. It must indeed be confessed that these advantages offered on our part do not come near what you propose to yourselves, and of which you leave no longer the least doubt. *You give us to understand that Trichinopoly is in your hands as a mortgage and security, and that you have a contract in good form.* The first form and most essential should be, that he who made it, has a right to what he disposes of, and this condition he most certainly fails in; but this is no difficulty with you; you have got possession, and you propose to keep it. As to the Arcot country, you content yourself with possessing a few Jageers there, in order that the French may pretend to no more; because your justice inclines you to establish equality between the two nations. For all the rest of the country, you are satisfied with being masters of it under the name of Mahomed Allee: it is for this you choose that this country should remain to him, and that every other person be incapable of possessing it. Mootis Allee Cawn of Velour, with whom you acknowledge to live in good intelligence, even since Salabatzing sent him the saned which was communicated to you, cannot get your consent, because he is not Mahomed Allee. Salabatzing himself cannot name any other; because his choice cannot be deemed free, if it falls on any other but Mahomed Allee; in such a case the right devolves on yourself to appoint this last. We offered this same Mahomed Allee a considerable establishment out of the Arcot country; the proposal is intolerable, it is treating a prince like a private person. This pretended prince was contented heretofore, but you are not satisfied. What is the meaning of all that, Sir? It is easy to divine; this is the method by which you seek to establish equality between the two nations, by remaining in possession of a considerable kingdom, protectors of Mahomed Allee in all the rest of the Carnateck, and making a particular distribution of a few Jageers to serve as a measure of the liberality Mahomed Allee is to shew the French. See there the end of these proposals, so full of reason and justice, so conformable to the laws of the country, and which we cannot reject, according to you; without declaring ourselves unreasonable, and something worse. *The commerce*, you add, *shall be free to the French*, just the same as to the English, although we may well be *persuaded that Mahomed Allee, out of gratitude and friendship, would distinguish the English in his favours.* However this preference need not alarm us; *the liberty of commerce in the Arcot country shall be guaranteed by the chief of the Marattas, the king of Tanjore, the Mysoreans, &c.* What again does this mean, Sir, and what can the present and the future lords of Deckan think of it? What! Shall a country of their dependence be subject to be guaranteed by the powers you have named? What! these powers which are

are tributary to them ſhall oppoſe the alterations they may think proper to make in this province; and it is in this manner that you would make it appear that you ſupport only the fundamental Laws of the Mogul Empire, while the very idea overthrows them utterly. This pretended guaranty which cannot take place, and which is little known to the Aſiaticks, preſents an idea quite different from that which you would lend it for the commerce of the Arcot country: we ſee the end of it, it is the maintaining Mahomed Allee and his deſcendants in the government of this province, in ſpite of the lords of Deckan, and of the emperor himſelf; it is the continuance of a war, the duration of which has already been too long; it is the ruin of Myſore and Tanjour, which will be the conſequence of the neceſſity this guaranty will put the maſters of Deckan to, in order to reduce theſe tributaries into the juſt bounds they ought to obſerve with regard to them: this is all that can be hoped from a guaranty as chimerical as it is oppoſite and injurious to the Mogul government. We do not aſk you what means you would purſue to engage theſe powers in this imaginary guaranty. We do not carry our curioſity ſo far; but ſuppoſing it had no other objection but the commerce, which aſſuredly is not the caſe, we beg you will permit us to offer the following reflections. If we ſhould meet with any moleſtation, any inſult, or any injuſtice, our reſource will be to arm all the people abovementioned, to make a league like that, which by many contrivances you at length formed againſt us, and to begin a war worſe than this, provided our guarantees will conſent to it. If a private Frenchman ſhould ſuffer the loſs of a thouſand pagodas the nation ſhall give lacks to Morarow to engage him to come and ravage the whole country, and get juſtice done to the perſon aggrieved. *It is thus that the Engliſh do not ſeek any advantage for themſelves alone, and propoſe to hold all in common with the French.*

In comparing, Sir, your propoſals with ours, three very juſt concluſions ſhould be drawn, with which we ſhall finiſh this letter.

The firſt concluſion, is, that very much is wanting to your deſiring a parity of treatment for the two nations, and to your having taken, for the rule of your pretenſions, and your propoſals, an equality of juſtice. Parity of treatment would be, that no more favour be ſhewn to one nation than the other; you are willing however, by your own confeſſion, to have as much as the French (and even infinitely more, as you ſhew without acknowledging it) while for this the French are obliged to ſtrip themſelves by the rights they have; and to inveſt you with thoſe you have not. Equality of juſtice demands that every one receive according to his rights. Thoſe of the French are

real

real and well founded, and your refusal to acknowledge them cannot weaken them, no more than your protestations annul them.

The second conclusion will be, that you have without the least title, an ambition more real and more unmeasurable, than that which you seek to infer from the titles of the marquis Dupleix. You exclaim for that the lawful masters of Deckan have associated him, to do him honour in the government of their country, as if he aspired to nothing less than the usurping the whole. What exercise, or what use has he hitherto made of this authority? Shew it us, and justify by some lawful instance, the dread you feign. He will not consent that you give for master of the Carnateck a man who is enslaved to you, who is a rebel against Salabatzing, to whom he is accountable, as well as to us, for the blood of Chundah Saib. See here the subject of your cries against him; the masters of the country have given him expresly the province of Arcot with that of Trichinopoly. He sees with pleasure the government of the first in the hands of him whom Salabatzing has chosen to govern it, and he is endeavouring to procure, by lawful means, the second for the Maissoreans, to whom you promised it, and whom you disappointed. Would you in his place have acted like him? It is very evident not, by your endeavouring to usurp the kingdom of Trichinopoly on a title as groundless as the cession of a man who has no manner of right to it, and who never can have that of alienating it. Let the country recover its tranquility, and the marquis Dupleix will astonish, by fresh strokes of disinterestedness and moderation, those that have not so much as he.

The third conclusion should be, that you are very far from wishing for peace as he does. He has endeavoured at it quite in a different manner from you, whether you consider his conduct or his offers. The affectation, which may be called immoderate, wherewith you strive to lay the rupture of the conferences he proposed to you at his door, shews plainly that you only endeavoured to save appearances, and to turn them against him, if the thing were possible.

Excuse, Sir, the length of this letter; one word advanced without proof requires often many reflections to refute it; we should have many others, but the equivalent will be found in former writings. If any thing should displease you, Sir, in what we have been exposing to you for our justification, we beg you will attribute it only to the necessity we were drove to, both by the end we were seeking and the matter we were treating.

The marquis Dupleix laughed when we requested of him on your part, Sir, that he would not forget to transmit your letters

ters to his superiors. He is not, says he, the person that wishes the least to give them a knowledge of pieces so favourable to his cause.

We have the honour to be, with profound respect,
Sir,

Pondichery, the 7th March, 1755.

Your most obedient and humble Servants,
Fr. L. Lavaur
Bausett.
De Kerjean.

PRIDEAUX's Account of the HEGIRA.

FROM the flight of Mahomet, the Hegira, which is the Æra of the Mahometans, begins its computation. It was first appointed by Omar, the Third Emperor of the Saracens, on this occasion. There happened a contest before him about a debt of money: the Creditor had from his Debtor a bill, wherein he acknowledged the debt, and obliged himself to pay it on such a day of such a month. The day and the month being pass'd, the Creditor sues his Debtor before Omar for the money. The Debtor acknowledged the debt, but denied the day of payment to be yet come, alledging the month in the bill mentioned, to be that month in the year next ensuing; but the Creditor contended that it was that month in the year last past; and for want of a date to the bill, it being impossible to decide this controversy, Omar called his council together, to consider of a method how to prevent this difficulty for the future; where it was decreed, that all bills and other instruments should ever after have inserted into them the date both of the day, of the month, and also of the year, in which they were signed. And as to the Year, he having consulted with Harmuzan, a learned Persian then with him, by his advice, ordained all computations to be made for the future from the flight of Mahomet from Mecca to Medina. And for this reason, this Æra was called the Hegira, which in the Arabick Language signifieth a Flight. It takes its beginning from the sixteenth day of July, in the year of our Lord six hundred twenty and two. And ever since this decree of Omar (which happened in the eighteenth year of it) it hath constantly been used among the Mahometans, in the same manner as the computation from the incarnation of our Lord Christ is with us Christians. The day that Mahomet left Mecca, was on the first of the Former Rabia, and he came to Medina on the twelfth of the same month. But the Hegira begins two months before, from the first of Moharram. For that being the first month of the Arabian Year, Omar would make no alteration as as to that, but anticipated the computation fifty-nine days, that he might begin his Æra from the beginning of that year in which this Flight of the Impostor happened, which gave name thereto. Till the appointing of this Æra, it was usual with the Arabians to compute from the last great war they were engaged in.

The Hegira being that, which all of the Mahometan Religion have, ever since the constitution of Omar, computed by; the subject matter of the History which I now write obligeth me henceforth to make use of this Æra through the remaining part of it. But because it computeth by Lunar Years only, and not by Solar, it is requisite that I here inform the reader of the nature of those years, and the manner how the Hegira computeth by them. Anciently the Arabs, although they always used Lunar Years, yet by intercalating seven months in nineteen years, in the manner as do the Jews, reduced them to Solar Years; and consequently had their months always fixed to the same season of the year. But this growing out of use about the time of Mahomet, their year hath ever since been strictly Lunar, consisting of only three hundred fifty-four days, eight hours, and forty-eight minutes, which odd hours and minutes in thirty years making eleven days exactly, they intercalate a day on the 2d, 5th, 7th, 10th, 13th, 15th, 18th, 21st, 24th, 26th, and 29th years of this Period. So that their year, in those years of this period, consists of three hundred fifty-five days, by reason of the intercalated day, which they then add to the last month of the year. And this year all that profess the Mahometan Religion have ever made use of; and there is a passage in the Alcoran whereby they are confined to it. For the Impostor there calls it Impiety to prolong the Year, that is, by adding an Intercalary month thereto. So that according to this account, the Mahometan Year falling eleven days short of the Solar; it hence comes to pass, that the beginning of the year of the Hegira is unfixed and ambulatory (the next year always beginning eleven days sooner than the former) and therefore sometimes it happens in Summer, sometimes in Spring, sometimes in Winter, and sometimes in Autumn; and in thirty and three years compass goes through all the different seasons of the year, and comes about again to the same time of the Solar Year, although not exactly to the same day. Which being like to create some confusion to us who are used to the Solar Year; to prevent this, after the year of the Hegira, in the margin I add the day of the month in the year of our Lord in which it begins. The months of the Arab Year are as follows; 1. *Moharram.* 2. *Saphar.* 3. *The former Rabia.* 4. *The later Rabia.* 5. *The former Jomada.* 6. *The latter Jomada.* 7. *Rajeb.* 8. *Shaban.* 9. *Ramadan.* 10. *Shawall.* 11. *Dulkaada.* 12. *Dulhagha.* The first hath thirty days, and the second twenty-nine, and so alternatively to the end of the year; only in the intercalary years, Dulhagha hath thirty days, because of the day added, but on all other years only twenty-nine.

A Chro-

A Chronological Table for thirty-five Years of the Hegira, with the Days of the Month on which they begin in the Solar Year.

Years of Christ from 1st Jan.	Years of the Hegira.	Years of Christ from 1st Jan.	Years of the Hegira.
622	1 - July 16	640	19 - Jan. 2
623	2 - July 5	640	20 - Dec. 21
624	3 - June 24	641	21 - Dec. 10
625	4 - June 13	642	22 - Nov. 30
626	5 - June 2	643	23 - Nov. 19
627	6 - May 23	644	24 - Nov. 7
628	7 - May 11	645	25 - Oct. 28
629	8 - May 1	646	26 - Oct. 17
630	9 - April 20	647	27 - Oct. 7
631	10 - April 9	648	28 - Sept. 25
632	11 - March 29	649	29 - Sept. 14
633	12 - March 18	650	30 - Sept. 4
634	13 - March 7	651	31 - Aug. 24
635	14 - Feb. 25	652	32 - Aug. 12
636	15 - Feb. 14	653	33 - Aug. 2
637	16 - Feb. 3	654	34 - July 22
638	17 - Jan. 23	655	35 - July 11
639	18 - Jan. 12		

THE END.

INDEX.

A

 ——his

INDEX.

I N D E X.

French

INDEX.

G

Monsoon

P

Pocock,

FINIS.